The
Only Language
They Understand

The
Only Language
They Understand

Forcing Compromise in
Israel and Palestine

Nathan Thrall

METROPOLITAN BOOKS

HENRY HOLT AND COMPANY

NEW YORK

Metropolitan Books
Henry Holt and Company
Publishers since 1866
175 Fifth Avenue
New York, New York 10010

www.henryholt.com

Metropolitan Books® and m® are registered trademarks of
Macmillan Publishing Group, LLC.

Portions of this book previously appeared, in different form, in the following
publications: *The New York Review of Books*, *London Review of Books*, and *Foreign Affairs*.

Library of Congress Cataloging-in-Publication data

Names: Thrall, Nathan, author.
Title: The only language they understand : forcing compromise in Israel and
Palestine / Nathan Thrall.
Description: New York, New York : Metropolitan Books, Henry Holt and Company,
2017. | Includes bibliographical references and index.
Identifiers: LCCN 2016036968| ISBN 9781627797092 (hardcover) | ISBN
9781627797108 (electronic book)
Subjects: LCSH: Arab-Israeli conflict. | Jewish-Arab relations. | Palestinian
Arabs—Israel—History.
Classification: LCC DS119.7 .T487 2017 | DDC 956.9405/5—dc23
LC record available at https://lccn.loc.gov/2016036968

Our books may be purchased in bulk for promotional, educational, or business use.
Please contact your local bookseller or the Macmillan Corporate and Premium
Sales Department at (800) 221-7945, extension 5442, or by e-mail at
MacmillanSpecialMarkets@macmillan.com.

First Edition 2017
Designed by Meryl Sussman Levavi
Printed in the United States of America
1   3   5   7   9   10   8   6   4   2

For my girls—
Zoe, Tessa, and Judy

Contents

V. NEGOTIATION
"Political Horizons" and Other Euphemisms for False Hope

The
Only Language
They Understand

Preface

Scattered over the land between the Jordan River and the Mediterranean Sea lie the remnants of failed peace plans, international summits, secret negotiations, United Nations resolutions, and state-building programs, most of them designed to partition this long-contested territory into two independent states, Israel and Palestine. By the accounts of many diplomats, journalists, and historians, these efforts at peacemaking were repeatedly thwarted by the use of violence, which destroyed the trust necessary for the two sides to reconcile.

The Only Language They Understand presents a different view of the conflict. The title comes from an old saying I've heard often in my years here, first in Gaza, where I spent an initial six weeks in an airy apartment overlooking the harbor in 2010, and then in Jerusalem, where I've lived with my family outside the Old City walls since 2011. Whether uttered by a Hamas leader sitting amid the rubble of his Gaza home destroyed by an Israeli F-16 or spoken by a West Bank yeshiva student mourning the loss of neighbors stabbed to death by Palestinian assailants, the phrase means one thing: talk is pointless, because the enemy will be persuaded only by force.

When I started writing this book, a number of Israeli and Palestinian colleagues, friends, and interview subjects asked me what I would call it. After I told them, the reaction was almost always the same: laughter and appreciation—from people in both camps and across the political spectrum, including, to my surprise, one veteran Israeli negotiator who yelled out "*kol hakavod!*" (well done!) in the lobby of the King David Hotel—and then a pause, followed by a question, somewhat hesitantly posed. "But is it about our side, too?"

Indeed it applies to Israelis and Palestinians alike. I argue that it is force—including but not limited to violence—that has impelled each side to make its largest concessions, from Palestinian acceptance of a two-state solution to Israeli territorial withdrawals. This simple fact has been neglected by the world powers, which have expended countless resources on self-defeating initiatives meant to diminish friction between the parties. By urging calm and restraint, quashing any hint of Palestinian confrontation, promising an imminent negotiated solution, facilitating security cooperation, developing the institutions of a still-unborn Palestinian state, and providing bounteous economic and military assistance, the United States and Europe have entrenched the conflict by lessening the incentives to end it.

The history of these doomed efforts plainly shows that compromise on each side has been driven less by the promise of peace than the aversion of pain. But the pain has not been limited to bloodshed. Economic sanctions, boycotts, threats, unarmed protests, and other forms of confrontation have been just as important in bringing about ideological concessions and territorial withdrawals. "Force" in this broader sense has, sadly, proved the only language "they" understand.

What remains to be seen is how much more of it Israelis and Palestinians will have to endure before bringing their conflict to an end.

I.

FORCING COMPROMISE

What has been taken by force can only be recovered by force.

—Gamal Abdel Nasser

1.

The Only Language They Understand

I. American Pressure

I would be willing to lose my election because I will alienate the Jewish community. . . . Thus, if necessary, be harder on the Israelis.

—President Jimmy Carter to Secretary of State Cyrus Vance

When Jimmy Carter entered the White House in January 1977, no one expected that he would quickly obtain two of the most significant agreements in the history of the Arab-Israeli conflict: the peace treaty between Israel and Egypt, and the Framework for Peace in the Middle East, which served as the blueprint for the 1993 Oslo Accord.

Essential to Carter's success was an approach wholly unlike those of his predecessors, one that was not expected by even the closest observers of the former peanut farmer from Plains, Georgia. In his presidential memoirs, Carter wrote that prior to his election he "had no strong feelings about the Arab countries. I had never visited one and knew no Arab leaders." Announcing his candidacy in December 1974, he highlighted his support for the integrity of Israel, to which he had traveled as governor of Georgia with his wife, Rosalynn, the previous year. The trip had special significance for Carter, a devout Southern

Baptist who had studied the Bible since childhood. He stood atop the Mount of Olives, worshipped in Bethlehem, waded in the Jordan River, floated in the Dead Sea, studied excavations in Jericho, toured Nazareth, walked along the escarpments of the Golan Heights, and handed out Hebrew Bibles to young Israeli soldiers at a graduation ceremony in the West Bank military outpost at Beit El. He was briefed on Israeli politics and security by future prime minister Yitzhak Rabin, foreign minister Abba Eban, former chief of staff Haim Bar-Lev, and prime minister Golda Meir. "My recent trip to Israel had a profound impact on my own life," he wrote after returning to Atlanta. "It gave me a greater insight into and appreciation for the Jewish faith and the long and heroic struggle of the Jewish people for basic human rights and freedom."[1]

It came as something of a shock, then, when early in his tenure Carter displayed an unprecedented willingness to confront Israel and withstand pressure from its supporters in the American Jewish community and Congress. He was the first American president to call publicly for an almost total Israeli withdrawal to the pre-1967 lines. Of even greater concern to Israel, he was also the first to see the Palestinian issue as central to resolving the Middle East conflict and the first to speak of a Palestinian right to self-determination. Israeli nerves were rattled when, less than two months after taking office, he said publicly, "There has to be a homeland provided for the Palestinian refugees who have suffered for many, many years." Carter believed the Palestine Liberation Organization was ready for compromise. At a time when Israel boycotted the group, he used the terms "Palestinian" and "PLO" interchangeably, another cause for Israeli alarm. Among his top White House advisers were Zbigniew Brzezinski and William Quandt, two participants in a 1975 Brookings Institution study group that recommended far-reaching shifts in US policy, including a push for Israel's withdrawal to the pre-1967 lines, Palestinian self-determination, and "strong encouragement" from the great powers.[2]

The departure from the positions of previous administrations could hardly have been clearer. Carter's predecessor Gerald Ford had issued a written assurance that the United States would "give great weight to . . . Israel remaining on the Golan Heights," Syrian territory conquered in the 1967 war; Carter, by contrast, spoke of Israel's return to the pre-1967 lines with only minor modifications. Ford promised Israel that the United States would not deal with the PLO until that body had recognized Israel's right to exist, whereas Carter—to the great consternation of Israel and its American Jewish supporters—shook hands with the PLO representative at the UN, reached out through intermediaries to its leader, Yasir Arafat, and sought to include it in negotiations. Ford provided a letter to Yitzhak Rabin that has since been held up as a US commitment not to coerce or surprise Israel, giving it the right to review, if not veto, any US peace initiative. The letter stated that the United States would "make every effort to coordinate with Israel its proposals," with a view to "refraining from putting forth" plans "that Israel would consider unsatisfactory." Carter, conversely, would seek to orchestrate what he called a "showdown" with Israel; he decided early in his administration that the United States should "put together our own concept of what should be done in the Middle East" and then "put as much pressure as we can on the different parties to accept the solution that we think is fair."[3]

Carter squeezed Israel harder on the Palestinian issue than any American president before or since. He believed Israel would make peace only if forced to by the United States, and he saw the denial of Palestinian self-determination as immoral. Summarizing his approach, he wrote:

> Since I had made our nation's commitment to human rights a central tenet of our foreign policy, it was impossible for me to ignore the very serious problems on the West Bank. The continued deprivation of Palestinian rights was not only used as the primary lever against Israel, but was contrary to the basic moral and ethical principles of both our countries. In my opinion it was imperative that the United States work to obtain for these people the right to vote, the right to assemble and to debate issues that affected their lives, the right to own property without fear of its being confiscated, and the right to be free of military rule. To deny these rights was an indefensible position for a free and democratic society.[4]

Carter made the Arab-Israeli conflict a priority and brought to it a sense of urgency that his predecessors had felt only in reaction to a crisis or war. He spent more time on the issue than on any other during his presidency. Unsatisfied with the small, iterative steps preferred by the Israelis, he began planning for an international peace conference in Geneva that would include the PLO and aim for a comprehensive resolution. Early in his administration, Carter blocked two deals for US weapons sought by Israel, and in each case he stood his ground in the face of an intense lobbying effort. At their first meeting together as heads of state, in March 1977, Carter was tough on Rabin, telling him that the administration would hold to its position that settlements in the Occupied Territories were illegal, enjoining him to adopt a "fresh perspective" on a permanent solution, informing him that only minor modifications to the pre-1967 lines could be made, and pressing him to allow PLO leaders to attend the Geneva peace conference then being prepared. He expressed frustration at Rabin's insistence that he would not deal with the PLO even if it accepted Israel's legitimacy and UN Security Council Resolution 242, which called for peace in exchange for Israel's withdrawal from territory occupied in 1967. Carter pointed out that the United States had talked to North Korea and that France had negotiated with the Algerian National Liberation Front, despite its use of terrorism. "It would be a blow to U.S. support for Israel," Carter warned, "if you refused to participate in the Geneva talks over the technicality of the PLO being in the negotiations."[5] The Israeli delegation left the White House deeply distraught.

A series of warm meetings between Carter and Arab heads of state did little to allay Israel's fears. Whereas Carter described Rabin as "very timid, very stubborn, and also somewhat ill at ease," he wrote of Jordan's King Hussein that "we all really liked him, enjoyed his visit, and believe he'll be a strong and staunch ally." Of meeting Syria's president, Hafez al-Assad, Carter wrote, "It was a very interesting and enjoyable experience. There was a lot of good humor between us, and I found him to be very constructive in his attitude." But Carter reserved his most glowing praise for the Egyptian president, who traveled to Washington on a state visit: "On April 4, 1977, a shining light burst on the Middle East scene for me. I had my first meetings with President Anwar Sadat." In his diary, he wrote: "he was a charming and frank and also very strong and courageous leader who has never shrunk from making difficult public decisions. . . . I believe he'll be a great aid if we get down to the final discussions on the Middle East. . . . my judgment is that he will deliver." At the end of Sadat's visit, Carter told his wife, "This had been my best day as President." Several weeks later he would write, "My own judgment at this time is that the Arab leaders want to settle it and the Israelis don't."[6]

* * *

A severe setback seemed to have been delivered to Carter's push for a comprehensive peace when, in May 1977, Menachem Begin's right-wing Likud Party won an upset victory over Labor, which together with its antecedent, Mapai, had dominated Israeli politics since the state's establishment, heading each of the country's first seventeen governments. Begin was largely unknown in Washington. Carter's advisers scrambled to provide him with material on the incoming prime minister's positions, history, and outlook. Begin was haunted by the Holocaust—in his hometown of Brest, in occupied Poland, nearly all of the Jews, including his parents and brother, were executed—and he viewed the world as inherently dangerous and anti-Semitic. In 1952 he opposed Israel's reparations agreement with West Germany, delivering a fiery speech as his supporters marched on the Knesset and stoned it. He was a disciple of the Revisionist Zionist leader Vladimir (Ze'ev) Jabotinsky, whom he called his master. After Jabotinsky's death in 1940 and Begin's release from the Soviet gulag in 1941, he arrived in Palestine and rose to command Jabotinsky's Zionist paramilitary organization, the Irgun, for which he would spearhead the use of improvised explosives and simultaneous bombings against the British. His memoir of his time with the Irgun, *The Revolt*, was admired as a manual of guerrilla warfare by members of the Irish Republican Army and the African National Congress, and his writings would later be found at an al-Qaeda training camp in Afghanistan and read by Osama bin Laden. In 1946, the Irgun blew up the King David Hotel in Jerusalem, site of the British Mandate's military and administrative headquarters, killing ninety-one people, most of them civilians. In April 1948, one month before Israel declared independence as the British withdrew, the Irgun detonated grenades and dynamite in civilian homes in the Palestinian village of Deir Yassin, leaving more than one hundred dead. Both operations had been approved by David Ben-Gurion's paramilitary organization, the Haganah, but Begin took most of the blame.[7]

Throughout his life, he was a staunch ideological opponent of Palestine's partition. He opposed it when the British first recommended it in 1937, and again in 1947 when the United Nations endorsed it in Resolution 181. The emblem of the Irgun was a map of the territory to which it laid claim, Palestine and Transjordan, over which a rifle was superimposed, and under which appeared the words "Only Thus." The platform of his political party, Herut—Likud's predecessor—asserted, "The Jordan has two banks; this one is ours, and that one too." By the time the Revisionists came to power in 1977, they no longer claimed the territory of Jordan. But the Likud's 1977 platform left no possibility of Israeli withdrawal from the West Bank, which it referred to by the biblical names Judea and Samaria:

> The right of the Jewish people to the Land of Israel is eternal, and is an integral part of its right to security and peace. Judea and Samaria shall therefore not be relinquished to foreign rule; between the sea and the Jordan, there will be Jewish sovereignty alone. Any plan that involves surrendering parts of the Western Land of Israel militates against our right to the Land, would inevitably lead to the establishment of a "Palestinian State," threaten the security of the civilian population, endanger the existence of the State of Israel, and defeat all prospects of peace.[8]

Begin's attachment to Sinai and the Golan Heights was not nearly as strong as his devotion to what he called the Western Land of Israel (that is, west of the Jordan River). Following the 1967 war, he did not oppose the government's expression of willingness to withdraw from the Golan Heights and Sinai, but in 1970 he forced his party to leave the coalition government when the latter had accepted an American plan based on UN Resolution 242, implying Israeli withdrawal from the West Bank as well. The day after his election in 1977, he visited a Jewish settlement in the West Bank and promised to establish many more. During that visit he corrected reporters who used the terms West Bank ("The world must get used to the area's real—biblical—name," he said: "Judea and Samaria") and annexation ("You annex foreign land, not your own country"). Tears nearly came to his eyes when he first described to Carter the perils of withdrawing from the West Bank. "Please," he said, "excuse my emotions." He considered this land to be the site of many of the most significant stories in the Bible, making it no less the divine birthright of the Jewish people than the 55 percent of mandatory Palestine allotted to the Jews by the UN in 1947, or the additional 23 percent they had conquered in the 1948 war. If Jews had no right to the land God promised them in Judea and Samaria, Begin believed, they had no right to Haifa and Tel Aviv. Begin would tell Carter that the Arab part of Jerusalem that Israel had conquered in the 1967 war was the heart of the Israeli nation: "The Eastern part is the real Jerusalem—West Jerusalem is an addition."[9]

The other members of Begin's government did not inspire more confidence in the possibility of peace. His defense minister, Ezer Weizman, a combat pilot and former deputy chief of staff who had overseen the total destruction of the Egyptian air force on the first day of the 1967 war, was a former member of the Irgun. Begin's agriculture minister, former major general Ariel Sharon, among the most accomplished commanders in Israel's history, was a champion of the settlement enterprise and had led the 1953 massacre of sixty-nine Palestinian residents of the West Bank village of Qibya, ordering "maximal killing and damage to property." To allay fears that the government would adopt extremist policies and to give it a sense of continuity with its predecessors, Begin named, as foreign minister—and key interlocutor with the United States—Moshe Dayan, a hawkish member of the Labor Party and a revered former chief of staff who had been defense minister during the 1967 war. Shortly after that war, when no Jewish settlements had yet been established, Dayan said that one of his primary goals was to prevent the West Bank from continuing to have an Arab majority. On another occasion, he said that it was better for Israel to have the Sinai beach resort of Sharm el-Sheikh without peace than to have peace without Sharm el-Sheikh. "The Arabs would not dare go to war against us," Begin said, "when in the government sit military leaders like Moshe Dayan, Ezer Weizman, and Ariel Sharon."[10]

The odds were stacked overwhelmingly against Carter and his aides.

But rather than reassess policies and objectives in light of the new government, Carter's team began to prepare for an inevitable confrontation. There were reasons not to abandon their strategy. It made little sense to wait indefinitely for a return to power of the Labor Party, which on many of the most important foreign policy issues was not all that different from Likud. The main difference between them concerning the West Bank was that Likud wanted to annex it or at least prevent any non-Israeli sovereignty there, whereas Labor was willing to divide it with Jordan, annexing to Israel approximately one-third, including Jerusalem.[11] But both ideas were totally unacceptable to the Palestinians and the Arab states. And, in at least one important respect, Carter's goals were more aligned with Begin's than with Rabin's: Begin wanted a full peace treaty with Egypt, whereas Rabin preferred to create new interim agreements.

There were, moreover, some in the administration who believed that Begin's election was not necessarily bad for Carter. National Security Adviser Zbigniew Brzezinski "seemed to think that Begin's election would ultimately be helpful to the administration's strategy, if only because it would be easier to pressure a government led by Begin than one in which Begin was leader of the opposition," wrote National Security Council staff member William Quandt. "In Brzezinski's analysis," he wrote, "the president should be able to count on the support of the Israeli opposition, as well as the bulk of the American Jewish community, if he ever faced a showdown with Begin."[12] This was perhaps too optimistic, but it contained a kernel of truth.

Much of the American Jewish community was uncomfortable with Begin's hard-line policies. And though Carter felt that his diplomacy was constrained by the criticisms of American Jews, some within the community encouraged him to confront Begin. Nahum Goldmann, the president of the World Jewish Congress and former president of the World Zionist Organization, told Secretary of State Cyrus Vance that Begin was a "retarded child." He mocked the prime minister for having told a group of American Jewish scholars that there was no need to fear an Arab majority if Israel annexed the West Bank, because within a few years the country would absorb two million new Jewish immigrants— this at a time when immigrants to Israel were few. Goldmann urged the administration to bear down on Israel. "The Jews are a very stubborn people," he said. "That is why they have survived, but they must often be forced to do what is in their own best interest. The Bible says that God brought the Jews out of Egypt 'with a strong arm,' because, as the Talmud notes, if He had not used 'a strong arm,' the Jews would never have left their bondage." Goldmann also pointed out that Carter had a majority in Congress and so could perhaps succeed where earlier presidents had not.[13]

* * *

Following Begin's election, Carter's drive toward Middle East peace was unrelenting. Days before Begin formed his government, Vice President Walter Mondale delivered a speech reasserting the administration's positions, including the call for a "Palestinian homeland." The next week, US diplomats launched a public campaign against Begin's interpretation of Resolution 242, rejecting his view that the resolution excluded Israeli withdrawal from the West Bank and Gaza and repeating the need to create a Palestinian homeland. The United States then prepared for further confrontation. It drafted principles for negotiations to take place at a peace conference in Geneva and resolved to take those principles to Arab leaders whether Israel agreed to them or not. When, as expected, Begin rejected two of them—Israeli withdrawal on "all fronts" and Palestinian self-determination—Vance planned a trip during which he would seek their approval by Arab leaders and thus isolate Begin.[14]

Additional pressure came from increasing contact between the United States and the PLO. Prior to Vance's trip, Arafat sent a message to Carter that he would publicly state the PLO's willingness to live in peace with Israel if the United States would support the creation of a Palestinian "state unit entity." Carter then instructed Vance to make ready for the PLO to attend the Geneva peace conference, and to welcome PLO acceptance of Resolution 242 even if it came with the PLO's well-known reservation, which was that the text did not speak of Palestinian self-determination. "If the PLO will meet our requirement of recognizing Israel's right to exist," he wrote to Vance, "you may wish to arrange for early discussions with them—either in private or publicly acknowledged." Begin pleaded with Carter not to allow Vance, in his discussions with the Arabs, to bring up Israel's withdrawal to the pre-1967 lines with minor modifications. Carter refused.[15]

As the United States concluded that it would not be able to obtain the necessary Israeli concessions for negotiations in Geneva, Carter turned to the idea of abandoning the principles and instead using the conference as a forum to corner Begin. On August 8, 1977, Vance sent a telegram from Saudi Arabia reporting that he had been urged to have official dealings with the PLO. That day, Carter sought to advance US-PLO dialogue by stating publicly that if the PLO accepted Resolution 242 with reservations, the United States would start discussions and be open to its participation in Geneva. As he left Saudi Arabia for Tel Aviv, Vance told the press that the United States would no longer insist on the PLO changing its charter. The Israelis were furious. Little more than two weeks after having declared that there was no confrontation between the United States and Israel, Begin compared Vance's willingness to recognize the PLO with Neville Chamberlain's appeasement of Adolf Hitler. In a meeting with Vance, Begin read from the PLO charter, called it a genocidal organization, and said that, concerning negotiations with Israel, the PLO would be "excluded forever."[16]

Tension was building, and Begin was beginning to feel trapped. Vance had asked the Israelis and the Arabs to submit draft peace treaties to the United States. He had also started to float ideas concerning Palestinian self-determination, including a transitional period of administrative self-rule in the West Bank and Gaza, to be followed by a Palestinian referendum determining the future status of the territory. The State Department announced in September that "the status of the Palestinians must be settled" and "cannot be ignored" and that the "Palestinians must be involved in the peacemaking process." US outreach to the PLO intensified, with an unofficial White House channel, in the person of Landrum Bolling—a political scientist and Quaker peace activist trusted by Carter—communicating directly with Arafat.[17]

To Begin's dismay, America seemed to be drifting away from Israel and toward the Arabs and the Palestinians. Dayan described a September meeting with Carter as "most unpleasant." The United States would not relent on its positions, all of which were objectionable to Israel. When Begin again asked that the United States not reiterate its stance on Israel's return to the pre-1967 lines, Carter refused once more. Adding to Begin's sense of encirclement, Arafat welcomed a US statement on the necessity of Palestinian participation in Geneva and said that the PLO would accept Resolution 242 if the United States declared its support for a Palestinian state. The PLO political department chief, Faruq Qaddumi, went further, saying that if Palestinian rights were recognized, the PLO would acknowledge Israel's right to exist, establish a state in the Occupied Territories, and abandon the armed struggle.[18]

What Begin most feared was the creation of a Palestinian state or the planting of the seed of one in the West Bank and Gaza. With each passing day, it seemed that Carter and the Arabs were colluding to make those fears come true. Begin grasped for a way out of the vise. Pleading had not worked, nor was the United States deterred or diverted by Israel's more confrontational steps, including settlement building and the extension of social services to the residents of the West Bank and Gaza. The latter move drew a strong rebuke from the United States, which feared it presaged annexation. A few days later, Israel approved the construction of three new settlements, resulting in a stern warning to Begin that repetition of such acts would "make it difficult for the President not to reaffirm publicly the US position regarding 1967 borders with minor modifications." By the end of August, Brzezinski felt that both Carter and Vance were fed up and in the mood for a "showdown." The United States began drafting its own model peace treaties, including, ominously for Begin, one that would establish a new transitional regime in the West Bank.[19]

* * *

The exits were closing on Begin, with only four visible paths of potential escape. Over the next few months, he would try each one: approach Egypt secretly to strike a separate deal on Sinai that would allow Israel to circumvent the United States and avoid the Palestinian issue; initiate a battle with the PLO at its base in Lebanon in an effort to cut off any possibility of US engagement with the organization; confront Carter with US domestic opposition and threats to turn the American Jewish community against him; and make an Israeli counterproposal that would give autonomy to Palestinians in the West Bank and Gaza without suggesting eventual self-determination.

The first two paths he pursued in parallel. Begin tried exploring a separate peace with individual Arab states days after Carter had threatened to insist publicly on a peace settlement resulting in only minor modifications to the pre-1967 lines. Israel approached Jordan first. But Jordan's King Hussein ruled out an agreement on anything less than full Israeli withdrawal from the Occupied Territories, including East Jerusalem, and refused to make a deal with Israel that would circumvent the PLO.[20]

Egypt was next. For secret talks in mid-September, the bald, eyepatch-wearing Dayan put on what he called a beatnik wig, a mustache, and sunglasses and flew to Rabat for the first meeting between representatives of Begin and Sadat. But, like Jordan, Egypt showed no interest in cutting out the Palestinians and forging a separate peace. Sadat's envoy, Dr. Hassan Tuhami, "was guided by one overriding principle: peace in exchange for our complete withdrawal from the territories we had occupied," Dayan wrote. "Arab sovereignty should be absolute and the Arab flag should fly in all these territories, including East Jerusalem." Tuhami insisted that the Palestinians must have nationhood, and said that Sadat would not sign a final peace agreement alone, without the participation of his Arab colleagues. These were not the answers Israel had hoped to hear. But Dayan refused to believe that the door had been entirely shut.[21]

* * *

Three days after Dayan left Morocco on September 17, Israel took its second tack, an invasion of Lebanon. The United States had seen it coming weeks in advance, since the day after Carter had so alarmed Israel with his August 8 statement welcoming PLO participation at Geneva and conditional dialogue with the United States. The morning after Carter's statement, Dayan had called on Samuel Lewis, America's highly popular ambassador to Israel. He told Lewis that the government wanted to "wipe out" some of the Palestinians in southern Lebanon, where Israel feared the PLO was consolidating its position. Israel had already been providing arms to Lebanese Christians fighting the Palestinians in Lebanon, and now it wished to back them up with an invasion. In a telegram entitled "Major Military Incursion by Israel Threatens in South Lebanon," Ambassador Lewis wrote:

> I have been trying to divine since leaving Dayan's house what the Israelis are up to. One unhappy hypothesis would be that they are now indeed worried that the PLO is on the point of accepting Resolution 242, which could produce a major split between us and the Israelis. One way to make sure that does not happen might be to do something militarily against the PLO which would preclude any change in their position toward Israel.[22]

Days later, on August 14, Carter sent a blunt warning to Begin that military action against the PLO in south Lebanon would have the "gravest consequences" for Israel. Begin replied that Israel wouldn't invade without first consulting the United States. But on September 20, 1977, Israeli forces invaded Lebanon with American-supplied armored personnel carriers. This was a violation of US agreements with Israel and of the 1976 Arms Export Control Act, which stated that exported American military equipment could be used only for defensive purposes. The United States confronted Israel with the charge and received the reply that the US equipment had been withdrawn. But US intelligence was able to confirm for Carter that this was not true.[23]

Carter was deeply offended at having been lied to. On September 24, which was the Jewish Sabbath, he had an urgent letter of warning hand-delivered to Begin. Carter demanded that Begin withdraw from Lebanon "immediately" and asked that he avoid "a serious and public difference between us over your use of American-supplied military equipment, on which our law is very explicit." He warned that he didn't want the situation to "develop into a major problem in US-Israeli relationships" and threatened that, if his words were not heeded, Congress would be informed of Israel's violation of arms exports agreements, and further deliveries of US military assistance to Israel "will have to be terminated." The pressure worked. Begin read the message in front of the American deputy chief of mission, immediately promised to withdraw his forces, and said he would convene his security cabinet that evening to determine the timing. He then pulled out a bottle of whiskey, poured two glasses, and raised his, as if to acknowledge Carter's victory.[24] The first of Begin's invasions of Lebanon came to an end.

* * *

It was not long before Begin tried his third tack: levying Israel's supporters in the American Jewish community and Congress to compel Carter to back down. With this strategy he would be more successful than with the first two. On October 1, 1977, the United States went over the heads of the regional parties and issued a joint statement of principles with the Soviet Union, the Geneva conference cochair. Much of the world was taken by surprise. The PLO welcomed the statement. Sadat called it a "brilliant maneuver." But Israel fumed. Most upsetting were the statement's calls for Palestinian participation in the Geneva talks, for Israeli withdrawal from territories occupied in 1967, and, especially, for "the resolution of the Palestinian question, including insuring the legitimate rights of the Palestinian people." Israel announced that the joint statement would "harden Arab demands and diminish the prospects of talks." To *The New York Times* correspondent in Jerusalem, it seemed that Israeli officials were hinting that "the growing strain between the Begin and Carter administrations would intensify."[25]

The administration had done little to cover its flanks. It had not fully consulted Congress, briefed the press, or contacted the American Jewish community. "Dayan, however, had been given a draft on September 29," wrote the National Security Council's William Quandt, "and therefore the Israelis knew what was coming and had time to put their friends on notice." Carter's press secretary, Jody Powell, said "the American Jewish [community] went bonkers. We had a very serious political problem off that." Jewish and neoconservative supporters of Israel in the Democratic and Republican parties attacked the administration for harming Israel and giving the Soviet Union a prominent role. The communiqué was condemned by the Conference of Presidents of Major American Jewish Organizations, the American Jewish Congress, the Anti-

Defamation League, and AIPAC, the American Israel Public Affairs Committee, which called it a victory for the PLO and said that the mention of the "legitimate rights of the Palestinian people" was "a euphemism for the creation of a Palestinian state and the dismemberment of Israel." Democrats in Congress said the statement put too much strain on Israel. "As a result," Quandt wrote, "an otherwise peaceful Saturday erupted into controversy, accusations, and recriminations."[26]

Israel's campaign against the statement was effective. Carter retreated within three days, clarifying at the UN that while the Arabs insisted on the "legitimate rights" of the Palestinians, "how these rights are to be defined and implemented is . . . not for us to dictate." He assured a group of Jewish members of Congress and supporters of Israel that the communiqué had not called for the PLO to participate in Geneva and that he had no intention of imposing a settlement, saying, "I'd rather commit political suicide than hurt Israel."[27]

More US concessions came when Carter met Dayan in New York. Dayan declared the US-Soviet statement on Geneva "totally unacceptable" and told Carter that his government feared that the Soviet Union and the United States planned to "impose a Palestinian state" on Israel. "What I would like is your assurance," he said, "that you will not use pressure or leverage on us to get us to accept a Palestinian state, even if it is tied to a Jordanian federation." Carter replied that he did not want to make such a statement, but nor did he "intend to pressure" Israel. In that case, Dayan bluntly asserted, he would have no choice but to state publicly that Israel had sought assurances from Carter and had been rejected. "It is not fair," Carter said, "to put me in this position."[28]

The tables had started to turn. Dayan understood that Carter needed his help to quell domestic criticism. At nearly every press conference during the preceding days, Carter had been forced to defend himself against the charge that he had sold out Israel and broken a US commitment not to deal with the PLO. Now, in New York, Dayan didn't shy from using tactics that Brzezinski would later refer to as "blackmail." As Carter revealed more of his vulnerability, Dayan pressed his advantage. It would make the American Jewish community "very happy," he said, if he and Carter were to reach the following agreement: Dayan would say that he had informed the United States of Israel's opposition to a Palestinian state, a return to the pre-1967 lines, and the US-Soviet Geneva statement, while the United States would announce that there would be no imposed settlement, no compulsion involving the use of economic and military aid, and no demand that Israel consent to the Geneva statement. If, however, "we say anything about the PLO or about the Palestinian state, and that this is bad for Israel," Dayan warned, "there will be screaming here and in Israel."[29]

At first, Carter pushed back. "If there is a confrontation and if we are cast in a role against Israel and with the Arabs, Israel would be isolated, and this would be very serious. It would be a blow to your position." But Dayan was not cowed, judging, correctly, that Carter feared confrontation more than he did. He "exploited the opportunity brilliantly," wrote a US official at the meeting, playing "a weak hand with consummate political skill." As Carter announced that he was going to bed, Dayan pushed hard. "It would be bad," he cautioned, "if we did not say anything tonight." Carter relented, and two hours later a joint US-Israel statement announced the reversal: Israel did not have to accept the Geneva statement in order to attend the peace conference. "For the first time," Quandt wrote, "Carter gave clear priority to domestic political concerns."[30]

* * *

What neither the United States nor Israel anticipated was that Begin's third tack, the use of Israel's American supporters, would backfire. Carter's surrender was seen by the Israeli government and its allies, as well as by the Arab states, as a setback to his peace efforts and a sign of his susceptibility to coercion. Many concluded that he was probably too weak to further confront Israel and achieve his goals. But rather than causing inaction and despair, Carter's retreat led to a new breakthrough.

Sadat was so deeply troubled by Carter's capitulation that he was prompted to act on his own. After receiving a handwritten note from the US president on October 21, imploring him in a "personal appeal" to help break the impasse, Sadat concluded that the United States was helpless and that Carter's plans were doomed. It was this note, Sadat later said, that convinced him of the need to reply to the entreaty with what he informed Carter would be a "bold step."[31]

By this time Sadat had already suggested to his foreign minister that he might address the Knesset in Jerusalem. He later credited Carter for having set the historic plan in motion. "When he wrote to me, I felt the weight of the Zionist lobby in the United States," he said. "I felt this was unfair to him." On November 9, Sadat made his shocking announcement before the Egyptian parliament: "I am prepared to go to the ends of the earth for peace, even to the Knesset itself."[32]

He arrived at Ben Gurion Airport ten days later. Not everyone was convinced that the visit heralded a breakthrough. Israel's chief of staff, Mordechai Gur, said it might be a ruse to hide Egyptian preparations for war. Deputy Prime Minister Yigael Yadin called for a mobilization of Israel's reserves in order to be ready for a new Egyptian surprise attack. In case Sadat's plane turned out to be a Trojan horse filled with terrorists, Israeli sharpshooters took aim from positions on the rooftop of the airport's main terminal. Upon hearing a suggestion that Begin and Sadat would go on to win a Nobel Peace Prize, former prime minister Golda Meir remarked, "I don't know about the Nobel Prize, but they certainly deserve an Oscar."[33]

Sadat's fateful speech did not please Begin. Delivered in Arabic, much of it was devoted to the Palestinian question, which Sadat called the crux of the Middle East conflict. He wasted no time in dispelling Israel's hope of an agreement that excluded the Palestinians. "Frankness makes it incumbent upon me to tell you the following: First, I have not come here for a separate agreement between Egypt and Israel," he announced from the dais. "Peace cannot be worth its name unless it is based on justice and not on the occupation of the land of others." He continued, "If you have found the moral and legal justification to set up a national home on a land that did not all belong to you, it is incumbent upon you to show understanding of the insistence of the people of Palestine for establishment once again of a state on their land." Defense Minister Ezer Weizman handed a note to Begin: "We have to prepare for war." The entire world, Sadat went on, "even the United States of America, your first ally," has come to acknowledge the legitimacy of Palestinian claims. Sweating profusely and drawing his speech to a close, he called on Israel to reach a peace agreement based on its withdrawal from every inch of territory occupied in 1967 and the "achievement of the fundamental rights of the Palestinian people and their right to self-determination, including their right to establish their own state."[34]

Sadat's proposals were a nonstarter for Begin. But the speech succeeded in putting the onus on Israel to reply. In one dramatic move, Sadat had rescued the United States's flailing diplomacy, neutralized much of the US domestic opposition to Carter's initiative, obliged Israel to put forward its own proposal, and deprived Begin of the comfortable position in which he found himself after Carter's retreat. Sadat had signaled to Israel and its American supporters that peace was possible, and he had conveyed the price of an agreement in no uncertain terms.[35]

US expectations added to the pressure. In the wake of Sadat's speech, for the first time, a minority of Americans said that Israel wanted peace while a majority said that the Arabs did. On December 10, Vance met Begin in Jerusalem, delivering a personal written appeal from Carter to publicly affirm two principles demanded by Sadat: a withdrawal to the pre-1967 lines, including in the West Bank, and a resolution of the Palestinian problem in all its aspects.[36]

* * *

Begin's back was against the wall. He had tried three exits from the American and Egyptian drive toward Palestinian self-determination, and each was now closed. Sadat's speech had put before Begin an impossible choice: peace, or Greater Israel. It was then that Begin decided to take his fourth and final tack, an Israeli counterproposal meant to avoid the choice and obtain both. Begin informed Vance that he had a blueprint for "home rule" for the Palestinians that he intended to bring to the White House the following week. "I hope the President will accept my plan," he said. "It is not a Palestinian state but it is a dignified solution for the Palestinian Arabs."[37] Carter didn't know it at the time, but he was about to receive from Begin the concessions that would form the basis of his historic achievement at Camp David.

The scheme Begin brought Carter had been approved by Israel's security cabinet. For Egypt, Israel would withdraw totally from Sinai, restoring Egyptian sovereignty up to the pre-1967 lines. For the Palestinians, Israel would abolish its military government and establish a Palestinian self-governing authority in the West Bank and Gaza, with elections, local policing, and a review of all arrangements—"including perhaps sovereignty," Begin said—after five years. Security would remain in Israel's hands, conflicting claims to sovereignty would be left open, and Israel would not extend its own sovereignty beyond the pre-1967 lines, except in Jerusalem. Begin told Carter that Sadat was responsible for his plan: "The idea of self-rule came from his visit. He can take credit for this. For the first time in history, the Palestinian Arabs will have self-rule."[38]

One of the most interesting aspects of Begin's proposal was to give the right of Israeli citizenship—including the right to vote for and be elected to the Knesset—to every Palestinian in the West Bank and Gaza, and to allow, regardless of citizenship, unrestricted purchase of land anywhere in Mandatory Palestine to all Palestinians and Jews. These rights were to be in addition to, not in place of, Palestinian self-rule. Begin's argument for granting them was essentially a moral one. "And now I want to explain why we proposed a free choice of citizenship, including Israeli citizenship," he declared. "The answer is: Fairness." Referring to the predecessor of present-day Zimbabwe, which was then ruled by a white minority, he added, "We never wanted to be like Rhodesia." Full citizenship for Palestinians "is a way to show our fairness to all men of goodwill," he said. "Here we propose total equality of rights—anti-racialism."[39]

* * *

To the great relief of subsequent Israeli governments, the plan for equal citizenship rights for Palestinians and Jews was dropped. It was one of the few aspects of Begin's proposal that was not incorporated into the Camp David Accords nine months later. But the rest of Begin's two proposals, one for Egypt and the other for the Palestinians, would form the basis of the two historic framework agreements signed at the White House on September 17, 1978.

One agreement established a framework for full peace between Israel

and Egypt in exchange for Israel's withdrawal from the Egyptian territory it had conquered in the June 1967 war. It ended the state of bellig-
erency between Israel and its most powerful Arab adversary, removing
the threat to Israel of another war against a united Arab front. "If you
take one wheel off a car, it won't drive," Dayan had said to Carter. "If
Egypt is out of the conflict, there will be no war."[40]

The second agreement, the "Framework for Peace in the Middle
East," was not finalized or implemented in Carter's time, but it, too,
proved to be of great importance. It served as the basis for both the 1991
Madrid peace conference that launched the next quarter century of
Israeli-Palestinian negotiations, and, more significantly, the 1993 Oslo I
Accord, which is, in essence, an expanded version of the 1978 framework agreement.[41] The Oslo I Accord, in turn, provided the semblance of
Israeli-Palestinian conciliation that Jordan required in order to sign a
formal peace treaty with Israel in 1994, after many years of tacit cooperation and alliance. And it has defined and circumscribed nearly
every aspect of Palestinian-Israeli relations from 1993 until the present. It is largely the result of pressure Carter and Sadat applied to
Begin in 1977 and 1978.

Oslo's main points and those of the 1978 framework are almost identical. Both promised the establishment of a Palestinian self-governing
authority in parts of the West Bank and Gaza; negotiation of an interim
agreement that would outline the self-governing body's powers and
responsibilities; redeployment of Israeli forces to specified locations;
withdrawal of the Israeli military government and civil administration;
introduction of Palestinian national elections; creation of a local police
force that would maintain liaison with Israel; prevention of immigration of Palestinian refugees to the West Bank and Gaza without Israel's
agreement; a time limitation of five years for Palestinian self-governance;
commitment to a solution that would recognize the legitimate rights of
the Palestinians; and, no later than the third year of the interim period,
commencement of negotiations on the final status of the West Bank and
Gaza, leading to a solution based on Resolution 242, which emphasizes
"the inadmissibility of the acquisition of territory by war" and calls for
a lasting peace in exchange for "withdrawal of Israeli armed forces from

territories occupied in the recent [June 1967] conflict."[42] In 1994, Yasir Arafat, Shimon Peres, and Yitzhak Rabin won the Nobel Peace Prize for having committed to an agreement created sixteen years earlier by Jimmy Carter, Anwar Sadat, and Menachem Begin.

* * *

Between Begin's 1977 proposal and the signing of the Camp David Accords, Carter faced numerous setbacks. To overcome them, he put tremendous strain on Israel. In February 1978, he colluded with Sadat on a nine-step plan to force an agreement on Begin. The following month, he told Begin sternly that the main "obstacle to peace, to a peace treaty with Egypt, is Israel's determination to keep political control over the West Bank and Gaza, not just now, but to perpetuate it even after five years." Dayan wrote, "Though Carter spoke in a dull monotone, there was fury in his cold blue eyes, and his glance was dagger sharp." Begin admitted to his aides that the meeting was one of the most diffi-cult moments of his life. Two days later, Carter told a group of Senate leaders, "We cannot support Israel's policy which is incompatible with the search for peace." He then pushed through an arms sale to the Saudis over vehement objections from Israel and its supporters in Congress. When Vice President Mondale visited Israel in July 1978, Ariel Sharon accused the administration of "sowing the seeds for war by over-pressuring Israel and over-promising the Arabs."[43] At Camp David itself, Carter squeezed the parties by putting forward his own propos-als, warning Sadat of the end of their personal friendship and the relationship between their two countries, and threatening Begin with American censure and the termination of US aid.[44] Israel's former deputy national security adviser Charles Freilich wrote in his book on the country's decision-making:

> On the tenth day [of the thirteen-day Camp David summit] Carter threatened to state publicly that whereas he had reached full under-standing with Sadat, Begin's refusal to dismantle the Sinai settle-ments and recognize the applicability of Resolution 242 to the West Bank had prevented agreement. American pressure came to a head

on the twelfth and penultimate day, as Carter threatened direct sanctions: "I will not be able to turn to Congress and say, 'Continue providing Israel with assistance,' when I am not sure that you really want peace." It was at that meeting that Begin finally conceded on the settlements and Palestinian clauses. He would later tell the Knesset: "there was the possibility of saying no to President Carter and the Camp David summit would have blown up that very day. . . . I knew that Israel would not be able to withstand it . . . not in the U.S., not in Europe, not before the Jews of the United States. . . . Israel could not have stood . . . facing the entire world."[45]

But most of the concessions in the Camp David Accords had been made by mid-December 1977, only six months after Begin took office the previous June. They were unprecedented for any Israeli government, and particularly striking for one so hawkish and wholly committed to Greater Israel. Begin consented to a full withdrawal from Sinai although his foreign minister had often said that he preferred keeping the territory to having peace. Begin was the first Israeli prime minister to agree even to the presence of Palestinians in official negotiations over the future of the West Bank and Gaza, and he was harshly attacked for it by the centrist Labor Party. Begin had gone from ruling out any possibility of ever negotiating with the PLO to accepting its members in negotiations. From insisting that Palestine was Jordan, he came around to proposing the establishment of Palestinian self-governance in Gaza and the West Bank.[46]

To many Palestinians, Begin's concessions were mere crumbs. But they were enormous compromises in the minds not just of the Likud but of the Israeli center and left. When implemented under Oslo, they changed the conflict irrevocably and brought about, for the first time since 1967, seemingly irreversible steps toward Palestinian self-determination.

In fairly short order, Jimmy Carter succeeded in forcing one of the most right-wing, annexationist figures in Israel's history to do precisely what he had most sought to avoid: plant the seed of a Palestinian state.

II. Israeli Withdrawals

Zionism will not evacuate a single yard of land without a political-military struggle that compels it to do so.[47]

—GEORGE HABASH

In the decades since the Camp David Accords, every American president has tried to finish what Jimmy Carter started. Each has failed, and these failures have led to a widespread conclusion, not just in the United States but throughout the world, that the Israeli-Palestinian conflict may be insoluble. The parties are intransigent, the issues are intractable, the interests of political leaders are too narrow, and on each side the power of constituencies opposed to partition is too great. Palestinian leaders are paralyzed by their lack of legitimacy. Israeli governments are constrained by fractious coalition politics. American presidents are shackled by the power of Israel's domestic supporters. Arab states are divided and distracted by more urgent concerns. The role of religion, dueling claims to sovereignty over sacred spaces, large refugee populations, demands for restitution too great to be satisfied, the smallness of the territory, Israel's vulnerability to surprise attack, the trauma of the Holocaust, the freshness of wounds from terrible violence, the absence of trust, and the irreconcilability of conflicting historical narratives—all, it would seem, render the conflict too difficult to resolve.

Yet Carter's experience suggests a different view. Faced with the threat of real losses—whether human, economic, or political—Israelis and Palestinians have made dramatic concessions to avert them. Through persistent coercion, both have taken steps toward accepting an international consensus around Palestine's partition into two states along the pre-1967 lines. Carter's achievement is but one of many examples demonstrating each party's responsiveness to force, that is, to all forms of pressure—including violence—that threaten significant costs.

In Israel's case, each of its territorial withdrawals was carried out under duress. Following the 1956 Suez Crisis, when Israel colluded with France and the United Kingdom to invade Egypt, Prime Minister David Ben-Gurion refused to withdraw from Sinai and Gaza. At the end of the war, he wrote that the Red Sea island of Tiran, off the coast of Sinai, would now be "part of the third kingdom of Israel," and in his victory speech he hinted at annexing Egyptian territory. International intimidation of Israel brought about a swift and complete reversal. The Soviet premier sent a letter threatening rocket attacks and the deployment of volunteer forces to assist the Egyptian army. President Dwight D. Eisenhower's administration issued an ultimatum: if Israel didn't unconditionally withdraw, it would lose all aid from the United States and from American Jews, and the US would not oppose Israel's expulsion from the UN.[48] Within a day and a half of his victory speech, Ben-Gurion announced Israel's withdrawal.

Israel's next retreats came on the heels of the devastating October 1973 war, which alerted the country to the necessity of peace with Egypt and the effectiveness of Egyptian and Syrian forces. The war had shaken Israel, at one point causing a teary-eyed Moshe Dayan to predict the "destruction of the third temple."[49] In the wake of the conflict, Israel signed three agreements to undertake limited withdrawals, one in Syria and two in Sinai. Each was made under acute pressure by the United States, which had been subjected to a painful Arab oil embargo in response to its support for Israel.

In its first Sinai withdrawal agreement, negotiated during a war of attrition with Egypt, Israel made greater concessions than those it had refused to make previously, which was among the reasons the Egyptians called the 1973 war a victory. Stalled talks on the second Sinai withdrawal were successfully concluded thanks only to a US threat in the form of a "reassessment" of relations with Israel—the prime minister called it "one of the worst periods in American-Israeli relations"—during which the United States suspended consideration of economic assistance and refused to provide any new arms deals. The agreement to withdraw from parts of Syria in 1974 was, like the first Sinai disengagement, completed under the strain of an ongoing war of attrition, with Syrian forces striking Israeli territory and IDF positions.[50]

* * *

In Lebanon, Israel withdrew four times between its first invasion in September 1977 and the end of its occupation in 2000. The first two evacuations were undertaken as a consequence of heavy international coercion; the second two, as a result of violence. The first, in September 1977, was brought about by Carter's fury at having been lied to about the use of American-supplied equipment in the offensive and by his threat to terminate US military aid. The second followed another Israeli incursion in response to the March 1978 Coastal Road massacre, an attack and bus hijacking carried out by PLO militants that left thirty-eight Israelis dead. Again the pullout came in reaction to strong-arming by the United States. Israel "grossly overreacted in Lebanon," the president wrote in his diary, "destroying hundreds of villages, killing many people, and making two hundred thousand Lebanese homeless." The United States condemned Israel's retaliation and pushed through a UN Security Council resolution—"the Israelis did their best," Carter wrote, "to prevent our sponsorship"—demanding Israel's immediate withdrawal and establishing an international peacekeeping force to supplant the IDF and confirm its departure.[51] After the resolution passed, Israel announced it would cooperate fully with the UN, and began to evacuate.

The next two pullouts from Lebanon were unilateral, driven by a desire to halt the growing number of fatalities among Israeli troops. The 1982 invasion quickly descended into a quagmire, with heavy Israeli losses from bombings and guerrilla attacks. By 1983, the army recommended unilateral withdrawal in order to reduce casualties. Begin was tormented by the deaths of young Jews in what he had called a "war of choice." He announced his resignation in August 1983, telling his cabinet, "I cannot go on." The occupation of Lebanon had tarnished Israel's international standing. An internal commission of inquiry found that Defense Minister Ariel Sharon bore "personal responsibility" for the massacre by Christian Phalange forces of civilians in the Palestinian refugee camps of Sabra and Shatila in south Beirut, and declared that the state of Israel had "indirect responsibility." Israel estimated that between seven hundred and eight hundred were killed during the two-day massacre, while the Palestinian Red Crescent put the total at over two thousand. Israel pulled out in stages: a limited withdrawal from the outskirts of Beirut in 1983, followed by a larger series of disengagements in 1985.[52]

The final retreat would not come until fifteen years later. It was set in motion in April 1996, when a sixteen-day conflict between Israel and

Hezbollah, known to Israelis as Operation Grapes of Wrath, resulted in widespread international condemnation of Israel for its killing of over one hundred Lebanese civilians taking refuge in a UN compound in the village of Qana. The next month, the newly elected prime minister, Benjamin Netanyahu, took the helm of the first government to propose a withdrawal from Lebanon without a peace treaty. Israelis had become increasingly critical of the costs of occupying southern Lebanon, referring to it as "our little Vietnam." Soldiers were losing their lives for no apparent strategic gain. Following the death of seventy-three soldiers in a crash of two helicopters on their way to Lebanon, a group of bereaved mothers began holding vigils outside the Defense Ministry each time another soldier died. Hezbollah was growing steadily stronger, and Israel's proxy force, the South Lebanon Army, was weakening, obliging Israel to carry more of the occupation's costs. In May 1999, Ehud Barak won the prime ministerial election after campaigning on a promise to extract Israel from the Lebanese morass within one year. Over the objections of the IDF chief of staff, who warned against sending a message of frailty by retreating under fire, Israel withdrew to the international border.[53]

* * *

In the West Bank and Gaza, too, Israel was forced to withdraw under duress. Mass protests in December 1987, the beginning of the First Intifada, convinced the government that the Occupied Territories had become ungovernable and direct military rule could not indefinitely be sustained. In the first three weeks of the uprising, the army doubled its presence in the West Bank and tripled it in Gaza, where more soldiers were deployed to suppress the rebellion than had been used to conquer the territory in 1967. The intifada frightened Israel by breathing new life into the struggle for Palestinian statehood. The strong assertion of Palestinian nationalism bolstered the PLO at the expense of two other claimants to the West Bank: Israel and Jordan. "It was the intifada," said Jordan's King Hussein, "that really caused our decision on disengagement [i.e., surrender of claims to the territory]" in July 1988, all but foreclosing the possibility of Jordan and Israel dividing it.[54] Filling the void left by Jordan's relinquishment, the Palestinians declared independence in November 1988. Weeks later, 104 UN member states acknowl-edged the proclamation of the State of Palestine, and in December 1988, the United States recognized the PLO.[55]

Israel's leaders understood that containing the intifada and the Pal-estinian march toward self-determination required more than mere military domination. They were being pushed by the United States to accept a new peace plan and later to come up with their own. In early 1989, just over a year after the revolt began, Defense Minister Yitzhak Rabin introduced a proposal for the Palestinians to gain autonomy in the West Bank and Gaza in exchange for aborting the uprising. Several months later, Likud Prime Minister Yitzhak Shamir, a vehement oppo-nent of ceding any part of the Land of Israel, and especially to Palestin-ians, was compelled to put forward a plan for Palestinian self-governance in the West Bank and Gaza, based on the Camp David Accords.[56]

To bring these ideas to fruition, however, would require additional forms of coercion, including violence. Rabin was elected prime minis-ter in 1992, as the intifada shifted from mass protests to increased mili-tarization. Hamas and Islamic Jihad were growing more powerful. In early 1993, Israel and the Occupied Territories descended into the worst period of violence and repression since the uprising began. In March, fifteen Israelis and twenty-eight Palestinians were killed; the next month, Hamas launched its first suicide bombing. Rabin sealed off the Occupied Territories "until further notice." Chiefs of the security ser-vices stressed the urgency of finding a political solution. Israeli nego-tiators in Oslo repeatedly asked the Palestinians to stop the intifada. A debate took shape about whether to unilaterally withdraw from Gaza, and a poll taken during the summer of 1993 showed 77 percent of Israelis in favor. In public, Rabin promised to separate from the Palestinians and "take Gaza out of Tel Aviv." "It is better," he said, "for the Arabs not to be swarming around here." In private, he received reports on the negotiations in Oslo, where Israel would soon commit to the withdrawal of its military government and the establishment of limited Palestinian self-rule.[57]

The intifada had not caused Israeli leaders to suddenly desire Pales-tinian self-determination for its own sake. The government would no doubt have preferred a return to full control over a largely quiescent

Palestinian population, as had been the case for most of the two decades prior to the uprising. But the intifada had rendered that option obsolete. For Israel, the concessions of Oslo were the next best thing. That they were grudgingly made and widely seen as far-reaching did not change the fact that they fell far short of ending occupation or of guaranteeing, as the Israeli right falsely charged, the eventual establishment of a Palestinian state. The accord was based, at Rabin's insistence, on the 1978 Camp David framework agreement, which itself was a modified version of Begin's 1977 autonomy plan, designed for the specific purpose not of establishing Palestinian self-determination but of thwarting it. Rabin's goal, as he told the Knesset one month before his assassination, was the establishment of "an entity which is less than a state."[58]

And so pressure on the Israeli government did not abate after the signing of the first Oslo agreement in September 1993. The following months saw a sharp rise in violence against Israeli citizens. Some Palestinians believed Oslo was more likely to prevent independence than to establish it; the plan for Israeli withdrawal in "Gaza and Jericho first" seemed like a trap. "Gaza and Jericho first—and last," went an oft-repeated quip.[59]

Oslo allowed Israel not to end the occupation but repackage it, from direct to indirect control. The agreement permitted Israeli forces to redeploy from populated Palestinian city centers to rural areas, where resistance was more difficult to organize and easier to contain. In the cities, the costs of Israel's rule were greatly lessened, as Palestinians took responsibility for the suppression of protests and violence. "The Palestinians will be better at it than we are," Rabin explained, "because they will allow no appeals to the Supreme Court and will prevent the Israeli Association for Civil Rights from criticizing the conditions there by denying it access to the area. They will rule by their own methods, freeing—and this is most important—the Israeli army soldiers from having to do what they will do."[60] Some Palestinians viewed their limited autonomy as little more than an Israeli ploy to tame the PLO and quash the intifada, but the fact remained that prior to the uprising even limited autonomy under the PLO had been unavailable to them.

Given that for Israel the driving force behind Oslo was the desire to protect soldiers and civilians from exposure to growing violence and unrest, it was only natural that the violence during negotiations and after the accord was signed would lead to further initiatives for separation and withdrawal. Between Yasir Arafat's return from exile to Gaza in July 1994 and the September 1995 agreement for additional IDF withdrawals from Palestinian urban areas (known as Oslo II), suicide bombings killed sixty-four, more than the number taken by terrorism in any of the preceding nineteen years.[61] The political rhetoric claimed that the country would not hand more territory to Palestinians until violence had ceased, but in reality Israel did not hand over territory until violence had started.

Despite all its criticism of Oslo and its vows to cancel the agreement, when the right came to power it behaved no differently, responding to unrest with further withdrawals. After Prime Minister Netanyahu formed a government in June 1996, he initially refused to honor the commitments of past governments to large parts of the Oslo agreements. This changed abruptly in late September, when he made a catastrophic decision that would lead to Palestinian violence and Israeli concessions to quell the unrest.

That month, Israel blasted open an exit to a Jerusalem archaeological tunnel that ran alongside the edge of the holy site known to Jews as the Temple Mount and to Muslims as the Noble Sanctuary or al-Aqsa Mosque compound. Palestinians had opposed opening the tunnel for ten years. The new exit was in the heart of the Muslim Quarter of the Old City, in territory Israel had occupied since 1967. Netanyahu claimed the tunnel had been opened merely to ease the flow of visitors to the site, but he later admitted that the act "expresses our sovereignty over Jerusalem." Several days of riots and bloody clashes ensued, leaving fifteen Israeli soldiers and some eighty Palestinians dead. It was the worst violence since the height of the intifada, perhaps since the occupation began. Palestinians referred to it as the "tunnel uprising."[62]

Within days, the UN Security Council passed a resolution calling for an immediate reversal of Israel's move. President Bill Clinton quickly convened a summit of Arab, Palestinian, and Israeli leaders, at the end of which he won from Netanyahu a promise to negotiate a withdrawal from the West Bank city of Hebron. In January, Israel signed the Hebron Protocol, which called for its withdrawal from 80 percent of the city, its release of thirty-one Palestinian women prisoners, and its commitment to three further withdrawals in the West Bank over the next eighteen months. These were negotiated in greater detail in a separate memorandum signed at Maryland's Wye River plantation the following year. Finalized in fall 1998, during the quietist period of the Oslo years, much of the Wye memorandum was never implemented.[63]

* * *

The decision to undertake Israel's most consequential withdrawal from the Occupied Territories was made in late 2003, during the bloodiest period of Israeli-Palestinian violence since the 1948 war. Ariel Sharon, the hard-line former general referred to as "the Bulldozer," took power when the Second Intifada was in its sixth month and spinning out of control. Contrary to all expectations of the man known as the father of the settlement movement—who had once demanded that a general be fired for saying that the First Intifada could not be defeated by military means alone—Sharon was prepared to make immediate concessions to halt the fighting. According to then US ambassador to Israel Martin Indyk, "Sharon offered a freeze on all settlement activity for six months if Arafat would make a serious attempt to stop the intifada violence."[64]

Sharon was under immense strain to halt the mounting death toll. The horrific violence occupied much of the world's attention, leading to cease-fire proposals, withdrawal demands, and new support, including from the United States, for the establishment of a Palestinian state. Saudi Arabia's de facto ruler, Crown Prince Abdullah, was so upset by American support for Israel during the intifada that he refused to visit Washington in 2001 to meet George W. Bush. Coming close to tears at a Paris hotel, he showed Secretary of State Colin Powell a stack of grisly photos of recently killed Palestinians, demanding, "How can you possibly tolerate such suffering? These are *your* weapons, and this is *your* ally." Soon after, the crown prince "rocked the White House with a letter, held in absolute secrecy in that summer of 2001 and still secret today, that put US-Saudi relations in the balance," wrote the deputy national security adviser Elliott Abrams. The Saudis threatened to break ties unless America did something to stop the violence. "Responding to Saudi pressure," Abrams wrote, "the United States would endorse Palestinian statehood" several days later.[65] Within months, the UN Security Council followed suit, passing a resolution calling for a State of Palestine for the first time. Bending to the new consensus, Sharon, too, accepted the idea of a Palestinian state, becoming the first Israeli prime minister to do so.[66]

Pressure on Sharon within Israel was also growing. As the violence intensified, support for territorial compromise increased. A series of public opinion polls asked Israelis about their willingness to approve a peace settlement first proposed by President Clinton, which offered Palestinians a capital in Jerusalem and sovereignty over the Noble Sanctuary/Temple Mount. Peak support for the plan—79 percent—was found in a March 12–14, 2002, poll, at the height of the Second Intifada and just days after two suicide bombings in Jerusalem. "The bloodshed was so great," wrote Abrams, that Sharon lifted his policy of demanding seven days of quiet before he would negotiate a cease-fire. In fall 2003, members of the nation's security elite condemned the occupation with unprecedented vehemence. Sharon received two open letters protesting his policies in the Occupied Territories: one from Israeli air force pilots pledging to "refuse to continue hitting innocent civilians" and objecting to the "long occupation which corrupts all of Israeli society"; another from members of the army's most prestigious special forces unit, Sayeret Matkal, vowing to "no longer participate in the regime of oppression in the territories [and] the denial of human rights to millions of Palestinians . . . [and to] no longer serve as a defensive shield for the settlement enterprise." Similarly harsh criticisms came in a joint interview with four former chiefs of the Shin Bet, among the most authoritative security figures in the country, who called for a dismantlement of settlements and a territorial withdrawal.[67]

No less difficult for Sharon were the mounting plans and peace proposals put forward in response to the violence. None of them was remotely appealing to the Israeli government. In April 2001, a US-led committee submitted a report recommending a freeze of all construction in settlements, including their so-called natural growth, and in October reports of a forthcoming American plan for a Palestinian state so worried Sharon that he stridently warned the United States against appeasing the Arabs as Western democracies had done with Adolf Hitler: "Israel will not be Czechoslovakia." In early 2002, the Saudis introduced the Arab Peace Initiative, which called for Israel's full with-drawal to the pre-1967 lines and was welcomed by the UN Security Council. The former Shin Bet chief Ami Ayalon and the Palestinian intellectual Sari Nusseibeh presented the People's Voice Initiative one year later, in June 2003, gaining a quarter million Israeli signatories and the backing of three other former heads of the Shin Bet. In December of the same year, a group of Palestinians and Israelis, among them for-mer negotiators, government officials, generals, and ministers, issued a draft peace treaty known as the Geneva Initiative, which, to Sharon's dismay, was greeted with official responses from Secretary of State Powell and President Bush.[68]

More significant than any of these was the Roadmap to Middle East Peace, a plan announced by the United States, together with the EU, UN, and Russia, in April 2003. It called for an end to the intifada, a withdrawal of Israeli forces from areas occupied since the violence began, a freeze of settlement activity, the dismantlement of all settle-ment outposts created since Sharon took office, and the establishment of a Palestinian state. Sharon yielded, accepting the Roadmap—albeit with fourteen reservations—and confronting his party with bitter truths about the inevitability of Palestinian independence. Speaking to a Likud conference while the intifada was raging, he said, "The idea that it is possible to continue keeping 3.5 million Palestinians under occupation— yes, it is occupation, you might not like the word, but what is happening is occupation—is bad for Israel and bad for the Palestinians, and bad for the Israeli economy. Controlling 3.5 million Palestinians cannot go on forever." Six months later, the UN Security Council endorsed the Roadmap, and Sharon told US officials of his intention to unilater-ally withdraw from Gaza. When Bush later asked why Sharon had decided to pull out, Sharon replied, "I didn't want other people, even you with all the problems you have, to press me. It was better to take steps ourselves."[69]

The unprecedented violence of the intifada had led Sharon to take two consequential measures. The first was to erect a barrier between Israel and over 90 percent of the West Bank, an idea that originated in Rabin's 1992–1995 government and his call for separation during the First Intifada. Now the stated goal of the barrier was to contain the plague of suicide bombings. Yet it displeased Israelis and Palestinians alike. Palestinians objected because it attached East Jerusalem and roughly 8.5 percent of the West Bank to the Israeli side; settlers also objected, viewing the barrier as a major step toward partition and relinquishment of territory. Sharon confirmed the settlers' fears in a December 18, 2003, speech, at which he announced the withdrawal from a then unspecified number of settlements in Gaza and the West Bank. "The relocation of settlements will be made, first and foremost, in order to draw the most efficient security line possible," he said, referring to the separation barrier. "Settlements which will be relocated are those which will not be included in the territory of the State of Israel."[70]

Sharon's final maneuver was the Gaza pullout. Israeli casualties there had been rising steadily from increased use of explosives smuggled through underground tunnels connected to Egypt. Rocket attacks from the territory had increased sevenfold in the year leading up to Sharon's decision. His goal, he said, was "to carry out an evacuation—sorry, a relocation—of settlements that cause us problems." He wanted to "reduce as much as possible the number of Israelis located in the heart of the Palestinian population" and thereby lessen "friction between us and the Palestinians."[71]

He completed the full withdrawal from Gaza and four northern West Bank settlements in late summer 2005. As with previous pullouts, the Gaza exit was undertaken in order to avoid something worse—in this case, the momentum building toward Palestinian statehood and the continued exposure of Israeli soldiers and civilians to attacks by Gaza militants, who were growing stronger by the day.

* * *

Four months later, Sharon suffered a stroke from which he would never recover. Hamas, which was seen as the first Palestinian group to have forced an Israeli territorial withdrawal, won legislative elections in the West Bank and Gaza several weeks later. With Sharon incapacitated, Israel's acting prime minister, Ehud Olmert, campaigned on a promise to finish what Sharon started by evacuating soldiers and settlers from the roughly 90 percent of the West Bank that lay east of the separation barrier. But Olmert's plan was never implemented, thanks both to the

2006 Lebanon War, which marked the beginning of the end of his political career, and to the Israeli loss of a sense of urgency with respect to the Palestinian question.[72] The population of the West Bank was exhausted and went through a period of post-intifada quiescence. With resistance diminished, so too was the pressure. Serious proposals for unilateral withdrawal were not raised for the next nine years.

Predictably enough, when the West Bank once more erupted in violence in the fall of 2015, the question of withdrawing resurfaced. During the first six months of the unrest—which included Palestinian stabbing, shooting, and car-ramming attacks and Israeli fire at West Bank and Gaza protests—some thirty Israelis and more than two hundred Palestinians were killed. Politicians and pundits referred to it as a third intifada, although in scale and intensity it was nowhere near a match for the first two uprisings. To quell the attacks, the army took steps to ease restrictions on Palestinian daily life and proposed pulling Israeli forces out from some areas; but some of the most senior generals said that larger political concessions would be needed to restore calm.[73]

In the middle of the violence, which was initially centered in Jerusalem, public opinion polls showed a newfound willingness to divide the city, with an unprecedented two-thirds in favor of relinquishing control of neighborhoods in the Palestinian-majority east. Responding to these shifts in opinion, the Labor Party, which led the opposition, revealed a new plan to separate from West Bank and Jerusalem Palestinians. It called for giving the Palestinian Authority (PA) greater control of the 91.5 percent of the West Bank that lay east of the separation barrier, dismantling settlement outposts, and withdrawing from many East Jerusalem neighborhoods by rerouting the wall, thereby cutting off hundreds of thousands of Palestinian Jerusalemites from Israel and the rest of the city, including the al-Aqsa Mosque.[74] The significance of the plan was not that it was likely to be implemented but that at a time when Israelis were frightened and under assault the party thought a proposal for unilateral withdrawal could help pave its return to power.

* * *

Despite the evidence that severe pressure, including violence, has repeatedly elicited Israeli compromise, many wish to deny the causal relationship, for fear that such an admission would lead to the application of still more coercive force. AIPAC, one of the most powerful lobbying groups in the United States, promotes the idea that US interests are best achieved not only by abstaining from exertions on Israel but by ensuring, in the words of George W. Bush, that there is "no daylight" between the two countries. It is a view upheld widely in Washington, and not just by the neoconservatives who shaped policy under George W. Bush. Even the numerous Obama administration officials who were unsympathetic to AIPAC's views felt impotent to firmly oppose them. A national security official who served in government under both Bush and Barack Obama privately compared the two experiences: "I don't know what's worse—working for an administration that enacts AIPAC's policies enthusiastically, out of conviction, or working for one that does so grudgingly, out of fear."[75]

Among the American officials who wielded the most influence over policy toward Israel during the sixteen years of the Clinton and Obama administrations were Martin Indyk and Dennis Ross. Both were veterans of the first and second Clinton administrations, with previous affiliation to the Washington Institute for Near East Policy, originally an offshoot of AIPAC's research department. In his memoir of his years under Clinton, written before he had become much more skeptical of Israel's willingness to compromise, Indyk encapsulated the central idea that AIPAC has promoted over the years: "The record . . . suggests that American presidents can be more successful when they put their arms around Israeli prime ministers and encourage them to move forward, rather than attempt to browbeat them into submission."[76] What the historical record in fact suggests is that something close to the opposite is true.

In 2015, Ross—an adviser to Obama and Hillary Clinton—published *Doomed to Succeed: The U.S.-Israel Relationship from Truman to Obama*, a book devoted to the thesis that "when the United States pressured Israel, we never benefited." For Ross, "to simultaneously distance from Israel and move on peace contained a built-in contradiction," since, as he believes, it is embracing Israel, not coercing it, that produces results. (Ross is usually careful to present his advocacy for US alignment with Israel as deriving from an impartial analysis of what will work to achieve peace. But at a private talk at a New York synagogue in 2016, he peeled back this veneer of objectivity, stating, "Plenty of others are advocates for Palestinians. We don't need to be advocates for Palestinians. We need to be advocates for Israel.")[77]

Describing policy differences among US officials, Ross wrote of "a long-standing split between those who saw working closely with the Israelis as the key to affecting Israeli behavior favorably, and those who did not." Ross counts himself among the first group. This gap, he wrote, could be found within "the Truman, Kennedy, Nixon, and both Bush administrations," but not in those of Eisenhower, Carter, or Clinton. In Clinton's case, Ross wrote, the gap wasn't present because "working closely with the Israelis was the norm." In the case of Eisenhower and Carter, by contrast, "this tension did not exist because there was little serious advocacy for working closely with the Israelis."[78]

In setting up this schema, Ross offered a neat test of his thesis—and inadvertently disproved it. The two presidents he faulted for threatening and keeping a distance—Eisenhower and Carter—were the only ones who succeeded in compelling Israel to undertake a full territorial withdrawal. Contrary to what most advocates for Israel try to argue, it's hardly the case that force—including but not limited to violence—has been ineffective in advancing accommodation between Israelis and their neighbors. All too often, it has been the primary driver of compromise.

III. Palestinian Concessions

The world does not pity the slaughtered. It only respects those who fight.[79]

—MENACHEM BEGIN

Pressure has been no less effective on Palestinians. The results have not been as tangible, because prior to Israel's evacuation from Gaza, the Palestinians never truly possessed any territory to give up, unless one counts the PLO bases in Jordan and Lebanon, from both of which they were forcibly expelled. Instead, repeated defeats and punishing measures exacted a series of ideological concessions, in which territorial ambitions were slowly narrowed from all of Mandatory Palestine to the 22 percent that Israel conquered in 1967. The coercion took three primary forms: military defeat, economic deprivation, and the threat of cutting off the path to a Palestinian state.[80]

More than any other factor, it was Israel's overwhelming military power that convinced Palestinians they could obtain no more than 22 percent of the land on which they had lived before 1948. A series of military campaigns made that clear. By the end of the 1948 war—at every stage of which Israeli forces outnumbered the combined total of Arab forces—Israel had expanded its boundaries to 78 percent of Mandatory Palestine; prior to the war, when Jews had made up one-third of the population and owned less than 7 percent of the land, the UN's partition plan had allotted 55 percent to Israel.[81] The success was decisive enough to preclude Israel from ever being forced to return to the borders of the partition plan. But it was not so decisive that the great powers favored a settlement in which Israel would keep all 78 percent.

Israel changed that through the use of additional force. As late as 1955, the United States and the United Kingdom proposed a peace plan in which the country would give up large parts of the Negev Desert, shrinking from its 1949 area to a size in between the 55 percent of the pre-war partition plan and the armistice lines of 78 percent. But one year later, following Israel's 1956 conquest of Sinai and Gaza, the world powers changed their view, seeing the existing boundaries as permanent. No serious partition proposals to give Israel anything less have since been raised.[82]

The Arabs, too, following their crushing defeat in June 1967, abandoned hope of taking any territory beyond what Israel conquered in the war. In Khartoum in September 1967, at the first Arab summit conference after the war, the Arab states famously declared the principles of "no peace with Israel, no recognition of Israel, no negotiations with it." What received far less notice was the resolution's preceding sentence, which affirmed not just that the Arab states sought Israel's withdrawal from only the "lands which have been occupied since the aggression of June 5" but that they sought to regain it nonviolently, through "political efforts at the international and diplomatic level." Following the summit,

Israel's director of military intelligence, Major General Aharon Yariv, informed the Knesset that the Arabs had decided to seek a political solution. But Israel was not eager to give up the land conquered in 1967. So it rushed to define the Khartoum Resolution as a display of intransigence, dubbing it the "three noes" when in fact it was a significant, capitulatory step toward formally accepting Israel in its pre-1967 boundaries.[83]

Once the Arabs had conceded Israeli control of 78 percent of Mandatory Palestine, the Palestinians, whose entire strategy at that time was premised on entangling the Arab states in a war to liberate all the land, stood no chance of gaining anything more than the remaining 22 percent—and even that they were far too weak to secure on their own. But it would take time, and considerable force, before the Palestinian national movement would come to admit the new reality.

* * *

The first significant step toward compromise came during the greatest defeat the PLO had yet suffered. In September 1970, the Jordanian army assaulted PLO forces that were based in the country and had challenged the monarchy's authority. The army killed about a thousand guerrillas and pushed the rest out, mostly toward Lebanon. Thousands more Palestinian civilians were killed in the conflict, which the PLO called "Black September." Several factions dwindled or disappeared, and one of the most hard-line groups moved to the pragmatic camp. A deputy chief of the PLO said the battles had threatened the organization with "total collapse."[84]

The traumatic confrontation had two important consequences. The first, a change in PLO means, came about because the rout had exposed the organization's weakness and thus undermined hopes of liberation through guerrilla fighting modeled on the people's wars of China and Vietnam. A shift in strategy toward increasing terrorism began.[85] The goal of this wave of hijackings, bombings, and shootings was not to pose a serious military challenge to Israel, which was far beyond Palestinian capabilities. Rather, it was to disguise the PLO's feebleness in the wake of Black September; score tactical and symbolic victories such as large prisoner exchanges; and embarrass the Arab states for their inaction and growing accommodation with Israel. It likewise put the Palestinian issue atop the world's agenda; asserted Palestinian identity and independence of decision-making; and mobilized a political constituency, instilling in Palestinians a sense that they were not helpless refugees but proud revolutionaries. Crucially, it also helped demonstrate that no peace could be reached without the participation of the PLO.

The second change, in PLO objectives, came swiftly too. In January 1971, three months after Jordan's main offensive, the organization issued a statement revealing a willingness to defer the liberation of all Palestinian land and accept Israel's withdrawal from only the territories occupied in 1967: "We are certainly not opposed to total Israeli withdrawal from the Occupied Territories," it said, as long as Palestinians retain the "right to struggle for the full liberation of Palestinian soil."[86]

The following month, the Palestinian National Council, the PLO's parliament in exile, made an additional move away from its maximalist goals. For years, the PLO's charter had stated that only those Jews who had resided in Palestine prior to "the beginning of the Zionist invasion" would be considered Palestinian and therefore endowed, together with their patrilineal descendants, with "a legal right to their homeland." The implication was that any other Jews would have to leave. But after Black September, the PNC resolved to "set up a free and democratic society in Palestine for all Palestinians, including Muslims, Christians, and Jews." Arafat said it was "a humanitarian plan which will allow the Jews to live in dignity, as they have always lived, under the aegis of an Arab state and within the framework of Arab society."[87]

* * *

The PLO's next compromise came after the October 1973 war, which extended Israel's boundaries still farther. The Arab states' failure to recover an inch of the territory they had lost in 1967 all but obliterated what remained of Palestinian hopes of an Arab-led liberation. Worse, Arab demands were steadily narrowing, now focused on partial withdrawals from territories Israel conquered in 1967, with no mention of Palestinian rights or aspirations. In the words of one PLO leader, the 1973 war transformed the national movement "from romanticism to realism."[88]

A diplomatic push to resolve the conflict without involving the PLO intensified the sense that the doors to independence were closing. Two months after the war, the United States and the Soviet Union cosponsored the Middle East peace conference in Geneva, excluding the Palestinians. This was followed by the US-brokered withdrawals from parts of Egyptian and Syrian territory. The Palestinians feared that Jordan would achieve its aim of regaining the West Bank by forging its own agreement with Israel. Secretary Kissinger argued for precisely this, telling Israel repeatedly that a deal with Jordan was the best way to sideline the PLO, which was then still fighting for influence in the Occupied Territories. Otherwise, he warned Israel's ambassador to the United States, "within a year, Arafat will be the spokesman for the West Bank." PLO angst was palpable. Its weekly publication declared that it regarded "the implementation of military disengagement talks on the Jordanian front as a handover of our Palestinian land from the Zionist enemy to the Jordanian regime under U.S. imperialist sponsorship." But merely denouncing a Jordanian-Israeli deal was unlikely to stop it. The head of one PLO faction described the dilemma: "If the PLO declares that it wishes to rule the Gaza Strip and West Bank, then it will seem to have abandoned the historic rights of the Palestinian people to the rest of the Palestinian land"; if it does not, however, then it "will have officially relinquished the Bank and Strip to the Jordanian regime."[89]

In June 1974, weeks after the Israeli-Syrian disengagement agreement, President Richard Nixon traveled to Jerusalem and urged Prime Minister Rabin to sign a deal with Jordan over the West Bank, leaving out the PLO. That same month, under the threat of a Jordanian-Israeli agreement, the PNC made a momentous shift away from the PLO charter's rejection of any partition of the homeland and toward accepting a state in less than all of Mandatory Palestine. The PNC adopted a new ten-point political program that resolved to establish an "independent fighting national authority on any part of the Palestinian territory to be liberated." The Arab League later endorsed the plan and affirmed, over Jordan's objections, the PLO's status as "the sole legitimate representative of the Palestinian people."[90]

Arafat then took a further step. He joined Egypt and Syria to sign a

Tripartite Communiqué that softened the PNC ten-point program with three amendments. First, it eliminated reference to a "fighting national" authority, thus intimating that a Palestinian government, once established, would not necessarily fight Israel. Second, it implied a willingness to negotiate, stating that the territory on which the Palestinian authority was established would be liberated by either military *or political* means. Third, it promised to work toward Israeli withdrawal "from all *occupied* Arab territories," which meant, in the view of Egypt and Syria—and now, by implication of its signature, the PLO—only those Israel had conquered in 1967. Coming less than a year after the 1973 war, this was the first signal that the PLO would agree to a state in the West Bank and Gaza alone. The Popular Front for the Liberation of Palestine (PFLP) withdrew from the PLO executive committee in protest, forming a Rejectionist Front with several other PLO factions and accusing the mainstream PLO of lulling the Palestinians into submitting to a negotiated settlement "drop by drop."[91]

* * *

The PLO's next major move toward acceptance of Israel and a two-state partition along the pre-1967 lines occurred two and a half years later, in 1977, following a series of painful military defeats in the Lebanese civil war. The conflict had begun with clashes between Christian militias and Palestinian fighters in 1975, and the Palestinians had fared well at first. But the following year, they suffered thousands of losses, first in the PLO-controlled Beirut slum of Karantina, and later, at the Palestinian refugee camp of Tel al-Za'tar. Fearing a Palestinian victory that could limit its ability to dominate Lebanon, Syria and its allies defeated PLO forces, turned some factions against their fellow Palestinians, and controlled two-thirds of the country by the end of 1976, imposing severe restrictions on the organization's presence.[92]

Once again, the pressure was not just military but political, with the specter of a Jordanian takeover of the West Bank looming. Exploiting the PLO's weakness, Jordan revived the idea of a Jordanian-Palestinian confederation. Much to the PLO's displeasure, Egypt followed suit, telling Secretary of State Cyrus Vance that it too favored the idea. The Carter administration was eager to set up a new Middle East peace conference in Geneva, and again the PLO feared a Jordanian-Israeli deal from which it would be excluded.[93]

The PLO quickly took several moderating steps designed to placate the world powers, establish itself as an interlocutor with the United States, and block an agreement between Israel and Jordan. In January 1977, under the supervision of Fatah Central Committee member Mahmoud Abbas, it initiated a dialogue with several Israeli doves, including former general Mattityahu Peled. The same month, the head of the pro-Syrian PLO faction Sa'iqa stated that "in return for liberating some land we may accept a truce, for a longer or shorter period, and we may cancel the embargo on dealings with [Israel]." In February, Arafat sent a message to the United States expressing interest in a dialogue and met with Egypt's foreign minister to discuss changing the PLO's charter. Several days later, the PLO announced it was willing to attend the new Middle East peace conference, which would mean negotiating with Israel.[94]

The biggest step came the following month, when the PNC convened in Cairo and removed much of the ambiguity concerning its ten-point program of 1974. Addressing the PNC, the head of the PLO's political department, Faruq Qaddumi, explicitly stated, for the first time, that the Palestinian national authority would be established only in the West Bank and Gaza. That summer, the PLO sent a message to the White House offering to announce publicly and unambiguously its readiness to live in peace with Israel, if the United States would commit to supporting the establishment of an independent Palestinian state. Next, Qaddumi expressed willingness to approve a modified version of Resolution 242, entailing recognition of Israel, and to abandon the armed struggle.[95]

* * *

Yet the PLO's greatest concessions were still to come. Israel's June 6, 1982, invasion of Lebanon utterly transformed the Palestinian national movement, driving it from its last base in a country bordering Israel and putting it on the path to the historic compromise that would result in a PLO-led government in the West Bank and Gaza. During the invasion,

Israel swiftly conquered the south, besieged Beirut, captured six thousand PLO guerrillas, and forced Arafat to capitulate. The PLO abandoned bases in Beirut, handed over weapons to the Lebanese National Movement and Lebanese army, and evacuated eleven thousand personnel. To facilitate the surrender, the United States gave the PLO explicit written assurances that Israel had committed itself to ensure the safety of Palestinian civilians after the retreat.[96]

It was a promise the US and Israel did not keep. Eleven days after Arafat sailed from Beirut, the US peacekeeping contingent also departed, leaving Palestinians vulnerable. The Israeli defense minister, Ariel Sharon, who had repeatedly told IDF officers that Christian militias should "clean out" West Beirut, now ordered the army to allow Christian militiamen to enter Beirut's Sabra and Shatila refugee camps, where they proceeded to massacre between seven hundred and several thousand Palestinian civilians—primarily children, women, and the elderly— with much of the killing done in plain view of Israeli soldiers on a ridge overhead. During the rampage of rape and execution, Israeli flares illuminated the darkened camps, and terrified refugees were turned back at Israeli roadblocks in Sabra.[97]

The PLO had reached its nadir. The defeat in Lebanon had demonstrated the futility of seeking to liberate Palestine from neighboring bases and of hoping for Arab assistance. Arab states could hardly be relied upon to liberate Palestine when they would not attempt to defend even sovereign Lebanon from Israeli attack. Deputy PLO chief Salah Khalaf, known as Abu Iyad, quipped that the bickering Arabs had finally agreed on something during Israel's invasion: to betray the PLO. The organization had now clashed or quarreled with every Arab country bordering Palestine and was welcome in none. Its fighters were dispersed throughout the region, with no central base. Palestinians fled Lebanon in record numbers, with some seventy thousand departing from the Beirut airport in 1983 alone. The flow of funds to the organization dried up as crude oil prices dropped, the Soviet Union disengaged, and the polarized Arab world turned its attention to the Iran-Iraq War.[98] The decline of Soviet-US competition marginalized the Palestinians. Arafat and the PLO leadership were forced to relocate to faraway Tunisia.

Once again, concessions came quickly—just days, in fact, after the

Palestinian expulsion from Beirut. On September 1, 1982, the PLO completed its evacuation and President Ronald Reagan announced a plan for Middle East peace that was based closely on the 1978 Camp David Accords. It explicitly ruled out the possibility of Palestinian statehood, called for autonomy in the West Bank and Gaza in association with Jordan, and excluded the PLO. Yet after the rout in Lebanon, the PLO's desperate leaders said that Reagan's plan, which Israel rejected, had "some positive elements" and Arafat agreed to negotiate on the basis of it several months later.[99]

More significant was the PLO's acceptance of a new peace plan for two states on the pre-1967 lines, approved at the Arab summit in Fez just over a week after the last ship of PLO fighters sailed from Beirut. Previously the PLO had offered only conditional willingness to state that it would live in peace with Israel. Now that conditionality was dropped. The Fez Initiative was almost identical to a two-state plan put forward by Crown Prince Fahd of Saudi Arabia in August 1981, which Arafat had quietly helped formulate but was rejected by the PLO at the time. After Lebanon, however, two tweaks to the Saudi plan were enough to ensure Palestinian ratification: boilerplate mention of the PLO as the representative of the Palestinians and naming the UN Security Council as guarantor of "peace between all States of the region."[100]

The PLO took another placating step one year later. In September 1983, it endorsed the Geneva Declaration, which affirmed support for the Fez plan and for a solution based on "the relevant United Nations resolutions concerning the question of Palestine."[101] The PLO thereby dropped its insistence on modifying Resolution 242 and in doing so met the principal precondition of its inclusion in US-sponsored negotiations.

* * *

None of these incremental concessions extracted the PLO from its post-Lebanon predicament. Over the next several years, Palestinians would grow still more isolated and fragmented. Arafat felt he had no choice but to engage with Jordan, for fear that it would otherwise strike a deal over the West Bank without him, especially after Israel's primary advocate of a Jordanian-Palestinian confederation, Shimon Peres, became prime minister in 1984. Arafat met with Jordan's King Hussein two months after his expulsion from Lebanon. Controversially, he persuaded his PLO faction, Fatah, to accept a peace plan that included a Jordanian-Palestinian union without any guarantee—such as making an initial step of Palestinian statehood a clear precondition of the union—that it would not amount to Jordanian domination. That same month, senior PLO officials broke the Arab boycott of Egypt launched after Camp David, another signal of the PLO's pivot toward the Arab countries that were allied with the United States and prepared to make peace with Israel.[102]

The PLO's various conciliatory steps were less successful in generating movement toward peace talks than in causing turmoil within the floundering organization. Arafat's initiatives had generated large antagonisms, causing a split within Fatah in 1983 and a decision by two leftist factions, the Democratic Front for the Liberation of Palestine and the Popular Front for the Liberation of Palestine, to suspend their activity in the PLO. When Arafat made a high-profile visit to Sadat's successor, President Hosni Mubarak, in December 1983, some PLO officials called for his overthrow.

By 1986, a close Arafat aide published a paper stating that the organization had fallen into such disarray that its primary aim should be mere survival. The bleak scene at Arafat's Tunis office around this time was described by Yezid Sayigh in his authoritative history of the PLO: "Visitors to his headquarters during the summer and autumn of 1987 found little of the frenetic bustle that had long been [its] hallmark. All but absent were the PLO officials, foreign dignitaries, and journalists waiting into the early hours of the morning for brief interviews, the telephone rarely rang, and the reams of papers to be scanned and signed had dwindled." When Arafat arrived for the November 1987 Arab Summit in Amman, he was snubbed by King Hussein, who overlooked the PLO in his opening address. Arafat couldn't convince the other Arab leaders to make more than ritual mention of the Palestinians in the summit's concluding statement.[103]

* * *

The Palestinian national movement could hardly have been more adrift when, one month after the Amman summit, an Israeli army tank-transport truck plowed into a line of cars and vans carrying Palestinian laborers from Gaza, killing four and leading to the unexpected outbreak of protests that marked the beginning of the First Intifada. The PLO grabbed on to the uprising as to a life preserver. Suddenly the long-sought peace talks that the past several years of concessions had failed to produce seemed like a realistic possibility. Days after the intifada began, Arafat gave an interview stressing his acceptance not just of all relevant UN resolutions on Palestine but specifically of Resolution 242. Mahmoud Abbas announced that the PLO sought an international peace conference. Like the official PLO weekly, he argued for capitalizing on the insurrection by setting up a government-in-exile, which, it was thought, could put the Palestinians on an equal footing with other states at a hoped-for peace conference and circumvent the American and Israeli refusal to deal with the PLO.[104]

Though the uprising indeed brought new opportunities, it generated new pressures, too. First among these were concerns about how to sustain the revolt financially and when to exploit it politically. The intifada's primary architect, Khalil al-Wazir, known as Abu Jihad, worried that Arafat would seek diplomatic gains prematurely; others feared that by waiting the PLO risked missing an opportunity, as the energy of activists and the means of supporting them inevitably dwindled. A second strain was the suffering of West Bank and Gaza residents, who bore the brunt of the arrests, interrogations, economic deprivation, beatings, and killings. Speaking on behalf of the outside PLO leadership, Abu Iyad said, "Seeing children risking their lives imposed on us the need to achieve a realistic peace."[105]

Third was anxiety over the possibility that Israel or the United States could try to strike a direct bargain with West Bank and Gaza Palestinians, shutting out the PLO. The intifada had shifted the national movement's center of gravity, for the first time, from the diaspora to the "inside"—the Occupied Territories. In fact, without the weakening of the outside PLO leadership, Palestinians inside might never have felt the need to take the struggle for liberation into their own hands. This was the view of Abu Iyad, who said that there would have been no uprising if the PLO had remained in Beirut, because the people would still have been waiting for outside leaders to save them. Though the PLO's fear of a separate Israeli accommodation with local Palestinians was likely exaggerated, it was nevertheless common and made worse by the publication, one month into the intifada, of a fourteen-point political program drafted by Palestinians in the West Bank and Gaza and delivered to the US Secretary of State. It called for a declaration of independence and the establishment of a provisional government in which local Palestinians and PLO leaders in exile would have equal representation.[106]

A fourth, critical form of pressure came from Jordan, but in a most unexpected manner. Less than eight months into the uprising, following a failed Jordanian attempt to reassert control in the Occupied Territories and an Arab League decision to direct all funds for the intifada to the PLO, Jordan made a dramatic decision to end its long struggle to take back the West Bank. To the shock of the PLO leadership, Jordan dissolved its West Bank organizations, stopped its development projects, cut every legal and administrative tie to the territory, and announced that it was surrendering all claims on the West Bank to the PLO. The PLO leadership could not contain its joy over one of the greatest achievements in the history of the national movement. "The Jordanian option is over," said a gloating Arafat adviser. "Now there is the PLO, and only the PLO."[107]

This satisfaction didn't last long, for it raised two urgent questions. First, with whom would Israel and the United States now negotiate over the West Bank, given their boycott of the PLO? The scale and intensity of the intifada had generated renewed interest in Middle East peace. With Jordan out of the picture, there was a strong drive to push the PLO to make concessions in order to gain admittance to talks. The PLO's most powerful patron, the Soviet Union, urged it to recognize Israel. The United States did so as well. Secretary of State George Shultz gave a policy speech in which he cautioned that the Palestinian uprising served as a reminder that the status quo could not continue. He called for addressing the "legitimate rights of the Palestinian people, including political rights," and said that Palestinians should be permitted to participate in direct negotiations if they were to renounce terrorism, recognize Israel, and accept Resolution 242. "History will not repeat itself," he said, alluding to the unique opportunity presented by the intifada and Jordan's disengagement. "Practical, realistic steps by Palestinians are required."[108]

The second question raised by the Jordanian decision was more troubling: now that King Hussein had relinquished claims to the West Bank, would the right-wing government of Prime Minister Yitzhak Shamir annex it? In his speech, Shultz warned both Israelis and Palestinians against unilateral moves: "Peace cannot be achieved through the creation of an independent Palestinian state," he said, "or through permanent Israeli control or annexation of the West Bank and Gaza." To prevent the latter, the PLO decided it had to act. Within weeks of Jordan's disengagement, a PLO leader announced that the organization would preemptively declare a Palestinian state.[109]

The declaration was written mostly by the poet Mahmoud Darwish and delivered by Yasir Arafat at a PNC meeting in Algiers on November 15, 1988. Together with an accompanying communiqué, it became known as the PLO's "historic compromise." The Palestinians acknowledged that their right to sovereignty derived from what the PLO had for decades rejected as illegal and unjust: the 1947 UN plan that "partitioned Palestine into two states, one Arab, one Jewish." The PNC approved the declaration, accepted negotiations for a political settlement on the basis of Resolution 242, and consented to a state on only 22 percent of the homeland, calling for the "withdrawal of Israel from all the Palestinian and Arab territories it occupied in 1967, including Arab Jerusalem."[110]

To the nations the PLO was addressing it was easy to miss the new constraints that had led to this decision. Although the organization had gained new leverage from the intifada, it had no way of knowing how long that would last. If it did not seize the moment, it risked not just Israeli annexation of the West Bank but losing the opportunity to make political gains from the uprising before it was extinguished, with hundreds of Palestinians dead and the PLO back in its old rut.[111] It was easy, too, to overlook the continuity between the proclamation and the many relinquishments made over the preceding years. The declaration was in reality less a new concession than an attempt to repackage and cash in on a series of old and unreciprocated compromises, chief of which was the endorsement of a two-state solution.

Yet to the members present, the PNC's "session of the intifada" was still understood to be momentous. Before a world audience that was now finally paying attention, they had loudly offered the biggest compromise of all: abandoning the claim of refugees to sovereignty over their lands in the state of Israel. Liberating this lost land had been the central aim of the PLO's main factions, almost all of them founded by refugees, since their inception. It was for that reason that some Fatah dissidents rejected the PLO decision, accusing the organization of having acceded to "surrender in the guise of independence" and exchanging "a homeland for a state."[112] A PLO official, Shafiq al-Hout, described the emotional scene:

> When the moment came to vote, I left my seat. I had tears in my eyes and mixed emotions in my heart. A foreign journalist asked me if I was shedding tears of joy or sadness. I had to admit that they were both, but in a moment of anger, I said, "Thank God my father did not live to witness this day. I do not know what I could say to him if he asked me what was to become of his home city of Jaffa in this state that we have just declared."[113]

The following month, Arafat renounced terrorism and recognized Israel's right to exist. The United States rescinded its boycott of the PLO, and an era came to an end. Through eighteen years of defeat and incremental compromise, the Palestinian national movement had, in al-Hout's words, abandoned what it long considered a just solution in the hope of achieving a possible one.[114]

* * *

What Palestinians saw as a historic concession, sacrificing justice for the sake of peace and consenting to a state on less than one-fourth of their homeland, Israel viewed as an unreasonable, unjust, and maximalist demand for withdrawal from every inch of the territory it had conquered in 1967. Israel bridled at the notion of giving to the feeble PLO the same total evacuation that it had granted to Egypt, the strongest Arab country. Still less was it inclined to hand over to its weakest adversary territory it had valued even more than the biblical lands of Sinai and Lebanon.[115] To contain the intifada, Israel was willing to offer no more than limited self-governance. The Palestinians had refused that for over a decade, although they had no capability to obtain more.

The stalemate was broken by more pressure on the Palestinians. Under the twin strains of economic asphyxiation and political isolation, the PLO would soon do the unthinkable and compromise on the "historic compromise," agreeing to postpone independence and accept limited autonomy under Israeli occupation.

The decisive event was Iraq's August 1990 invasion of Kuwait, which placed the PLO in an acute dilemma. On one hand, some four hundred thousand Palestinians lived in Kuwait, and the PLO relied on funding from Kuwait's Gulf Arab allies, which felt threatened by Iraq and joined the US-led coalition against it. On the other hand, the PLO had forged strategic and financial ties to Iraq, and many Palestinians supported Saddam Hussein's invasion. To oppose Iraq, moreover, was to risk inviting its retaliation against those hundreds of thousands of Palestinians in Kuwait. And Arafat was angry with the Gulf states because they had supported his Islamist rivals, offered minimal support to the intifada, and given over seven times more aid to the Afghan mujahiddin since the early 1980s than they had provided to the PLO since its founding.[116]

Arafat sought at first to take a position of ostensible neutrality. But not long after the invasion, the PLO was seen as backing Iraq unmistakably. At an Arab summit it initially voted against a resolution denouncing Iraq's threats to the Gulf states and supporting Saudi Arabia's request for US forces to defend it against Iraq; by late August 1990, however, the PLO and its main factions were arguing that Iraq's invasion was a preemptive, defensive move against an American conspiracy.[117]

It was a decision from which the PLO never recovered. Hundreds of thousands of Palestinians fled Kuwait after the war. Many Arab states, which had been contributing less and less money to the PLO, now cut off funds altogether, putting stress both on the weakened organization and the waning intifada. Strikes in the West Bank and Gaza could not be maintained when the PLO couldn't afford to pay the families of workers. In the summer of 1991, a leader of the PFLP remarked: "We burdened the uprising with more than it could bear." The PLO was politically isolated—not just condemned by the Arab states but estranged from both superpowers. The United States had already cut off dialogue with the organization after guerrillas from one of its factions launched a thwarted attack at an Israeli beach in May 1990. Then, as the Soviet Union was foundering, senior PLO officials made the mistake of publicly exulting in an abortive August 1991 coup attempt.[118]

The Soviet collapse several months later brought new hardships. The states of the region shifted toward alliance with the United States, Israel's closest ally. The Arabs were without a military option against Israel. The PLO lost a vital patron. And the fall of communism dealt a near fatal blow to the Marxist, Leninist, and pan-Arab factions once promoted by the Soviets. In its final two years, the Soviet Union lifted restrictions on Jewish emigration, leading several hundred thousand citizens to move to Israel by the end of 1991, with hundreds of thousands more to follow.[119] These immigrants posed a twofold threat to Palestinian statehood: first, the increase in the number of Jews in Israel and the territories it occupied lessened the country's demographic need for partition; second, Prime Minister Shamir had vowed to settle the new immigrants in the West Bank and Gaza, complicating any future withdrawal.

The PLO was quick to adapt to its weakened position. At the US- and Soviet-sponsored peace conference in Madrid in October 1991, the Palestinians accepted terms of attendance set by Israel and the United States: they would not form their own delegation but would rather be part of a joint Jordanian-Palestinian group; they would be represented by neither PLO officials nor Jerusalem residents nor members of the diaspora but instead by leaders in the West Bank and Gaza not affiliated with the organization, relegating PLO heavyweights to a behind-the-scenes role outside the negotiating room; their talks with Israel would be on limited autonomy in Gaza and the West Bank, excluding Jerusalem, and not on statehood or a final peace agreement; the conference would have no power to impose a solution to the conflict; and Israeli settlements would continue to be built during the negotiations. These were largely the terms of the 1978 Camp David Accords that the PLO had adamantly refused. Explaining the reversal, Faruq Qaddumi said the Palestinians had no choice: it was either join the peace process or exit history.[120]

The Madrid conference led to a series of bilateral negotiations in Washington that lasted until mid-1993 and went nowhere. In large part this was because the talks offered the PLO no incentive to support an agreement from which it would have been shut out. Shimon Peres remarked that expecting the PLO to allow local leaders to reach an agreement with Israel was like asking the turkey to help prepare Thanksgiving dinner. Arafat believed the United States wanted him to approve the talks, agree to a non-PLO delegation, and disappear, like "a male bee that fertilizes once and then dies." A member of the Executive Committee wrote, "As if Abu Ammar [Arafat] was not paranoid enough already, with his insistence on keeping all the cards in his hand and remaining the sole decision maker, some people started whispering to him about the possibility of an alternative leadership in the Occupied Territories." Yezid Sayigh wrote that Arafat "privately resented the delegation's access to the US administration, and feared that such recognition could presage the emergence of an alternative 'insider' leadership."[121] To deal with the threat, he used his influence over the Palestinian negotiators to delay and obstruct the Washington talks, in the hope of forcing the United States or Israel to engage him directly.[122]

The strategy worked. In January 1993, Israel launched direct negotiations with the PLO in Sarpsborg, Norway, south of Oslo, under the auspices of Arafat and Mahmoud Abbas for the PLO and Foreign Minister Shimon Peres and his deputy, Yossi Beilin, for Israel. The Israeli government saw an opportunity in the PLO's predicament. Rabin correctly observed that the organization was "on the ropes" and was therefore likely to make new concessions. Israel's head of military intelligence told Rabin that Arafat was now the best possible interlocutor, because the PLO's situation had become so dire that it risked imminent collapse.

This was hardly an exaggeration. Beginning in March 1993, while the fateful talks were taking place in Norway, the PLO cut payments to as many as one in three of its personnel. Assistance to the West Bank and Gaza dropped over 90 percent by mid-1993. The PLO budget had been halved, the Palestinian National Fund could not meet its obligations, numerous media outlets were closed, and thousands of Fatah guerrillas had been laid off. In Lebanon, the lack of funds resulted in medical emergencies that went untreated, the deaths of Palestinians who couldn't afford dialysis for their failing kidneys, unrest in the refugee camps, and protests in front of the PLO representative's home.[123] The leadership ranks of the national movement had thinned after senior figures like Abu Jihad and Abu Iyad were assassinated. All the while, Islamists were steadily gaining on the PLO in Gaza and the West Bank.

Under the greatest strain in its history, the PLO made its greatest concession. Insolvency, political isolation, and competition with local leaders induced compromises that even the 1982 military defeat in Lebanon had not. Less than eight months after the first meeting in Norway, the PLO agreed to what it had categorically rejected since Camp David: a plan for limited self-governance under Israeli occupation, closely based on Menachem Begin's 1977 autonomy proposal, which had been designed for the specific purpose of forestalling Carter's push for Palestinian self-determination. Although the plan offered real gains to the Palestinians and contained unprecedented concessions from Israel—unimaginable in the absence of severe American pressure—it fell far short of American and Palestinian goals. To Zbigniew Brzezinski, it amounted to little more than a "Basutoland for the Arabs"—a reference to a former African kingdom under British colonial administration.

When the PLO finally relented in 1993, giving up fifteen years of resistance to the plan, the Israeli novelist Amos Oz said it was a triumph surpassed only by the establishment of the Jewish state—"the second biggest victory in the history of Zionism."[124] This assessment was merited insofar as the Palestinians had taken the most concrete step yet toward giving up 78 percent of their homeland, but it ignored the fact that the victory also contained unprecedented Zionist concessions—the first post-1967 steps toward partition of Mandatory Palestine, establishment of Palestinian self-governance, and diminishment of Israeli control over large parts of the West Bank and Gaza—concessions that were not only coerced but that constituted an outcome far less desirable to the Israeli government than the status quo before the intifada: full control of the Occupied Territories, with no Palestinian autonomy and minimal resistance.

Some Palestinians overstated the benefits of the deal. Mahmoud Abbas, whom the Norwegian, Israeli, and Palestinian participants at Oslo had called the "Holy Spirit" of the talks, referred to the agreement as an "achievement" that "ended a twentieth-century conflict." The PLO negotiator Nabil Sha'ath said the accord meant "a full peace with Israel, with totally open borders." Arafat's assessment was more cautious: "I know many of you here think Oslo is a bad agreement," he said after arriving in Gaza in July 1994. "It is a bad agreement. But it's the best we can get in the worst situation."[125]

Not everyone agreed. Several in the Palestinian leadership foresaw the catastrophe they would face at the close of Oslo's so-called interim period of five years: expansion of Israeli settlements; increased unemployment and economic dependence on Israel; greater restrictions on Palestinian movement; newfound Israeli control over PLO leaders no longer in exile; the discrediting of former strugglers for Palestinian national liberation, now regarded as the occupation's collaborators and lowly clerks; and no end in sight to Israeli military control.[126]

The objection of these critics, many of them leading advocates of accommodation with Israel, was not that Oslo restricted the Palestinians to only 22 percent of their homeland. It was that the deal had not provided even that. By failing to obtain Israeli agreement just to the mere possibility of eventually establishing a Palestinian state, the PLO had consented to what risked becoming indefinite occupation. Edward Said, among the harshest critics of Oslo and also then one of the most prominent supporters of a two-state solution, wrote: "For the first time in the twentieth century, an anticolonial liberation movement had . . . made an agreement to cooperate with a military occupation before that occupation had ended." Unlike Nelson Mandela's African National Congress, which had refused to supply the white South African government with police officers until parity between white and black South Africans had been reached, the PLO had agreed to become Israel's enforcer. Through Oslo, wrote Said, "the Israelis are rid of an unwanted insurrectionary problem, represented by Gaza, that Arafat must now work at solving for them." The leaders of the intifada would become officers in the Palestinian intelligence services, tasked with suppressing dissent; men who had once thrown themselves as wrenches into the gears of occupation became its chief lubricants instead. Two independent members of the PLO Executive Committee, Mahmoud Darwish and Shafiq al-Hout, resigned in protest.[127]

On the other hand, Oslo's proponents argued, what had the Palestinians really conceded? The PLO had already accepted a state on

22 percent of the homeland in 1988, and by the time of Oslo the organization was a spent force, with little ability to procure better terms. By
signing Oslo, the PLO acquired, for the first time, recognition from
Israel and the large boost in international legitimacy that went with it;
return from exile; and, in the eyes of Arafat, at least the prospect of a
Palestinian state. It also gave the PLO a government based in part of its
homeland, the transfer of authority from Israel's military to the Palestinians, limited Israeli withdrawals, and a major step toward partitioning Mandatory Palestine, all without renouncing the claim to a sovereign
state. Though this was less than full independence, it was more than
Israel had previously been willing to give. Critics maligned the modest
gains of Oslo, but there was little reason to believe that refusal of it would
have brought full independence within grasp.

In bringing the PLO into the West Bank and Gaza, Oslo carried risks
for both sides. For Israel, the risk was that when temporary autonomy
began to look permanent, after the five-year interim period had expired,
Palestinian factions could turn the weapons of the authority's security
forces against Israel. For the Palestinians, the risk was that the struggle
for national liberation would be replaced by the struggle for mortgages,
government salaries, donor aid, reduced Israeli incursions into cities
ostensibly under Palestinian control, and higher numbers of exit
permits. The Palestinians would become so dependent on their self-
governing authority, and that authority so dependent on Israel, that
there would be little chance of confronting their occupiers in a manner
that jeopardized the existence of the Oslo system. The dangers for both
parties eventually materialized, but the Palestinian liability turned out
to be the greater and more enduring one. Israel proved quite capable of
dealing with the military threat of Palestinian security officers and their
light arms. The Palestinians, by contrast, are still struggling to wean
themselves from their enfeebling dependency on the Oslo apparatus.

More important than what Oslo modified was what both it and the
Camp David Accords left out. Neither one offered any guarantee that
the interim period would finish after five years; neither demanded a
removal of settlements nor even a halt in their expansion; neither stated
that Palestinians would have a capital in any part of Jerusalem; neither
suggested how the refugee problem would be resolved; neither described

what Israel's borders would be or whether there would be a withdrawal to something close to the pre-1967 lines; neither indicated that the Palestinians would eventually achieve self-determination; and, most critically, neither specified what would happen if negotiations on the final status of the West Bank and Gaza did not successfully conclude.

Oslo was ostensibly meant to lead to a final agreement, but it provided Israel with little incentive to reach one. In this respect, the germ of Oslo—Begin's 1977 plan for Palestinian self-rule—had a much better chance at ushering in a full disengagement from the Occupied Territories. By offering citizenship to all residents of Mandatory Palestine during the interim period, Begin's plan would have given Israel a strong demographic incentive to bring that period to an end—or else accept a Palestinian majority controlling the parliament and government of the Jewish state. In Oslo, by contrast, Israel was granted indefinite control of all the land without having to give equal rights to all its residents. So long as Oslo's so-called interim period continued, Israel could postpone choosing between the two painful options—a full partition or equal rights for Palestinians—that it most sought to avoid. Israel would have every incentive to keep Oslo going indefinitely, forestall the choice, and perpetuate Palestinian self-governance under occupation. In the meantime, it could build settlements across the Occupied Territories in order to unilaterally shape the contours of any future partition.[128]

* * *

Twenty years after Oslo, the population of Jewish settlers in Jerusalem and the West Bank had reached well over half a million, and Likud Prime Minister Benjamin Netanyahu was advancing a boom in construction of new settlement housing while conducting still more rounds of inconclusive, US-mediated talks.[129] In the years between, the Palestinians tried every method of breaking out of the Oslo trap. They conducted years of peaceful weekly demonstrations in West Bank villages where land was expropriated. They sent spokesmen and diplomats around the world to present their case. They put forward UN resolutions and gave evidence to the International Criminal Court. They joined international institutions where they could pursue their claims, and, at the behest of their financial donors, especially the United States, they refrained from joining others. They engaged in economic cooperation with Israel, and they made limited attempts at boycotts as well. They worked hand-in-glove with Israeli security forces to arrest Palestinian militants and stifle even nonviolent protests, and at other times they also looked away to let some of the militants attack. They elected as president the man who had stood most resolutely against violence, Mahmoud Abbas, and they elected as prime minister Ismail Haniyeh, a leader of the Islamic Resistance Movement, Hamas.

They strengthened governing institutions, dismantled militias, and implemented a reform of their security forces under Salam Fayyad, an appointed technocrat who replaced the Hamas prime minister and was hailed in capitals across the globe. They fought multiple wars from Gaza, and they enforced years-long cease-fires in between. They launched a 2000–2005 intifada that was taken over by militias, and they initiated an "orphaned uprising" of unorganized, individual attacks in 2015. Following Abbas's 2005 election, they provided Israel with a decade of unprecedented quiet in the West Bank. When that didn't work, they threatened to dismantle the self-governing authority on which they had become financially dependent, and not long after that they vowed never to give it up. Above all, and with greater consistency than with any other approach, they engaged in every possible form of negotiation: international summit conferences, proximity talks, draft peace treaties, secret bilateral talks mediated by the United States, secret bilateral meetings without mediators, and high-profile official negotiations facilitated by US presidents and secretaries of state.

In all that time, Israel never presented the Palestinians with what it offered to every neighboring Arab state: a full withdrawal from occupied territory. Egypt regained sovereignty over each grain of sand in Sinai, with no Israeli settlement left standing. Jordan established peace based on the international boundary as defined under the British Mandate, forcing Israel to give back 147 square miles. Lebanon obtained disengagement to the international border without providing Israel with recognition, peace, or even a cease-fire agreement. And Syria received a 1998 proposal from Netanyahu—on which the prime minister subsequently backtracked—for full departure from the Golan Heights.[130]

But the Palestinians have never secured such an offer, despite being the only party to the Arab-Israeli conflict that has a legal and moral claim to *more* territory than that which Israel conquered in 1967. Shimon Peres was among the few Israeli officials to acknowledge the magnitude of the concession made by the Palestinians when they agreed to a state on the pre-1967 lines, 22 percent of their homeland. Before this shift, he said, "the Palestinian state's size should have been according to the 1947 map," in which Palestinians were to receive 44 percent. "Arafat moved from the 1947 map to the 1967 one," giving up half the land allotted to the Palestinians. "I don't know any Arab leader," he said, "who would give up 2 or 3 percent."[131]

Peres said Arafat's relinquishment was Israel's "greatest achievement." But instead of seizing on this greatest of achievements, Israel pocketed it, taking the compromise as a starting point for negotiations on dividing the remaining 22 percent. Those talks have failed repeatedly, in no small part because Palestinians have had no leverage with which to insist that a state on the pre-1967 lines with Jerusalem as its capital was not intended as an opening bid but rather as the bare minimum of a peace agreement like those reached with Jordan and Egypt.

Palestinians have failed where other Arab nations have succeeded because they never posed a real threat to Israel and were too weak to protect their concessions from further erosion. One year before fully withdrawing from Lebanon, Ehud Barak explained the reason for prioritizing peace with the Syrians over the Palestinians and for the discrepancy in Israel's approach to the two nations: "The Syrians have 700 war planes, 4,000 tanks, 2,500 artillery pieces, and surface-to-surface missiles that are neatly organized and can cover the country with nerve gas," he said. "The Palestinians are the source of legitimacy for the continuation of the conflict, but they are the weakest of all our adversaries. As a military threat they are ludicrous. They pose no military threat of any kind."[132]

* * *

During the past two and a half decades of intermittent negotiations, Palestinian powerlessness has induced further compromises, from consent to Israel's annexation of settlement blocs, to giving up large parts of Jerusalem that were conquered in 1967, to acquiescing in demilitarization and other restrictions on the sovereignty of their future state. Despite these concessions, the Palestinians remained far too weak to obtain what has been granted to them by international law, including, for example, a 1980 UN Security Council resolution calling on Israel to dismantle all settlements in the territories occupied in 1967.[132] In fact, on every major issue of peace negotiations—from borders, Jerusalem, and refugees to settlements, water, and security—the Palestinians have demanded no more, and often considerably less, than what international law and the majority of the world's nations ostensibly support. Yet Israeli governments continue to claim that Palestinian demands are unreasonable and that Israel has no partner for peace.

Through years of coercion and defeat, Palestinians have been compelled to accept the positions of the UN Security Council, Europe, and the United States. But these same parties have failed to put similar pressure on Israel to respect those positions as well. As a result, the Palestinians have been stuck in limbo: not strong enough to resist international demands and too weak to prevail upon Israel to comply. The Palestinian leadership has thus been left to engage in one round of stalemated talks after another, while its frustrated constituents cycle through bursts of violence, Israeli counterviolence, and periods of wearied, submissive quiescence, each new capitulation strengthening the Israeli view that force is the only language the Palestinians understand.

IV. Peace Industry Illusions

> *History teaches us that men and nations behave wisely once they have exhausted all other alternatives.*[134]
>
> —ABBA EBAN

It has now been more than a quarter century since Israelis and Palestinians first started negotiating under US auspices in Madrid. There is no shortage of explanations for why each particular round of talks failed. The rationalizations appear and reappear in the speeches of presidents, the reports of think tanks, and the memoirs of former officials and negotiators: bad timing; artificial deadlines; insufficient preparation; no agreed terms of reference; inadequate confidence-building measures; coalition politics; or leaders devoid of courage. Many blame imbalanced mediation; poor coordination among separate negotiating channels; scant attention from the US president; want of support from regional states; exclusion of key stakeholders; or clumsily choreographed public diplomacy. Among the most common refrains are that extremists were allowed to set the agenda and there was a neglect of bottom-up economic development and state-building. And then there are those who point at negative messaging, insurmountable skepticism, or the absence of personal chemistry (a particularly fanciful explanation for anyone who has witnessed the warm familiarity of Palestinian and Israeli negotiators as they reunite in luxury hotels and reminisce about old jokes and ex-comrades over breakfast buffets and post-meeting toasts). If none of the above works, there is always the worst cliché of them all—lack of trust.[135]

Postmortem accounts vary in their apportionment of blame; itemization of tactics mistakenly applied; and mix of frustration, hope, and despair. But nearly all of them share a deep-seated belief that both societies desire a two-state agreement and therefore need only the right conditions—together with a bit of nudging, trust-building, and perhaps a few more positive inducements—to take the final step.

In this view, Oslo would have led to peace had it not been for the tragic assassination of Yitzhak Rabin. The 1998 Wye River Memorandum and its commitment to further Israeli withdrawals in the West Bank would have been implemented if only the Labor Party had joined Netanyahu's coalition to back the agreement. The Camp David summit in July 2000 would have succeeded if the United States had been less sensitive to Israeli domestic concerns, insisted on a written Israeli proposal, consulted the Arab states at an earlier phase, and taken the more firm and balanced position adopted half a year later, in December 2000, when President Clinton outlined parameters for an agreement. Both parties could have accepted the Clinton parameters with only minimal reservations had the proposal not been presented so fleetingly, as a one-time offer that would disappear when Clinton stepped down less than a month later. The negotiations in Taba, Egypt, in January 2001 were on the brink of agreement but failed because time ran out, with Clinton just out of office, and Ehud Barak facing almost certain electoral defeat to Ariel Sharon. The two major peace plans of 2003—the US-sponsored Roadmap to Middle East Peace and the unofficial Geneva Accord—could have been embraced had it not been for a bloody intifada and a hawkish Likud prime minister in power.

And on it goes: the Annapolis negotiations of 2007–2008 came very close to a breakthrough but were thwarted by Ehud Olmert's corruption scandals, unprecedentedly low popularity, and resignation just days after he suggested the most far-reaching proposal of the talks. Direct negotiations between Abbas and Netanyahu in 2010 could have lasted more than thirteen days if only Israel had agreed to temporarily halt construction of some illegal settlements in exchange for an extra $3 billion package from the United States. Several years of secret back-channel negotiations between the envoys of Netanyahu and Abbas could have made history if only they weren't forced to conclude prematurely in late 2013, because of an artificial deadline imposed by separate talks led by Secretary of State John Kerry. And, finally, the Kerry negotiations of 2013–2014 could have led to a framework agreement if the secretary of state had spent even a sixth as much time negotiating the text with the Palestinians as he did with the Israelis, and if he hadn't made inconsistent promises to the two sides regarding the guidelines for the talks, the release of Palestinian prisoners, curtailing Israeli settlement construction, and the presence of US mediators in the negotiating room.[136]

* * *

Each of these rounds of diplomacy began with vows to succeed where predecessors had failed. Each included affirmations of the urgency of peace or warnings of the closing window, perhaps even the last chance, for a two-state solution. Each ended with a list of tactical mistakes and unforeseen developments that resulted in failure. And, just as surely, each neglected to offer the most logical and parsimonious explanation for failure: no agreement was reached because at least one of the parties preferred to maintain the impasse.

The Palestinians chose no agreement over one that did not meet the bare minimum supported by international law and most nations of the world. For years this consensus view supported the establishment of a

Palestinian state on the pre-1967 lines with minor, equivalent land swaps that would allow Israel to annex some settlements. The Palestinian capital would be in East Jerusalem, with sovereignty over the al-Aqsa Mosque compound and overland contiguity with the rest of the Palestinian state. Israel would withdraw its forces from the West Bank and release Palestinian prisoners. And Palestinian refugees would be offered compensation, a right to return not to their homes but to their homeland in the State of Palestine, acknowledgment of Israel's partial responsibility for the refugee problem, and, on a scale that would not perceptibly change Israel's demography, a return of some refugees to their pre-1948 lands and homes.

Although years of violence and repression have led Palestinians to make some small concessions that chipped away at this compromise, they have not fundamentally abandoned it. They continue to hope that the support of the majority of the world's states for a plan along these lines will eventually result in an agreement. In the meantime, the status quo has been made more bearable thanks to the architects of the peace process, who have spent billions to prop up the PA, create conditions of prosperity for decision-makers in Ramallah, and dissuade the population from confronting the occupying force.

Israel, for its part, has consistently opted for stalemate rather than the sort of agreement outlined above. The reason is obvious: the deal's cost is much higher than the cost of making no deal. The damages Israel would risk incurring through such an accord are massive. They include perhaps the greatest political upheaval in the country's history; enormous demonstrations against—if not majority rejection of—Palestinian sovereignty in Jerusalem and over the Temple Mount/Noble Sanctuary; and violent rebellion by some Jewish settlers and their supporters. There could be bloodshed during forcible evacuations of West Bank settlements and rifts within the body implementing the evictions, the Israeli army, whose share of religious infantry officers now surpasses one-third. Israel would lose military control over the West Bank, resulting in less intelligence gathering, less room for maneuver in future wars, and less time to react to a surprise attack. It would face increased security risks from a Gaza–West Bank corridor, which would allow militants, ideology, and weapons-production techniques to spread from

Gaza training camps to the West Bank hills overlooking Israel's airport. Israeli intelligence services would no longer control which Palestinians enter and exit the Occupied Territories. The country would cease extraction of West Bank natural resources, including water, lose profits from managing Palestinian customs and trade, and pay the large economic and social price of relocating tens of thousands of settlers.[137]

Only a fraction of these costs could be offset by a peace agreement's benefits. Chief among these would be the blow dealt to efforts to delegitimate the country and the normalization of relations with other nations of the region. Israeli businesses would be able to operate more openly in Arab states, and government cooperation with such countries as Saudi Arabia and the United Arab Emirates would go from covert to overt. Through a treaty with the Palestinians, Israel could attain the relocation of every Tel Aviv embassy to Jerusalem, and receive additional financial and security benefits from the United States and Europe. But all of these combined do not come close to outweighing the deficits.

Nor have the moral costs of occupation for Israeli society been high enough to change the calculus. Ending international opprobrium is indeed important to the country's elites, and as they find themselves increasingly shunned, the incentive to withdraw from the Occupied Territories will likely increase. But so far Israel has proven quite capable of living with the decades-old label of "pariah," the stain of occupation, and the associated impact on the country's internal harmony and relations with Diaspora Jews. For all the recent fretting about decreasing American Jewish support for Israel, the conversation today is not so different than it was at the time of the first Likud-led governments decades ago. Similarly enduring—and endurable—are the worries that occupation delegitimates Zionism and causes discord within Israel. As far back as over thirty years ago, former deputy mayor of Jerusalem Meron Benvenisti wrote of growing numbers of Israelis who had doubts about Zionism, "expressed in the forms of alienation, emigration of young Israelis, the emergence of racist Jews, violence in society, the widening gap between Israel and the Diaspora, and a general feeling of inadequacy."[138] Israelis have grown adept at tuning such criticisms out.

It was, is, and will remain irrational for Israel to absorb the costs of an agreement when the price of the alternative is so comparatively low. The consequences of choosing impasse are hardly threatening: mutual recriminations over the cause of stalemate, new rounds of talks, and retaining control of all of the West Bank from within and much of Gaza from without. Meanwhile Israel continues to receive more US military aid per year than goes to all the world's nations combined and presides over a growing economy, rising standards of living, and a population that reports one of the world's highest levels of subjective well-being.[139] Israel will go on absorbing the annoying but so-far tolerable costs of complaints about settlement policies. And it will likely witness several more countries bestowing the State of Palestine with symbolic recognition, a few more negative votes in impotent university student councils, limited calls for boycotts of settlement goods, and occasional bursts of violence that the greatly overpowered Palestinians are too weak to sustain. There is no contest.

* * *

The real explanation for the past decades of failed peace negotiations is not mistaken tactics or imperfect circumstances but that no strategy can succeed if it is premised on Israel behaving irrationally. Most arguments put to Israel for agreeing to a partition are that it is preferable to an imagined, frightening future in which the country ceases to be either a Jewish state, a democracy, or both. But these assertions contain the implicit acknowledgment that it makes no sense for Israel to strike a deal today rather than wait to see if such imagined threats actually materialize; if and when they do come to be, Israel can then make a deal. Perhaps in the interim, the hardship of Palestinian life will cause enough emigration that Israel may annex the West Bank without giving up the state's Jewish majority. Or, perhaps, the West Bank will be absorbed by Jordan, and Gaza by Egypt, a better outcome than Palestinian statehood, in the view of many Israeli officials.

It is hard to argue that forestalling a settlement in the present makes a worse deal more likely in the future: the international community and the PLO have already established the ceiling of their demands—22 percent of the land now under Israeli control—while providing far less clarity about the floor, which Israel can try to lower. Israel has continued to reject the same Palestinian claims made since the 1980s, albeit with a few added Palestinian concessions. In fact, history suggests that a strategy of waiting would serve the country well: from the British government's 1937 Peel Commission partition plan and the UN partition plan of 1947 to UN Security Council Resolution 242 and the Oslo Accords, every formative initiative endorsed by the great powers has given more to the Jewish community in Palestine than the previous one. Even if an Israeli prime minister knew that one day the world's nations would impose sanctions on Israel if it did not accept a two-state agreement, it would still be irrational to strike such a deal now. Israel could instead wait until that day comes and thereby enjoy many more years of West Bank control and the security advantages that go with it, particularly valuable at a time of cataclysm in the region.

Israel is frequently admonished to make peace in order to avoid becoming a single, Palestinian-majority state ruling all the territory from the Jordan River to the Mediterranean Sea. But that threat does not have much credibility when it is Israel that holds all the power and will therefore decide whether or not it annexes territory and offers citizenship to all its inhabitants. A single state will not materialize until a majority of Israelis want it, and so far they overwhelmingly do not. The reason Israel has not annexed the West Bank and Gaza is not for fear of international slaps on the wrist, but because the strong preference of most of the country's citizens is to have a Jewish-majority homeland, the raison d'être of Zionism. If and when Israel is confronted with the threat of a single state, it can enact a unilateral withdrawal and count on the support of the great powers in doing so. But that threat is still quite distant.

In fact, Israelis and Palestinians are now farther from a single state than they have been at any time since the occupation began in 1967. From Begin's autonomy plan to Oslo and the withdrawal from Gaza, Israel and Palestine have been inching steadily toward partition. Walls and fences separate Israel from Gaza and over 90 percent of the West Bank. Palestinians have a quasi state in the Occupied Territories, with its own parliament, courts, intelligence services, and Foreign Ministry. Israelis no longer shop in Nablus and Gaza the way they did before Oslo. Palestinians no longer travel freely to Tel Aviv. And the supposed reason that partition is often claimed to be impossible—the difficulty of a probable relocation of over 150,000 settlers—is grossly overstated: in the 1990s Israel absorbed several times as many Russian immigrants, many of them far more difficult to integrate than settlers, who already have Israeli jobs, fully formed networks of family support, and a command of Hebrew.[140]

As long as the Palestinian government and the Oslo system are in place, the world's nations will not demand that Israel grant citizenship to Palestinians. Indeed, Israel has had a non-Jewish majority in the territory it controls for several years.[141] Yet even in their sternest warnings, Western governments invariably refer to an undemocratic Israel as a mere hypothetical possibility. Most of the world's nations will refuse to call Israel's control of the West Bank a form of apartheid—defined by the International Criminal Court as a regime of systematic oppression and domination of a racial group with the intention of maintaining that regime—so long as there is a chance, however slim, that Oslo remains a transitional phase to an independent Palestinian state.

* * *

Contrary to what nearly every US mediator has asserted, it is not that Israel greatly desires a peace agreement but has a pretty good fallback option. It is that Israel greatly prefers the fallback option to a peace agreement. No tactical brilliance in negotiations, no amount of expert preparation, no perfect alignment of the stars can overcome that obstacle. Only two things can: a more attractive agreement, or a less attractive fallback. The first of these options has been tried extensively, from offering Israel full normalization with most Arab and Islamic states to promising upgraded relations with Europe, US security guarantees, and increased financial and military assistance. But for Israel these inducements pale in comparison to the perceived costs.

The second option is to make the fallback worse. This is what President Eisenhower did when he threatened economic sanctions to get Israel to withdraw from Sinai and Gaza. This is what President Ford did when he reassessed US relations with Israel, refusing to provide it with new arms deals until it agreed to a second Sinai withdrawal. This is what President Carter did when he raised the spectre of terminating US military assistance if Israel did not immediately evacuate Lebanon in September 1977. And this is what Carter did when he made clear to both sides at Camp David that the United States would withhold aid and downgrade relations if they did not sign an agreement. This, likewise, is what Secretary of State James Baker did in 1991, when he forced a reluctant Prime Minister Shamir to attend negotiations in Madrid by withholding a $10 billion loan guarantee that Israel needed to absorb the immigration of Soviet Jews.[142] That was the last time the United States applied pressure of this sort.

The Palestinians, too, have endeavored to make Israel's fallback option less attractive through two uprisings and other periodic bouts of violence. But the extraordinary price they paid proved unsustainable, and on the whole they have been too weak to worsen Israel's fallback for very long. As a result, Palestinians have been unable to induce more from Israel than tactical concessions, steps meant to reduce friction between the populations in order not to end occupation but to mitigate it and restore its low cost.

Forcing Israel to make larger, conflict-ending concessions would require making its fallback option so unappealing that Israel would view a peace agreement as an escape from something worse. That demands more leverage than the Palestinians have so far possessed, while those who do have sufficient power have not been eager to use it. Since Oslo, in fact, the United States has done quite the reverse, working to maintain the low cost of Israel's fallback option. Successive US administrations have financed the PA, trained its resistance-crushing security forces, pressured the PLO not to confront Israel in international institutions, vetoed UN Security Council resolutions that were not to Israel's liking, shielded Israel's arsenal from calls for a nuclear-free Middle East, ensured Israel's military superiority over all of its neighbors, provided the country with over $3 billion in military aid each year, and exercised its influence to defend Israel from criticism.

No less important, the United States has consistently sheltered Israel from accountability for its policies in the West Bank by putting up a facade of opposition to settlements that in practice is a bulwark against more significant pressure to dismantle them. Both the United States and most of Europe draw a sharp distinction between Israel and the Occupied

Territories, refusing to recognize Israeli sovereignty beyond the pre-1967 lines. When the limousine of the US president travels from West to East Jerusalem, the Israeli flag comes down from the driver-side front corner. US officials must obtain special permission to meet Israelis at the IDF's central command headquarters in the Jerusalem settlement of Neve Yaakov or at the Justice Ministry in the heart of downtown East Jerusalem. And US regulations, not consistently enforced, stipulate that products from the settlements should not bear a made-in-Israel label.

Israel vehemently protests against this policy of so-called differentiation between Israel and the Occupied Territories, believing that it delegitimates the settlements and the state, and could lead to boycotts and sanctions of the country. But the policy does precisely the opposite: it acts not as a complement to punitive measures against Israel but as an alternative to them. Differentiation creates an illusion of US castigation, but in reality it insulates Israel from answering for its actions in the Occupied Territories, by assuring that only settlements and not the government that creates them will suffer consequences for repeated violations of international law. Opponents of settlements and occupation who would otherwise call to impose costs on Israel instead channel their energies into a distraction that creates headlines but has no chance of changing Israeli behavior. It is in this sense that the policy of differentiation, of which Europeans and US liberals are quite proud, does not so much constitute pressure on Israel as serve as a substitute for it, thereby helping to prolong an occupation it is ostensibly meant to bring to an end.

Support for the policy of differentiation is widespread, from governments to numerous self-identified liberal Zionists, US advocacy groups like J Street, and the editorial board of *The New York Times*. Differentiation allows them to thread the needle of being both pro-Israel and anti-occupation, the accepted view in polite society. There are of course variations among these opponents of the settlements, but all agree that Israeli products that are created in the West Bank should be treated differently, whether through labeling or even some sort of boycott. What supporters of differentiation commonly reject, however, is no less important. Not one of these groups or governments calls for penalizing the Israeli financial institutions, real estate businesses, construction companies, communications firms, and, above all, government ministries that profit from operations in the Occupied Territories but are not headquartered in them. Sanctions on those institutions could change Israeli policy overnight. But the possibility of imposing them has been delayed if not thwarted by the fact that critics of occupation have instead advocated for a reasonable-sounding yet ineffective alternative.

Supporters of differentiation hold the view that while it may be justifiable to do more than label the products of West Bank settlements, it is inconceivable that sanctions might be imposed on the democratically elected government that established the settlements, legalized the outposts, confiscated Palestinian land, provided its citizens with financial incentives to move to the Occupied Territories, connected the illegally built houses to roads, water, electricity, and sanitation, and provided settlers with heavy army protection.[143] They have accepted the argument that to resolve the conflict more force is needed, but they cannot bring themselves to apply it to the state actually maintaining the regime of settlement, occupation, and land expropriation that they oppose.

* * *

Since the end of the Cold War, the United States has not so much as considered using the sort of pressure it once did, and its achievements during the past quarter century have been accordingly meager.[144] US policymakers debate how to influence Israel but without using almost any of the power at their disposal, including conditioning aid on changes in Israeli behavior, a standard tool of diplomacy that officials deem unthinkable in this case. Listening to them discuss how to devise an end to occupation is like listening to the operator of a bulldozer ask how to demolish a building with a hammer. Moshe Dayan once said, "Our American friends offer us money, arms, and advice. We take the money, we take the arms, and we decline the advice." Those words have become only more resonant in the decades since they were uttered.[145]

Until the United States and Europe formulate a strategy to make Israel's circumstances less desirable than a peace agreement, they will shoulder responsibility for the oppressive military regime they continue to preserve and fund. When peaceful opposition to Israel's policies is squelched and those with the capacity to dismantle the occupation don't raise a finger against it, violence invariably becomes more attractive to those who have few other means of upsetting the status quo.

Through pressure on the parties, a peaceful partition of Palestine is achievable. But too many insist on sparing Israelis and Palestinians the pain of outside force, so that they may instead continue to be generous with one another in the suffering they inflict.

II.

DOMINATION

Israeli Conquest and
Its Justifications

I gave you a land you did not till and cities you did not build, to dwell in; you ate of vineyards and olive groves you did not plant.

—Joshua 24:13–14

2.

Feeling Good About Feeling Bad

In April 1897, the British lawyer Herbert Bentwich sailed for Jaffa, lead-ing a delegation of twenty-one Zionists who were investigating whether Palestine would make a suitable site for a Jewish national home. Bent-wich was an acquaintance of Theodor Herzl, whose pamphlet "The Jewish State" had been published the year before. Herzl, who had never been to Palestine, hoped Bentwich's group would produce a comprehen-sive report of its visit for the First Zionist Congress, which was to be held in Basel later that year.[1]

Bentwich was well-to-do, Western European, and, like many of the early Zionists, religious. Herzl was chiefly interested in helping the impoverished and persecuted Jews of Eastern Europe, but Bentwich was more worried about the number of secular and emancipated Jews in Western Europe who were becoming assimilated.[2] A solution to the problems of both groups, he believed, could be found by resurrecting the Land of Israel in Palestine.

At the end of the eighteenth century, roughly 250,000 people lived in Palestine, including some 6,500 Jews, most of them Sephardic, con-centrated in the holy cities of Hebron, Jerusalem, Safed, and Tiberias. By 1897, when Bentwich's delegation made its visit, the Jewish share of the population had more than tripled, with Ashkenazi Zionist immigra-tion pushing it up toward 5 to 8 percent.[3]

Bentwich seems not to have noticed the large majority of Gentiles, writes his great-grandson, the *Haaretz* columnist Ari Shavit, in the award-winning book *My Promised Land*. In his white suit and white cork hat, Bentwich failed to observe the Arab stevedores who carried him ashore, the Arab peddlers in the Jaffa market, the Arab guides and servants in his convoy. Looking out from the top of a water tower in central Palestine, Bentwich didn't register the thousands of Muslims and Christians below, or the more than half a million Arabs living in Palestine's twenty towns and cities and hundreds of villages. He didn't see them, Shavit tells us, because most lived in hamlets surrounded by vacant territory; because he saw the Land of Israel as stretching far beyond the settlements of Palestine into the deserts of present-day Jordan; and because there wasn't yet a concept of Palestinian national identity and therefore there were no Palestinians.[4]

Bentwich's blindness was tragic, Shavit laments, but it was necessary to save the Jews. In April 1903, forty-nine Jews were murdered in a pogrom in Kishinev, the capital of Moldova. More than a million Jews fled Eastern Europe over the next decade, the majority of them to America. Most of the 35,000–40,000 who immigrated to Palestine were secular and idealistic.[5] They believed Palestine could accommodate Arabs and Jews. Many lived in agrarian communal settlements, which helped to transform the image of the pale, effete Jew of the ghetto into the tanned, masculine pioneer of the socialist kibbutz.

By 1935, Jews made up more than a quarter of the territory's population, and in dozens of places Palestinian tenant farmers had been evicted to make way for Jewish orange groves and agricultural communities. But the arrival of Jewish capital, technology, and medicine, Shavit writes, didn't benefit only the Jews. He cites a 1936 article by the leader of Rehovot's orange growers: "Never did a colonial project bring so much blessing as the blessing brought upon the country and its inhabitants by our project."[6]

With Hitler's rise, many more Jews sought to move to Palestine. The violence of the 1936–1939 Arab Revolt, a nationalist uprising against the British Mandate and mass Jewish immigration, resulted in the deaths of five thousand Palestinians and several hundred Jews and shocked the local Jewish community. Opposition to Jewish immigration wasn't new, but before this, riots and violence had been brief and sporadic.

Zionism's utopian phase came to an abrupt end, Shavit writes, to be replaced by the realization that ethnic conflict and population transfer were unavoidable.[7]

When the United Nations proposed partition in 1947, Jews made up less than 32 percent of the population and owned under 7 percent of the land. The UN proposal, which was rejected by the Palestinian leadership and the Arab League, granted the majority of the land— 55 percent—to the Jewish minority. The plan was approved by the UN General Assembly even so, and war broke out the following day, November 30, 1947. By the time Arab armies invaded in May 1948, around two thousand Jews and four thousand Palestinians had been killed and some 250,000–350,000 Palestinians had fled or been driven out.[8]

In July 1948, the Israeli army attacked the Palestinian village of Lydda, located between Tel Aviv and Jerusalem. Soldiers threw hand grenades into houses, fired an antitank shell at a crowded mosque, and sprayed the survivors with machine-gun fire. More than two hundred were killed. The prime minister, David Ben-Gurion, instructed Yigal Allon, the operation's leader, to deport the surviving residents. Another commander, Yitzhak Rabin, issued the order: "The inhabitants of Lydda must be expelled quickly, without regard to age."[9]

These and other episodes of what Shavit calls "cleansing" were not an aberration, he writes, but an integral part of the Zionist mission to create a state with the largest possible Jewish majority. "If Zionism was to be, Lydda could not be," he writes. "If Lydda was to be, Zionism could not be." "One thing is clear to me," Shavit goes on:

> the brigade commander and the military governor [of Lydda, both of whom Shavit interviewed] were right to get angry at the bleeding-heart Israeli liberals of later years who condemn what they did in Lydda but enjoy the fruits of their deed.... If need be, I'll stand by the damned. Because I know that if it wasn't for them, the state of Israel would not have been born.[10]

After the war, progress took precedence over reflection, Shavit writes. Survival was all. Denial took root: the Holocaust was not mentioned; Sephardic and Middle-Eastern Jewish culture were marginalized;

Palestinian refugees were forgotten. History was erased. Hebrew patronyms replaced Eastern European ones. The names of biblical locations supplanted those of Arab cities. In the decade after the war, four hundred now empty Palestinian villages were demolished and four hundred new Israeli ones were built.[11]

Enormous challenges confronted the fledgling state: rationing, poverty, an influx of traumatized Holocaust survivors. In less than four years, the Jewish population more than doubled. Against all odds, it thrived, Shavit writes, and became an egalitarian social-democratic state. Science, industry, and agriculture flourished. In the desert, a nuclear reactor was built.[12]

Much to Shavit's regret, however, the enlightened Israel built by Ben-Gurion didn't last long. After the triumph of 1967, when Israel conquered Sinai, the Golan Heights, and the rest of Mandatory Palestine, there came the devastating surprise attack led by Egypt and Syria in 1973. The Labor Party, which under various names had been the dominant political force since before the founding of the state, never recovered. Seeking to fill the void left by the old Labor Zionist settlement movement, religious Zionists spread out across the hills of Judea and Samaria, land of greater biblical significance than the coastal territory held by Israel before 1967.

A peace movement grew from Labor's ashes. Shavit considered himself a member, but over time he came to see its faults. Its base was a narrow Ashkenazi elite and its leaders were dilettantes, he writes. It used calls for peace as a cudgel against settlers and the right wing. Its moralizing, misleading focus on the relatively straightforward issue of the 1967 occupation was a way of avoiding a reckoning with what Shavit views as the irresolvable tragedy of 1948. It concentrated on West Bank settlements, he believes, in order to distract attention from the evacuated Palestinian villages in Israel proper where the movement's leaders now lived. Promising a utopian vision no less messianic than that of the settlers, it conflated an end to occupation with peace, ignoring Arab political culture and Palestinian aspirations for all of Mandatory Palestine. It counted, Shavit believed, on a peace partner that didn't exist and deluded itself about the nature of the conflict and the brutality of the Middle East. Clashes between Palestinians and Israelis didn't begin in

1967; an end to the occupation isn't the Palestinians' only demand. Even if the occupation ends, Palestinian citizens of Israel will still want to change the Jewish character of the state. The refugees will not give up on returning to Lydda. The essence of the conflict is Lydda, Shavit writes.[13] And Lydda has no solution.

* * *

Equal parts memoir, popular history, and polemic, *My Promised Land* makes a forceful argument about the unlikelihood of a two-state solution, but not from either of the political standpoints typically associated with this position, the far left and the hard right. Instead, it provides a window into the thinking of the largest section of the Israeli electorate, the amorphous, conflicted center, which, after Oslo's failure, the Second Intifada, and the thousands of rockets fired from Gaza, has come to the view that Jewish and Palestinian nationalism can't be reconciled. The book is a sympathetic portrait of the Holocaust survivors who eked out an existence in the cramped housing estates of a recently founded country; the technology entrepreneurs propping up an economy that includes a dangerously large and growing nonworking population; and the young West Bank settlers in their knitted yarmulkes, who "admired the historical Labor Movement" but "despised what Labor had become."[14]

Shavit is critical of his own tribe, the Ashkenazi Labor Zionist elite: he describes its debasement of Jews who came to Israel from Arab countries and were indiscriminately sprayed with DDT and forced into camps, some of them surrounded by barbed wire; its fear that Arabic-speaking Jews and ultra-Orthodox yeshiva graduates would overtake "their" country, turning it into another religious Middle Eastern state and destroying its Western foundations from within; its blurring of the line between condemnation of the right's politics and contempt for the right's lower-status supporters; and its hollow vision of peace, which "had no Arabs," as Shavit puts it, and was used as a means of attacking the underclasses who brought Menachem Begin's Likud to power in 1977.[15]

Central to Shavit's critique of this elite is the claim that it has refused to face up to the meaning of Palestinian dispossession in

1948, concentrating on the 1967 occupation instead. But in Shavit's focus on the events of 1948, he himself does something similar, drawing attention to the war while overlooking the way Palestinians view the decades before and after it. Palestinians do not merely seek an apology for the expulsions and losses that occurred during the heat of battle. They want Israelis to recognize what they see as the injustice of the displacement they've suffered since the dawn of Zionism. Shavit is to be commended for not glossing over the misdeeds of Israeli soldiers in 1948—documented over the past few decades by Benny Morris, Avi Shlaim, Ilan Pappé, Simha Flapan, and other revisionists known as the New Historians—even if he congratulates himself rather too many times for having dared "touch the fire."[16] But he doesn't merely describe what happened in 1948; he attempts to justify it, and his book is in part a moral defense of Zionism's costs to the local population.

Curiously for a text so concerned with the legitimacy of Zionism, *My Promised Land* doesn't make the most powerful and obvious arguments for the right of Jews to self-determination in what is now the state of Israel: first, the fact of its being enshrined in international law, in the form of UN Resolution 181, which was reaffirmed in the declarations of independence of both Israel, in 1948, and Palestine, in 1988. Second, that no matter the actions of their forebears, there are now more than six million Jews in Israel, 75 percent of its population, and the majority of them are second- and third-generation Israelis who want self-determination in their own state. And third, that to deny Jews a country would be to seek redress for past injustices by creating new ones.

Rather than make Israel's case on these narrow and fairly uncontroversial grounds, Shavit chooses a more ambitious, and fraught, approach: a history of Israel in which the 1948 war emerges as an exception that proves the rule of his country's morality. Shavit relegates other difficult aspects of Israeli dealings with the Palestinians to the shadows. The resulting mélange of legend and fact is not firm ground on which to stake a moral claim, and he makes many assertions that are easy to dispute: that early Zionists were oblivious to the existence of a native population; that there were few alternatives available to Jews in Eastern Europe; that a historic right of the Jewish people to establish sovereignty in their ancient homeland trumped the rights and wishes of the local population who had lived there for more than a thousand years; that Zionist immigration offered an economic boon to local Arabs; that the Holocaust retroactively justified the Zionist settlement that preceded it by more than half a century; and that the government established after Israel's founding was democratic and fair.[17] Several of these points have some merit, but all are presented with glaring omissions and misrepresentations, even by the standards of mainstream Zionist historiography.

* * *

Shavit is a secularist, who sees the decision to establish a Jewish national home in Palestine as based on broad universal grounds—the need of a persecuted people for asylum—and not on the belief that the Jews own the land by virtue of God's promise to Abraham. Save for several references to the Holy Land and the Jews' ancient homeland, religion is almost entirely absent from his description of early Zionism.[18] Yet, as Anita Shapira, among the strongest critics of the New Historians, shows in a recent book, *Israel: A History*, religious ideas, traditions, and texts were at the heart of the enterprise from the start. In the Yishuv, the pre-state Jewish community, "the Bible was the seminal text," Shapira writes. "It preserved historical memory . . . and also concretized the Land of Israel, forming a direct connection between past and present." The piety of Eastern European Jews was the main reason the secular leaders of the Zionist movement chose to settle in Palestine and not in Argentina, as Herzl had contemplated in "The Jewish State," or the East African territory offered by the British government and considered by the Sixth Zionist Congress in 1903.[19]

Shavit writes that if Jews hadn't come to Palestine at the turn of the twentieth century they would have had no future. This was hardly the case, as Shapira points out: millions of Eastern European Jews fled to the West, mostly to America. Even among the small Zionist minority, large numbers chose not to remain in Palestine. Of the thousands of men and women who arrived during the first wave of Zionist immigration, from 1881 to 1904, more than half did not stay; the same was true of the 35,000–40,000 immigrants of the second wave. Ahad Ha'am, one of Zionism's most influential thinkers, whom Shavit calls "the national moral leader," believed that most Jews should go to live in the United States and only a select few should establish a spiritual center in Palestine, a model society for the diaspora to emulate.[20]

Ahad Ha'am and other prominent Zionists of the time also contradict the much-echoed notion of Palestine's emptiness. They noticed the local Arabs who made up more than 90 percent of Palestine's inhabitants, and foresaw war with them. Six years before Shavit's relative, Bentwich, arrived in Palestine, Ahad Ha'am had written:

> We must surely learn, from both our past and present history, how careful we must be not to provoke the anger of the native people by doing them wrong. . . . And what do our brothers do? Exactly the opposite! . . . They deal with the Arabs with hostility and cruelty, trespass unjustly, beat them shamefully for no sufficient reason, and even boast about their actions . . . even if [the Arabs] are silent and endlessly reserved, they keep their anger in their hearts. And these people will be revengeful like no other. . . . This society . . . will have to face the prospects of both internal and external war.[21]

As Shapira shows, after the Seventh Zionist Congress in Basel in 1905 a heated debate arose about the suitability of Palestine as a national home, given its large Arab population. A lecture by Yitzhak Epstein, "The Hidden Question," helped spark the debate, exacerbating tensions between the territorialists, who wanted to establish Jewish self-rule wherever they could, and the Zionists of Zion, who insisted on a national home in Palestine. "Will those who are dispossessed remain silent and accept what is being done to them?" Epstein asked. "In the end, they will wake up and return to us in blows what we have looted from them with our gold!"[22]

These ethical debates are almost entirely ignored in Shavit's narrative, a striking omission in a book so concerned with moral defense. He asserts that Zionist settlement was justified by the need of Eastern European Jews to escape persecution, but passes over the attendant normative questions: Did persecution in Europe mean that Jewish refugees had to be accommodated anywhere that could take them, or was there a special obligation on Palestine? Did the persecuted Jews have a right merely to refuge in Palestine, or to their own state there, even if that meant displacing the local population? Was it legitimate for the British to promise the Jews a national home in Palestine? In avoiding these issues, Shavit brings us no closer to understanding the way Palestinians view their history, and he entrenches a narrative of moral righteousness that will hinder any reconciliation.

Although he questions the Zionists' actions in the 1948 war, Shavit has no doubts about the rectitude of their cause before that point. "In the spring of 1935," he writes, "Zionism is a just national movement" representing "an absolute, universal justice that cannot be refuted. At this point in time the injustice caused to native Arabs by the Zionist project is still limited." This blunt assessment, and others like it, might be more convincing if Shavit could explain why Israel's second prime minister, Moshe Sharett, then going by the name Shertok, said in 1936 that "there is not a single Arab who has not been hurt by the entry of Jews into Palestine." Or the reason Ben-Gurion said in 1938: "When we say that the Arabs are the aggressors and we defend ourselves—this is only half the truth.... The fighting is only one aspect of the conflict which is in its essence a political one. And politically we are the aggressors and they defend themselves."[23] More than seventy years after the most prominent Zionists uttered these words, Shavit by comparison displays a Manichean obtuseness.

He repeatedly invokes the socialist egalitarianism of the kibbutz as a moral justification for Zionism, as if the harmony of the kibbutz could excuse the Zionists' behavior toward non-Jews. "Without the communal aspect of kibbutz," he writes, "socialist Zionism will lack legitimacy and will be perceived as an unjust colonialist movement.... By working the land with their bare hands and by living in poverty and undertaking a daring, unprecedented social experiment, they refute any charge that they are about to seize a land that is not theirs." The egalitarian kibbutz, the orange grove, being close to nature—these are presented by Shavit as the essence of life in Palestine during the British Mandate. Arabs flourished alongside Jews; injustices to the locals were offset by the progress Zionism brought. All of this fits nicely with the story told to children at Zionist summer camps, but crucial parts are missing from Shavit's picture: the promotion of "Hebrew labor," "Hebrew land," and "Hebrew produce," and the efforts to close the Jewish economy to

Arab workers; the repeated Arab petitions against Jewish immigration dating back to 1891; and the bourgeois urban lifestyle chosen by most immigrants in spite of the promotion of a rustic, pioneering ideal. "Despite all the preaching," Shapira writes, "in 1931 only 19 percent of the Jews in Palestine lived in agricultural settlements, and subsequently this figure dwindled."[24]

The Arab Revolt of 1936–1939, Shavit writes, "pushed Zionism from a state of utopian bliss to a state of dystopian conflict," paving the way for 1948. But this era of innocence is a figment of his imagination. In 1886, an Arab riot against Jewish settlers was described in the Zionist press as a pogrom; subsequent riots took place in 1920, 1921, 1929, and 1933.[25]

When Shavit asserts that the 1948 war was an unavoidable consequence of Zionism, he seems to forget his depiction of happy coexistence in the early years of the Yishuv. "The conquest of Lydda and the expulsion of Lydda were no accident," he writes. "They were an inevitable phase of the Zionist revolution that laid the foundation for the Zionist state. Lydda is an integral and essential part of our story. And when I try to be honest about it, I see that the choice is stark: either reject Zionism because of Lydda, or accept Zionism along with Lydda." But Shavit doesn't back up his claim that the expulsion of Lydda was inevitable. Lydda was situated on land granted to the Arab state in the 1947 UN partition plan. Unlike the capture of the southern village of Isdud (present-day Ashdod) or the northern town of Nazareth, Lydda's conquest wasn't necessary to correct the flawed borders of the partition plan, which divided the Jewish state into discontinuous thirds. At the time of Lydda's July 1948 defeat, Shapira writes, the Arab combatants were "ill-equipped, partially trained soldiers," outnumbered by Jewish forces (as they remained for the rest of the war) and with "no coordination and no central command." Shavit writes that taking over Lydda, ejecting its residents, and forbidding their return were necessary, but he doesn't explain why this wasn't also true of Bethlehem, Qalqilya, the Old City of Jerusalem, or any number of other Palestinian towns that abutted the new state. As Shapira shows, Israeli leaders decided after some discussion not to conquer other areas and drive out their Palestinian residents, even though they had the capacity to do so.

Toward the end of the war, she writes, Ben-Gurion "rejected Yigal Allon's proposals to conquer the West Bank, which at the time was militarily achievable. He was sensitive to the demographic problem of governing hundreds of thousands of Arabs, and did his utmost to avoid that snare."[26]

In a broader sense, however, Shavit may be right that the displacement of Palestinians was in the cards from early on, and that the expulsions of 1948 were a natural extension of the goals of the mainstream Zionists, who sought to create a Jewish state for a largely Eastern European minority population despite the objections of the native Arab majority. "The partial dispossession of another people," Shavit writes, "is at the core of the Zionist enterprise." Yet Shavit leaves curiously unexamined the decades-old ideology that he says drove this dispossession. He shrugs off questions about it by saying one either accepts Zionism or one doesn't. He does not try to reply to the universalist questions put to Zionism from its earliest days, such as the argument made by a delegation of Palestinian Muslim and Christian leaders in response to a 1921 report by the British Mandatory authorities: "What confusion would ensue all the world over if this principle on which the Jews base their 'legitimate' claim were carried out in other parts of the world! What migrations of nations must follow! The Spaniards in Spain would have to make room for the Arabs and Moors who conquered and ruled their country for over seven hundred years."[27]

Shavit also fails to trace the roots of Zionist ideology to the romantic, exclusivist, *völkisch* nationalism of the Eastern European and German lands from which most early Zionists came. With one exception, he doesn't ask whether that ideology played a role in driving the expulsions of 1948 and the state policies that followed the war, some of which continue to this day. The exception is West Bank settlement: he asks whether it is "a benign continuation of Zionism or a malignant mutation of Zionism," and he concludes that, though its modus operandi is similar to that of early Zionist settlement, "the historic and conceptual context is completely different" and so it is "an aberration, a grotesque reincarnation."[28]

Throughout the book, Shavit writes misleadingly of a unitary Zionism, ignoring the considerable diversity within the movement. His version of Zionism goes without contestation from its late nineteenth-century birth until today, with the sole setback of 1948. It's as if he'd taken the crudest anticolonialist and anti-imperialist critiques of Israel—in which every misdeed in the history of Zionism is a predetermined consequence of Zionism *tout court*—and inverted them. In every case except 1948, the connections between Zionist ideologies and Israeli actions toward Palestinians, particularly those who hold Israeli citizenship, are minimized.

Shavit is right to make the point that Arabs weren't just passive victims. Many of the Zionist movement's actions have been driven by a very real sense of threat caused by Arab antagonism: the 1929 Hebron massacre, the support of Nazi Germany by the Grand Mufti of Jerusalem, the anti-Semitism pervasive in Arab propaganda, the numerous military attacks against Israel, the suicide bombings of civilians in Israeli cities during the Second Intifada. But Shavit does his defense a disservice by obfuscating so much. His telling of Israel's story glosses over or entirely omits some inconvenient facts. In the years after the armistice, as Shapira, Morris, and other historians have recounted, several thousand of the 750,000 Palestinians expelled from their lands were shot and killed when they tried to sneak back home under cover of darkness; Israel destroyed, expropriated, and tried to erase signs of past life in former Palestinian villages, including those where Israel's 75,000 internally displaced Palestinian citizens had lived; and between 1949 and 1956 tens of thousands of Palestinians, including residents of present-day Ashkelon and Bedouin in the north and the Negev, were encouraged to leave or forcibly displaced to Sinai, Gaza, Syria, and elsewhere.[29]

Shavit doesn't mention that Israel's prime minister approved plans in the early 1950s to transfer thousands of Christian Arabs to Argentina and Brazil, or that the state imposed military government on its Arab citizens until the end of 1966, denied them access to the judicial system, censored their press, made employment in schools and municipalities contingent on the military administration's consent, and restricted their movement by requiring them to obtain permits to leave their villages. For Shavit, "the Israel of the 1950s was a just social democracy," one of "the most egalitarian . . . in the world."[30]

Shavit ignores the post-1948 acceleration of the settlement project, which restricted the growth of Arab villages within Israel, expropriated their lands, and surrounded them with new settlements that were intended, in the words of government officials, to "Judaize" the Arab-inhabited areas and borderlands. And he disregards the fact that after the 1967 conquest of the West Bank, Gaza, Sinai, and the Golan, it was mainly Israel's Labor Party leaders and leading intellectuals—not religious zealots—who pushed for territorial expansion.[31]

Most glaringly, Shavit doesn't explore the continuities between Israeli actions in 1948 and current policies: the restrictions on the sale and lease of land to Arabs; the punishment of organizations that commemorate the Nakba, the Palestinian catastrophe of 1948; and the plans of the World Zionist Organization's Settlement Division to "Judaize the Galilee" and expand Jewish territorial contiguity into areas inhabited by Palestinian citizens. The headline of an editorial commenting on these government-supported plans in *Haaretz* stated, " 'Judaization' = racism."[32] Each week the newspapers describe the struggle to strengthen the state's Jewish character at the expense of its Palestinian citizens, yet in Shavit's account it's as though the 1948 war was the last time Israel curtailed the rights of the quarter of the country that isn't Jewish.

* * *

My Promised Land was written for an American audience, in English not Hebrew, and has received more praise from American Jews than any other book on Israel published in the past decade. The director of the Anti-Defamation League, Abraham Foxman, the *Atlantic* correspondent Jeffrey Goldberg, and the *New Republic*'s editor, Franklin Foer, offered gushing blurbs for the book, as did the former Israeli prime minister Ehud Barak. It received the Natan Book Award, a prize that funds publicity, marketing, and distribution for the winning titles. The American Israel Public Affairs Committee had its staff distribute copies to youth activists. Thomas Friedman and David Brooks each dedicated a laudatory *New York Times* column to it. *The New Yorker*'s editor, David Remnick, whom Shavit describes as his book's "godfather," spoke on multiple panels to publicize the work, which he helped edit, extracted in his magazine, and called "the most extraordinary book" on Israel in decades and "an argument for liberal Zionism." In a panegyric in *The New York Times Book Review,* Leon Wieseltier, who was then literary editor of *The New Republic,* described it as "a Zionist book unblinkered by Zionism."[33]

Opinion polls suggest that most American Jews identify themselves as liberals and Democrats and feel affection for Israel. Many dislike the suggestion that there is any tension between their commitment to liberalism and their Zionism. Shavit's fundamentally uplifting tale, his celebration of Israel, tells American liberal Jews that there is not. The findings of the New Historians concerning the darker sides of Zionism can be acknowledged, and the magnanimity of the acknowledgment can be wielded to hold Israel in a still firmer embrace. Shavit's display of mournful soul-searching about Lydda allows him and his readers to feel good about feeling bad. He can tell Palestinian refugees to get over it, while shedding a tear himself. As he admonished a hypothetical Palestinian interlocutor in a radio interview: "I acknowledge Lydda, but you must not get addicted to Lydda. You have to leave that behind." Palestinians are commanded to forget their history, and in the same interview Jews are told to remember theirs: "We've lost this basic understanding that we are the ultimate victims of the 20th century."[34]

Shavit's emphasis on the tragic inevitability of Israel's predicament reassures his readers that they can absolve the country of its past wrongdoing—what happened was, after all, unavoidable—and that there is little Israel or its advocates can do today to make up for it. He chastises the left for failing to acknowledge the centrality of the Palestinian refugee issue, but not because he thinks the refugees' needs must be addressed. Shavit, like Israeli officials, brings up Palestinian refugees only to assert that the conflict can't be resolved. In short, he justifies inaction, but cloaks it in empathy.

At a discussion with Remnick, Shavit said he wouldn't "condemn" those who perpetrated massacres in 1948:

> SHAVIT: [The soldiers] complained about some Israeli bleeding heart authors that are very well known. They said, "We did the dirty work. They live on the land that we cleared for them, and then they say, 'These guys committed war crimes.'" And that's a valid argument.

Now I think it's very important to remember, and I said it to you on some other occasions, I mean, this country [the United States] is based on crimes that are much worse than Lydda, much worse than Lydda. I mean when I hear American liberals, Canadian liberals, Australian liberals, and New Zealand liberals, their liberalism, and their universal values, are based on the fact they basically murdered the other, and therefore they can criticize us—

REMNICK: What is the difference?

SHAVIT: A hundred years.

REMNICK: Exactly.[35]

Not quite. Of course, Shavit is right that during the centuries prior to 1948, Native Americans suffered a much worse fate than the Palestinians, who were not killed in numbers so great as to deprive them of their current numerical advantage over Israeli Jews. But that doesn't make the attention now paid to the plight of Palestinians hypocritical, or simply a result of Zionism emerging at a later time. It's hard to imagine an American commentator getting away with telling Native Americans that he refused to condemn past misdeeds, that Native American anguish was necessary for the greater good of America, and that it was the Native Americans' "moral and reasonable obligation to overcome that trauma," as Shavit said to Charlie Rose about the massacres and expulsions of 1948.[36]

Shavit offers American Jews a seemingly liberal Israeli voice with which many of them can identify—one that's neither too chauvinist, like portions of the Israeli right, nor too despairing and critical, like sections of the Israeli left. Inside Israel, however, Shavit's views aren't considered liberal. In his columns he presents himself as the voice of the reasonable silent majority, and so his positions in recent years, though inconsistent, have followed the steadily rightward-moving center, whose members include the more hawkish parts of Labor as well as Netanyahu and the more moderate elements of the Likud. Shavit is there to reassure the Israeli political consensus of its wisdom.

As far back as 1997, he opposed the Oslo Accords, referring to them as "a collective act of messianic drunkenness" and defending their most prominent opponent, Netanyahu, against charges that he was partly to blame for their failure. During the Second Intifada, he praised Sharon for having "conducted the military campaign patiently, wisely and calmly" and "the diplomatic campaign with impressive talent." In the final week of the 2014 war in Gaza that took the lives of 71 Israelis and more than 2,250 Palestinians, Shavit wrote that strong objection to Israeli conduct was illegitimate and amounted to anti-Semitic bigotry: "We're a tiny minority nation under attack, and sweeping criticism of this nation is like sweeping criticism of the black, gay, or Yazidi minority." Shavit has been among the most prominent advocates of the view that there was and is "no partner" for peace in the Palestinian leadership, claiming that Barak had "offered the whole world to the Palestinians." He says he supports an end to occupation but in the same breath cautions that this step is "problematic" and "liable to foment tidal waves of violence that will rock Israel and jeopardize its existence." In 2006, he repeatedly attacked Ehud Olmert's plan to withdraw from large parts of the West Bank, calling it the "unconditional surrender of Zionism" and "the beginning of the end" of Israel, and argued during a panel discussion at the Council on Foreign Relations that a withdrawal even to the West Bank separation barrier, which would leave the vast majority of settlers on the Israeli side of the wall, would be a mistake. Shavit has often predicted an Iranian nuclear bomb or a military strike against Iran, thus making himself seem like a mouthpiece for Netanyahu. In the West Bank, he advocates slow, cautious, and gradual change while Israeli soldiers and bases remain in place.[37] But in the United States all this is somehow packaged as liberalism.

In his review for *The New York Times*, Wieseltier called *My Promised Land* "the least tendentious book about Israel I have ever read." But defending the positions of the hawkish center while calling himself a liberal doesn't make Shavit or his book unbiased. It makes his narrative more like a Trojan horse of liberalism that conceals in its belly a slickly promoted, refined version of Ze'ev Jabotinsky, the founder of the Revisionist Zionist Party that, after many transformations, now rules Israel. The book's final chapter contains several approving references to Jabotinsky's influential 1923 essay "The Iron Wall" and to its "prophet." Jabotinsky wrote:

Zionist colonization, even the most restricted, must either be terminated or carried out in defiance of the will of the native population.
This colonization can, therefore, continue and develop only under
the protection of a force independent of the local population—an
iron wall which the native population cannot break through. . . . if
anyone objects that this point of view is immoral, I answer: It is not
true; either Zionism is moral and just or it is immoral and unjust.
But that is a question that we should have settled before we became
Zionists. Actually we have settled that question, and in the affirma-
tive. We hold that Zionism is moral and just. And since it is moral
and just, justice must be done, no matter whether Joseph or Simon
or Ivan or Achmet agree with it or not.[38]

Shavit's argument, like Jabotinsky's, rests on a tautology. Both
assume that Zionism was just from its inception, and so conclude that
what was required by it was justified. In "The Iron Wall," Jabotinsky
disparaged the distinctions among various strands of Zionism, writing
that there were "no meaningful differences between our 'militarists' and
our 'vegetarians.'" Shavit, who markets militarist ideas in the language
of a latter-day vegetarian, serves as living proof of Jabotinsky's view that
the vegetarians are merely more prone to handwringing.

—October 2014

3.

Going Native

In the final months of 2015, Israel confronted the greatest unrest it had faced since the Second Intifada had ended more than ten years earlier. Palestinian protests and clashes with Israeli forces spread from East Jerusalem to the rest of the West Bank, as well as to Gaza and Palestinian towns inside Israel. During the first three weeks of October, ten Israelis were killed and more than one hundred injured in stabbings and shootings and by drivers ramming cars into pedestrians. Over the same period, Israeli forces killed fifty-three Palestinians and injured around two thousand.[1] Compared with the Second Intifada, the demonstrations were smaller, the influence of Palestinian political factions weaker, and the violence far less lethal. But the attacks came more frequently, with several of them, uncoordinated, on most days.

In Jerusalem, police units, reinforced by the army, deployed on buses and trains and at major intersections. Private security guards stood at the entrances to restaurants and cafés. Bomb squads detonated half-empty shopping bags left in the streets. Darker-skinned Israelis boarding buses sometimes shouted out to the other passengers that they were Jewish; a man printed a T-shirt that read, "Calm down, I'm a Yemenite"—that is, a Jewish Israeli of Yemeni descent, who shouldn't be confused with an Arab. One man was mistaken for a Palestinian and stabbed. Another was shot and killed by Israeli soldiers. An innocent

Eritrean asylum seeker at the site of an attack was shot and then, as he lay bleeding to death, kicked repeatedly in the head.[2]

The government took harsher measures than the security establishment recommended. Palestinians in East Jerusalem, the source of much of the violence, suffered most from the crackdown. Nearly five hundred East Jerusalem Palestinians were arrested in five weeks beginning in mid-September, more than twice as many as had been arrested for security-related offenses between 2000 and 2008, a period that included the Second Intifada. One government minister proposed destroying all illegally built Palestinian houses in East Jerusalem, a measure that, because of restrictive zoning, would have threatened at least one-third of the city's Palestinian homes.[3]

In the forty-eight years since Israel conquered the eastern half of what it calls its eternal, unified capital, Jerusalem had never been more divided. Checkpoints and police trucks with flashing lights marked the line between West and East. Large concrete blocks cut off the exits from Palestinian neighborhoods. New obstructions, long queues, and heavy traffic deterred residents from leaving. In one neighborhood, additional bus routes operated on either side of the divide, one for trips outside the area, the other for movement within it. Elsewhere, a barricade was erected to separate Palestinian homes from a nearby Jewish settlement. At some intersections, Palestinians were stopped at random, told to lift up their shirts, and then frisked against a wall. Police units with dogs made frequent raids into Palestinian neighborhoods. The houses of people alleged to have carried out attacks were demolished, and the interior minister called to deport Palestinian perpetrators from East Jerusalem and revoke some of the rights of their relatives. The government refused to return the bodies of about a dozen Palestinians killed in the violence, both as a punishment and for fear that funerals would lead to new clashes.[4]

As a result of years of efforts to quash Palestinian political organization in Jerusalem, there was no leadership Israel could engage with to help tackle the unrest. The Palestinian government in Ramallah was prevented from acting in Jerusalem, as was the PLO, whose institutions in the city Israel closed down years ago. Jerusalem's representatives to the Palestinian parliament had been deported to the West Bank. Israel's security agency monitored "political subversion," including lawful opposition to Israel's occupation, in effect criminalizing all Palestinian political activity.[5]

Young Palestinians in Jerusalem felt they had been abandoned. Many of them loathed the political leadership in Ramallah, which they believed stood by as Israel slowly transformed and took over the city's east, cutting it off from the rest of the West Bank. The international community barely reacted as settlement growth in East Jerusalem soared. When Israel imposed new restrictions on the ability of Palestinians to access the al-Aqsa Mosque, its official custodian, the Jordanian government, failed to reverse them. The rest of the world called for calm and a return to the status quo, which in practice meant continued Israeli control of the site. As steadily increasing numbers of Jews visited the al-Aqsa compound, which they revere as the Temple Mount, Palestinian residents of East Jerusalem continued to be forbidden from entering the plaza of the Western Wall (regarded by Muslims as the Buraq Wall), which is located on the ruins of a Palestinian neighborhood forcibly evacuated and destroyed by Israel at the end of the 1967 war.

The leaders of other Arab states were largely silent, much as they were when over 2,250 Palestinians were killed by Israeli forces in the 2014 Gaza War. Israel's tacit alliance with many of the Arab states was one of the reasons for the Palestinians' sense of abandonment and despair. It was once thought that the need to achieve peace with the Arabs would be a strong incentive for Israel to grant the Palestinians statehood. Yet de facto peace had come to the Jewish state without its having to end the occupation, a significant victory for Israel in the history of its conflict with the Arabs. Even so, the 2015–2016 unrest—despite Arab indifference, Palestinian weakness, and overwhelming Israeli military and economic strength—reminded Israel that its greatest challenge, as well as its oldest, remained unmet.

* * *

In 1923, Ze'ev Jabotinsky argued against those Zionists who wanted to avoid dealing with the Palestinians by first making peace with Arabs outside Palestine:

A plan that seems to attract many Zionists goes like this: if it is impossible to get an endorsement of Zionism by Palestine's Arabs, then it must be obtained from the Arabs of Syria, Iraq, Saudi Arabia and perhaps of Egypt. Even if this were possible, it . . . would not change the attitude of the Arabs in the Land of Israel towards us. . . . If it were possible (and I doubt this) to discuss Palestine with the Arabs of Baghdad and Mecca as if it were some kind of small, immaterial borderland, then Palestine would still remain for the Palestinians not a borderland, but their birthplace, the center and basis of their own national existence. Therefore it would be necessary to carry on colonization against the will of the Palestinian Arabs, which is the same condition that exists now.[6]

Jabotinsky's bleak conclusion, which proved prescient during the next half century, was that acceptance of Zionism would not come from Palestinians or other Arabs voluntarily. It would come only after the Palestinians, Arabs, and Muslims of the region had concluded through bitter experience that Zionism could not be overcome. Until then, Palestine's Jewish community would remain isolated and insecure, rejected by its neighbors as a foreign entity imposed by colonial powers.

This was the condition that prevailed for the first three decades of Israel's existence, though there were several notable exceptions to Arab rejection: in 1948, Egypt offered to grant Israel de facto recognition in exchange for Egypt's annexation of territory in the Negev; in 1949, President Husni al-Za'im of Syria proposed to take in three hundred thousand Palestinian refugees and sign a peace treaty with Israel if Syria was given control over half of the Sea of Galilee; shortly before his assassination in 1951, King Abdullah I of Jordan, too, sought a peace treaty with Israel; Syria advanced a formal agreement over the armistice line in 1953; in February 1973, President Anwar Sadat of Egypt volunteered to sign a peace treaty with Israel if it withdrew from the territory it conquered in the 1967 war; and, in 1974, Jordan suggested the same.[7]

But for the most part Israel learned to live alone, the only state between Morocco and Pakistan that is neither Arab nor Muslim. Initially outgunned, outnumbered, and convinced of the enduring animosity of its neighbors, Israel prepared itself for the battles that Jabotinsky predicted it would have to win, and win decisively, if it was eventually to gain Palestinian and Arab acceptance. Without that acceptance, fenced-off Israel would be less Promised Land than Middle Eastern ghetto, unable to provide its inhabitants the safe haven that is at the heart of the Zionist goal.

Though Israel never formulated an official national security doctrine, its strategy against its regional adversaries could be said to have rested on several pillars: bringing in diaspora Jews to consolidate a Jewish majority; securing the support of a great power (before Israel's independence, the United Kingdom, followed by France and, after 1967, the United States); establishing a nuclear deterrent; building up conventional-weapons capabilities; forging regional alliances with non-Arab states; and undermining enemies through military aid to minority populations. Several of these strategic priorities were advanced in what came to be known as the periphery doctrine, put in place in the 1950s by Prime Minister David Ben-Gurion and the first heads of the Mossad, the foreign intelligence service.[8] The strategy's basic premise was that Israel faced a proximate "core" of implacable Arab hostility, which could be countered only through action at its edges.

According to *Periphery: Israel's Search for Middle East Allies*, by the Mossad veteran Yossi Alpher, the strategy, though often ad hoc, consisted of three primary components: alliances with non-Arab states such as Iran, Turkey, Ethiopia, Uganda, Kenya, and, briefly, Sudan; secret cooperation with Arab states at the outer edges of Arab-controlled territory, including Oman, Yemen, and Morocco; and support for religious and ethnic minorities who were opposed to their Muslim or Arab neighbors—Maronites in Lebanon, black Africans in south Sudan, and Kurds in Iraq (though not, of course, in the allied states of Iran and Turkey, where the Kurdish populations are much larger).[9]

The periphery doctrine had several aims, not all of them directed at Israel's adversaries. Perhaps the most important was for Israel to market its usefulness to the great power it was courting even before 1967, the United States. Israel collected information on US adversaries, shared intelligence with US allies, and presented its alliances as a counter to Soviet influence in the region. Another aim was military. The very fact of Israel's trilateral alliance in 1958 with Turkey and Iran, two of the region's strongest powers, was meant to deter Arab attacks, in particular from Syria and Egypt after they briefly formed a union—the United Arab Republic—in the same year. Israel's close ties with Ethiopia and with south Sudanese rebels provided another sort of deterrence, by playing on Egypt's fears that those two countries could reduce the northward flow of Nile River water, on which the Egyptian people and economy depend. Military support of the Kurds meant that Iraq couldn't safely devote all its armed forces to the wars with Israel in 1967 and 1973. During the 1962–1970 civil war in Yemen, in which Saudi Arabia and Egypt backed opposing sides, Israel undermined Egypt's army by supplying the Zaidi royalists with airdrops of arms and materiel, indirectly financed by the Saudis. The effect was to sap Egypt's army and, more important, to help keep a substantial part of it tied down in Yemen when Israel launched a surprise attack at the outset of the June 1967 war. In July 1976, Israel's peripheral alliances facilitated the rescue of more than a hundred passengers on a hijacked plane held at Entebbe Airport in Uganda; the raid would have been impossible, Alpher writes, had the air force "not been able to overfly Ethiopia and Kenya and land for refueling in Nairobi, all fruits of Israel's southern periphery effort."[10] Taken together, these policies and alliances forced Arab states to regard Israel as a regional power, not simply a colonial implant.

What Israel's partners sought from these alliances included money (Morocco, for example, received financial compensation and investment in return for allowing the clandestine immigration of Jews to Israel); arms (weapons captured by Israel in its wars with the Arabs were later transferred to Maronites and Iran-supported Shiite clans in Lebanon, insurgents in southern Sudan, Kurds in northern Iraq, and Zaidi royalists in Yemen); training (the Ethiopian army, the Moroccan intelligence agency, and rebel groups in Iraqi Kurdistan and southern Sudan); and intelligence sharing, especially in the cases of Iran and Turkey. No less alluring to these allies was what they took to be Israel's extraordinary power over Washington. Alpher says that Israeli operatives sometimes cultivated their allies' exaggerated and anti-Semitic beliefs about Jewish influence: "We knew that the issue of the *Protocols of the Elders of Zion* plays a very important role for them. To a certain degree even, we played that card, so they'd think we . . . could manipulate US policy in their favor."[11]

Not all Israelis were supportive of the periphery doctrine. Some security officials warned that these alliances, with the exceptions of those with Morocco and Oman, came at the expense of efforts to achieve a more strategically valuable Arab-Israeli peace: they had the effect of convincing Arab neighbors of Israel's enduring antagonism, refusal to integrate in the region, and preference for achieving security without making the necessary concessions. It was argued that the doctrine even encouraged Israel to spurn outstretched Arab hands, such as those of Sadat in 1973.

Another criticism of the periphery strategy was that, on matters of greatest importance, it was simply ineffective. In the 1967 war, Israel's allies didn't lift a finger to help it. In the 1973 war, Morocco sent a division to bolster Syria and Iraq in the Golan, and assurances made by Iran gave Iraq the confidence to leave the homeland less defended and send forces to fight Israel. The Kurds failed to fulfill their promise to open a front against Iraq and were pressured by both Iran and the United States not to help Israel. After the war, Iran supported the Arab oil embargo. At this point it wasn't even clear, Alpher writes, that Washington placed much value on these peripheral alliances.[12]

During the decade that followed the 1973 war, the periphery doctrine collapsed. In 1975, the shah of Iran signed the Algiers Agreement with Iraq, ending Iran's support for the Iraqi Kurds and Israel's access to them. By 1979, the shah had been deposed and replaced by Ayatollah Khomeini, turning what had been Israel's most valuable regional ally into a principal adversary. Three years later, Israel invaded Lebanon and sought to bring to power a pro-Israel Maronite regime that would expel the Palestinians to Jordan, where they could establish a Palestinian state—thereby, it was hoped, allowing Israel to keep the West Bank. The endeavor was a total failure, serving as a warning to subsequent Israeli leaders of the dangers of meddling in Arab politics.[13]

* * *

But what truly ended the periphery doctrine was the 1979 peace treaty with Egypt, which invalidated the central premise of the strategy: that no peace could be reached with the Arab core. The agreement with Israel's best-armed enemy marked the beginning of the end of the Israeli-Arab conflict, to be slowly replaced by the less menacing but more intractable Israeli-Palestinian one. It set the precedent—followed by the accord with Jordan—of an Arab-Israeli peace that ignored the demands of the Palestinians. As Yasir Arafat ruefully remarked, "Sadat has sold Jerusalem, Palestine, and the rights of the Palestinian people for a handful of Sinai sand."[14] Postponing the call for Israeli withdrawal from the West Bank and Gaza was the price Egypt and the United States chose to pay for restoring Egyptian sovereignty in Sinai.

In his useful book *Thirteen Days in September: Carter, Begin, and Sadat at Camp David,* Lawrence Wright recounts a conversation between Sadat and his foreign minister, Mohamed Kamel, on the day before the signing ceremony, moments before Kamel resigned. Kamel warned Sadat against "a separate peace between Egypt and Israel which would be completely independent of what might happen in the West Bank and Gaza." It would isolate Egypt from other Arab states, doom Palestinian national aspirations, and provide Israel with the cover to build settlements and continue its occupation. Every one of Kamel's predictions was borne out in subsequent years. But Sadat did not believe that refusing to sign would protect the Palestinians or make likely a future Arab liberation of their land. Even if he turned down the chance for Egyptian-Israeli peace, he told Kamel, the other Arab states on their own would "never solve the problems [in Palestine]. . . . Israel will end by engulfing the occupied Arab territories, with the Arabs not lifting a finger to stop them, contenting themselves with bluster and empty slogans, as they have done from the very beginning."[15]

It wasn't long before others started to follow Sadat's lead. For a few years after the agreement, Egypt seemed to be diplomatically isolated in the region, but the Arab states soon reopened their embassies in Cairo. In 1982, they put forward a plan that offered implicit recognition to Israel, calling for peace among all states in the region in exchange for the dismantling of Israeli settlements and the establishment of a Palestinian state on the pre-1967 lines with East Jerusalem as its capital. The plan represented a dramatic advance in Arab willingness to live in peace with Israel, but was denounced by the Israeli government as something close to the opposite. Yitzhak Shamir, then foreign minister, called it "a renewed declaration of war"; the plan's proposal for a Palestinian state, the Foreign Ministry's official announcement concluded, "constitutes a danger to Israel's existence."[16]

During the following decade, Israel's position in the region grew progressively stronger. The peace with Egypt had greatly reduced the threat of a simultaneous attack on two fronts. Arab attention had turned toward the Iran-Iraq War, further relieving pressure. After Israel's invasion of Lebanon, the PLO was destroyed as a military force and relegated to distant Tunis. The fall of the Soviet Union in 1991 removed military backing from Israel's fiercest adversaries and supplied the country with nearly a million Jewish immigrants over the next fifteen years—a significant aid in the demographic battle. The US invasion of Iraq in 1991 neutralized another primary threat. The First Intifada, which lasted from December 1987 until 1993, finally pushed Israel toward accommodation with the PLO.

The Madrid-Oslo peace process brought the country to heights of cooperation with the Arabs that were unimaginable in the days of the periphery doctrine. Jordan signed a peace agreement in 1994. Seven Arabic-speaking countries—Egypt, Jordan, Morocco, Mauritania, Tunisia, Oman, and Qatar—had diplomatic representation in Israel. Foreign Minister Shimon Peres said that Israel's next goal should be to join the Arab League.[17]

Although the euphoria didn't last, the collapse of Oslo, the outbreak of the Second Intifada, and the attendant cooling of relations with the Arabs didn't have significant strategic implications for Israel or affect its military dominance. Comprehensive peace with the Arabs had become less important as their ability to wage a successful war had decreased and as Israel came to be able to depend on the even stronger backing of the United States after 9/11: the two countries now shared a sense of threat that brought them into tighter cooperation. The United States increased its already heavy presence in the Middle East, and the 2003 invasion of Iraq was enthusiastically supported by Netanyahu and other Israeli leaders. Iran and Syria worried that they could be next in line for US invasion. Libya volunteered to give up a clandestine nuclear weapons program. As the preeminent Middle East ally of a hegemon at the height of its power, Israel had little to fear from its adversaries.

* * *

For the first five decades of its existence, Israel's chief concern had been how to deter surrounding Arab states from attacking and how to prevail over them if deterrence failed. In 2016 Israel faced no threat of conventional warfare from any Arab state. Syria, Iraq, Libya, and Yemen had all but disintegrated. Syria's chemical weapons program, for many years among Israel's top national security threats, had been neutralized. The leaders of Egypt and Jordan had intensified security cooperation with Israel. Against Salafist jihadis in Sinai, as well as Hamas in Gaza, Egypt and Israel were working together more concertedly than at any time since the peace treaty was signed. In many respects, they considered themselves to be closer allies to each other than each was to the United States. Jordan recognized that Israel was a guarantor of its security, the regional power most likely to intervene on its behalf if it faced a serious threat.

The Palestinian national movement was crushed. Since agreeing in 1993 to establish limited self-governance before achieving independence, the Palestinians had been stuck in an impossible situation: on the one hand, a quasi state, on the other, a quasi liberation movement, neither of which was a success on its own terms. The PLO had gradually been drained of all its power and turned into an empty body with no plan for achieving independence. Palestinian political division—with Hamas controlling Gaza and the Fatah-dominated Palestinian Authority controlling the West Bank—greatly reduced the pressure on Israel to allow the establishment of a Palestinian state. The main pockets of opposition to the occupation—militants firing from Gaza, lone wolf attackers in Jerusalem, protesters against Israeli visits at the al-Aqsa compound, weekly demonstrations in villages in parts of the West Bank controlled by Israel, the Boycott, Divestment, and Sanctions (BDS) movement in the diaspora, and hunger strikers in Israeli prisons—had one thing in common: all of them fell outside the Palestinian Authority's control. Suppression of resistance—whether violent or peaceful—was one reason the PA was held in contempt by many Palestinians, though most were still too dependent on it to seek its collapse.

The Muslim Brotherhood had been subdued throughout the region: overthrown in a military coup in Egypt, besieged in Gaza, split into rival factions in Jordan, defeated in Tunisia's 2014 elections, and outlawed in the Gulf. Sunni jihadists in Syria were not only refraining from attacking Israel but were receiving medical treatment in Israeli hospitals. They were a containable threat, not because they couldn't one day turn their guns toward Israel, but because if they were in control of a state they could be deterred; and if they weren't, they would remain, in the words of the former head of military intelligence Amos Yadlin, "third-order threats." Hezbollah was preoccupied with a battle for its survival in Syria. Hamas was severely constrained by Israel and by the Palestinian Authority in the West Bank, and in Gaza it was suffocated and seeking a long-term cease-fire.[18] Israel had few good solutions to the 2015–2016 unrest, but it had also grown accustomed to putting up checkpoints and walls.

Saudi Arabia, Oman, the PA, and the UAE were allies in all but name. They sided with Israel against Hamas in the 2014 war in Gaza. Since then, Saudi Arabia publicly acknowledged some of its previously secret cooperation with Israel, even permitting a delegation to visit the country to meet officials and members of parliament. The UAE allowed Israel to open a diplomatic office in Abu Dhabi and was among several nations, including Pakistan, that joined the Israeli air force in a US-sponsored aerial combat training exercise. Even Qatar, which hosted several senior Hamas leaders, worked openly with Israel on the reconstruction of Gaza, and Sudan announced its willingness to consider normalizing relations. In December 2013, President Shimon Peres was invited to address twenty-nine Arab and Muslim foreign ministers. The Arab League unilaterally enhanced its standing 2002 offer of comprehensive peace, disproving Israeli claims that it was a take-it-or-leave-it proposal that couldn't be adjusted or negotiated. In 2015 and 2016, diplomats searched for a way to help Israel and its Arab allies work together to reach an Israeli-Palestinian peace.[19]

In Syria, the bloodletting between Sunni jihadists and the Iran-Hezbollah-Assad alliance was hardly harmful to Israel. A victory for either was seen as worse for Israel than the prolongation of the war. As Menachem Begin is said to have remarked about the Iran-Iraq War, Israel wished great success to both sides. For the first time in Israel's history, an old idea of a Druze buffer state in southern Syria had become imaginable, as had an Alawite state on Syria's coast, and even, in the dreams of Israel's right, the possibility of gaining international recognition of the country's annexation of the Golan Heights.[20] The Kurds were closer to independence than they had ever been. Israel's hope was that the establishment of other minority states in the region would not only create new allies but also increase its own acceptance by Arabs and Muslims.

As the civil war spilled over Syria's borders, Turkey's problems steadily mounted, lessening its capacity to apply pressure on the Israeli government and pushing it toward reconciling with Israel in summer 2016. Even during the years of downgraded ties, trade between the two had increased. Goods that Turkey once transported on trucks through Syria to the rest of the Arab world arrived on ships in the port of Haifa, where they were loaded onto vehicles bound for Jordan and the Gulf. Despite a great deal of noise about Israel's international isolation, its trade with Europe, too, was increasing. It remained one of the top sellers of arms in the world. And with the discovery of large natural gas reserves in the Mediterranean, Israel signed contracts to begin exports, including to Arab states. As the government would often mention when tensions with Europe increased over West Bank settlements, Israel had steadily strengthened ties with China and India (the latter even started giving its support at the UN); gained the backing of several states for joining the African Union as an observer; established a mission at NATO headquarters; and, in 2016, it was elected chair of a UN permanent committee for the first time.[21]

Israel's principal adversary, Iran, agreed to significant restrictions on its nuclear program, and, for all the talk of it spreading its tentacles and attaining Middle Eastern dominance, was overstretched throughout the region. Unlike ISIS, Iran, as a Shiite power, had limited ability to penetrate other states in the region, most of them overwhelmingly Sunni. Israel continued to be the region's sole nuclear power, retained second-strike capabilities, and was not a signatory to the July 2015 nuclear agreement, so had no commitment not to attack Iran. The former head of the Mossad, Tamir Pardo, stated that the Palestinian issue was a greater danger to Israel than Iran's nuclear program, which, he said, didn't pose an existential threat.[22]

The United States, meanwhile, was still devoted to maintaining Israel's military superiority over all its neighbors. More than half of US spending on military aid went to Israel alone, with the amount set to increase in 2019.[23] The United States protected Israel's nuclear program from Arab countries calling for a nuclear-free zone in the Middle East and stood behind Israel in the UN Security Council and other international bodies, blocking any move more threatening than a toothless condemnation of settlements. It was unwilling to contemplate sanctions against companies and institutions operating in the Occupied Territories. With a few exceptions, it even insisted on referring to Israeli "neighborhoods," not "settlements," in East Jerusalem. It refused to recognize a Palestinian state. Israel was unyielding toward the Obama administration because it knew it had so little to fear.

The greatest challenges Israel faced as it approached its seventieth anniversary weren't regional but internal: the need to subsidize a large nonworking population, comprised largely of ultra-Orthodox men and Arab women; demographic growth among Palestinian citizens and ultra-Orthodox Jews; an excluded Palestinian minority; attacks against Israelis, particularly in Jerusalem; and indecision about where to draw the still nonexistent borders and what rights to grant Palestinians in Gaza and the West Bank.

In its search for regional integration, Israel was remarkably successful, even without having paid the price of Israeli-Palestinian peace. This was not to say it wouldn't fight future wars with Arab enemies such as Hamas and Hezbollah. But in those conflicts it now stood to have the backing of the preponderance of major Arab states.

Jabotinsky, it turns out, was wrong to doubt that the Palestinians could be ignored. But he was right that an accommodation with the Arabs outside Palestine would not end the resistance of Arabs within it, as the 2015–2016 unrest in the West Bank and Jerusalem showed. Absent peace with the Palestinians, relations with other Arabs could go only so far. It had always been the case that only the Palestinians themselves could confer the legitimacy and acceptance that Zionism craved. This was at the heart of Israel's demand to be recognized as the national homeland of the Jewish people. That the demand was made of Palestinians, and not of Jordanians or Egyptians, reflects Israel's recognition, at least implicit, that Palestinian claims are legitimate. Until they are relinquished, Zionism cannot achieve its purpose.

In the meantime, Israel continues to become more like its neighbors. It struggles with the separation of religion and state, excludes a substantial minority group from the country's identity, has grown rich in natural resources, and is plagued by high-level corruption. It endures growing Western complaints over failure to uphold democratic practices. Its relationship with Washington is increasingly based on security. And, with its neighbors, it grumbles about American naiveté. Sixty-eight years after its founding, Israel has become much more a part of the region, for better and also for worse.

—October 2015

III.

COLLABORATION

Easing Occupation as a Failed Strategy of Liberation

Security coordination is sacred and will continue whether we agree or disagree on policy.

—Mahmoud Abbas, speaking to
a group of Israelis in 2014

4.

Our Man in Palestine

On August 31, 2010, the night before President Barack Obama's dinner inaugurating direct talks between Israeli and Palestinian leaders, Hamas gunmen shot and killed four Jewish settlers in Hebron, the West Bank's largest and most populous governorate. The attack—the deadliest against Israeli citizens in over two years—was condemned by officials from both sides, who said that it was meant to thwart the upcoming negotiations. According to a Hamas spokesman, however, the shooting had a more specific purpose: to demonstrate the futility of the recent cooperation between Israeli and Palestinian security forces. This cooperation had expanded under the quiet direction of a three-star US Army general, Keith Dayton, commander of a little-publicized American mission to build up Palestinian security capability in the West Bank.[1]

Referred to by Hamas as "the Dayton forces," the security apparatus was formally under the authority of Mahmoud Abbas, the Palestinian president and head of Hamas's rival party, Fatah, but it was, in practice, controlled by Salam Fayyad, the unelected prime minister, a diminutive, mild-mannered technocrat.[2] Abbas appointed Fayyad following Hamas's grim takeover of Gaza in June 2007 and entrusted him with preventing the same thing from happening in the West Bank.

Fayyad received a doctorate in economics from the University of Texas at Austin and held positions at the Federal Reserve Bank of St. Louis, the World Bank, and the International Monetary Fund

(IMF) before becoming finance minister under Yasir Arafat.[3] His reputation as a fiscally responsible and trustworthy manager ensured the
steady supply of international aid on which the Palestinian economy
depends. Though he had neither a popular following nor backing from
a large political party (his Third Way list received a mere 2.4 percent of
the votes in the 2006 legislative elections), he was in charge of nearly
every aspect of Palestinian governance. He didn't, however, participate
in the negotiations over a settlement with Israel, which are the prov-
ince of the PLO (Fayyad is not a member of its leadership) and are han-
dled by its chairman, Abbas, who turned eighty-one in 2016.

Fayyad was criticized at home for many of the same reasons he was
lauded abroad. He condemned violence against Israel as antithetical to
his people's national aspirations, stated that Palestinian refugees could
be resettled not in Israel but in a future Palestinian state, and suggested
that this state would offer citizenship to Jews. He was praised in the
opinion pages of *The Washington Post*, *The Wall Street Journal*, and *The
New York Times*, and had good relations with foreign leaders unpopular in Palestine: on Fayyad's first visit to the Oval Office, in 2003,
George W. Bush greeted him with index and pinky fingers extended to
display UT Austin's "Hook 'em Horns" sign. When the daughter of Ariel
Sharon's chief of staff was married two years later, Fayyad sat next to
Sharon at the wedding and talked with him for several hours.[4]

* * *

In February 2010, Fayyad spoke before Israel's security establishment at
the annual Herzliya Conference, where he was compared by Shimon
Peres to David Ben-Gurion. Much of Fayyad's speech concerned his
ambitious plan, made public in late August 2009, to establish unilaterally a de facto Palestinian state within two years. By that time, according to Fayyad, "the reality of the state will impose itself on the world."
Fayyad's goal to "build" a state—he did not say he would declare one—
was endorsed by the Middle East Quartet and supported eagerly by
international donors.[5]

Some Palestinians rejected Fayyad's plan as too closely resembling
Benjamin Netanyahu's notion of "economic peace," which proposes
that development precede independence. And a number of Israelis

expressed suspicions that Palestine would seek UN recognition of its statehood when the plan was complete. Israel's then foreign minister Avigdor Lieberman warned that any unilateral steps Fayyad took toward a state could prompt Israel to annul past agreements and annex parts of the West Bank.[6]

Fayyad said that his idea was "intended to generate pressure" on negotiations. Mike Herzog, chief of staff to defense minister Ehud Barak, speculated that Fayyad thought political negotiations would not succeed, making his plan "the only game in town." The danger, for Israel and the Palestinian Authority alike, was what would happen if both initiatives failed. Israel, Herzog said, would not withdraw from territory in response to a declaration or a UN resolution. The risk was that Hamas would be able to present a persuasive argument that violence was the only means of achieving national liberation.[7]

During its first year, Fayyad's strategy was succeeding. His administration started more than one thousand development projects, which included paving roads, planting trees, digging wells, and constructing new buildings, most prominently in the twin cities of Ramallah and al-Bireh. He reduced dependence on foreign aid and began carrying out plans to build new hospitals, classrooms, courthouses, industrial parks, homes, and even a new city, Rawabi, between Ramallah and Nablus. But "reforming the security forces," Ghassan Khatib, a spokesman for the Palestinian Authority, told me, was "the main and integral part of the Fayyad plan. Many of the government's other successes, such as economic growth, came as a result."[8]

To its constituents, Fayyad's government presented reform of the police and other security forces as principally a matter of providing law and order—apprehending criminal gangs, consolidating competing security services, forbidding public displays of weapons, and locating stolen cars. But its program for "counterterrorism"—directed mainly against Hamas and viewed by many Palestinians as collaboration with Israel—was its most important element: the targeting of Hamas members and suspected sympathizers was intended to reduce the likelihood of a West Bank takeover and, as important, helped Fayyad make a plausible case that he was in control and that Israel could safely withdraw from the territory.

In 2009, Palestinian and Israeli forces took part in nearly thirteen hundred coordinated activities, many of them against militant Palestinian groups, a 72 percent increase over the previous year.[9] Together they largely disbanded the al-Aqsa Martyrs Brigades, a principal Fatah militia; attacked Islamic Jihad cells; and all but eliminated Hamas's social institutions, financial arrangements, and military operations in the West Bank.

According to the 2009 annual report of the Shin Bet, Israel's internal security agency, "continuous [counterterrorist] activity conducted by Israel and the Palestinian security apparatuses is the main reason" that attacks from residents of the West Bank and East Jerusalem declined to their lowest numbers since 2000.[10] Under Fayyad the level of cooperation, Herzog said, was "better than before the Second Intifada even—it's excellent." Mona Mansour, a Hamas legislator in the Palestinian parliament and widow of an assassinated senior leader of the movement, told me, "The PA has succeeded more than the Israelis in crushing Hamas in the West Bank."[11]

* * *

At the center of the security reforms were nine "special battalions" of the National Security Forces, which in 2010 was an eight-thousand-member gendarmerie that made up the largest unit of the then twenty-five thousand-strong Palestinian armed forces in the West Bank.[12] The officer in charge of the vetting, training, equipping, and strategic planning of these special battalions was Lieutenant General Keith Dayton, the US security coordinator for Israel and the Palestinian Authority from 2005 to 2010.

In a desert town sixteen miles southeast of Amman, more than three thousand Palestinians completed nineteen-week military courses under Dayton's supervision at the Jordan International Police Training Center, built with American funds in 2003 for the instruction of Iraqi police. In Hebron, Jenin, Jericho, and Ramallah, the Dayton mission organized the construction and renovation of garrisons, training colleges, facilities for the Interior Ministry, and security headquarters—some of which, like the one I visited on a hilltop in central Hebron in 2010, had been destroyed by Israel during the Second Intifada. The office of the

US Security Coordinator (USSC) planned to build new camps in Bethlehem, Tubas, and Tulkarm, and additional facilities in Hebron and
Ramallah. It offered two-month leadership courses to senior PA officers
and created and appointed advisers to a Strategic Planning Directorate
in the Ministry of Interior. Between 2007 and 2010, the US State Department allocated $392 million to the Dayton mission, with another $320
million granted between 2011 and 2013.[13]

At its headquarters in a nineteenth-century stone building at the US
consulate in West Jerusalem, the USSC had a forty-five-person core staff
composed primarily of American and Canadian but also British and
Turkish military officers. In addition, it employed twenty-eight private
contractors from the Virginia-based DynCorp International. By late
2011—a date that dovetailed with Fayyad's deadline—the USSC planned
to have supervised the training of one NSF battalion for every West
Bank governorate except Jerusalem.[14]

General Dayton reported to Secretary of State Hillary Clinton and
Admiral Mike Mullen, then chairman of the Joint Chiefs of Staff. He
advised George Mitchell, the special envoy for Middle East peace, and
was praised by influential senators, representatives, and Middle East
analysts, who viewed the work of the USSC as a singular achievement.
As a result of Dayton's activity, Israel granted greater responsibility to
Palestinian security forces, expanding their geographical areas of operation, sharing higher-quality intelligence, and lifting the midnight-to-
five-a.m. curfews in several of the largest West Bank cities. Israel also
reduced the travel time between most urban centers in the West Bank by
opening roads, relaxing controls at checkpoints, lifting vehicle permit
requirements, and removing physical obstacles, which were reduced to
nearly their lowest number since 2005.[15]

Colonel Philip J. Dermer, a member of the USSC, wrote in a
March 2010 report circulated among senior White House and military
staff that the "mission has arguably achieved more progress on the
ground than any other US effort in Israeli-Palestinian peacemaking."
Michael Oren, Israel's ambassador to the United States, remarked, "You
can send George Mitchell back and forth to the Middle East as much
as you like, but expanding what Dayton is doing in the security realm

to other sectors of Palestinian governance and society is really the only viable model for progress."[16]

* * *

The first US security coordinator, Lieutenant General William (Kip) Ward, arrived in Jerusalem in March 2005. Elliott Abrams, deputy national security adviser to George W. Bush, told me that Ward's mission was organized in response to three closely coinciding events: the 2004 reelection of Bush, who wanted to rebuild Palestinian security forces as a part of his Roadmap to Middle East Peace; the death, nine days later, of Arafat, who had resisted American attempts to reform the security services; and the victory of America's favored candidate, Mahmoud Abbas, in the January 2005 presidential election.[17]

Ward's mission concentrated initially on security reform but soon focused on preparing for Sharon's disengagement from Gaza and four northern West Bank settlements. The withdrawal went fairly smoothly for Israel, but Ward failed to prevent violence on the Palestinian side. Settler greenhouses were looted, empty synagogues were burned, and Palestinians began fighting one another for control of Gaza.[18]

Weeks after Dayton took over from Ward, Hamas defeated Fatah in the January 2006 parliamentary election. Overnight, Dayton's task changed from reforming the security forces to preventing a Hamas-led government from controlling them. State Department lawyers sought ways to continue assisting the Fatah-dominated security forces of the Palestinian Authority, which were soon to be led by Hamas, a group the United States had declared a terrorist organization. The solution was to send direct aid to President Abbas, who was elected separately and could be considered detached from the incoming government and legislature. In a reversal of its long-standing policy of pressuring the Palestinian president to give power to the cabinet, the United States advised Abbas to issue decrees and make appointments that would limit the new government's rule, particularly over the security forces. Hamas reacted by establishing a security service of its own. Abbas banned the Hamas force in a decree that the cabinet then declared illegal. During the next year, Hamas and Fatah engaged in a series of violent clashes in which cadres on both sides were assassinated.[19]

Khalid Mish'al, the chief of Hamas's political bureau, delivered a fiery speech denouncing the "security coup" as a "conspiracy" supported by "the Zionists and the Americans"—charges Fatah denied. In February 2007, on the brink of civil war, Fatah and Hamas leaders traveled to Mecca, where they agreed to form a national unity government, a deal the United States opposed because it preferred that Fatah continue to isolate Hamas. Fayyad became finance minister in the new government, despite, he said, American pressure not to join. The Peruvian diplomat Alvaro de Soto, who had been the UN envoy to the Quartet, wrote in a confidential "End of Mission Report" that the violence between Hamas and Fatah could have been avoided had the United States not strongly opposed Palestinian reconciliation. "The US," he wrote, "clearly pushed for a confrontation between Fatah and Hamas."[20]

One month before taking control of Gaza in June 2007, Hamas forces attacked USSC-trained troops at their base, killing seven and withdrawing only after three Israeli tanks approached. Testifying before Congress the following week, Dayton claimed that the attack had been repulsed, and he denied that Hamas was on the rise—a claim not borne out during the following weeks. In Gaza, "it took [Hamas] just a few days," said Raji Sourani, director of the Palestinian Center for Human Rights, "to flush away a 53,000-strong PA security apparatus which was a fourteen-year Western investment."[21]

Yet the defeat of American-backed Fatah forces offered a rather different lesson to the small circle that had influence over the USSC. "We didn't regard this as proof the project wasn't working," Abrams said, "but rather that the project was needed."[22]

* * *

Gaza was lost, but in Abbas's appointment of an emergency cabinet led by Salam Fayyad, the United States felt it had "the best Palestinian Authority government in history." So I was told by David Welch, a former assistant secretary of state who helped oversee the Dayton mission. The Bush administration ended its fourteen-month embargo of the PA, Israel released $500 million in withheld taxes, Palestinian and Israeli security forces increased their coordination, and the USSC rapidly expanded its operations. In Fayyad's first three and a half months as prime minister, the PA mounted a campaign in the West Bank against charities, businesses, preachers, and civil servants affiliated with Hamas, arresting some fifteen hundred of the movement's members and suspected sympathizers. "Once it became clear that Hamas had won in Gaza," Welch said, "then the whole thing was a lot cleaner to do in the West Bank."[23]

By late October 2007, the government was making an intensive effort to maintain order in Nablus, one of the West Bank's most turbulent cities; in Jenin the following May, a special battalion trained by the USSC led the largest operation ever mounted by the PA.[24] Both operations won approval from local residents, who were grateful for improved security. But these actions were dependent not only on restraint by Hamas and Islamic Jihad but also on the support of Israel, including the amnesty it offered to Fatah gunmen.

Many Palestinians saw the campaigns by their security forces as an effort to suppress Hamas—the victors in free and fair elections—and also to prevent attacks against Israel. "The challenge for Fayyad and Abbas," Ghaith al-Omari, a former foreign policy adviser to Abbas, told me, "is that for many Palestinians violence against Israel is a nationalist, respectable endeavor." This view was confirmed by reactions to a February 2008 suicide bombing at a shopping center in Dimona, Israel, and the shooting one month later of eight students at a yeshiva in West Jerusalem. More than three-quarters of polled Palestinians supported the attacks, which were praised by Hamas and condemned by the PA.[25]

Over the following year, the PA alienated itself from the public still further, and with little aid from Hamas. At an Israeli base north of Ramallah, the journalist Nahum Barnea attended a meeting between Palestinian and Israeli commanders. Barnea reported in *Yediot Aharonot*, one of Israel's two most widely circulated newspapers, that the head of the Palestinian National Security Forces told the Israelis, "We have a common enemy," and the chief of Palestinian military intelligence said, "We are taking care of every Hamas institution in accordance with your instructions."[26] The article was later translated in the Palestinian press.

Another blow to the PA's popularity came when Israeli forces evicted some two hundred Jews from a contested building in Hebron, and settlers in the area vandalized ambulances and mosques, set fire to cars and homes, and shot and wounded Palestinian residents. Prime Minister Ehud Olmert said he was "ashamed at the scenes of Jews opening fire at innocent Arabs," an event he called a "pogrom." When the riots spread to the Palestinian-controlled part of the city, Hebron locals watched as their security forces quietly disappeared. Both the former governor, later appointed Abbas's chief of staff, and the NSF commander of Hebron, a Hamas stronghold, told me that Israeli soldiers regularly made incursions into PA-controlled areas, forcing, the governor said, "humiliated and insulted" Palestinian troops to withdraw to their barracks.[27] Perceptions of collaboration were heightened, they added, by Israel's frequent practice of arresting people who had just been released from Palestinian detention.

* * *

The greatest damage to the reputation of the Palestinian security forces occurred during the December 2008–January 2009 Israeli war in Gaza. In plainclothes and uniform, PA officers in the West Bank surrounded mosques, kept young men from approaching Israeli checkpoints, arrested protesters chanting Hamas slogans, and dispersed demonstrators with batons, pepper spray, and tear gas. The trust between Israeli and Palestinian forces was so great, Dayton said, that "a good portion of the Israeli army went off to Gaza." Barak Ben-Zur, a former head of counterterrorism in Israeli military intelligence and later special assistant to the director of the Shin Bet, told me that "in Israeli Arab cities there were more protests against the war than in the West Bank," thanks to the "total quiet kept by the Palestinian security services." Avigdor Lieberman later said, "Mahmoud Abbas himself called and asked us, pressured us to continue the military campaign and overthrow Hamas."[28]

Following the war in Gaza, Dayton spoke before an influential group of politicians and analysts at the Washington Institute for Near East Policy, where he boasted of his mission's accomplishments: building a force that worked against Hamas and cooperated with Israel during the war, and creating "new men" through USSC training of Palestinian troops. Israeli commanders, he said, asked him how quickly he could produce more. His comments were not well received in Palestine, where they reinforced the image of the United States and Israel as puppeteers. The Palestinian Authority sent a formal complaint about Dayton's "unacceptable declarations"; senior Palestinian officials, including Fayyad, refused to attend meetings with Dayton; and, according to *Jane's Defence Weekly*, "owing to tensions in the relationship between Dayton and the civilian Palestinian leadership, his role [was] scaled down."[29]

For Fayyad, Dayton's speech could not have been more poorly timed; it followed the release of a widely publicized poll that had found the Palestinian Authority's legitimacy among West Bank residents at record lows, and it occurred just weeks after Palestinians held large demonstrations protesting an alleged attempt by PA security forces to assassinate Sheikh Hamed al-Beitawi, a prominent Hamas leader in the West Bank. Beitawi, a member of parliament, chairman of the Palestinian Islamic Scholars Association, and a cleric well known for his sermons at the al-Aqsa Mosque, had escaped an attack by unidentified assailants once before. The Palestinian Authority later banned him from preaching, and two of his sons were arrested. Yet Beitawi said he was confident that the Fayyad government would not last. "Fatah and the PA are going down for two reasons," he told me in Nablus: "corruption and coordination with the Israelis."[30]

In December 2009, when Israeli forces in Nablus, allegedly acting on a tip from PA security services, killed three militants suspected of murdering a West Bank rabbi, more than twenty-thousand Palestinians attended the funeral, which turned into a protest against the PA's security cooperation with Israel. Several days later, Hamas's al-Aqsa TV broadcast a cartoon with a chorus singing, "We swear that we will not be terrorized by Dayton."[31] The cartoon revolved around a character named Balool, a Palestinian commander who could be seen kissing the boots of Israeli soldiers, wearing a beret bearing the insignia "Dayton," and claiming not to represent any political faction, upon which his pants fell to reveal underwear colored in Fatah's yellow.

On the day the cartoon was shown on television, Abbas, who was depicted in it as an Israeli soldier's marionette, told an interviewer, "We are not Israel's security guards." Yusuf al-Qaradawi, a Doha-based television preacher who is watched by an audience of tens of millions, said in a sermon broadcast on Qatar TV that "if it is proven that [Abbas] incited Israel to strike Gaza, he deserves not merely to be executed, but to be stoned to death."[32]

* * *

Islamists have hardly been the only critics of Dayton and the security forces. In an op-ed entitled "Jericho's Stasi," a former Palestinian human rights advocate and strong critic of the PA wrote, "I would like to suggest that General Dayton not just train agents in the use of weapons, beating, and torture . . . but also train them how to behave among their own people." The NSF trained by Dayton were not authorized to make arrests, but they regularly led joint operations with other security services whose leaders were trained by the USSC, and that had, according to Human Rights Watch and Palestinian human rights groups, practiced torture. A year into Fayyad's first term, Mamdouh al-Aker, head of the Palestinian Independent Commission for Human Rights, spoke of the government's "militarization" and asserted that "a state of lawlessness had shifted to a sort of a security state, a police state."[33]

Charges of authoritarianism subsequently intensified. Abbas, whose term expired during the war in Gaza, was ruling by presidential decree. There had been no legislature since June 2007, and judicial rulings were frequently ignored by the security services. Fayyad, for all his commitment to accountability and transparency, was repeatedly found in polls to be seen as less legitimate than the Hamas prime minister in Gaza, Ismail Haniyeh, and he oversaw a government that a 2008 Global Integrity Index ranked, in a tie with Iraq, as the sixth most corrupt in the world.[34]

In other respects, too, the Palestinian Authority's practices came under severe criticism.[35] According to Shawan Jabarin, the director of the human rights group al-Haq, torture had become routine. In polls taken after Fayyad took office, West Bank residents consistently reported feeling less safe than Gazans, whose lives under Hamas rule were in many respects worse. The West Bank Ministry of Religious Affairs dictated Friday sermons to be read by imams. Palestinian journalists, according to Amnesty International, were detained and threatened during the Gaza war for reporting on government suppression. During the first three years Fayyad was prime minister, the Palestinian Authority twice ranked lower in the Reporters Without Borders Press Freedom Index than any other Arab government. And in 2010 Freedom House gave the Palestinian Authority the same rating for political rights that it did for civil liberties—"not free."[36]

Fayyad attempted to strengthen his credibility with Palestinians by participating in acts of "peaceful resistance"—demonstrations against Israel's security wall and burnings of products made in Israeli settlements. But in the view of Sam Bahour, a Palestinian entrepreneur and advocate of civil rights, the government's decision "to adopt one small element" of an existing and more comprehensive boycott was mere "window dressing" meant to cover up "a heavy-handed security state whose primary goals are to keep Hamas and criticism of the government in check." On August 25, 2010, when leftist and independent political parties held a rally against direct talks with Israel, it was violently broken up by PA security forces.[37]

Earlier that year, the Palestinian Authority prepared for municipal elections, which Hamas, citing political repression, announced it would boycott. Khalil Shikaki, the most prominent Palestinian pollster, told me that the purpose of the elections was "to further weaken Hamas and bolster the government's legitimacy." When Fatah's internal divisions prevented it from agreeing on candidate lists, the Palestinian Authority canceled the elections, denying that it had done so because Fatah feared losing. But Shawan Jabarin told me that the government's denial was not credible: "In May and June, we learned of tens or hundreds of cases where Hamas followers were questioned by the security forces about the municipal elections and asked if they want to run or not, if they want to vote or not, to whom they want to give their vote." At his office in Ramallah, Shikaki said that because people in Gaza felt freer to express their political views to his staff, "We get more accurate reporting on how people voted in the last election in Gaza than we do here."[38]

In his 2010 report, the USSC's Colonel Dermer wrote, "While Israelis and [US] officials view recent PA successes in the field rather myopically as a win against terror, wary Palestinians view them as new regime protection." A shortcoming of US efforts, he wrote, was "the undefined nature of the USSC mission and its desired end state. Is the aim for the PA to take on and defeat Hamas militarily? To seek vengeance for the loss of Gaza? To maintain order on Israel's behalf? Or is it to lay the security groundwork for a free and independent democratic Palestinian state?" Ghandi Amin, a director at the Independent Commission for Human Rights, told me, "I have no hope for the Fayyad plan. I look on the ground and see only an increased role for security agencies."[39]

In 2011, Lieutenant General Michael Moeller, who replaced Dayton, received the USSC's largest ever appropriation. His task, as the deadlines for both the Fayyad plan and the end of Israeli-Palestinian negotiations approached, was to advance two irreconcilable goals: building a Palestinian force that could guarantee Israeli security while, at the same time, lessening the perception that the United States was firmly supporting what many residents of the West Bank, like the independent politician Mustafa Barghouti, had come to describe not as one occupation but two.[40]

—September 2010

5.

Palestinian Paralysis

In April 2013, when Prime Minister Fayyad resigned, fed up with political attacks from President Abbas's Fatah, a number of observers worried that it marked "the beginning of the end of the PA."[1] Western governments viewed Fayyad as indispensable, the only uncorrupted figure both aligned with their interests and sufficiently independent of Fatah to check its unelected rule in the West Bank.

Although Fayyad was unpopular locally, he was a capable technocrat, successfully administering the Palestinian Authority's scattered municipalities. He spoke a common tongue with international donors, having formerly served as the International Monetary Fund's representative to the PA, and was valued in Washington primarily because of his reputation for transparency, his efforts at reforming the security forces, and his close collaboration with Israel. He was appreciated not in spite of his poor relations with the two largest Palestinian political parties but because of them. And he displayed a keen sense for what US officials might like to hear, proclaiming his "open-ended commitment" to fire any individuals Washington disliked from boards of Islamic charities; his hostility to Hamas, which he described as "our problem much more than it's Israel's or the U.S.'s"; and his "better relationship with the Central Bank of Israel than with the PMA," the Palestine Monetary Authority."[2]

Yet Fayyad's Israeli and US champions were also a cause of his down-fall. The United States reduced its aid to the Palestinian Authority, helping contribute to a financial crisis that Fatah then used to whip up protests against Fayyad's economic policies. After Abbas's decision to apply for Palestine's upgrade in status at the UN General Assembly in November 2012—a decision Fayyad opposed so vigorously that he reportedly broke a bone in his hand while pounding his fist on a con-ference table—Israel imposed debilitating financial sanctions, leading to a new round of demonstrations against Fayyad, cynically fueled by Fatah.[3] Above all the United States and Israel failed to show the Pales-tinian people that Fayyad's program of strong cooperation would advance them toward independence.

Many of the obstacles Fayyad faced were structural, not personal. Any Palestinian prime minister, especially one who is not on good terms with Fatah, has to manage the same inverse relationship between domes-tic support and closeness to Israel and the United States. Fayyad bore responsibility for collecting the Israeli tax transfers and Western aid on which the Palestinian Authority depends, both of which were regularly withheld for reasons outside his control. The prime minister has never been responsible for overall Palestinian strategy; instead, decisions over whether to fight, file suit against, negotiate, or cooperate with Israel lay with the Palestine Liberation Organization and its chairman, Abbas. In the end, Fayyad resigned because he became a scapegoat for the deeper problems of the Palestinian national movement and the political malaise induced by the PLO's indecisiveness.

* * *

Since the failure of Oslo and the end of the Second Intifada, the PLO has had the ability to choose between one of two broad strategies, both of them within the bounds of its 1993 commitment to nonviolence: defying Israel or cooperating with it. On the one hand, Palestinian leaders could have taken up a domestically popular but potentially dan-gerous strategy of challenging Israel more aggressively. This approach could have involved encouraging popular protest (and risking violence); reconciling with Hamas by disregarding US and European preferences to exclude it from decision-making; or taking steps toward internation-alizing the conflict, for example by ignoring US calls for restraint and joining UN organizations at which claims against Israel could be pursued. Any of these moves could have put additional pressure on a complacent Israel and the feckless international community to at least begin reassessing the status quo. But they might also have spurred retaliation and large reductions in foreign aid.

On the other hand, Palestinian leaders could have opted to cooperate more with Israel and Western powers. This strategy might have included returning to the incremental, confidence-building steps on which the Oslo process was based. Much before 2013, the PLO might have considered entering sustained public talks even in the absence of Israeli commitments to freeze all settlement construction or to agree to the pre-1967 lines as the basis for negotiations.[4] It could also have launched discussions on arrangements—such as the establishment of a state with provisional borders—that fell short of a conflict-ending agreement but would have given the Palestinians more territory, sovereignty, and international recognition. But Abbas feared that such steps would take pressure off Israel to agree to a final settlement, open him to severe domestic criticism, and further weaken the legitimacy of the PLO and Fatah. Fayyad's resignation was no doubt a reminder for Abbas of the perils of cooperating too closely with the West.

Faced with two unappealing options, Palestinian leaders tried to stand on a less perilous middle ground, threatening to edge slowly toward confrontation through steps that were not large enough to risk substantial costs but that were too small to win much domestic favor. They offered mild support for popular protests (even as they worked behind the scenes against them), took half steps toward reconciling with Hamas, feinted at and eventually inched toward challenging Israel in international agencies, and, prior to 2013, refused to negotiate peace without an Israeli settlement freeze and commitment to the pre-1967 lines, even while still holding "exploratory meetings" and secret talks.[5]

Fence straddling of this sort had its own price. The PLO had essentially chosen not to choose, and, in so doing, continued its slow enfeeblement, leaving Palestinians increasingly dissatisfied and allowing greater room for other events and actors to shape the conflict. Indeed, much of the protest activity in the months preceding Fayyad's resignation—from hunger strikes by Palestinian prisoners to demonstrations against the Palestinian government and Israeli settlers—reflected an attempt to fill this leadership void. In the absence of a clearly articulated PLO strategy, calls for bolder steps toward confrontation only grew.

* * *

The PLO's indecision allowed the public to pull it—gradually and grudgingly—toward defiance, though with such reluctance that it hardly appeased its critics. Likewise, by refusing to engage in greater cooperation, the PLO was forgoing the potential benefits of doing so, such as having prisoners released from Israeli jails, acquiring weapons for PA security forces, regularly receiving tax transfers and foreign aid, gaining greater international sympathy, enduring fewer Israeli incursions into Palestinian-controlled areas, and expanding PA jurisdiction in the West Bank. Equivocation and vacillation left no one happy.

There was, furthermore, little reason for West Bank leaders to be so hesitant about committing to one of these strategic directions. Joining additional UN bodies such as the World Intellectual Property Organization, for example, might have provoked some backlash, but the PA would collapse only in the highly improbable event that the United States, European countries, and Israel wanted it to. Instead, all three parties believed that the PA's relatively intransigent but peaceful leadership was much more attractive than any of the alternatives. This was illustrated repeatedly. Israeli and Palestinian leaders negotiated with one another by pointing a gun at the PA's head, but each side knew that the other would not actually pull the trigger. In November 2012, Israeli leaders spoke of annulling the Oslo agreements and forcing a PA collapse if Abbas pursued an upgrade in Palestine's status at the UN General Assembly. Abbas did just that and, not surprisingly, the Israeli threats turned out to be empty. The next month, Abbas threatened PA dismantlement in response to a planned expansion of Israeli settlements around Jerusalem, but this talk also turned out to be hot air. When the Palestinians used what Israelis referred to as the "nuclear option" and the "doomsday weapon"— joining the International Criminal Court, in 2015—Israel swallowed it and kept pushing for heightened cooperation with the PA.[6]

Similarly, a Palestinian decision to increase cooperation with Israel and Western donors could have prompted some domestic criticism, but nothing that would have brought down the government. In January 2012, Palestinian objections to the PLO's direct talks with Israel barely reached a murmur. Even if Palestinian leaders had agreed to break the taboo of refusing a state on provisional borders, domestic opposition might have been far less than expected: in effect, Palestinians were already living within a state, as decreed by the UN General Assembly, with provisional borders, as set by the Oslo Accords. Nor would the de jure creation of a state with provisional borders have been likely to harm Palestinian interests by removing what little pressure Israel faced to reach a final agreement; so long as no peace accord had been reached, there would almost certainly have been continued protests against land confiscations and the separation barrier; calls to sanction and boycott Israel; and legal challenges to settlement construction, home demolitions, displacement of families, and restrictions on movement. Such agitation would be manageable for Israel if there were greater cooperation with the PLO, but it has also proven manageable without it.

Indignation against "negotiations for the sake of negotiations"—as many have come to view talks—distracted Palestinians from the costs of inaction. During the years that Palestinian leaders refused to enter formal, direct talks, Israel advanced settlement construction in the West Bank, consolidated control over East Jerusalem, and further isolated Gaza. The PLO gained nothing in return. If it had come to the table, it might not have been able to slow Israel's advance, but it likely would have gained some concessions.

Of course, Palestinian leaders were not exclusively to blame for the standstill. Most were responding to the contradictory demands of their constituents. West Bankers seemed to want to have it both ways: to wage a more effective resistance to the occupation but without reducing living standards or suffering the effects of another intifada. The West Bank leadership indulged the contradiction, failing to communicate clearly to its people—and possibly even to itself—that these two objectives were at odds with each other.

There was little incentive for Palestinian leaders to pull the national movement out of this tangle, since the public had already made its preferences known, protesting vociferously against stalled salary payments and increases in the cost of living while expressing only muted criticism of intermittent negotiations, security cooperation with Israel, and the Palestinian Authority's recurrent antagonism toward popular protests. And so the PLO leadership continued to muddle along, even after it no longer had Fayyad to blame for the choices it was not making.

—April 2013

6.

The End of the Abbas Era

One of the greatest challenges posed to the more than decade-long rule of Mahmoud Abbas and his strategy of bilateral negotiations, diplomacy, and security cooperation with Israel came in late 2015 and early 2016. Young Palestinians in Jerusalem and the West Bank, most of them unaffiliated with any political faction, initiated a series of stabbings, shootings, protests, and clashes, resulting in the deaths of some thirty Israelis and more than two hundred Palestinians in a six-month period.[1] The violence reflected a sense among Palestinians that their leadership had failed, that national rights had to be defended in defiance of their leaders if necessary, and that the Abbas era was coming to an end.

Abbas came to power with a limited window to achieve political results. More a drab functionary than a charismatic revolutionary leader like Yasir Arafat, he was seen as a bridge to recovery from the ruinous years of the Second Intifada. At the time of his election, in January 2005, Palestinians were battered, exhausted, and in need of an internationally accepted, violence-abhorring figure who could secure the political and financial support necessary to rebuild a shattered society. The Fatah movement was divided and discredited by the failure of Oslo, by corruption scandals, and by the abandonment of its liberation strategy before independence had been achieved. Abbas, who had led outreach to the Israelis since the 1970s, seemed a sufficiently unthreatening transitional figure. He had few serious challengers: Hamas abstained from the presidential election; Fatah's founding leaders had been assassinated many years earlier; Marwan Barghouti, who had been in an Israeli prison since 2002, withdrew from the race. And the Bush administration, newly reelected, favored Abbas.[2]

No one expected these conditions to last. Palestinian fatigue from fighting Israel would wear off. The West Bank and Gaza would be rebuilt. Hamas wouldn't stay out of politics forever. Continuing occupation would foment resistance. Leaders who suppressed that resistance would be discredited. And a new generation of Palestinians would grow up with no memory of the costs of the intifadas and no understanding of why their parents had agreed not only to refrain from fighting the Israeli army but to cooperate with it, under agreements that Abbas had negotiated.

For Abbas, political survival depended on making significant gains before any of this occurred. His approach entailed several gambles: First, that providing Israel with security, informing on fellow Palestinians, and suppressing opposition to the occupation would convince Israel's government that Palestinians could be trusted with independence. Second, that after Palestinians had met US demands to abandon violence, build institutions, and hold democratic elections, the United States would put pressure on Israel to make the concessions necessary to establish a Palestinian state. Third, that after being invited to participate in legislative elections, Hamas would win enough seats to be co-opted but too few to take over. Fourth, that by improving the PA economy and rebuilding its institutions, Abbas would buy enough time to achieve statehood.

In all four respects, he came up short. Israel took his security cooperation for granted and its citizens did not demand that their government reward Abbas for his peaceful strategy. The United States did not apply the necessary pressure to extract significant concessions from Israel. Hamas won the legislative elections, took over Gaza, and refused to adopt Abbas's political program (though the victory also strengthened foreign support for Abbas, as the international community sought to undermine the Islamists). And West Bankers, though dependent on the jobs and economic infrastructure provided by the Palestinian Authority, also resented it, and lost whatever faith they once had that Abbas's plan could succeed. According to several opinion polls taken in 2015 and 2016, two-thirds of West Bankers and Gazans wanted him to resign.[3]

As Abbas's failures mounted, Palestinians took matters into their own hands. They did so gradually at first, in areas outside PA control: Jerusalem, Gaza, Israeli prisons, and villages and refugee camps not under PA jurisdiction. Finally, in October 2015, the process accelerated, as violence and protests against Israel proliferated, even in parts of PA-controlled territory in the West Bank.

For Abbas, this presented a substantial threat. A true uprising could have made security cooperation with the occupier untenable, leaving him with limited means to suppress, marginalize, and imprison his only significant political challenger, Hamas, while opening the door for new contenders. By definition, violence would have represented a weakening of Abbas's hand, since his principal asset was always his international respectability. If attacks had intensified, he could have been condemned internationally for not doing enough to stop them and discredited domestically for doing too much. If security had broken down, Israel would have found him increasingly irrelevant and been tempted to start empowering those it believed capable of quelling the unrest.

Yet the odds were still stacked overwhelmingly against those seeking to turn the clashes and violence into a sustained uprising. The attacks and protests were dispersed, unorganized, and uncoordinated, without a strategy or clear goals. Many Palestinians believed that enormous sacrifices could achieve results, but few wished to pay that price again. Protesters did not show up in numbers approaching those of the First or Second Intifada, and they did not turn against the Palestinian Authority, which together with Israel remained the greatest obstacle to over-turning the status quo. Palestinians were certain that Abbas's cooperative strategy would fail, but they had little faith that the alternatives would do better.

PA security forces mostly avoided the embarrassment of violently quashing protests against Israel and managed to keep their collaboration with it out of the public eye. The IDF appeared to have learned lessons from two intifadas and was taking pains not to exacerbate tensions by imposing closures or withholding permits to leave Palestinian territory or work in Israel. Huge numbers of people continued to depend on a PA whose existence would have been threatened by a new uprising.

* * *

As Israel's occupation of the West Bank and East Jerusalem approached its fiftieth anniversary, it was hard to defend the notion that it was unsustainable. But sustainable is not the same as cost-free.

The violence of late 2015 and early 2016 was a resurgence of occupation's costs, which, though unpleasant for Israel, remained the bearable price of holding on to East Jerusalem and the West Bank. For the Palestinians, the violence and protests were an announcement that although their crushed and divided national movement may not have been strong enough to achieve its goals, its constituents were not so weak that they would no longer pursue them.

—October 2015

IV.

CONFRONTATION

Palestinian Pressure and Its Limits

The guns will talk.

—Yasir Arafat

7.

Not Popular Enough

The Palestinian national struggle has been identified with images of hijacked airplanes, homemade rockets, charred wreckage of exploded buses, and, more recently, teenagers wielding scissors and knives, but in over a century of Zionist-Arab conflict it has been the unarmed—or, as Palestinians call it, "popular"—form of resistance that has been more prevalent and deeply rooted. During the first decades of Zionist immigration to Palestine, Jews barely encountered violent opposition.[1] Palestinians instead protested by witholding cooperation, appealing to the Ottoman and British authorities to slow Zionist immigration, and refusing to sell their property. Through such means, more than 93 percent of Palestine's territory remained outside Jewish hands at the outset of the 1948 war, and even the less than 7 percent owned by Jews had been sold mostly by absentee landlords residing abroad, many of whom weren't Palestinian.[2]

In the four major wars Israel fought, Palestinian participation was extraordinarily low. In 1948, of a population of 1.3 million, only a few thousand Palestinians joined irregular forces or the Arab Salvation Army; in the 1956, 1967, and 1973 wars, Palestinian contributions were also slight.[3] The violence that Palestinians did lead over the decades was many times less deadly than struggles against foreign occupiers elsewhere in the world. From the first Palestinian riots in 1920 until the end of June 2016, according to Israeli government sources, fewer than four thousand Jews (forty per year) were killed as a result of Palestinian violence, including the intifadas and wars in Gaza.[4]

The four most notable acts of Palestinian rebellion all began in non-violent protest. These periods are the most highly revered in Palestinian national memory, precisely because nonviolence permitted and encouraged the sort of collectivism, solidarity, and broad-based participation that violence did not. The 1936–1939 Arab Revolt started with a general strike, demonstrations, boycotts, and nonpayment of taxes. The British repressed it brutally, making use of torture, home demolitions, deportations, raids, collective punishment, and aerial bombardment. The strike was called off within six months, after approximately one thousand Palestinians had been killed, and the revolt then turned violent, resulting in the deaths of another Palestinians and several hundred Jews and Britons.[5]

The second large Palestinian rebellion took place on March 30, 1976, when tens of thousands of Palestinian citizens of Israel went on marches and joined a general strike to protest against increased land confiscations by the Israeli government in the Galilee; the event, known as Land Day, has been commemorated with demonstrations each year since. During the third rebellion, known as the First Intifada (for many of the Palestinians old enough to have participated in it, the "real" intifada), people took part in mass protests, strikes, and boycotts; refused to pay taxes; flew banned Palestinian flags; threw stones; and engaged in other largely unarmed acts, particularly during the intifada's initial phase. In the first year of the uprising, 4 Israeli soldiers were killed, while Israeli security forces and settlers killed at least 326 Palestinians. This revolt is sometimes known as the Intifada of the Stones and is seen by Palestinians as providing the model for popular resistance, of which they consider stone throwing to be a legitimate part. The IDF views stone throwing as a violent act but admits that not a single soldier has died as a result of it. Court testimony by members of the Israeli security forces and videos made by journalists record numerous occasions, some as recent as 2015, when undercover Israeli agents infiltrated protests, incited Palestinians to violence, and threw stones at soldiers themselves in an attempt to entrap protesters.[6]

The far bloodier Second Intifada also began with unarmed protests and stone throwing over Ariel Sharon's visit to Jerusalem's al-Aqsa Mosque compound, or Temple Mount. Israeli forces killed 7 Palestinian demonstrators the day after the visit, 13 the following day, and, several days later, 12 Palestinian citizens of Israel, who had called a general strike and launched unarmed protests in solidarity.[7] Large demonstrations and other peaceful forms of resistance dwindled as violence took over, but they were not entirely extinguished. Alongside the militarization of the intifada there grew a new incarnation of popular resistance, which began spreading across West Bank villages in 2002.

* * *

Initially, these popular protests, which were seen as a return to the methods of the First Intifada, were aimed at stopping the construction of the separation barrier, which de facto annexed parts of the West Bank to Israel, dividing and surrounding many Palestinian communities and cutting them off from their lands.

The resistance began in the agricultural village of Jayyous, the largest olive-producing region of the West Bank governorate of Qalqilya. In September 2002, residents found signs affixed to the trees informing them that the separation barrier would be routed several miles east of the pre-1967 line, coming within ninety feet of some of Jayyous's homes and separating the village from twelve thousand of its olive trees, each of its groundwater wells, and all of its irrigated land.[8] Residents held demonstrations, welcomed Israeli and international solidarity activists, stood in front of bulldozers, and temporarily slowed the army's advance. But in the end, the barrier was erected and the protests stopped. A similar pattern emerged in Mes'ha, Beit Liqya, Beit Ijza, Biddu, and Ni'lin. Men, women, and children stood before bulldozers, hugged olive trees to prevent their uprooting, marched, were arrested, tear-gassed, shot, and sometimes killed, but failed to stop the barrier from going up.

There were a few isolated successes, however. In 2004, the International Court of Justice issued an advisory opinion stating that "the construction of the wall being built by Israel . . . [is] contrary to international law" and that Israel was obligated to dismantle it forthwith. Israel ignored the ICJ, but the village protests did not stop. After dozens of demonstrations in Budrus, west of Ramallah, the IDF recommended changing the planned route of the separation barrier so that it would no longer encircle Budrus and eight other villages, closing them off from both Israel and the rest of the West Bank. In 2005, the government approved a new route that intruded on less of Budrus's land, kept closer to the pre-1967 line in that small section of the barrier, and no longer confined the nine villages.[9]

The following year, Israeli courts ruled that the inhabitants of a single home near Jerusalem—entirely encircled by the barrier, encroached on by a settlement, and locked in by a gate that could be opened only by the army—were no longer to be trapped inside, their relatives prevented from visiting unless they obtained permits. In 2007, after two and a half years of protests in nearby Bil'in, the Israeli Supreme Court ruled unanimously that the barrier should be rerouted: "We were not convinced," the chief justice wrote in her decision, "that it is necessary for security-military reasons to retain the current route that passes on Bil'in's lands."[10]

The protests spread and were no longer concerned only with the location of the barrier. In Kafr Qaddum, villagers held weekly demonstrations against the closure of their main road and exit, shut down after the neighboring settlement of Kedumim added a new neighborhood. All the settlements outside Jerusalem are located in the 60 percent of the West Bank designated Area C by the Israeli military, and Palestinians there have had much to protest. The majority of Area C is off-limits to its Palestinian inhabitants. The army can expel residents by declaring that their land is to be used as a "firing zone" for military training, and it has failed to prevent attacks on people and property by Israeli settlers. Building permits are hard to come by: of the thousands of applications submitted by Palestinians between 2000 and 2012, only 5.6 percent were approved, and in practice building by Palestinians is permitted in less than 1 percent of Area C. Homes and other structures built without permits are routinely demolished: in the same years, nearly three thousand were destroyed, displacing thousands of people.[11]

In 2008, a group in Hebron called Youth Against Settlements organized nonviolent protests against the army's extinction of Palestinian life in the center of the city: the IDF had erected more than a hundred obstructions to restrict movement; forced hundreds of businesses to shut down; enforced what it calls "sterile" streets, where Jewish settlers can walk but Palestinians cannot (the front doors of Palestinian houses on these streets were welded shut, obliging their residents to use roofs and ladders to get out); and shut down what was once Hebron's main market and liveliest thoroughfare, Shuhada Street. Curfews for Palestinians and restrictions on access to Shuhada Street were first imposed in 1994, in response not to Palestinian but to Israeli violence: an American-born settler, Baruch Goldstein, forced his way into the back of the Ibrahimi mosque and fired 111 rounds at the rows of worshippers kneeling in Friday morning prayer, killing twenty-nine.[12] The Palestinians of Hebron have been punished for this massacre ever since.

Elsewhere, in Nabi Saleh, a village of some six hundred people, residents challenged the confiscation of their land and their main spring by the settlement of Halamish. Israeli government statistics obtained by the NGO Peace Now show that one-third of the area registered to Halamish was stolen from private Palestinian owners. The figure is almost identical to the amount—over 32 percent—of West Bank settlement land that is privately owned by Palestinians. During the Second Intifada, in a common practice, the IDF declared territory adjacent to Halamish a closed military zone. The army prevented the villagers from farming their lands there, while allowing the settlers in; that is, it was essentially a closed military zone for Jewish-only farming. In protest against these and other usurpations, every Friday dozens and sometimes hundreds of people would march from Nabi Saleh toward the spring, where settlers had built an arbor, a swing, and pools. After two and a half years of demonstrations, the villagers finally managed to reach the spring. They spent an hour there before settlers demanded the army expel them, and they have remained banned from it ever since.[13]

In 2011, protests moved beyond the West Bank. As upheaval spread throughout the Middle East, thousands of unarmed demonstrators marched on Israel's borders on May 15, the day commemorating the Nakba, the loss of Palestinian land and homes in the 1948 war. In other places abroad, particularly on university campuses, another form of peaceful resistance—the movement to boycott, divest from, and sanction Israel—markedly grew.[14]

In the West Bank, meanwhile, new tactics emerged. A group of young Palestinian activists calling themselves Freedom Riders invited foreign journalists to accompany them when they boarded a public bus in the West Bank used by settlers to travel to and from Israel. When the bus arrived at the outskirts of occupied East Jerusalem, to which Palestinian but not Jewish residents of the West Bank require entry permits, the police ordered the activists to get off the bus; they refused, comparing themselves to Rosa Parks as they were arrested. The next year a group of protesters blocked a road near Ramallah that is for Israeli cars only.[15]

At the same time, the PLO leadership pursued—haltingly, and primarily as a means of leveraging new talks with the Israeli government— what it considered a peaceful resistance strategy in the international sphere: it advanced a UN Security Council resolution on the illegality of settlements, which the United States vetoed; joined UNESCO as a member state; won Palestine's admission to the UN as a nonmember observer state; and, following the collapse of US-led negotiations in April 2014, signed instruments of accession to numerous international treaty bodies, as well as, in December, the International Criminal Court.[16] Although these diplomatic moves did not put a dent in the machinery of occupation and had no impact on Palestinians' daily lives, they nevertheless helped give rise to a sense that momentum for nonviolent resistance was building.

Palestinian activists also turned to a new approach, adopting the settler tactic of "creating facts on the ground": on a contentious site known as E1, a plot of land east of Jerusalem that had been picked out for settlement expansion, they put up two dozen tents to form a protest "village" called Bab al-Shams. In stark contrast to the Israeli government's years of inaction toward Jewish-inhabited, illegally constructed settlement outposts, which are not only left alone but guarded by the military, connected to water and electricity, and often retroactively legalized, Israeli forces acted swiftly at Bab al-Shams, evicting the protesters within forty-eight hours. The idea nevertheless caught on, and over the next several weeks four more protest villages were set up.[17]

For a period, there was hope that this wave of popular resistance could start the next great Palestinian rebellion—a peaceful, grassroots, non-factional uprising led by a new generation. But this hope faded quickly. Participation, never high to begin with, shrank. Political leaders showed little interest. Media attention turned elsewhere.

Some battles by individual towns and villages continued, but they remained disparate, localized struggles against specific aspects of the occupation of the West Bank, never coalescing into a larger revolt against occupation itself. Why they failed to do so is one of the central questions of the novelist and journalist Ben Ehrenreich's *The Way to the Spring*, a compassionate and eloquent account of popular resistance and Israeli military repression in the West Bank.

* * *

For those active in the popular resistance movement, there is little mystery about why Israel has not faced a sustained, widely supported campaign of Palestinian civil disobedience and unarmed struggle since the First Intifada. It can be summarized in a single word: Oslo.

The Oslo agreements brought the First Intifada to an end, established limited Palestinian self-governance in parts of Gaza and the West Bank, outsourced to the new Palestinian government many of Israel's responsibilities as an occupying power, and to a significant degree immunized Israel against the forms of protest to which it had previously been vulnerable: boycotts, strikes, nonpayment of taxes, and mass demonstrations. Israel protected itself from the damage of possible labor strikes by replacing Palestinian workers with foreigners: prior to Oslo, over one-third of the Palestinian labor force worked in Israel or its settlements, but by 1997, three years after the inception of the PA, the figure had dropped to 16 percent. Unemployment soared.[18] Palestinian leaders who just several years earlier had been directing intifada labor strikes against Israel were now in official government positions begging the Israeli authorities to issue more work permits.

Nonpayment of taxes, which had been an Israeli liability, now became a Palestinian one, as the PA began collecting income taxes. At the same time, the Palestinian economy became more vulnerable, since basic services once provided by the occupying power were no longer guaranteed: the PA depended on Israel to hand over the far larger taxes on imports, which it collected for a 3 percent fee, and sometimes with-held when the Palestinians didn't behave themselves.[19]

Large-scale protests ceased to pose the sort of threat to Israel that they once did, as Gaza was fenced off and over 90 percent of the population of the West Bank was divided into 165 islands of ostensible PA control (Area A islands, the 18 percent of the West Bank in which the PA has security and civil jurisdiction, and Area B islands, the 22 percent where the PA has only civil authority). These islands are surrounded by Area C, the spatially contiguous 60 percent of the West Bank that the Palestinian Authority may not enter.[20] This territorial arrangement ensures that the largest population centers, in Area A, are removed from direct contact with Israelis; indirectly managed by the IDF, through its close cooperation with Palestinian security forces; and encircled by zones of Israeli control, which make any large demonstration containable, less likely to spread, and easily sealed off from incomers.

That leaves Area C as the main realm of protest in the West Bank. But most Area C communities are small, isolated villages and hamlets in valleys, deserts, or on hills. Their sparseness and topography make mass demonstrations nearly impossible, which in turn means less attention from the media and less ability to influence a fairly oblivious Israeli public, most of whom in their daily lives are hardly conscious of the occupation.

Those who continue to demonstrate also face a daunting set of legal obstacles. Protests in the West Bank are effectively criminalized. Israel's Military Order 101, in place since 1967, makes illegal any "procession, gathering, or rally . . . held without a permit issued by a military commander," with a procession or rally defined as "any group of ten or more persons" assembled "for a political purpose or for a matter that could be interpreted as political." Incitement, defined as "orally or in any other way attempt[ing] to influence public opinion in the region in a way that is liable to disturb public peace or order," is outlawed too. Another regulation allows local IDF commanders to declare any area—for example, the Palestinian-owned land on which a protest is taking place—a "closed military zone," thereby enabling them to shut down demonstrations and arrest the participants.[21]

Thanks to laws and regulations such as these, some 40 percent of all Palestinian men in the West Bank and Gaza have been confined in Israeli jails. Once arrested, Palestinian protesters, unlike Israeli ones, are subject to the military justice system, in which they may be placed in "administrative detention" indefinitely, without charge or trial. By his forty-fourth birthday, Bassem Tamimi, one of the leaders of the protests in Nabi Saleh, had been arrested ten times and "spent three years of his life in Israeli prisons without ever being convicted of a crime." When he was finally tried, in 2011, he was charged with "incitement," "solicitation to stone throwing," "disruption of legal proceedings," and "organizing and participating in unauthorized processions." The trial dragged on; more than a year after his arrest he was convicted of two of the charges, and sentenced to thirteen months in prison. Tamimi's conviction was hardly in doubt: in 2010, the last year for which records are available, 99.74 percent of Palestinians tried in Israel's military courts were found guilty.[22]

The odds were not much better for Palestinians attempting to use this same justice system to address Israeli wrongdoing. Of all complaints filed against soldiers between 2010 and 2013, only 1.4 percent resulted in an indictment, and this doesn't take into account the large number of cases Palestinians never bothered to file. There were roughly three hundred charges of torture at the hands of the Shin Bet that resulted in official inquiries between 2013 and 2016, but not one precipitated a criminal investigation.[23]

There were also internal obstacles to a new popular uprising. Fatah feared that Hamas might use popular protest to undermine its authority in the West Bank, and Hamas feared Fatah would do the same in Gaza. Many Palestinians were still exhausted from the Second Intifada. In Area C villages like Nabi Saleh, Ehrenreich writes, residents were divided over the utility of the protests, which had exacted a heavy price: after fourteen months of weekly demonstrations, 155 residents had been injured, 70 had been arrested, 15 were in prison, 6 were in hiding, and nearly every home had been either damaged in Israeli raids, burned by gas grenades, or sprayed with a feculent liquid the army calls skunk. During the following twenty months, 2 protesters were killed by the army.[24]

Palestinian politicians were of little help. They were profoundly distrusted and seen as having squandered the sacrifices of the First Intifada on a set of agreements that had in fact given Israel's occupation new life. Palestinians saw enormous gaps between the rhetoric of their leaders and the reality of their positions. Rhetoric was the PLO Central Council voting to end security cooperation with Israel and Mahmoud Abbas threatening to dismantle the PA. Reality was Abbas calling security cooperation "sacred" and vowing that "the PA is our achievement and we will not give it up." Rhetoric was official support for boycotts of Israeli products. Reality was Israeli settlements constructed largely by Palestinian workers. Rhetoric was the Palestinian president promising, "Our people will continue their popular peaceful resistance to the Israeli occupation." Reality was a movement that was never supported by Palestinian leaders and that was sometimes suppressed by PA security forces, helping ensure that demonstrations failed to sustain the attention of a fickle press, hardly made an impression on Israelis, and were little more than a ritualized nuisance for the occupying power.[25]

Political figures might have wanted to claim that popular protest and civil disobedience were of a piece with the PLO's nonviolent strategy of joining international institutions and asserting the PA's statelike quality. But there was a fundamental contradiction between the two paths. The message the PA's constituents heard was that they should keep quiet, put faith in their leaders, do their jobs, pay their mortgages, and allow the guys in nice suits who use such phrases as "capacity building" and "institutional development" to deliver an independent state. It was a model of liberation without struggle—elite-driven and antiparticipatory. Popular resistance was closer to the opposite. It was of and by the people: devolving power to local committees, villages, and municipal councils; disrupting the status quo; collectively enduring closures, curfews, and revocations of work and exit permits; risking damage to PA institutions and their technocrats with seven- and eight-word job titles; and losing sons and daughters to Israeli bullets and jails.

Near the end of his book, Ehrenreich recounts a vivid instance of the security coordination that Palestinian leaders frequently claim to oppose. A little after one a.m. on June 22, 2014, Israeli forces entered

Ramallah and took up positions in a downtown building housing the police station. The Palestinian police put up no resistance and, in the view of many bystanders, appeared complicit in the operation. Young people then marched through the streets, yelling, "Traitors!" and "The PA is a whore!" To put down the demonstration, Ehrenreich writes, Israeli soldiers "began firing tear gas and both live and rubber-coated bullets from a few blocks away as the Palestinian police battled the crowd around the station. The streets were thick with smoke and gas, but for a few minutes before the jeeps sped off again, everything was perfectly clear. The Israelis were shooting from one direction and the PA from another, the two security forces acting in concert against the same opponent—the young men who had come out in defense of their city."[26]

That Israel and the Palestinian Authority largely succeeded in containing any real challenge to their symbiotic control of the West Bank created a sense of despair among many activists. Some members of a once hopeful movement began wondering whether the popular resistance that grew after the Second Intifada was less the spark of a new revolution than the last embers of an old one.

First Intifada leaders who had ruthlessly crushed collaboration became, post-Oslo, officially sanctioned overseers of it. Palestinians in Gaza and the West Bank saw the PLO transformed from a protector against an occupying army into an agglomeration of self-interested businessmen securing exclusive contracts from it. Nationalism gave way to individualism, and compromise with Israel, as a necessary means of survival, was legitimized from the top down. Resistance came to seem futile, if not foolish.

Worse still, no Palestinian could fully escape feeling implicated in the collaboration that was inherent in the daily functions of the Palestinian Authority and the lives of the people who depend on it. In the years since Oslo, the line between resistance and collaboration has been blurred. Too many rely on the Palestinian Authority's existence, and too few can determine its true function: is it an instrument of indirect Israeli control, or a means of achieving independence against the wishes of the occupier?

Life in the West Bank has become discordant, absurd. Businessmen and ministers in expensive Mercedes and Audi sedans drive past refugee camps where children burn tires or throw stones. For many, the popular resistance movement that sprouted in isolated West Bank villages was a reminder of purer and prouder days of struggle. It was an echo and an inspiration, but never quite popular enough.

—September 2016

8.

Rage in Jerusalem

What the government of Israel calls its eternal, undivided capital is among the most precarious, divided cities in the world. In 1967, when it conquered the eastern part of Jerusalem and the West Bank—both then administered by Jordan—Israel expanded the city's municipal boundaries threefold. As a result, approximately 37 percent of Jerusalem's current residents are Palestinian. They have separate buses, schools, health facilities, and commercial centers, and they speak a different language. In eastern neighborhoods, Israeli settlers and border police are frequently pelted with stones, while Palestinians have on several occasions been beaten by Jewish nationalist youths in the western half of the city. Balloons equipped with cameras hover above East Jerusalem, maintaining surveillance over the Palestinian population. Most Israelis have never visited and don't even know the names of the Palestinian areas their government insists on calling its own. Municipal workers come to these neighborhoods with police escorts.[1]

Palestinian residents of Jerusalem have the right to apply for Israeli citizenship, but in order to acquire it they have to demonstrate a moderate acquaintance with Hebrew, renounce their Jordanian or other citizenship, and swear loyalty to Israel. More than 95 percent have refused to do this, on the grounds that it would signal acquiescence in and legitimation of Israel's occupation. For those who have applied, permissions have been scarce: in 2015, only 2.9 percent of applications were approved.

Between the year the city was first occupied and 2014, more than 14,400 Palestinians had their residency revoked. As permanent residents, Palestinians in Jerusalem are entitled to vote in municipal (but not national) elections, yet more than 99 percent boycott them.[2] With no electoral incentive to satisfy the needs of Palestinians, the city's politicians neglect them.

All Jerusalemites pay taxes, but the proportion of the municipal budget allocated to the roughly 316,000 Palestinian residents of a city with a population of 850,000 doesn't exceed 10 percent. Service provision is grossly unequal. In the East, there are five benefit offices, compared with the West's eighteen; four health centers for mothers and babies, compared with the West's twenty-five; and eleven mail carriers, compared with the West's 133. Palestinian neighborhoods have one-thirtieth as many playgrounds per resident as Jewish neighborhoods. Many roads are in disrepair and are too narrow to accommodate garbage trucks, forcing Palestinians to burn trash outside their homes. There is a shortage of sewage pipes, so Palestinian residents have to use septic tanks that often overflow. Students are stuffed into overcrowded schools or converted apartments; 2,200 additional classrooms are needed. More than three-quarters of the city's Palestinians live below the poverty line.[3]

Since 1967, no new Palestinian neighborhoods have been established in the city, while Jewish settlements surrounding existing Palestinian areas have mushroomed. Restrictive zoning and grossly unequal permit allocation prevent Palestinians from building legally. Israel has designated 52 percent of land in East Jerusalem as unavailable for development and set aside 35 percent for Jewish settlements, leaving the Palestinian population with only 13 percent, most of which is already built on. Those with growing families are forced to choose between building illegally and leaving the city. Roughly a third of them decide to build, meaning that 93,000 residents are under constant threat that their homes will be demolished.[4]

The government has no shortage of bureaucratic explanations for this unequal treatment, but it doesn't always try to hide the ethno-religious basis of its discrimination. After terrorist attacks by both Jews and Palestinians in Jerusalem and the West Bank, in summer and fall 2014, the government demolished the homes of only the Palestinian perpetrators. Palestinians who live in houses abandoned during the 1948 war have been evicted to make room for Jewish former owners and their descendants, but the reverse has yet to occur.[5]

Jerusalem was once the cultural, political, and commercial capital for Palestinians, connected to Bethlehem in the south and Ramallah in the north. But the construction of the separation wall cut Jerusalemites off from the West Bank and from one another. The route of the barrier was chosen to encompass as many East Jerusalem and West Bank Jewish settlements as possible while excluding the maximum number of Palestinians. In the Jerusalem area, only 3 percent of it follows the pre-1967 line. The wall divides the Palestinians in Jerusalem into two groups: between two-thirds and three-quarters are on the Israeli side, disconnected from Palestinians in the West Bank; between a quarter and one-third have found themselves on the West Bank side, and are now forced to wait in long lines at checkpoints to get to schools and services.[6]

Because areas on the West Bank side of the barrier are still within Jerusalem's municipal boundaries, the Ramallah-based PA is forbidden to enter them. Although the Israeli police, in common with the providers of other basic municipal services, largely refuse to go to these places, residents are still obliged to pay municipal taxes to qualify for health care and benefits. These neighborhoods have become a no-man's-land where criminals can escape from both Israel and the Palestinian Authority.[7]

In Palestinian areas on the Jerusalem side of the wall, too, crime has become pervasive. Israeli forces tend to enter these neighborhoods only when there's a threat to Jews. The Israeli security presence in East Jerusalem is made up mostly of paramilitary units, which are there essentially to quash dissent and prevent attacks on settlers rather than to protect Palestinians. Noncooperation with Israeli forces, because of rejection of their authority or out of fear of being seen as collaborating, has allowed gangs to proliferate. They are involved in robberies, drug smuggling, gun running, and extortion, which affects large numbers of Palestinian businesses.[8] Rising crime and insecurity have helped make East Jerusalem a ghost town at night.

Unrest and ethnic tension have been increasing for several years, but only after July 2014 did people begin referring to the protests and violence as an intifada. At the end of June 2014, the Israeli army discovered the bodies of three teenage students at West Bank yeshivas who had been kidnapped and murdered earlier that month. The next day, hundreds of Jews demonstrated in West Jerusalem, chanting "Death to the Arabs," "Muhammad is dead," and similar slogans. Several dozen protesters attacked Palestinian workers and passersby. Before sunrise the next morning, three Jewish nationalists drove to the upper-middle-class Palestinian neighborhood of Shuafat, abducted a randomly selected sixteen-year-old called Muhammad Abu Khdeir, beat him, and burned him alive.[9]

In the days following his murder, riots broke out in Palestinian areas of Jerusalem. A light railway that passes through Shuafat on its way to the nearby settlement of Pisgat Ze'ev was repeatedly stoned and the service suspended.[10] Demonstrations spread when the war in Gaza broke out a week after Abu Khdeir's murder. In the following months, there were protests in East Jerusalem nearly every day.

Two of the focal points were Silwan, southeast of the Old City walls, where Jewish settlers with state-funded private security guards have taken over numerous buildings, and the al-Aqsa Mosque compound, or Temple Mount, where Israel has frequently restricted Palestinian access while facilitating visits by a small but vocal Jewish minority, doubling the number of Jewish visitors between 2009 and 2014. This minority, which has boasted high-ranking Knesset members, ministers, and deputy ministers, ignores ultra-Orthodox injunctions by advocating prayer and, in some cases, even the construction of a third Jewish temple on the site.[11]

Jerusalem's mayor, Nir Barkat, said that the number of incidents involving stone throwing and Molotov cocktails had risen from two hundred per month in the period preceding the Gaza War to five thousand per month afterward. More than a thousand Palestinians in Jerusalem, most of them minors, were detained in the several months after Abu Khdeir's murder—four times the total arrested in East Jerusalem for security-related offenses between the start of the Second Intifada and 2008.[12]

To counter the unrest, the Israeli government seconded a thousand special forces officers to the Jerusalem police; deployed four extra border police units; conducted large-scale raids; increased the presence of paramilitary forces in East Jerusalem; established checkpoints and barricades around Palestinian areas; called on Israelis who have firearms licenses to join a volunteer security force; ordered the houses of Palestinian attackers to be demolished and their relatives arrested; dispersed crowds by hosing them with skunk; erected concrete fortifications at bus stations; threatened to penalize parents of teenage demonstrators; proposed prison sentences of up to twenty years for throwing stones; and handed out fines in Palestinian neighborhoods for such minor offenses as jaywalking and spitting out the shells of sunflower seeds.[13]

None of these measures had much effect. Growing numbers of Palestinians, particularly in East Jerusalem, were injured by Israeli forces; several were killed. In November 2014, another Palestinian teenager in East Jerusalem was abducted and beaten, but left alive. Several Palestinians in the West Bank were run over. Attacks on Israelis increased sharply. A leading supporter of Jewish prayer in the Temple Mount/ Noble Sanctuary, who would become a member of the Knesset in 2016, was shot. Two ax-, knife-, and gun-wielding Palestinians from East Jerusalem killed a police officer, a worshipper, and four ultra-Orthodox rabbis at a West Jerusalem synagogue. There were gruesome attacks on Israeli soldiers and civilians by Palestinians using guns and knives and vehicles. More Israelis died in such incidents in fall 2014 than in 2012 and 2013 combined.[14]

Israel's ministers and official spokespersons claimed that Mahmoud Abbas was inciting the violence. But that assertion was aimed more at thwarting Abbas's diplomatic initiatives than at providing a sober assessment of the causes of the unrest. As Israel's senior security officials stated, the fall 2014 attacks were actually the work of "lone wolves"—spontaneous acts of violence, not committed by followers of a particular political faction. They stemmed precisely from the absence of Palestinian political leadership.[15]

* * *

The Palestinian sense of abandonment by their leaders is particularly acute in Jerusalem, where the PA is forbidden from acting and to which Ramallah, like most of the Arab world, devotes many lofty words but very few deeds. When he assented to the five-year interim arrangements for self-governance in the Oslo Accords, Yasir Arafat agreed to exclude Jerusalem from the areas to be governed pro tempore by the PA. Local figures, notably the late Faisal Husseini, had refused to agree to this, which is one reason Yitzhak Rabin, who resolutely opposed dividing Jerusalem and said he would rather abandon peace than give up a united capital, chose to bypass Husseini and instead completed secret negotiations in Oslo with Arafat's emissaries.[16]

Palestinians in Jerusalem have been bereft of leadership since Husseini's death in 2001. Jerusalem's four representatives in the Palestinian parliament—all of them members of Hamas, elected in 2006—have been deported. The Shin Bet monitors "political subversion," which includes opposition to the occupation.[17] Since all Palestinian political parties oppose the occupation, they and their activities have, in effect, been criminalized. Even innocuous institutions such as the Arab Chamber of Commerce and Industry have been shut down. Years of Israeli suppression of political activity have ensured that when violence does erupt in Jerusalem, there is no legitimate authority to quell it, making the spontaneous, unorganized protests and attacks far more difficult for the security forces to thwart and contain.

The notion that Abbas incited the protests was laughable to Palestinians in Jerusalem. When permitted entry to the city, Abbas's representatives and associates have been verbally and physically attacked by Palestinians. A former religious affairs minister and his bodyguards were hospitalized after an assault while they were in the Noble Sanctuary, and a PA minister was shouted out of the mourning tent of the family of Abu Khdeir.[18] The PA was accused of standing idly by as a withering East Jerusalem was encircled, divided, and constricted.

Abbas was adamantly opposed to leading an intifada, peaceful or otherwise, and he would almost certainly have resigned if a new one began. Understanding his deep-seated abhorrence of violence, Hamas agreed in 2011 and again in 2013 to a joint campaign of peaceful protest with Fatah in the West Bank, but Abbas and the security forces under his command continued to act against such demonstrations. Even after Hamas's rise in popularity following the Gaza War and the subsequent Palestinian agitation in Jerusalem and cities within Israel, Abbas continued to eschew even the nonviolent means of pressuring Israel that had been available to him for several years.[19] When the PLO's strategy amounted to submitting resolutions to the UN Security Council that it knew in advance would be vetoed, it was little wonder that Palestinians in Jerusalem started acting on their own.

The result, in just a few weeks of heightened protest and violence, was a swift reversal of Israeli policies at the Temple Mount/Noble Sanctuary. In November 2014, Prime Minister Netanyahu flew to Jordan and privately committed to ease tensions at the holy site by barring Knesset members and provocative Jewish activists, limiting the size of visiting religious Jewish groups, and removing age and gender restrictions on Muslim access. When Israel breached these commitments in late summer 2015, reimposing age and gender restrictions on Muslim access and allowing entry to larger groups of Jewish activists, including a government minister, clashes broke out again.[20]

* * *

The 2014–2015 upsurge in protests and violence was called the silent intifada, the individual intifada, the children's intifada, the firecracker intifada, the car intifada, the run-over intifada, the knives intifada, the Jerusalem intifada, and the third intifada. But what it most closely resembled wasn't the First or the Second Intifada but the spike in uncoordinated, leaderless attacks that preceded the First Intifada in 1987. Then, as in 2014–2015, such violence was blamed wrongly on the PLO leadership. Then, too, that leadership appeared defeated and in decline. Then, too, there was the memory of elections, held in the previous decade, whose results Israel sought to undo.[21] Then, too, with no organized political structure in the West Bank and Gaza offering a clear strategy of national liberation, sporadic assaults on Israelis, not attributable to any political faction, were on the increase.

The crucial difference between the mid-1980s and 2014–2015 is that Palestinian civil society had become much weaker, and so, too, had the likelihood of coherent political organization of the kind that emerged soon after the First Intifada began. The groups that were then active have been supplanted, either by the institutions of a Palestinian Authority whose existence is premised on close cooperation with Israel, or by

NGOs whose foreign funders make assistance conditional on the pursuit of apolitical development projects or vague peace-building strategies that explicitly rule out nonviolent confrontation with Israel and any initiative likely to drive up the costs of military occupation. Palestinian society is afflicted with dependency, and it is dependent on forces that wish to preserve the status quo.

—November 2014

9.

Hamas's Chances

Neither Israel nor Hamas sought the summer 2014 war in Gaza. But both were certain that a new confrontation would come. The cease-fire in 2012 that ended an eight-day-long exchange of Gaza-based rocket launchings and Israeli aerial bombardment was never implemented. It stipulated that all Palestinian factions in Gaza would stop hostilities, that Israel would end attacks against Gaza by land, sea, and air—including the "targeting of individuals" (assassinations, typically by drone-fired missile)—and that the closure of Gaza would essentially end as a result of Israel's "opening the crossings and facilitating the movements of people and transfer of goods, and refraining from restricting residents' free movements and targeting residents in border areas." An additional clause noted that "other matters as may be requested shall be addressed," a reference to private commitments by Egypt and the United States to help thwart weapons smuggling into Gaza, though Hamas has rejected this interpretation of the clause.[1]

During the three months that followed the cease-fire, the Shin Bet recorded only a single attack: two mortar shells fired from Gaza in December 2012. Israeli officials were impressed. But they convinced themselves that the quiet on Gaza's border was primarily the result of their own deterrence and Palestinian self-interest. Israel therefore saw little incentive in upholding its end of the deal. Its forces made regular incursions into Gaza, strafed Palestinian farmers and those collecting scrap and rubble across the border, and fired at boats, preventing fishermen from reaching the majority of Gaza's waters.[2]

The end of the closure never came. Crossings were repeatedly shut. So-called buffer zones—agricultural lands that Palestinian farmers couldn't enter without being fired on—were reinstated. Imports declined, exports were blocked, and fewer Gazans were given exit permits to Israel and the West Bank.[3]

Israel had committed to holding indirect negotiations over the implementation of the cease-fire but repeatedly delayed them, at first because it wanted to see whether Hamas would stick to its side of the deal, then because Prime Minister Netanyahu couldn't afford to make further concessions to Hamas in the weeks leading up to the January 2013 elections, and then because a new Israeli coalition was being formed and needed time to settle in. Substantive talks never took place.[4] The lesson for Hamas was clear: even if an agreement was brokered by the United States and Egypt, Israel could still fail to honor it.

Yet Hamas largely continued to maintain the cease-fire to Israel's satisfaction. It set up a new police force tasked with arresting Palestinians who tried to fire at Israel. In 2013, fewer rockets were launched from Gaza than in any year since 2003, soon after the first primitive projectiles were shot across the border. Hamas needed time to rebuild its arsenal, fortify its defenses, and prepare for the next battle, when it would again seek an end to Gaza's closure by force of arms. But it also hoped that Egypt would open itself to Gaza, thereby making less important an easing of the closure by Israel and putting an end to Egypt and Israel's years-long practice of trying to dump on each other responsibility for the territory and its impoverished inhabitants.

In July 2013, the Egyptian coup led by General Sisi dashed Hamas's hopes. His military regime blamed all of the country's woes on the ousted president, Mohamed Morsi of the Muslim Brotherhood, and Hamas, the Brotherhood's Palestinian offshoot. Morsi was formally charged with conspiring with Hamas to destabilize the country. The leader of the Muslim Brotherhood and hundreds of Morsi's supporters were sentenced to death. The Egyptian military used increasingly threatening rhetoric against Hamas, which feared that Egypt, Israel, and the Palestinian Authority would take advantage of its weakness to launch a coordinated military campaign. Travel bans were imposed on Hamas officials. The number of Gazans allowed to cross to Egypt was reduced to a small fraction of what it had been before the coup. Nearly all of the hundreds of tunnels that had brought goods from Egypt to Gaza were closed. Hamas had used taxes levied on those goods to pay the salaries of more than forty thousand civil servants in Gaza.[5]

Hamas's former allies and primary supporters, Iran and Syria, would not help unless it betrayed the Muslim Brotherhood by switching its support in the Syrian war to the Alawite Bashar al-Assad as he fought against an overwhelmingly Sunni opposition. Hamas's remaining allies had their own problems: Turkey was preoccupied with domestic turmoil; Qatar was being pushed by its neighbors to reduce its support for the Brotherhood, which the most powerful Gulf monarchies perceived as their primary political threat. Saudi Arabia declared the Brotherhood a terrorist organization; other Gulf states continued to repress it. In the West Bank, Hamas couldn't wave a flag, hold a meeting, or give a speech without facing arrest by Israeli or PA security forces.

With pressure mounting and no strong ally to turn to, Gaza experienced a quick descent. Though Israel reacted to Egypt's closure of tunnels and the pedestrian crossing by slightly increasing its own supply of goods and exit permits, there was no change in its fundamental policy. Electricity shortages increased, with daily blackouts lasting between twelve and eighteen hours. Those in need of treatment in Egyptian hospitals paid bribes as high as $3,000 to cross the border when it was occasionally opened for a day. Shortages of fuel led to queues stretching several blocks at petrol stations, and fights broke out at the pumps. Trash piled up because the government couldn't afford fuel for garbage trucks. In December, sanitation plants shut down and sewage flowed through the streets. The water crisis worsened: more than 90 percent of Gaza's aquifer was contaminated.[6]

As it became clear that unrest in Egypt wouldn't lead to Sisi's ouster or to the return of the Brotherhood, Hamas saw only four possible exits. The first was to effect a rapprochement with Iran—at the unacceptable price of betraying the Brotherhood in Syria and weakening support for Hamas among Palestinians and the majority of Sunni Muslims everywhere. The second was to levy new taxes in Gaza, but these couldn't make up for the loss in revenue from the tunnels, and would risk stirring up opposition to Hamas rule. The third was to launch rockets at Israel in the hope of obtaining a new cease-fire that would bring an improvement in conditions in Gaza. This prospect worried US officials: it would undermine the quiescent Palestinian leadership in Ramallah and disrupt the Israeli-Palestinian peace talks that Secretary of State John Kerry had recently launched. But Hamas felt too vulnerable, especially because of Sisi's potential role in any new conflict between Gaza and Israel, to take this route. It was sure that the peace talks would fail on their own. The fourth and final option, which Hamas eventually chose, was to hand over responsibility for governing Gaza to appointees of the Fatah-dominated Palestinian leadership in Ramallah, even though Hamas had defeated it in the 2006 elections.

Hamas paid a high price, acceding to nearly all of Fatah's demands. The new PA government didn't contain a single Hamas figure, and its senior ministers remained unchanged. Hamas consented to allow the Palestinian Authority to move several thousand members of its security forces back to Gaza and to place its guards at borders and crossings, with no reciprocal positions for Hamas in the West Bank security apparatus. Most important, the new government agreed to comply with the three conditions for Western aid long demanded by the United States and its European allies: nonviolence, adherence to past agreements, and recognition of Israel. Though the agreement stipulated that the PA government would limit its mandate to technocratic matters, Abbas said it would pursue his political program.[7] Hamas barely protested.

The agreement was signed on April 23, 2014, after Kerry's peace talks had broken down; had the negotiations been making progress, the United States would have done its best to block the move. But the Obama administration was disappointed in the positions Israel took during the talks, and publicly blamed it for its part in their failure. Frustration helped push the United States to recognize the new Palestinian government despite Israel's objections. But that was as far as the United States was prepared to go. Behind the scenes, it pressured Abbas to avoid a true reconciliation between Hamas and Fatah. Hamas sought—and the agreement called for—the reactivation of the long-dormant

Palestinian legislative council as a check on the new government. But because the legislature contained a majority of Hamas members, the United States warned Abbas that it would cut financial and political support for the new government if the legislature met.

The reconciliation agreement was unpopular inside Hamas, from the grass roots to the second-highest tier of leadership. Musa Abu Marzouk, a senior leader in its political bureau, spent weeks in Gaza meeting Hamas cadres, listening to their concerns, and trying to convince them of the deal's wisdom. Militants worried that Fatah security personnel would try to avenge the deaths that resulted from the fighting between Hamas and Fatah in 2006–2007 and start a new civil war. Hamas officials wanted assurances that the Palestinian Authority wouldn't extend its collaboration with Israel against Hamas from the West Bank into Gaza. Employees of the government, thousands of whom were not affiliated with Hamas, worried about being fired or demoted, or simply going unpaid. Others said Hamas had conceded everything with no assurance that Fatah would fulfill its obligations. Among the rationales that Hamas leaders provided for signing the agreement was that it would allow the movement to focus on its original mission, military resistance against Israel.

The fears of the skeptics were confirmed after the government was formed. The most basic conditions of the deal—payment of the government employees who run Gaza and opening the crossing with Egypt— were not fulfilled. For years, Gazans had been told that the cause of their immiseration was Hamas rule. Now it was officially over, and conditions only got worse.

* * *

On June 12, 2014, ten days after the new government was formed, the kidnapping and murder of three Israeli yeshiva students in the West Bank radically changed Hamas's fortunes. Israel blamed Hamas for the murders, and one Hamas leader said that members of the military wing had conducted the operation, though several Israeli security officials said they believed the perpetrators were part of an independent cell that hadn't acted on orders from above.[8]

In its search for the suspects, Israel carried out its largest West Bank campaign against Hamas since the Second Intifada, closing its offices and arresting hundreds of members at all levels. Hamas officially denied organizational, top-down responsibility for the abductions and said Israel's accusations were a pretext to launch a new offensive. Among those arrested were more than 50 of the 1,027 security prisoners released in 2011 by Israel in exchange for the soldier Gilad Shalit. Hamas saw the arrests as a violation of the agreement made at the time of Shalit's release, which specified the circumstances under which the prisoners could be rearrested and also contained unfulfilled commitments by Israel to improve conditions and visitation rights for other Palestinian detainees.[9]

The Palestinian leadership in Ramallah worked closely with Israel to catch the militants. It had rarely been so discredited among its constituents, many of whom believed that abducting Israelis had proved the only effective means of gaining the release of prisoners widely regarded as national heroes. In several West Bank cities, residents protested against the security cooperation. In Jerusalem, Palestinians assaulted and censured allies of Abbas.[10]

As protests spread, militants in Gaza from non-Hamas factions began firing rockets and mortars in solidarity. Sensing Israel's vulnerability and the Ramallah leadership's weakness, Hamas called for the protests to grow into a third intifada. When the rocket fire increased, they found themselves drawn into a new confrontation, for they couldn't be seen to suppress the rocket attacks while they called for a mass uprising. Israel's retaliation for the projectile fire culminated in a series of bombings that killed nine militants, seven of them from Hamas, the largest number of fatalities inflicted on the group in several months. The next day, Hamas began taking responsibility for the rockets. Israel then announced Operation Protective Edge.[11]

For Hamas, the choice wasn't so much between peace and war as between slow strangulation and a battle that had a chance, however slim, of loosening the chokehold. It saw itself in a struggle for its survival, with its future in Gaza hanging on the outcome. Like Israel, Hamas was careful to set rather limited aims, selecting goals to which much of the international community was sympathetic. Its primary objective was that Israel honor three existing agreements: the Shalit exchange, including the release of the rearrested prisoners; the 2012 cease-fire, which called for an end to Gaza's closure; and the Hamas-PLO reconciliation agreement, which required Israeli acquiescence in order for the Palestinian government to pay salaries in Gaza, staff its borders, receive much-needed construction materials, and open the pedestrian crossing with Egypt.

These were not unrealistic goals. Obama and Kerry said they believed a cease-fire should be based on the 2012 agreement. The United States also proposed, in a draft framework for a cease-fire submitted to Israel, that funds be transferred to government employees in Gaza, a reversal of the previous US position. And over the course of the war, Israel came to think that it could solve its Gaza problem with help from the new government in Ramallah that it had formally boycotted. The Israeli defense minister hoped a cease-fire would place the PA's security forces at Gaza's border crossings. Netanyahu softened his tone toward Abbas. Near the end of the third week of fighting, Israel and the United States quietly looked away as the Palestinian government made payments to all employees in Gaza for the first time. Israeli officials across the political spectrum began to admit privately that the previous policy toward Gaza was a mistake. All parties involved in mediating a cease-fire envisioned postwar arrangements that effectively strengthened the new Palestinian government and its role in Gaza—and, by extension, Gaza itself.[12]

Achieving the release of the rearrested prisoners was a less attainable objective. But Hamas calculated that as the war dragged on, its chances of capturing a live Israeli soldier would increase. During the first three weeks of the war, it made at least four tries and said it had succeeded in two; Israel denied the claims, but has not offered convincing evidence that the missing soldiers are dead. Two years after the war, Israel reclassified the status of the two from "killed in action" to "missing in action or captive."[13] Few things would do more to discredit the Ramallah leadership than a new prisoner exchange deal between Hamas and Israel, even if on a smaller scale than the Shalit agreement. When Hamas announced it had captured the first soldier, crowds rushed into the streets of Gaza, Jerusalem, and the West Bank, setting off fireworks and passing out sweets, with new hope that their friends and relatives in Israeli prisons would soon be released.

Palestinian protests in solidarity with Gaza rapidly spread. Hamas flags outnumbered those of Fatah at a rally in Nablus. The Ramallah leadership, not altogether convincingly, adopted some of Hamas's rhetoric, using the word "resistance" and praising Hamas's fight. Throughout the war, clashes with Israeli forces took place in the West Bank and East Jerusalem nearly every night. On July 24, during the Muslim holy night of Laylat al-Qadr, the Qalandiya checkpoint in northern Jerusalem was the site of the largest demonstration in the West Bank since the Second Intifada.[14] Hamas knew it couldn't defeat the Israeli military, but the Gaza war held out the possibility of a distant though no less important prize: stirring up the West Bank, and thereby undermining the Ramallah leadership and the program of perpetual negotiation, accommodation, and US dependency that it stands for.

For many Palestinians, Hamas had once again proved the comparative effectiveness of militancy. Tunnels, which were central to its successes in the war, had long been the source of attacks against Israelis in Gaza. Hamas could point to a series of tunnel-based operations, including a deadly December 2004 explosion underneath an IDF post in southern Gaza, that helped precipitate Israel's pullout.[15] During the fighting in Gaza, Israel did not announce a single new settlement and expressed willingness to make certain concessions to Palestinian demands— achievements the Ramallah leadership had not been able to match in years of negotiations. At stake in the war was the future path of the Palestinian national movement.

The real barrier to a West Bank uprising prior to the war was not, as Hamas had claimed, Abbas's collaboration with Israel. It was, rather, social and political fragmentation and the widespread Palestinian acceptance of the notion that national liberation should come second to the largely apolitical and technocratic projects of state building and economic development. These were far greater obstacles for Hamas. To the extent that the war instilled pride in Palestinians who said they'd grown accustomed to feeling shame at the way their leaders groveled at American and Israeli feet, Hamas's achievement was not small.

But Hamas also risked a great deal. It stood to lose everything if

Israelis decided to reassess their long-standing reliance on it as Gaza's policeman, a strategy that had led Israel to keep Hamas powerful enough to exercise a near monopoly on the use of force in Gaza. An irony of the final weeks of ground combat was that Hamas's strong showing had put its position at risk. Israel might have felt that Hamas had become too big a threat. Hamas slowed the IDF's ground invasion and inflicted dozens of losses on Israeli troops, far more than most expected. Two weeks after the incursion began, the army hadn't made it past the first line of densely populated urban housing. Thanks to the vast tunnel network leading not just into Israel but under Gaza, the IDF would almost certainly have faced increased casualties had it decided to enter the city centers. During Operation Cast Lead in 2008–2009, Israel went far deeper into Gaza and lost only ten soldiers, four of them to friendly fire; in the 2014 war, its ground forces lost sixty-six.[16]

The tunnels also spared Hamas militants from much heavier losses. For the first time in decades, Israel was defending itself against an army that had penetrated its pre-1967 boundaries, by means of tunnels and naval incursions. Hamas rockets that were natively produced in Gaza could reach all of Israel's largest cities, including Haifa, and Hamas had developed armed drones. It was able to shut down Israel's main airport for two days. Israelis who lived near Gaza left their homes and were afraid to go back; the IDF admitted that there were probably still tunnels it didn't know about. Rockets from Gaza kept Israelis returning to shelters day after day, demonstrating the IDF's inability to deal with the threat. The war is estimated to have cost the country billions of dollars.[17]

The greatest costs, of course, were borne by Gaza's civilians, who made up the majority of the more than 2,250 lives lost by the time a cease-fire was announced on August 26.[18] Fifty days of conflict wiped out entire families, devastated neighborhoods, destroyed homes, cut off all electricity, and greatly limited access to water.

The war demonstrated both the power and the limits of Hamas's strategy. The Islamist group was strong enough to deter Israel from reoccupying the territory, which was no small feat for a tiny, besieged group facing the most powerful military in the region. But it was too weak to force Israel to make concessions other than those deemed to be in its own long-term interest, such as permitting the Palestinian Authority to operate in Gaza and easing some restrictions on the population. Where Hamas's strategy proved far more effective, however, was in domestic politics, where its stature and credibility were revitalized at the expense of Fatah and the Palestinian Authority. That was quite an accomplishment for the Islamist group, which understood that it was in the West Bank, not Gaza, that the future strategy and objectives of the national movement would be determined.

—August 2014

10.

Trapped in Gaza

Within a year of the 2014 Gaza War, the conditions that precipitated it had grown considerably worse. The Palestinian government of national consensus, formed in June 2014, never exercised authority in Gaza. Just over a year later, that government was reshuffled without Hamas's inclusion or input, dropping all pretense of consensus. Nominally, the consensus government persisted, because Hamas still saw it as offering the best chance of disowning responsibility for Gaza's miserable conditions. But it had not taken over managing the territory—not the payment of employees who administered Gaza; not the functions or operating costs of major ministries; and not the control of the border crossings that remained closed or highly restricted. The result for Gaza's population was unprecedented misery, a sense of abandonment by Palestinian leaders, and economic regression, with per capita income far lower than it had been over two decades earlier.[1]

Many diplomats who had hoped to resolve Gaza's problems by restoring PA control had lost faith that such a transfer of power was in the offing or would even substantially change conditions. Instead, lip service was paid to the ideal of Palestinian unity, which in reality Israel, the United States, and Europe opposed in any serious incarnation, and which they deemed unlikely to come about.

And why should it have? Via Israel, which collects taxes on the PA's behalf for a 3 percent fee, the Palestinian Authority in Ramallah received revenues from levies on all goods entering Gaza but did not have to spend them on the majority of its residents. Instead it paid tens of thousands of Gaza-based, Fatah-affiliated former PA workers, most of whom had been ordered to boycott the Hamas government on pain of losing their salaries. Egypt's closure of the network of Gaza–Sinai tunnels in 2013 meant that Hamas lost most of its tax income, while PA revenues greatly increased: goods that had previously come from Egypt and were levied by Hamas now entered through Israel, which collected the taxes on the PA's behalf.[2]

More important, leaders in Ramallah viewed governing Gaza as a trap: they would be given responsibility for the territory's enormous problems but no real authority to solve them. Were they to oversee Gaza's crossings, they argued, Hamas checkpoints would exist a few dozen yards behind them; true control, including over war and peace, would have remained beyond their grasp. PA leaders would be blamed for future violence without having the tools to prevent it. Nor were solutions on offer to fix the poverty, poor services, donor neglect, and energy and water crises for which the government would be held to account.

Egypt, which had ousted the Morsi government only a year before the war broke out, viewed Hamas as an extension of the Muslim Brotherhood and therefore a threat to its national security. More than at any time since Israel's 2005 withdrawal from Gaza, Egypt had succeeded in offloading responsibility for the territory onto Israel. It understood, too, that the Palestinian Authority was not being given sufficient incentive to take over. In Egypt's view, a superficial PA presence at the crossings would not weaken Hamas or substantially reduce the flow of militants and weapons between Gaza and Sinai. To put real pressure on the PA to return to Gaza, Egypt wanted something Israel was reluctant to provide: substantive links between Gaza and the West Bank. Such links would reduce Cairo's concerns that the two territories would remain separate indefinitely, leaving Gaza's growing population with no place to move but Egypt.

For Israel, a reversal of its policy of separating Gaza from the West Bank was viewed as a serious security threat; the separation was thought to prevent Hamas from transferring knowledge, weapons, funding, and, perhaps most dangerously, ideological and political influence to the West Bank. Keeping the rapidly growing Gaza population out of the West Bank also served a demographic interest for Israel, helping it boost the percentage of Jewish residents in what it refers to as Judea and Samaria.[3] For Israelis who opposed a two-state solution, the separation provided the added benefits of making a peace agreement more remote and calling into question Abbas's ability to speak on behalf of all Palestinians or claim a monopoly on the use of force, without which he could not credibly offer an end to the conflict.

Though Israel had arrived at a greater appreciation of the need to strengthen Gaza's economy to lessen the likelihood of renewed fighting, its preference was to do so by means other than connecting Gaza to the West Bank. It desired greater PA influence in Gaza, and PA control over Gaza's crossings, but only insofar as these elements of Palestinian unity were not accompanied by reciprocal steps in the West Bank that would have empowered Hamas.

What could be done to improve conditions in Gaza, therefore, was constrained by what Israel and the Palestinian Authority would allow in the West Bank. But because the West Bank was a greater priority than Gaza for both Israel and the Palestinian Authority, and because they remained committed to preventing Hamas from sharing power there, the most that Gazans could hope for were small economic improvements and relaxations of the closure regime. For Gazans, these were welcome, necessary steps that seemed likely to forestall a future war, but they were almost certainly not sufficient to prevent one.

* * *

As a result of the enormous shortfall in funding from donors who were reluctant to pay for projects that would likely be ruined in renewed fighting, Gazans saw little relief after the war. One year after the ceasefire, 17,863 families—100,000 people—who had lost dwellings during the conflict were still homeless and living with relatives or in temporary accommodations or in tents on the remains of their homes. For the first ten months after the war, no totally destroyed homes were allowed to be rebuilt, as the Palestinian Authority and Israel argued over how much construction material was needed for each square meter.[4]

Until mid-June 2015, 5,600 people lived in temporary shelters in United Nations Relief and Works Agency (UNRWA) schools. Because such small amounts of construction supplies entered Gaza after the war, poor families with partially destroyed homes resold materials on the black market for two or three times their cost to put food on the table or pay rent. An estimated 23 million tons of construction materials were needed to repair Gaza and to complete infrastructure and other projects begun before the war. Less than 6 percent of this amount arrived in the year following the fighting.[5]

In 2015, Gaza had the highest unemployment of any economy in the world; 80 percent of the population relied on donor aid, and 39 percent lived below the poverty line. Even before the war, more than half the population was "food insecure." The once-important manufacturing sector had shrunk by 60 percent. The war destroyed a third of Gaza's agricultural land and 40 percent of its livestock.[6]

A functioning economy requires exports, which had become virtually nonexistent. In 2005, the year of Israel's withdrawal, 9,319 truckloads of goods left Gaza, going mostly to Israel and the West Bank. By 2014, these figures had shrunk by more than 4,000 percent: 136 truckloads went abroad and 92 to the West Bank.[7]

Unions were on strike, the health sector was collapsing, and it was estimated that the barely commenced reconstruction of damage from the last several rounds of conflict would take decades to complete. Electricity shortages, already chronic before the war, worsened considerably, with frequent blackouts of sixteen hours per day in 2016. Widespread use of generators, far more expensive than power-company electricity, resulted in many burns and electrical shocks.[8]

Electricity shortages affected water supply, wastewater treatment, agriculture, and health services. Two of every five homes were not connected to sewerage; the vast majority of waste was untreated, with 100 million liters dumped in the sea daily; over 90 percent of the water from Gaza's aquifer continued to be unfit for humans; and one-third of residents had access to water for only six to eight hours every four days. Water-related diseases accounted for over one-fourth of illnesses and were the primary cause of child morbidity. For the first time in five decades, the infant mortality rate started to rise.[9]

Lawlessness and criminality began to spread. Bombs were placed at the homes and offices of Fatah leaders. Fights within Fatah—many between supporters of Abbas and those of the former Gaza Preventive Security chief Muhammad Dahlan—occurred in the universities and streets.[10] Ministers and other PA officials received death threats.

Boys and young men eagerly joined Hamas's military wing, the Qassam Brigades, one of Gaza's few growth sectors. Desperate families knowingly risked their lives to escape with the help of shady maritime smugglers in Egypt, at whose hands hundreds of Palestinians died in the year after the war. Others risked death by crossing the heavily fortified border into Israel, in the hope of finding work or sometimes a jail cell with regular meals and a bed.[11]

Salafi-jihadi groups grew in boldness and strength. They did not threaten Hamas rule but challenged the movement politically and ideologically, while tearing at Gaza's social fabric and undermining the internal security that was among Hamas's core achievements. They attacked hair salons and symbols of Western influence, such as the French Cultural Center, as well as Hamas government facilities and military personnel. In response, Hamas conducted a large arrest campaign and put up dozens of temporary checkpoints throughout Gaza; in some parts of Gaza City, residents passed through four of them in an area encompassing no more than several blocks. The militants did not back down. In July 2015, unknown assailants detonated bombs targeting five cars belonging to members of the armed wings of Islamic Jihad and Hamas.[12]

These tensions threatened to further erode the cease-fire with Israel through the old pattern of non-Hamas militants firing a trickle of rockets, prompting Israeli strikes against Hamas. In June 2015, Hamas killed a Salafi-jihadi leader suspected of involvement in a spate of Gaza bombings; in retaliation, a Salafi-jihadi group claiming affiliation to the Islamic State launched four rockets toward Israel, two of which fell within Gaza, and unidentified assailants set off an IED near the Gaza City pier. It was the second set of rockets shot toward Israel in little over a week. In both cases Hamas arrested the perpetrators and disavowed responsibility, while Israel responded with several strikes, including at Hamas sites.[13]

Gazans asked themselves not whether a new war would erupt but when. A Hamas leader with close ties to the military wing said, "Anyone who has a problem with his faction can fire a rocket at Israel in order to express his resentment. We're trying to do what we can to stop it, but the militants keep asking us why they should hold their fire when the blockade is still in place."[14]

* * *

For many years, Egypt had been the main portal for Gazans to reach the outside world (far fewer, mostly merchants and medical patients, left via Israel, and all of them were subject to Shin Bet vetting and, in many cases, interrogations). In 2012, 420,000 people transited through the Rafah terminal, the sole border crossing between Egypt and Gaza. In 2015, less than one-fourteenth as many—29,000 people—did so. For fully one-third of the year, none at all crossed; the pattern worsened in 2016, when not a single person passed during three of the first four months of the year. An Egyptian official said that, despite Saudi requests to ease pressures on Gaza, the terminal would remain mostly closed for the foreseeable future.[15]

Egypt also demolished, plugged, or flooded nearly all Gaza–Sinai tunnels. In an effort to prevent the construction of new ones, the Egyptian army razed the Sinai part of Rafah, replacing it with a buffer zone and relocating its inhabitants, many of whom have relatives in Gaza. Following the closure, Hamas and the Gaza government have been strangled. Struggling to find the money to keep the government running, Hamas imposed new taxes and fees that were met with widespread complaints, sometimes resulting in retraction, as with those temporarily imposed on new cars in 2012, or non-implementation, as with an April 2015 draft law for a "solidarity tax" on high-earning businesses. Employees hired by the Hamas government received sporadic, partial payments ranging from one-third to one-half their salaries. Even members of Hamas's military wing were affected.[16]

As Israel began to recognize its increased responsibility for Gaza's residents, the need to prevent or delay another war, and the unlikelihood of Egypt or the Palestinian Authority improving Gaza's conditions, it started to relax aspects of the closure regime. This reflected an understanding, particularly on the part of the Defense Ministry, that economic conditions had to be improved in order to forestall a new conflagration. Israel cooperated directly with Qatar to facilitate its reconstruction projects in Gaza and permitted it to make a one-time payment, in October 2014, to a portion of the employees of the Hamas government—a move that Israel had refused prior to the war.[17] But these steps did not address the fundamental problem of providing a stable source of revenue to the acting government in Gaza. They were insufficient to restore the economy, and they left the vast majority of Gazans trapped, without access to the outside world. Israel had learned some lessons from the war, but hadn't learned them well enough. Leaving these issues unresolved was a recipe for renewed conflict.

* * *

Since the Palestinian Authority lost control of Gaza in June 2007, Israel and Hamas have engaged in numerous short escalations and three major confrontations, in the last of which, the longest and bloodiest, over 2,250 Palestinians died (1,462 of whom, the UN found, were civilians), as did 71 Israelis (66 of them soldiers).[18]

During those eight years, Israel and Hamas have pursued irreconcilable goals. Israel sought to deter Hamas from attacking it or letting others do so, and to prevent the organization from increasing its materiel, the primary declared goal of the blockade. Hamas aimed to maintain its grip on power, strengthen its military might, and inflict higher costs on Israel in each successive battle. In the years leading up to the 2014 war, Hamas, far from being deterred or contained, prepared for and fought larger and larger conflicts, while its capabilities and its threat to Israeli life and property steadily increased. Those capabilities were weakened during the 2014 war, but only temporarily. Less than a year after the cease-fire, the head of the Shin Bet stated that Hamas had already rebuilt many tunnels leading into Israel and could wage a significant new war. As after past battles, Hamas didn't wait to begin rebuilding its stockpile, including by manufacturing, in Gaza, longer-range, more accurate rockets, which it started test-firing into the sea within weeks of the cease-fire.[19]

Israel may one day decide on an all-out invasion of Gaza, but its security establishment has indicated it very much prefers to avoid this. Its goal is to deter, not topple Hamas, because it fears Hamas's absence more. Most officials state that in the next round of conflict, unless an attack causes major civilian casualties, Israel is unlikely to reoccupy Gaza—for the same reason the army argued against doing so in 2014: the lack of any viable exit strategy other than returning the territory to Hamas. The IDF believes the PA and Fatah are too weak to wrest control from Hamas and stay in power, and that international forces would likely do no better. In the words of the then head of the IDF Southern Command, responsible for Gaza, "There is no substitute for Hamas as sovereign in the Strip. The substitute is the IDF and chaotic rule . . . and then the security situation would be much more problematic."[20]

Though the army's professional recommendation is unlikely to change, a minority opinion in the government does not rule out reoccupation. An Israeli official noted that at several points during the 2014 war, Benjamin Netanyahu did not believe he had majority support for his plans in the security cabinet—several members sought stronger action against Hamas—so did not convene it, including when Israel approved the final cease-fire.[21]

In a future war, particularly one in which residents of border communities are evacuated, as is now planned for towns within roughly four miles of Gaza, politicians may be particularly sensitive to the argument that Operation Protective Edge failed to meet Israel's objectives. There could be a slippery slope toward reoccupation, with an initial phase of partial seizure of strategic points, or a full ground invasion aimed at eradicating all Hamas's tunnels and most of its rockets and rocket-production facilities. The Israeli public—85 percent of which supported continued ground operations, according to a poll conducted three weeks into the war—does not want to undergo cycles of sustained rocket fire every few years, and may be persuaded by politicians that eradicating Hamas is the only solution.[22] On the other hand, Israelis have not held their politicians to account for failing to live up to previous pledges to destroy Hamas, and very few wish to see their troops once again policing Gaza's streets.

In Gaza, too, there was considerable war-weariness. Many residents professed readiness for a new conflict but in the same breath asked, with evident concern, whether one was coming. That the population wished to avoid war was not lost on the territory's rulers, who faced high dissatisfaction as taxes soared and reconstruction stalled. Several Hamas officials proposed a potentially renewable cease-fire of several years, during which economic life would be normalized and dependency on Israel reduced by establishing a floating pier off the coast of Gaza, from which ships could transit to a port in Cyprus. In the meantime, as the head of Israeli military intelligence reported to the Knesset in February 2016, Hamas was "restraining" other armed groups in Gaza, "making an effort to prevent rocket fire," and "doing everything it [could] to stop an escalation."[23]

During the period after the war, neither side was interested in a new confrontation. Hamas needed time to rebuild and improve its capabilities. It awaited a change in regional circumstances that could allow a new conflict to deliver achievements that the last one did not. Israel was not sufficiently threatened by Hamas to launch a preventive attack, and the difficulties Hamas faced in smuggling in weapons gave Israel a sense of reduced pressure in comparison with earlier periods of virtually unrestricted arms trafficking.[24]

As important, neither side had reason to believe a new war would have a different outcome. Two years later, conditions in the region had not changed substantially. Egypt was only more hostile toward Hamas and would not impede an Israeli operation against it, even one aimed at toppling the movement and reoccupying Gaza. The Palestinian Authority had no more intention of taking over Gaza than it did in 2014. It continued to abhor concessions by Israel that it feared would prolong Hamas rule. Qatar and Turkey were capable of offering Hamas diplomatic support but were still unable to bypass Egyptian mediation in order to help Hamas obtain concessions from Israel. Israel and the international community maintained their opposition to direct relations with Hamas, to an end to the blockade not premised on Hamas's disarmament, and to any steps that would significantly stabilize its power.[25]

But though Israel and Hamas did not seek a new war, resumed fighting was a constant risk. Events in Jerusalem and the West Bank threatened to trigger attacks from Gaza, as before the 2014 war. There remained the possibility of error. Hamas's control over other armed groups in Gaza was not total. Islamic Jihad threatened to break the cease-fire if a Palestinian prisoner on hunger strike died in custody. Israeli incursions into Gaza and destruction of tunnels caused a short flare-up in 2016; improvements in Israel's ability to locate tunnels posed the risk of larger escalations. Months after the 2014 cease-fire, a non-Hamas militant shot in the direction of IDF soldiers near Israel's side of the border fence, injuring one, and the army retaliated by killing a nearby Hamas commander responsible for monitoring and maintaining the cease-fire. "All it would have taken," a Hamas political committee member in Gaza said, "was for someone next to the Qassam commander to have fired a rocket in the heat of the moment, and we could have found ourselves in a new war."[26]

* * *

Of the four central stakeholders in Gaza—Egypt, Israel, Hamas, and the Palestinian Authority—Hamas and Israel were the most intent on avoiding war. Both recognized this. But both also believed that they were far more likely to continue periodic escalation and war than to find an arrangement that could substantially forestall the next confrontation.

Israel was as determined to maintain the closure that would lead to a new eruption as Hamas was resolved to build up its capabilities, without which Israel would have eliminated it long ago. In the words of former Mossad head Efraim Halevy, "Imagine that Hamas does disperse its military units and they lay down their arms. What will Israel do if it doesn't kill them? What incentive will we have to negotiate with them if they are no longer a threat to us?"[27]

In May 2016, the Israeli newspaper *Haaretz* obtained a leaked copy of a state comptroller's report on the 2014 war. According to *Haaretz*'s summary, the audit stated "that the Israeli leadership didn't seriously consider easing the economic restrictions on Gaza, which might have delayed the eruption of the 50-day war in the summer of 2014." Yet well before the appearance of the leaked draft, the government appeared to have understood some of its past mistakes: it reversed its refusal to recognize the Palestinian consensus government; retracted its veto over the payment of salaries to Gaza government employees hired by Hamas;

permitted limited exports to the West Bank; expanded the quantity and variety of imports to Gaza; and increased the number of Gaza patients and traders allowed to exit the territory.[28]

For Gazans, who lived under worse conditions in 2016 than they had at any time since Israel's occupation began in 1967, the lesson of the 2014 conflict was rather different: although a devastating war had brought only limited and meager relaxations of the closure, the benefits of cooperating—indeed, of continuing to provide Israel with the sort of security that its top generals openly praised—were more meager still.

—August 2015

V.

NEGOTIATION

*"Political Horizons" and
Other Euphemisms
for False Hope*

*I would have carried on autonomy talks for ten years,
and meanwhile we would have reached half a million
people in Judea and Samaria.*

—Yitzhak Shamir

11.

More Than One State, Less Than Two

At his Jerusalem residence on September 16, 2008, Prime Minister Ehud Olmert showed President Mahmoud Abbas a map representing the most far-reaching territorial compromise ever proposed by an Israeli premier. According to Olmert, his plan granted the Palestinians a state with a land area equal to 99.5 percent of the West Bank and Gaza. Israel would annex 6.3 percent of Palestinian territory, compensating the Palestinians with Israeli lands equivalent to 5.8 percent, as well as a corridor that would connect the two regions but remain under Israeli sovereignty. Jerusalem would be home to two capitals—its eastern, Arab neighborhoods part of Palestine, its Jewish neighborhoods in both halves of the city part of Israel—and a roughly two-square-kilometer area encompassing the Old City would be under international administration.[1]

Olmert has said to numerous interviewers that he told Abbas it was the best offer any Israeli leader would give in the next fifty years. Abbas asked to take the map to his experts. Olmert refused, fearing that Abbas would insist that it serve as a new starting point for future talks. The two agreed that their negotiators would meet the following day. In the years that followed, Olmert frequently asserted that he never heard from Abbas again. "I've been waiting," he later said, "ever since."[2]

This story, which is widely accepted in Israel and has done much to discredit the idea of a negotiated settlement, contains a number of inaccuracies. First, Olmert and Abbas did negotiate again on more than one occasion, as noted in former US deputy national security adviser Elliott Abrams's *Tested by Zion*, a detailed, frank, and perceptive account of the George W. Bush administration's involvement in the Israeli-Palestinian conflict. Second, Abrams writes that rather than ignoring the proposal, the Palestinians asked for clarifications and then said it was they who never heard back. Third, Olmert's descriptions of the offer, which he has not shown to the public or to anyone who could attest to its accuracy, have been inconsistent, adding credibility to Palestinian claims that it was less far-reaching and more vague than he has suggested.[3]

Olmert never provided absolute numbers when describing the territory he proposed to annex. Palestinian negotiators weren't able to ascertain whether the percentages he cited were of the entire Palestinian area that Israel conquered from Jordan and Egypt in 1967 or of a much smaller tract, excluding East Jerusalem and Gaza, among other regions. On top of this, calculations of the West Bank's size differ by several hundred square kilometers, according to the source of the figures. In some Palestinian accounts, Abbas couldn't be sure whether Olmert's proposed annexation of 6.3 to 6.8 percent of the West Bank and Gaza was not in fact closer to 8.5 percent—more than four times the 1.9 percent limit Abbas had placed on any swap.[4]

Adding to Palestinian doubts was that Foreign Minister Tzipi Livni had presented her own maps; these annexed 8 to 10 percent of the Occupied Territories, yet, Abrams notes, to the Palestinians "they looked very much the same [as Olmert's] . . . So how could the maps be so similar?"[5] The parties never agreed which Jewish settlements would be removed; Palestinians balked at Olmert's insistence on retaining Ariel, whose eastern border extends nearly halfway across the West Bank.

Still larger than these territorial discrepancies were ones concerning the division of Jerusalem, Palestinian refugees, and security arrangements. Olmert suggested that 5,000 refugees could return to Israel over five years while Abbas wanted 150,000 over ten years, with the possibility of renewal. Israel refused to acknowledge responsibility for the refugee problem, as Abbas insisted it do. Olmert's diplomatic adviser told Abrams that Israel demanded its armed forces remain in the future

Palestinian state, a condition Abbas rejected. As the lead Palestinian negotiator, Ahmed Qurei, told Abrams and other US officials, "Territory is the easiest issue."[6]

* * *

Abrams didn't think Abbas should take the deal. Olmert was mired in corruption scandals. He had been polling in the single digits for months and had promised to resign as soon as his party, Kadima, selected a successor. He presented his map the day before Livni was named as his replacement. Several days later, he formally resigned. "The weaker he became politically," Abrams writes, "the more Olmert seemed willing to risk."[7]

Abbas had good reason to be cautious. The legal standing of a peace treaty made with a lame-duck Israeli prime minister was less than clear. Abbas would be making painful concessions in a deal that could not be carried out until he somehow regained control of Gaza from Hamas. There seemed to be little prospect of Hamas accepting such an agreement. There were, Abrams writes, "too many lacunae in this deal." At a meeting with Bush in New York days after Olmert put forward his map, Abbas said that "many people in the Israeli government were encouraging him to break off with Olmert," an assertion later confirmed by Secretary of State Condoleezza Rice. Bush told Abbas that he "worried that any deal Olmert negotiated would be dead simply because he was its sponsor."[8]

Few of these details are known to Israeli voters, and even if better known would likely do little to alter the conclusion most of them have drawn: there is no Palestinian partner for peace. Ari Shavit, the author of *My Promised Land*, is a leading promoter of this view: "To this day Abbas has not responded positively to the offer of 100 percent made to him by . . . Olmert." In a column about the futility of further negotiations, Shavit wrote: "Shimon Peres, Ehud Barak, Ehud Olmert, and Tzipi Livni offered the whole world to the Palestinians, and the Palestinians were not satisfied."[9]

Whatever the public's misperceptions regarding Olmert's proposal and Abbas's calculations, they are right about three key points. First, over the past two decades, Palestinian positions have not changed significantly.

The PLO has remained fixed in its demand for territory equivalent to all of the West Bank and Gaza; in its view, it has already made major concessions by formally recognizing Israel, in 1993, and agreeing, in 1988, to a state on 22 percent of Mandatory Palestine.[10]

Second, Olmert offered far more land than any other Israeli leader, continuing a trend of increased territorial concessions in each successive round of official negotiations. In May 2000, Israel offered 66 percent of the West Bank, annexing 17 percent with another 17 percent not annexed but under its control and no swap of Israeli land; the numbers steadily rose until Olmert's proposal of 99.5 percent, including swaps. Third, Abbas did not accept the deal. As he has explained, "The gaps were wide."[11] In the years since, they have only widened.

* * *

In 2013, Israel's highest-rated television station, Channel 2, showed a news segment asking whether the possibility of a two-state solution to the conflict was not already dead. The answer, as presented in the anchor's concluding remarks and by most interviewees—left, right, religious, secular—was that two states had become unattainable.

Even as Secretary of State John Kerry expressed renewed American hope of resolving the conflict—within "a year and a half to two years or it's over," he said before launching talks in 2013—the Israeli public had never been more skeptical about the prospect of a negotiated settlement.[12] Some of this pessimism surely derived from familiar, frequently cited reasons: the failure of Palestinian leaders to accept what most Israelis view as generous offers; the suicide bombings during the Second Intifada; increased rocket fire from Gaza following Israel's withdrawal; Hamas's electoral victory.

But these causes cannot fully account for Israeli doubts. None of them explains how in March 2006—weeks after Palestinians nominated Hamas's Ismail Haniyeh as prime minister, and months after Israel's retreat from Gaza was met with continued projectile fire—Israelis gave an overwhelming plurality of their votes to the Kadima Party, which advocated further negotiations and a unilateral withdrawal from much of the West Bank if those talks were to fail. This election and the subsequent one, three years later, took place amid heightened tensions with

the Palestinians, yet parties proposing compromise and territorial withdrawal were embraced.

By June 2009, even Benjamin Netanyahu, leader of Likud, home to
many supporters of annexation, had declared conditional support for
two states. A founder of the settler movement called Netanyahu's declaration "a revolutionary ideological turn equivalent to the shattering
of the party's Ten Commandments." Others were and have remained
skeptical that Netanyahu meant it—not only his liberal critics but also
many of his allies. The Likud charter still maintained its rejection of a
Palestinian state. Yet Netanyahu's declared support for Palestinian
statehood grew only firmer. In May 2013—when the share of Jews had
already shrunk to less than half the population of Israel, the West
Bank, and Gaza—for the first time he used a demographic argument:
the purpose of an agreement was to prevent the eventuality of a binational state.[13]

* * *

By 2013, Israel's government represented a significant rightward shift in
mainstream Israeli thought. More than one in six of the coalition's
members resided beyond the pre-1967 lines. Roughly one-third of Knesset members were religious, a record. Another overlapping third were
members of the Land of Israel caucus, dedicated to strengthening the
settlements. And many government ministers advocated some form of
annexation of the West Bank. Like Netanyahu, however, most Israeli
Jews said they would accept a two-state solution (even though they also
believed it unlikely to materialize), but the terms on which they were
willing to do so were hardly realistic. As the leader of the pro-annexation
Jewish Home Party, Naftali Bennett, pointed out, "Some say they are
against the division of Jerusalem but they are in favor of a Palestinian
state. And I ask, where exactly would the Palestinian capital be? In
Jericho? In Bethlehem? In Berlin?"[14]

The right grew stronger as the arguments of the left and center were
discredited. Promoters of negotiations failed to convey how high a price
a peace agreement would exact. They told themselves and the public that
the outlines of a deal were well known and asserted that agreement
existed where it did not. Ambassador Stuart E. Eizenstat, a veteran of the

Carter and Clinton administrations, writes in *The Future of the Jews* that it is "commonly understood that the largest settlement blocks would remain under Israeli control in any final peace agreement." Israelis, likewise, speak of "consensus" settlements. But the common understanding of which Eizenstat writes was shared only by Israelis and their supporters. Leaked Palestinian transcripts from the Annapolis talks of 2007–2008 record the two sides fighting fiercely over the future status of what Israelis consider one of the most "consensus" settlements of all, Ma'ale Adumim, east of Jerusalem, with some forty thousand residents.[15]

Claims that peace is within grasp have been as overstated as warnings that the perpetually closing window for a two-state solution has nearly shut or that the occupation of the West Bank will make Israel an international pariah. In the countries in which the movement to boycott, divest from, and sanction Israel have made the largest gains— South Africa and the United Kingdom—Israeli exports have in fact sharply risen. Israelis are not overly worried that the EU will go significantly beyond wringing its hands over the way its financial support of the PA effectively underwrites Israel's occupation.[16]

Even if boycotts of Israeli companies headquartered in the West Bank gained steam, they would not stop the country's banks, cable television companies, or supermarkets from operating beyond the 1967 lines; nor would they significantly reduce the number of settlers, most of whom work not at factories adjacent to Ariel but in government jobs in settlements and in the private sector in Israel proper—at places like Intel, Bank Leumi, and Teva Pharmaceutical Industries.[17] And while elite attitudes toward Israel in the United States are changing, the share of Americans who support Israel over the Palestinians is as large a majority today as it was a decade ago.[18]

Years of relative quiet in the West Bank following the Second Intifada undermined the charge that the half-decade-old military occupation was unsustainable. Secretary Kerry warned that Israel would "be left to choose between being a Jewish state or a democratic state."[19] But limited Palestinian self-governance, including close security cooperation with Israel, has protected the country from having to make any such choice.

Thanks in part to a well-financed international support system for the occupation, Israelis could afford to be supportive of a two-state solution on unrealistic terms, justifiably skeptical that such a deal would be made, and apathetic about the consequences of not reaching one. And since partial territorial withdrawals had not put an end to Palestinian violence, the right was able to advance its argument that the conflict is neither primarily territorial nor based on grievances stemming from Israel's 1967 conquest. In this view, the century-long struggle is insoluble, because for Palestinians the core of it is not occupation but their displacement due to Zionist settlement.

Among intellectuals, too, there was growing skepticism that the old model of land for peace could work in Israel-Palestine. The assumption of American and Israeli negotiators that solving the problems of 1967 would close the door on those of 1948 came under powerful rebuke in two original books, published in 2011 and 2012, from distant points on the Israeli political spectrum: the historian Asher Susser's *Israel, Jordan, and Palestine: The Two-State Imperative* and the sociologist Yehouda Shenhav's *Beyond the Two-State Solution*. Susser documents how the gaps between the two sides, or at least some leading spokesmen from the two sides, have narrowed on issues deriving from the 1967 war—borders, settlements, and security arrangements—while "little if any real progress was made in resolving the 1948 question of refugee return."[21]

The right's case was further bolstered as strife expanded on each side of the Green Line. The border between Israel and Palestine seemed to fade: it was systematically buried under Israeli settlement housing and infrastructure, and its prominence further eroded as Jewish nationalist attacks spread from the Occupied Territories to Israel, taking the form of arson, vandalism, and violence against Palestinian citizens of the state. Jewish activists extended their demographic battle to cities in Israel proper, buying homes in Palestinian neighborhoods in Ramla, Akko, and Lod. Dozens of Israel's municipal chief rabbis signed a ruling forbidding the rental of homes to non-Jews.[20] Palestinian citizens of Israel forged closer ties with communities in the West Bank, and, in the Palestinian diaspora, the BDS movement grew.

But these trends, which to many seemed to signal the hopelessness of territorial division, could also be seen as a backlash against the more powerful forces of partition. Rather than ruin the chance of separation, the Second Intifada had accelerated it, culminating in the evacuation of all settlers from Gaza. After the Gaza withdrawal, right-wing and national religious Jews strove to reverse the division of Mandatory Palestine, their efforts reflecting the desperation of those who identified a seemingly inevitable partition that they had little ability to stop.

* * *

Alongside Israel's diminishing faith in a territorial resolution came an overdue shift in focus from the borders of the state to what lies within them. Among the country's citizens, Jews but not Palestinians have collective rights to land, immigration, symbols such as their own flag, and commemorations. Jews may not legally marry non-Jews in Israel. Current residents of Jerusalem homes that were abandoned during the 1948 war have been evicted to make room for former owners and their descendants—but only when the deed holders are Jews.[22]

The inequality of Jews and non-Jews within Israel's pre-1967 lines prepared the ground for still more unequal arrangements in the West Bank after 1967. Both were created by the Ashkenazi Labor Zionist elite that later criticized the settlers for dynamics it set in place. On what grounds, Shenhav asks, is the idea of Jewish settlement in ruined Palestinian villages within the pre-1967 boundaries—some of them formerly inhabited by Palestinians who were internally displaced by war—considered more moral than Jewish settlement on Palestinian agricultural lands of the West Bank? The former, he argues, involved far more human suffering. Susser, indeed any Zionist, would surely object to comparisons that would cast doubt on Israeli claims to its pre-1967 territory. But he offers strong support for the underlying premise that the root of the conflict lies in the more than century-old project of Zionist settlement itself.[23]

The growing awareness of these deeper, pre-1967 disputes initiated a gradual breaking with illusions and a return to the true nature of the conflict: a struggle between two ethnic groups between the Jordan River and the Mediterranean Sea. The peaceful arrangements they had so far discussed had all fallen short of both the full sovereignty Palestinians desired and the hard ethnic separation the Israeli mainstream sought. As Susser writes: "The Palestinian state that the Israelis were willing to endorse was never a fully sovereign and independent member of the family of nations, but an emasculated, demilitarized, and supervised entity, with Israeli control of its airspace and possibly of its borders too, and some element of Israeli and/or foreign military presence."[24] This was as true for Netanyahu as for Olmert, Barak, Peres, and Yitzhak Rabin, who a month before his assassination told the Knesset that the Palestinians would have "less than a state."[25]

In addition, Susser argues, Israel almost certainly will not achieve an end of conflict, much less recognition of a Jewish state, unless it meets Palestinian demands to admit responsibility for the flight and expulsion of refugees of the 1948 war.[26] Israeli leaders have been unwilling to answer these calls, fearing that any such acknowledgment or acceptance of claims to return would shake the foundations of the state, undermine its international legitimacy, and upend decades of Zionist teaching by conceding that at its birth Israel was responsible for forcibly dispossessing large numbers of Palestinian civilians from their homes.

Kerry's talks, like those between Olmert and Abbas, did not come close to resolving the 1967 issues, much less the 1948 ones. As the list of failed negotiations grows, Israelis will be more prone to ask themselves whether the time has come to postpone hopes of a full peace in order to achieve—perhaps through cease-fires or additional withdrawals—a further separation. They would thereby fortify an arrangement that is more than one state but less than two, which is, in fact, all that was ever on offer.

—July 2013

12.

Faith-Based Diplomacy

Even by the standard of his recent predecessors, John Kerry, who became secretary of state in February 2013, took on the Israeli-Palestinian conflict with extraordinary intensity. It was not an obvious choice, given the record of past diplomatic efforts, the bitter experience of President Barack Obama's first term, the many factors that had made the conflict only more difficult to resolve, and the far larger scale and importance of other challenges facing the United States: the slaughter in Syria, where the number of dead was approaching one hundred thousand and steadily rising; sectarian violence and anti-American militancy spreading throughout the Middle East; and an effort to shift US priorities to counter the growing power of China.

Despite all of these, America's ambitious new secretary found it particularly urgent to resolve the more than century-old conflict between Jews and Arabs in a territory smaller than his home state of Massachusetts. Between Kerry's swearing-in and the launch of talks half a year later, Israeli-Palestinian violence claimed fewer than ten lives.

The attention Kerry paid to the issue was matched by the resources the United States provides to Israel, which receives more American military aid than the rest of the world combined—about $3.5 billion annually and set to increase to $3.8 billion in 2019, making up over one fifth of the Israeli defense budget. As for the Palestinian government, it too secures close to half a billion per year and is among the largest per capita recipients of US aid.[1] Over these two small and highly dependent clients, the United States might be expected to possess considerable leverage. Yet its efforts to broker a peace agreement between them have been repeatedly frustrated, suggesting not just mismanagement of American taxpayer dollars but also the apparent impotence of the world's most powerful nation.

Still, Kerry's temptation to enter the morass was not difficult to understand. Most US officials believe without question that the foreclosure of a possibility of a two-state solution, whatever that might mean, would significantly harm American (as opposed to Israeli) interests. To many outsiders, the conflict seems to have a simple resolution—an ethnic partition of the territory into two nation-states separated by the pre-1967 lines—and the United States seems well placed to settle it. Confronted with accusations of US retreat from the Middle East and the seeming insolubility of problems elsewhere in the world, Kerry focused on what looked achievable.

He appeared, moreover, to think that securing an agreement was of great importance. The demography of Gaza, the West Bank, and Israel—where, collectively, the number of gentiles recently surpassed the number of Jews—led Kerry to assert that soon Israel would face the choice between "either being an apartheid state with second-class citizens—or it ends up being a state that destroys the capacity of Israel to be a Jewish state." Not for the first time and not for the last, he declared that "the window for a two-state solution is shutting."[2]

So Kerry pressed on, winning accolades not for any new strategy or tactic but rather for the sincerity of his faith in the possibility of brokering a deal. He was convinced an agreement could be reached if only he could drag the parties to the negotiating table and mediate it. He operated under the misapprehension that after decades of failed efforts, peace had remained elusive not because Israel and Palestine held irreconcilable positions but primarily because they did not trust each other.

Normally, the two parties, whatever their doubts, are willing to appease a determined, legacy-seeking American secretary of state. But Kerry found that months of shuttle diplomacy and earnest cajoling were

not enough to surmount the obstacles that had prevented direct negotiations for years.

* * *

Since the beginning of Obama's first term, there had been only three
meetings between Mahmoud Abbas and Benjamin Netanyahu, all of
them in September 2010. There had also been secret talks and, in
January 2012, unproductive "exploratory" meetings between lower-
level officials, held in Amman. The Palestinians concluded that Netanyahu was not serious about a two-state settlement and so they had
refused to enter official, publicly acknowledged talks unless Israel met
two conditions: first, agreement to a freeze in settlement activity; second, an understanding that the final borders of the two states would be
based on the pre-1967 lines, stipulations all Israeli prime ministers before
Netanyahu had rejected.[3] In the end, as American, Israeli, and Palestinian officials with direct knowledge of the talks have told me, Kerry
arrived at a formula to launch new negotiations: he made inconsistent
promises to each side.

To the Israelis, Kerry said he had gotten the Palestinians to acqui-
esce to hold talks in exchange for the release of prisoners, without the
demands for a settlement freeze or acceptance of the pre-1967 lines. To
the Palestinians, he suggested that he had nearly obtained agreement
to both: First, he told them, Israel would commit during the talks to
exhibit restraint within the settlement blocs and, according to several
Abbas confidants, to stop issuing new tenders for construction outside
them.[4] Second, Kerry gave a letter to the Palestinians affirming that the
goal of the United States was to create a Palestinian state with borders
based on the pre-1967 lines and mutually agreed swaps. The implication
was that the United States had secured private assurances from Netanyahu that he would meet or come close to meeting both conditions, but
that this could not be acknowledged, since it would likely be rejected by
the Israeli government or lead to its dissolution, and that the United States
would work to ensure that both pledges were respected.

Palestinian negotiators say Kerry gave them three other important
assurances. First, he understood that, if he were to succeed, the Israeli
government coalition would have to change at some point during the

negotiations. Second, the talks would begin with a focus on borders and security before turning to other issues. And third, the United States would be present for the discussions, a commitment Palestinians wanted because they see such mediation, even by Israel's closest ally, as preferable to negotiating with their occupier alone. As an added inducement, Kerry announced an ambitious plan to invest $4 billion in the West Bank.

None of these commitments was kept. Far from being restrained, new building in the settlement blocs surged. There was no halt in construction tenders issued outside the blocs, no initial focus on borders, no assurance that the discussions would be based on the pre-1967 lines, no $4 billion investment. At Israel's insistence and over Palestinian objections, there was almost no US presence in the room during the first several months of negotiations. And there was no choice forced on Netanyahu between accepting US guidelines for continued negotiations or breaking up his government. Quite the opposite: for all but the final, desperate weeks of the talks, US positions were formulated specifically to avoid posing problems for Israel's coalition government, many of whose members opposed the establishment of a Palestinian state.

Kerry made one more empty promise and it proved fatal. In exchange for Israel's agreement to release all 104 Palestinian prisoners who had been in jail since before Oslo, in 1993, Kerry secured a Palestinian commitment to halt any steps toward joining international conventions, treaty bodies, and organizations. For Israel, this promise had been a primary inducement to enter the talks.

Netanyahu insisted that the prisoners be released in four groups, spaced roughly two months apart. The Palestinians provided Kerry with a list that included fourteen Palestinian citizens of Israel, and Kerry assured them that Israel had accepted. Israel had not. Netanyahu never agreed to release these fourteen prisoners, which the Israeli cabinet decided would require a separate vote. But the Palestinian negotiators say they were led to believe the opposite.

Wishful thinking appeared to underlie the decision to mislead the parties. Had Kerry been on the brink of an agreement at the time of the planned fourth prisoner release, as he expected to be, he could reasonably have expected the pardons to be approved, and he said the United

States would compensate Israel by freeing Jonathan Pollard, the American intelligence analyst convicted of spying for Israel. But Kerry's plans didn't come to be. After the deadline for the fourth group had passed and it became clear that the fourteen prisoners would not be released to their homes, despite several days during which the United States made repeated assurances to the contrary, Palestinians felt they were no longer under obligation to refrain from signing international agreements.[5] They gave the United States several warnings of their intentions— enough time for the Israeli government to change its mind—and then joined fifteen conventions and treaty bodies as the State of Palestine. The talks collapsed.

* * *

At the start of the negotiations, Kerry's stated objective was a comprehensive peace treaty within nine months, and he maintained this goal in the face of widespread skepticism. Yet his critics failed to understand that there was little penalty for wrongly forecasting success when the world had grown so accustomed to failure. Ahead of the Camp David summit in 2000, Bill Clinton said a peace agreement could be achieved in several days. At the outset of the 2007–2008 Annapolis talks, Bush and Condoleezza Rice expressed confidence that talks could be concluded within one year. Three years later, in 2010, Obama and Secretary of State Hillary Clinton renewed Bush's one-year vow as they launched meetings that lasted all of three weeks.[6]

In each case, reaching an agreement was not the only reason for the two sides to engage in talks. Palestinian leaders have understood that their livelihoods and the foreign aid on which their government depends would be jeopardized if the peace process were somehow to come to a definitive end. Even ebbs in the process have financial consequences for Palestinians, who suffered a large dip in Western funding when negotiations were all but nonexistent for most of 2012. Each year they must show Western donors their "performance" in making progress toward statehood, despite the fact that more than seventeen years have passed since the date at which, according to the time-limited Oslo Accords, five years of interim governance by the PA were to end. Without the fiction of movement in peace talks, it becomes uncomfortably obvious to donors to the PA that the "state-building project" they are financing is not part of a "roadmap" or a pathway to independence but a treadmill.

For Israel, the process is no less instrumental. It has brought increased military aid; US vetoes of UN resolutions that Israel sees as unfavorable; and heightened stature on the global stage. Talks have won the appeasement of nagging leftists, human rights activists, and European officials; decreased support for boycotts and sanctions of Israel and settlement products; and a halt in steps toward international recognition of Palestinian statehood. Negotiations are thought—often wrongly—to have helped lessen Palestinian agitation against occupation by modestly reigniting hopes of achieving independence and thereby bolstering the PA's claim to its people that it is less a cover for occupation than a tool for ending it. In shoring up international support for Israel, talks can serve as a bulwark against criticism of military operations in Gaza and elsewhere. At times negotiations have enabled Israel to construct settlements with impunity, in violation of international law. This was seen in the Kerry talks, during which settlement activity—justified as necessary to keep the Israeli governing coalition intact while the prime minister prepared to make a far-reaching offer of peace—rose to levels far higher than in the months before or after. Finally, negotiations reduce the pressure to roll back military occupation, since, it is argued, they will shortly end it in any event.

These, however, are not among the primary reasons the United States engages in the peace process. In contrast to cynics like Israel's defense minister and former foreign minister, Avigdor Lieberman, who says he does not believe negotiations will succeed but supports them as a form of conflict management, the motives of American officials are at once more earnest and more dispiriting.[7]

Though there are important divisions among US policy makers, including a few who want the country to disinvest from peacemaking and a group of neoconservatives who oppose US-brokered talks because they believe Arabs will never agree to recognize Israel, the majority of senior officials who have worked on the conflict—including, and especially, presidents and secretaries of state—have believed with each new round that they had a good chance of reaching a comprehensive agreement.

Lack of experience is not at fault, for many of the advisers involved have played key roles in multiple administrations. Their views are echoed in the halls of Washington think tanks whose experts have encouraged each new miscarriage. In a 2009 memoir, Martin Indyk, who was ambassador to Israel during the Camp David summit and later Kerry's special envoy to the Middle East peace process, sought to diagnose the disease:

> Hope and optimism are critical components of the innocence that is the hallmark of America's engagement with the Middle East. Why would we bother to try to transform such a troubled region unless we somehow believed we could, and should? But the dark side of that innocence is a naiveté bred of ignorance and arrogance that generate a chronic inability to comprehend.[8]

II.

American officials involved in the peace process—as well as the think tanks, NGOs, advocates, journalists, and analysts who seek to influence them—can be divided into three groups. Their differing approaches to policy have dominated Middle East decision-making for over two decades and contributed to the failures of each administration.[9]

The first and smallest of these groups, which I shall call Skeptics, comprises conservatives and neoconservatives who believe that Arabs will not make peace with Israel, or, in the more nuanced version, that they will not agree to peace on terms acceptable to Israel's center-right majority. Much of their suspicion derives from their assessment that past Israeli offers have fallen far short of Palestinian demands. On the latter point, they are surely correct.

Prominent people and institutions associated with the Skeptic camp include senior officials of the George W. Bush administration, such as Elliott Abrams, John Bolton, and Douglas Feith; the more hawkish parts of AIPAC; the American Enterprise Institute; and *The Weekly Standard*, *Commentary*, and the editorial board of *The Wall Street Journal*.

Because many Skeptics oppose the peace process, they have had less influence on US-brokered negotiations. A few Skeptics still oppose the establishment of a Palestinian state, even after the George W. Bush administration officially endorsed the goal of creating one, but their voices have been largely muted.

Skeptics tend to consider negotiations not simply a waste of time but dangerous; they cite as evidence the Second Intifada, which followed the failure of the 2000 Camp David summit. They believe that every significant agreement signed between Israel and its Arab neighbors—from the Oslo Accords with the PLO to the peace treaties with Egypt and Jordan—was initiated without the United States. (Skeptics tend to downplay the importance of US efforts to encourage, finalize, or support these agreements.) Because of their antipathy to top-down negotiations, they have focused instead on bottom-up changes, most notably Salam Fayyad's project of institution building. That program remains, according to nearly all Washington officials, one of the few policy successes concerning the conflict in recent years.[10]

The record shows that, in the years since Oslo, the Skeptics who held positions of influence during the George W. Bush administration were responsible for changes that most Washington policymakers consider to be more positive and consequential than those of their predecessors and successors in the Clinton and Obama administrations. Skeptics helped bring about the first official approval, both from an Israeli prime minister, Ariel Sharon, and a US president, Bush, not of Palestinian autonomy but of statehood. They pushed in 2003 for the Palestinian Authority to create the post of prime minister, in which they helped install a US favorite, Mahmoud Abbas, the most moderate leader in Palestinian history.

After the end of the Second Intifada, in early 2005, Skeptics created a program that used US advisers to transition the Palestinian security forces under Abbas's command from sometimes fighting Israel to cooperating closely with it, a goal shared by all American officials. Skeptics worked to reduce the number of checkpoints in the West Bank. They encouraged the popular though not altogether effective attempts by Fayyad to lessen corruption and reform Palestinian institutions. And Skeptics supported the Israeli withdrawal from Gaza, perhaps the most significant change in the conflict since 1967. Skeptics of the Bush administration argue that their successes came precisely because they opposed fruitless peace talks—at least, until they were outmaneuvered by Condoleezza Rice, who made such talks a priority near the end of her tenure—and focused instead on smaller, incremental goals.

The Bush Skeptics also presided over no small number of failures. Grossly underestimating the strength of Hamas, they pushed for Palestinian legislative elections in 2006, convinced that Hamas—which had boycotted all previous national elections—would be discredited and defeated. The Skeptics then orchestrated a US-led policy to isolate the Islamist party and deprive it of its democratically elected power. In the view of Skeptics, the results of this isolation were mixed. On one hand, their policy succeeded: it prevented Hamas rule in the West Bank; demonstrated to Palestinians that the election of Islamists would exact a heavy collective price; and undermined the chance of a unified Palestinian government. On the other, the same policy also failed to achieve their aim of bringing down Hamas. Instead, it became stronger politically and militarily, while US collusion in thwarting Hamas's victory undermined the legitimacy of the unelected Palestinian government that the Skeptics had sought to support.

* * *

The proponents of a second, more activist approach toward negotiations—I'll call them Reproachers—reject the limited goals of the Skeptics, dismissing their doubts and believing that the conflict could be resolved if the United States were to put sufficient pressure on Israel (within the bounds of what they think American domestic politics can permit—which is to say, sufficient *verbal* pressure). Reproachers seek to be more balanced mediators, to forcefully criticize the expansion of Israeli settlements, and to dedicate greater effort toward conducting final-status talks.

A number of influential Reproachers are self-described realists and veterans of the peace process who are critical of themselves and other American officials for having acted, in the words of the former State Department official Aaron David Miller, as "Israel's lawyer." Prominent people and institutions associated with the Reproacher school include Obama during his first term, former Middle East envoy George Mitchell, Foreign Service officers at the US consulate in Jerusalem, Americans for Peace Now, J Street, and the editorial board of *The New York Times*.

Reproachers hold that most Israelis see little short-term incentive to change a status quo consisting of prolonged military occupation and increasing settlement activity in the West Bank. Large Israeli protests during recent years have been against the high cost of living and the military draft of ultra-Orthodox Jews, not against the occupation, which has become a normal, accepted, and easily ignored part of life for most people. In the absence of pressure, Reproachers argue, Israelis will continue to prefer this status quo to the principal alternatives. Few Israelis want to withdraw unilaterally, even from territory well short of what Palestinians demand, especially because doing so would not put an end to the conflict or to agitation against what remains of the occupation. Fewer still want to grant citizenship to all Palestinians living under their control, although that path is advocated by growing numbers on the Israeli right. And almost none seek an agreement on terms Palestinians say they can accept, fearing the possibility of granting sovereignty to a nation that may one day reelect Hamas.

Reproachers differ from other groups mainly in their sense of urgency about Israel's need to reach an agreement and in how willing they are to scold their ally publicly. Concerned that the country's more radical elements will drive it to ruin, Reproachers aim to act with "tough love" to help Israel achieve what they believe is in its own interest.

Reproachers such as Obama often claim that the half-century-old occupation is "unsustainable," that time is running out, that Israel faces demographic annihilation, and that the current circumstances present the last chance for peace—claims repeated so frequently as to be largely ignored by Palestinians and Israelis alike.[11] Seeing active US mediation as a necessary condition for peace, Reproachers reject the notion of Skeptics that, as with past treaties, an agreement will have to await the initiative of the parties themselves. Some Reproachers doubt the chance of peace under Netanyahu or other right-wing Israeli leaders (indeed, after the Kerry talks broke down, Obama administration Reproachers behaved more like Skeptics, calling for a "pause" in negotiations in the hope that the parties would eventually beg the United

States to reengage) but this does not translate into skepticism about the peace process in general.

Reproachers argue that the conflict has remained unresolved not because the maximum Israelis will concede is less than the minimum Palestinians will accept, as Skeptics claim. Rather, they say, it is because the United States has not been bold enough in seeking to bridge the differences. Reproachers tend to focus more on settlements and territory than on the thornier issues of sovereignty over Jerusalem's Noble Sanctuary/Temple Mount and the Palestinian refugee problem. They often state that the outlines of a final peace treaty are well known, and they tend to dismiss the possibility that failure thus far can be explained by the inadequacy of the arrangements they have suggested and seen rejected.

Nothing has done more to discredit Reproachers than holding power. No US administration had been more stacked with Reproachers than Barack Obama's, and no American president had been more sympathetic to Palestinians. But during their eight years in power, Obama and his advisers achieved much less for them than did George W. Bush.

This is partly the result of circumstance. Both the Bush Skeptics and the Obama Reproachers began their first terms at roughly the same time as a newly elected Likud prime minister who had still not accepted the idea of Palestinian statehood. Ariel Sharon in 2001 and Benjamin Netanyahu in 2009 entered office just months after the collapse of what in each case had been the most far-reaching Israeli-Palestinian negotiations to date. Both prime ministers refused to continue talks where their predecessors—first Ehud Barak and then Ehud Olmert—had left off, despite Palestinian pleas for them to do so.

Barak and Olmert had made offers that were unsatisfactory to Palestinians yet far ahead of mainstream Israeli public opinion. Each prime minister had made his proposal at a time when he was losing power and a historic agreement offered his only chance at keeping his job. The two US administrations were sure that the new Likud prime minister could not match, much less surpass, the offers of several months earlier. But whereas the Bush Skeptics concluded that renewed negotiations were pointless, the Obama Reproachers believed that talks could succeed if they employed the right mix of seduction and pressure, and so sought to start negotiations between the Palestinians and Netanyahu. They did so despite a deafening chorus of analysts and former officials stating that Netanyahu could not be brought to make even the concessions of his predecessor, which Palestinians had so recently found insufficient.

So in the early days of Obama's presidency, the Reproachers, led by White House Chief of Staff Rahm Emanuel, pushed for a settlement freeze, believing, incorrectly, that this would win respect, and subsequent steps toward normalization, from Arab states. But the Arab states offered Obama little more than indifference. After more than ten months of painful failure at appreciable domestic cost, the Reproachers succeeded in obtaining from Israel—in exchange for Abbas's politically damaging commitment to postpone a vote at the United Nation endorsing the Goldstone Report on the 2008–2009 war in Gaza—not a freeze but a so-called moratorium on settlements that was filled with loopholes. These included a large number of exemptions: for construction begun just beforehand; for educational, religious, cultural, and sport facilities; for planning and public infrastructure; and for building in East Jerusalem, where settlement is most consequential. The 2010 moratorium—which Obama asked to extend for ninety days in exchange for twenty F-35 stealth fighter aircraft worth $3 billion and a US pledge to veto moves toward Palestinian statehood at the UN—was immediately preceded and succeeded by so much construction as to render it meaningless. In West Bank settlements, the number of construction starts dropped less than 7 percent from the previous year, while in East Jerusalem, the number of tenders issued for new housing nearly quadrupled.[12]

Bush, by contrast, was offered a full freeze in settlement construction during Sharon's first months in office in 2001, as Indyk, who was then ambassador to Israel, writes in his memoir.[13] The principal difference was that Sharon offered it in exchange for a halt in the Palestinian violence then raging, whereas when Obama entered office, the Second Intifada had long since ended.

US pressure on Israel during Obama's first year consisted mostly of reprimands, which were more costly to his domestic political agenda than to Netanyahu. Though Reproachers were willing to take a different tone with Israel—and this received much attention in the often melodramatic coverage of US-Israel relations in the press—substantively it was clear that there was little appetite for more than rhetorical and symbolic confrontation. Frustrated with the failures of the Reproachers, Obama was reported by *The Washington Post* to have eventually asked them, "I see you want the moratorium [on settlements], but how does it get us where we want to be? Tell me the relationship between what we are doing and our objective."[14] It wasn't long before he brought in a senior figure from a rival ideological camp, whose members I'll call Embracers.

* * *

Embracers, the third and most influential group, combine the Skeptics' unconditional backing of Israel with the Reproachers' unwavering faith in the peace process. Prominent institutions associated with the Embracer school include the Anti-Defamation League, the more moderate parts of AIPAC, the US embassy in Tel Aviv, and the editorial board of *The Washington Post*. Like Skeptics, Embracers think a US focus on settlements is mistaken. Like Reproachers, they firmly believe that US involvement is necessary to achieving an agreement. Yet they argue that peace can be brokered only by embracing Israel tightly, reassuring it, and alleviating its fears. Israel, the Embracers reason, is the stronger party, with both more to give and more to lose; for Israel to have the confidence necessary to take generous steps, it needs unwavering American support.[15]

The most prominent Embracer is Dennis Ross, a George H. W. Bush and Clinton administration veteran who was asked to lead Obama's Middle East policy when the Reproacher strategy hit a wall. Ross and other Embracers opposed the push for a settlement freeze and leaned on Obama to avoid calling for a Palestinian capital in Jerusalem in an important policy speech.[16]

Embracers are popular with US presidents because they tell them precisely what they want to hear: that you can achieve your goals by remaining closely allied with Israel; that Palestinians will ultimately be happy because your cradling of Israel will lead to the peace they desire; and that along the way you'll win plaudits from Israel's supporters in the United States, thus paying no domestic political price.

So far this dream has not come true, but the words have been too sweet to resist.

Obama, who fell under the Embracers' spell quite early in his first term, adopted an approach toward the peace process not unlike that of Goldilocks. He entered office thinking the Bush Skeptics were too warm toward Israel, telling a group of Jewish leaders in 2009 that the Bush administration's intimacy with Israel had not produced results. But he soon concluded that his Reproachers were too cold. So he handed responsibility to the Embracers, who he believed would be just right.

Kerry's appointment as secretary of state heralded a reemphasis on the Embracers' strategy. When Israel put forward plans for extensive settlement expansion with each new prisoner release, Kerry did little more than call the announcements "illegitimate" and "unhelpful," while angering Palestinians by describing the sharp rise as "expected" and urging them not to abandon the talks.[17] He made it a priority to try to find a way to meet Netanyahu's demands for an Israeli security presence in the West Bank's Jordan Valley and for Palestinian recognition of Israel as a Jewish state, a position the United States had already failed to get even the Middle East Quartet to endorse. And he sought to avoid presenting Israel with any choice that might break up Netanyahu's coalition. On difficult issues such as the division of sovereignty in Jerusalem, he used evasive rhetoric—referring, for example, to Palestinian "aspirations" for a capital there—to imply to Palestinians that they would enjoy sovereignty in the city while suggesting to the Israeli right that no division would take place.

Following repeated disappointments, the Palestinians came to believe that the negotiations presented a greater risk than they had anticipated. As the 2013–2014 talks foundered and the United States' objective was steadily downgraded—from a comprehensive peace treaty, to a framework agreement between the parties, to an American framework proposal from which the parties could distance themselves, to a mere extension of talks without a framework—they feared that Kerry would put forward his vision of the outlines of an agreement, a vision that looked increasingly as if it would represent several steps backward from what they perceived as commitments already secured.

Palestinians recalled that in 2003, Bush's Roadmap to Middle East

204 THE ONLY LANGUAGE THEY UNDERSTAND

Peace, which was endorsed by the Quartet and the UN Security Council, promised that all settlement activity would be frozen and that settler outposts would be immediately dismantled. The Roadmap also stated that a final resolution to the conflict would be based on (though not identical to) the Arab Peace Initiative of 2002. This proposed a Palestinian capital in East Jerusalem; a just solution of the Palestinian refugee problem in accordance with the relevant 1948 UN General Assembly resolution (which the United States voted for); and a full withdrawal to Israel's pre-1967 boundaries, with no mention of accommodation for settlement blocs or land swaps.[18]

Palestinian representatives do not insist that a comprehensive agreement entail no modifications of the Arab Peace Initiative or other possible bases for future talks. But unless their hand is forced by binding parameters enshrined in international law, they have little incentive to accept negotiations predicated on less favorable terms than had been offered in the past.[19]

* * *

Kerry was surprised at his inability to obtain Palestinian acceptance of parameters that fell short of previous US proposals.[20] This despite the fact that there was no precedent for a Palestinian leader to make hugely controversial concessions in exchange for the mere opportunity to hold or extend talks, much less talks with an Israeli government whose intentions Palestinians had strong reasons to doubt. To concede, in the absence of a comprehensive peace treaty or even the reasonable probability of achieving one, that almost no refugees would have the choice of returning to Israel would be an act of political hara-kiri that any Palestinian leader would naturally avoid. Yet the United States asked Abbas to do just that, and expressed great disappointment when he refused to take the sword.

Reproachers repeatedly call on the United States to issue its vision of a final peace deal. They think that parameters for a comprehensive agreement, once proposed, would either serve as the basis for renewed negotiations or force the Israeli coalition to break apart (and be replaced, they hope, with a more amenable one). But there is little reason to believe the parties would accept such nonbinding guidelines in the absence of heavy pressure—the sort of pressure that no stream of American policymakers has been willing to apply. No one has yet drafted a set of substantive parameters on all final-status issues that, in the absence of significant coercion, including codification in a legally binding UN Security Council Resolution, could be publicly defended by both Abbas and the Israeli left, to say nothing of the country's right and center. (A Palestinian capital in historic Jerusalem, for example, is a sine qua non of any agreement that a Palestinian leader could sign, yet even the head of the Israeli Labor Party has publicly supported Likud's insistence on a "united" Jerusalem.)[21] And unless Abbas were to accept US parameters unequivocally, without issuing a set of nullifying reservations, the Israeli government would be under no pressure to do so.

At a White House meeting in March 2014, the Obama administration read Abbas a draft framework for continued negotiations, telling him that he could add reservations to it, as could the Israelis. But the proposal had not been seen or accepted by Israel. In fact, the Israelis had held extensive negotiations with the United States over a separate document, less favorable to Palestinians than the one shown to Abbas. The Palestinians complained about this: as with previous Palestinian acceptance of land swaps, the United States and Israel could take Abbas's concessions as a starting point to be further eroded in future talks. American officials were suspicious of this resistance, accusing the Palestinians of wanting to have it both ways: when an offer had not been approved by Israel, the Palestinians said it was "not serious"; when it had been approved, they called it "pre-cooked." At the same time, some conceded that Abbas had every reason to doubt that the United States would have forced Israel to accept the framework, rather than returning to him for further compromises.[22]

Reportedly the draft was more favorable to the Palestinians than the December 2000 proposal presented by President Clinton on one issue, territory. Whereas Clinton stated that Israel could annex up to 6 percent of the West Bank and give the Palestinians as little as 1 percent in compensation, Obama indicated that territorial swaps should be equivalent. But those with first-hand knowledge of the paper say the rest of the terms were less favorable or in some cases more vague, a disadvantage for the weaker negotiating party. They provided no end date for the withdrawal of Israeli security forces from Palestinian territory. There was no mention of even the symbolic formulations on refugees that Clinton had proposed: "the right of Palestinian refugees to return to historic Palestine" or "to their homeland." The plan did suggest a capital in Jerusalem, but it did not state that Palestinians would be sovereign over specific areas that Clinton had named, including the Muslim Quarter of the Old City and the al-Aqsa Mosque.[23]

The Obama administration expressed great frustration at Abbas's refusal to accept the framework. Obama said that Abbas was "too weak" to make peace, a seemingly defensible yet incomplete assessment of what went wrong with the Kerry talks. Obama failed to mention that Abbas's inability to accept the framework was exacerbated by the fact that Abbas does not represent huge parts of Palestinian society, including the many supporters of Hamas. American officials privately lament the lack of vision or courage among Palestinian leaders. But instead of seeking to help establish a leadership with bolstered legitimacy, the United States prioritizes the exclusion from Palestinian decision-making of all but the most dovish voices surrounding Abbas. Not just Islamists are shut out but other large, neglected constituencies, including refugees and the diaspora. This makes it more likely that the doves will be too weak to gather consensus around possible compromises, too afraid in the absence of such consensus to sign a deal, and too isolated to sell one successfully. It should not have been surprising, then, that given the choice between making politically explosive concessions and rejecting the US framework, the PLO moved in April 2014 to end the talks, join international conventions and treaties as the State of Palestine, and sign an agreement with Hamas to form a new government of technocrats acceptable to the PLO.[24]

III.

Despite the tactical differences among Skeptics, Reproachers, and Embracers, there is more uniting the three approaches than distinguishing them. If they were to draw up the outlines of a peace treaty, they might fight over the size of land swaps, the number of settlers Israel would evacuate, the location of the border dividing Jerusalem, how long Israeli security forces would remain in a Palestinian state, and the language used to rule out the return of nearly all Palestinian refugees. But to a nonexpert observer it would be difficult to discern the importance of such distinctions.

On questions of broader significance, their opinions largely overlap. Members of all three groups consider themselves pro-Israel and are concerned with preserving Israel as a Jewish state. All favor a two-state solution, the annexation by Israel of large settlement blocs in the West Bank, and a Palestinian capital in some part of East Jerusalem. When they speak of dividing Jerusalem, they mean dividing only occupied East Jerusalem, while forcing Palestinians wishing to go from Ramallah to the al-Aqsa Mosque to travel in tunnels running beneath East Jerusalem settlements annexed by Israel. All wish to deny Palestinian refugees anything more than a symbolic return to Israel, and all underestimate the moral significance to Palestinians of Israeli recognition of at least partial responsibility for the refugee problem. All imagine amounts of financial compensation to refugees that are orders of magnitude lower than refugees expect. (A 2003 survey showed that among those refugees willing to choose compensation instead of a return to Israel, 65 percent believed a fair amount would be $100,000–$500,000 per family. Prior to the Camp David negotiations in 2000, US officials estimated that a combined total of up to $20 billion might be available to Palestinian refugees and Jewish refugees from Arab countries, meaning that Palestinians could expect to receive no more than $1,000–$3,000 per refugee.) All neglect how unacceptable their proposals are to refugees, whose support will be indispensable for a lasting agreement, since they make up a majority of Palestinians worldwide and roughly 45 percent of the population of the West Bank and Gaza.[25]

All three groups back the Israeli demand to place severe restrictions on the sovereignty of a future Palestinian state, with limits on armament, border control, airspace, and ability to form alliances, as well as the placement within the state of international security forces, Israeli early-warning stations, routes for Israeli emergency deployments, and, for some considerable period, Israeli troops. Some of these restrictions are acceptable to PLO leaders, but they remain highly unpopular with the Palestinian public.

Most important, all three groups underrate how ineffectual and often detrimental US actions and policies have been, whether the incremental steps favored by the Skeptics or the final-status talks promoted by Embracers and Reproachers. The groups justify their positions on the grounds that they advance the parties toward a two-state peace. Yet the effect, in practice if not in intention, has been to create false hopes.

For two decades, the notion that peace may come in the near future has excused taking little more than minimal and inadequate steps to lessen the hardships imposed by occupation today. Had Israel and the United States demanded that a peace treaty precede a withdrawal from Gaza or southern Lebanon, the IDF might still be in both places. In point of fact, the United States' earnest and patient search for peace serves to entrench a one-state reality: Israeli Arabs deepen their ties to Palestinians in the West Bank; settlements spread; outposts are legalized; and annexationist Israelis grow in power. New roads and parks cut through Arab East Jerusalem and make any reasonable division of the city untenable. Palestinian residents of an intended future capital are surrounded by settlements, threatened with the loss of their residency, or compelled to move to the other side of the separation wall. All the while, a series of fruitless negotiations helps to discredit the two-state model and confirm the depth of the chasm between the two sides.

Despite the good intentions American officials express, the United States is less a cure than a cause of stasis. It deprives other third parties—whether European or Arab—of a meaningful part in the process. It negotiates and drafts proposals without adequately consulting or considering the concerns of communities whose support would be crucial for a lasting peace: religious Zionists and ultra-Orthodox Jews as well as Islamists, Palestinian citizens of Israel, and refugees. And the United States tells the Palestinians that peace talks, as well as Western support, are conditional on a halt in Palestinian steps to place more pressure on Israel.

Those steps—which, though popular with the public, are opposed or regarded warily by many Palestinian leaders—include popular protests, boycotts, sanctions, lawsuits, pursuit of recognition of a Palestinian state in various international institutions, and limits on security cooperation with Israel. They also include reforms within the PLO to admit

Hamas and other excluded Palestinian factions. The United States opposes such reforms, which are necessary for true Palestinian reconciliation, but fails to see that PLO negotiators will have little legitimacy without them.

No political incentives exist for the United States to change its policies, exert its considerable leverage over the parties, and overturn the status quo. The potential benefits of creating a small, poor, and strategically inconsequential Palestinian state are tiny when compared with the costs of heavily pressuring a close ally that wields significant regional and US domestic power. American policy thus remains designed to thwart actions that would raise the costs of the status quo, and so in effect sustains it.

—September 2014

13.

Obama's Palestine Legacy

In no American president did Palestinians invest higher hopes than Barack Obama, and in none did they come to feel more profound disappointment. Obama entered the White House more deeply informed about and supportive of the Palestinian cause than any incoming president before him. He had attended and spoken at numerous events organized by the Arab American and Palestinian American communities, in which he had numerous contacts, and he had repeatedly criticized American policy, calling for a more even-handed approach toward Israel.[1]

In a 2003 toast to Rashid Khalidi, the Palestinian American historian of the University of Chicago and later Columbia University, Obama reminisced about meals prepared by Khalidi's wife, Mona, and the many talks that had been "consistent reminders to me of my own blind spots and my own biases." He had dined with and attended lectures by such figures as Edward Said, the most famous and eloquent Palestinian critic of the Oslo Accords, and he had offered words of encouragement to Ali Abunimah, the Palestinian American activist, writer, cofounder of the Electronic Intifada, and leading advocate of a one-state solution.[2]

It is hardly an exaggeration to say that Palestinians looked to Obama as a potentially historic figure capable of ending their occupation. For the first time, they had the prospect of an American president who was not only sympathetic to their plight and motivated to resolve it but could connect to it viscerally. Obama could draw parallels with Britain's colonization of Kenya, where his Muslim father was born, and the African American struggle for civil rights that had culminated in his presidency. Palestinians recalled that in 2007, during the previous administration, Condoleezza Rice had said that Israel's restrictions on Palestinian life and movement were similar to the oppressive conditions that had angered her as a black child in racially segregated Alabama. Now the Palestinians had a black United States president who had cast himself as a champion of civil rights and replaced George W. Bush's Oval Office bust of Winston Churchill with one of Martin Luther King, Jr.[3]

In his first days on the job, Obama did not disappoint. Within hours of taking office, he made one of his first phone calls to a foreign leader, Palestinian president Mahmoud Abbas. "We were not expecting such a quick call from President Obama," a pleased Abbas adviser said, "but we knew how serious he is about the Palestinian problem."[4] Obama and his inner circle shared a strong conviction that a two-state agreement could be reached, and that a new approach was necessary for them to be the ones to reach it.

On his second day, Obama appointed a special envoy for Middle East Peace, Senator George Mitchell, author of a 2001 fact-finding report that called for a freeze in Israeli settlement construction. Four months later, ahead of a White House visit by Abbas, the administration publicly confronted Israel with a call for a complete freeze in settlement building in the West Bank, including East Jerusalem, and said that in discussing settlements it would not limit itself to the mealy-mouthed criticism of its recent predecessors, which had called them "unhelpful." A senior official who accompanied Mitchell and Secretary of State Hillary Clinton on a drive from Israel to the West Bank later recalled the delegation's discomfort as it entered the Occupied Territories: "my God, you crossed that border and it was apartheid."[5]

Visitors to the White House said they had never heard Bill Clinton, Ronald Reagan, or either Bush speaking about Israel and Palestine in the same way. Days after Abbas's visit, Obama traveled to the Middle East, skipping what for another president would have been a requisite stop in Israel, and delivered an address in Cairo in which he said that

212 THE ONLY LANGUAGE THEY UNDERSTAND

"the situation for the Palestinian people is intolerable," and spoke of the struggle of African Americans for full and equal rights.[6]

The shift was also felt by American Jewish leaders. At a White House meeting, Obama responded to the suggestion that Israelis "must know that the United States is right next to them," by replying: "Look at the past eight years. During those eight years, there was no space between us and Israel, and what did we get from that?"[7]

The president's rhetorical question implied the obvious answer: precious little. But that was still considerably more than what the Palestinians would receive during the coming years from Obama. If there was a distinguishing feature of Obama's record on Israel-Palestine, it was that, unlike his recent predecessors, he had not a single achievement to his name.

The presidents in the three decades before him had all fallen far short of ending occupation or achieving peace, but each had at least inched the parties toward greater partition and Palestinian self-rule. Jimmy Carter had obtained a framework peace agreement in which Israel committed to permit the establishment of a Palestinian self-governing authority, to negotiate with the Palestinians on a territorial withdrawal based on UN Security Council Resolution 242, and to recognize the legitimate rights of the Palestinian people. Ronald Reagan opened a dialogue with the PLO after it had recognized Israel, accepted Resolution 242, and renounced terrorism. George H. W. Bush laid the foundation of what is known as the peace process, dragging Prime Minister Yitzhak Shamir to the first official negotiations with the Palestinians at the 1991 conference in Madrid, which was followed by bilateral talks in Washington that led directly to Oslo. Bill Clinton supported the establishment of the PA in 1994 and helped broker subsequent agreements that expanded Palestinian territorial jurisdiction and secured limited Israeli withdrawals. George W. Bush was the first to make it US policy to support Palestinian statehood, advanced the first UN Security Council resolution explicitly calling for two states, obtained the first endorsement of Palestinian statehood from an Israeli prime minister, Ariel Sharon, and supported Israel's withdrawal from Gaza and its dismantling of four West Bank settlements.[8]

And Obama? After giving up on his short-lived demand for a settlement freeze in September 2009, his envoys pressured the Palestinians to accept two wildly inconsistent preconditions for negotiations: first, that during the talks Israel could continue building new settlements, in violation of the Fourth Geneva Convention; second, that while Israel violated international law, the Palestinians had to refrain from peacefully employing it, including by exercising their right to join multilateral institutions, a step which, unlike Israel's settlement construction, the United States said it would consider an act of "bad faith."[9]

Then, in 2013, following the failure of these efforts, Obama authorized Secretary of State John Kerry to initiate yet another round of doomed negotiations, which served as cover for settlement building by Benjamin Netanyahu, on a scale unmatched during the preceding decade and with US complicity. Obama even ordered his UN ambassador to issue his sole veto of a UN Security Council resolution, one that called for a halt in settlement activity in words nearly identical to those already used by the administration. Meanwhile the president had provided more money and weapons than any of his predecessors to the Israeli government. His aides spent much of their final year not on advancing Obama's goal of an end to occupation but rather on negotiating a substantial increase in US aid for the military that imposes it— to $38 billion over ten years—the most generous pledge of military assistance to any country in US history.[10]

Many in the administration hoped that this was merely a prelude to Obama's final act, which was exactly what concerned the Israeli government. It dragged out the military aid talks, demanded a still larger subsidy, and displayed reluctance to accept the unprecedented package of assistance. It did so not only because some believed that Obama's successor might provide an even more lucrative offer on more lenient terms, but also because it sensed a trap. By pointing to Israel's receipt of the military package, Obama was more able to take steps not to Israel's liking, including a last-gasp effort to secure a different sort of Palestine legacy.[11]

* * *

What legacy did Obama hope to leave? In his final months, there were only a few options that seemed politically feasible, which is to say they did not depend on the cooperation of the parties, the support of

Congress, or the absence of vociferous opposition from pro-Israel groups. One was to follow in the footsteps of Sweden by offering a largely symbolic recognition of the State of Palestine, without specifying its borders or the location of its capital. (Even in the realm of symbolism, Sweden's recognition hadn't amounted to much: two years later, the country's representative to the Palestinians did not refer to herself as an ambassador and her office was not called an embassy.)[12] But recognition was deemed to be a bridge too far.

A second was to support a UN Security Council resolution condemning Israeli settlements. That, however, had been done several times already, decades earlier, to little effect, and doing it again was not expected to alter Israeli behavior or Palestinian living conditions, although it would have allowed Obama to say that he had done something, without actually having done much. A third was for the administration to deliver a speech that outlined the terms on which it thought the conflict should be settled, or to seek multilateral endorsement of such terms, perhaps through the Middle East Quartet. But the announcement of a proposal risked having no lasting effect, either on the parties or on US policy, and the prospects of yet another plan were unpromising.

This left only one option that wasn't seen as unrealistic, unpalatable, or insignificant: to set down the guidelines or "parameters" of a peace agreement—on the four core issues of borders, security, refugees, and Jerusalem—in a US-supported UN Security Council resolution.[13] Once passed, with US support, these parameters would become international law, binding, in theory, on all future presidents and peace brokers.

Top US officials saw a parameters resolution as Obama's only chance at a lasting, positive legacy, one that history might even show to have been more important to peace than the achievements of his predecessors. Once Kerry's efforts extinguished the administration's last hopes of an agreement on their watch, a parameters resolution became their brass ring; after that, Israel-Palestine policy in Washington and capitals throughout Europe was largely at a standstill, hanging on the question of whether Obama would decide to grab it.

Proponents of such a resolution argued that it would form the guidelines for any future negotiations; decrease the likelihood of more talks like Kerry's that went nowhere, in part because they had no established terms of reference; reduce the incentives for the parties to hold out for better terms, since the resolution would not be subject to renegotiation; give each side the political cover of multilateral insistence on the concessions required of them; and present the parties with an international consensus that they could dislike but not reject indefinitely. Once Israelis and Palestinians succumbed to the weight of months or years of pressure to negotiate on the basis of a Security Council resolution—as eventually happened with Resolution 242, the basis of Israel's only peace treaties with its Arab neighbors—the parameters, if sufficiently detailed, the argument went, would greatly improve the chance that talks would have a successful outcome, by having secured, in advance, the most painful compromises on each side.

This was precisely the move that the Israeli government feared most. In his March 2016 speech to AIPAC, Netanyahu assaulted the idea, warning against those who

> seek to impose terms on Israel in the UN Security Council. And those terms would undoubtedly be stacked against us, they always are. So such an effort in the UN would only convince the Palestinians that they can stab their way to a state. . . . A Security Council resolution to pressure Israel would further harden Palestinian positions, and thereby it could actually kill the chances of peace for many, many years. And that is why I hope the United States will maintain its longstanding position to reject such a UN resolution.[14]

* * *

The idea that the United States should lay out the terms of an Israeli settlement with its neighbors has a long history, dating at least as far back as a 1977 *Foreign Affairs* article, "How to Save Israel in Spite of Herself," by George Ball, the former undersecretary of state and ambassador to the UN. "The parties will never come anywhere near agreement by the traditional processes of diplomatic haggling," Ball wrote, "unless the United States first defines the terms of that agreement, relates them to established international principles, and makes clear that America's continued involvement in the area depends upon acceptance by both sides of the terms it prescribes."[15]

Subsequent experience gave credence to the idea. Each of the US-mediated Israeli-Palestinian talks that failed was conducted without agreed guidelines, while each negotiation Israel concluded with its Arab neighbors was premised on internationally endorsed terms of reference. The land-for-peace formula of UN Security Council Resolution 242 was the foundation of Israel's agreements with Egypt and Jordan and of the interim agreement on Palestinian self-governance brokered in Oslo, which itself provided the terms of reference for successful subsequent negotiations on Palestinian self-rule.

But Resolution 242 was designed to achieve peace between Israel and the Arab states it had fought against in 1967, not between Israel and a yet-to-be established Palestinian state. It made no specific mention of the Palestinians—referring to them only obliquely, in a call for "a just settlement of the refugee problem"—or their right to statehood and self-determination, which was a primary reason that the Palestinians had for so many years objected to accepting it without reservations. Once the PLO had done so, in 1988, its leaders felt that they had finally agreed to parameters established by the international community, only to find that the United States backed the Israeli view that the Palestinians' acceptance of a state on less than one-fourth of their homeland was not a historic concession but a maximalist demand to be whittled down in future talks.

In round after round of negotiations since then, the Palestinians have reiterated that the guidelines of the discussion must be the UN resolutions they had been pressured to accept: from General Assembly Resolution 194, issued during the final phase of the 1948 war, which resolved that "refugees wishing to return to their homes and live at peace with their neighbors should be permitted to do so at the earliest practicable date"; to the Security Council resolutions that condemned settlement activity as a violation of the Fourth Geneva Convention (446, 452, 465, 478), demanded the dismantlement of all settlements, including in Jerusalem (465), urged an immediate halt to Israel's changes to the demographic composition of East Jerusalem and other Occupied Territories (446), affirmed the necessity of Israel's withdrawal from territories occupied in the 1967 war (242), and called for the creation of a Palestinian state (1397).

But as a mediator, the United States never insisted on these or other specific guidelines, and each final-status negotiation ended in failure and regret, with senior US officials belatedly seeking to draft parameters in order to salvage some lasting achievement from their wasted efforts.[16]

* * *

Obama had plenty of reasons to refuse to back a parameters resolution in his final months in office. Both the Israelis and the Palestinians had the ability to lobby their allies against such an approach, dragging the United States into exhausting negotiations and uncomfortable compromises. Reaching a consensus in the Security Council that would be acceptable to the United States was not assured, particularly given European and Russian reluctance to recognize Israel as a Jewish state.[17] Once passed, a resolution was unlikely to be accepted anytime soon by either side or to produce negotiations over a comprehensive agreement, which was its ostensible purpose.

Rather than generating hope that an agreement is possible, a resolution would risk causing a significant deterioration in relations as leaders on both sides would face pressure to assure key constituencies that they had not succumbed to the international community's diktat. Israel might build settlements in particularly sensitive areas, formally annex parts of the West Bank, or pass a law requiring a parliamentary supermajority to authorize any negotiations over Jerusalem; Palestinians could limit cooperation with Israel and pursue new claims against it in international institutions.[18]

Indeed, in the short run, a parameters resolution seemed to offer few advantages. The two sides would get no changes on the ground and no immediate prospect of ending the conflict. For Palestinians, the price of gaining American backing for international law would be that the United States would rewrite it in Israel's favor, and even then without exerting the pressure necessary to force Israel to accept the terms. Such a resolution would thus weaken their position in international law—one of the only realms in which they once held some advantage. For Israel, a parameters resolution would mean a set of US-backed, internationally endorsed terms of reference where previously it had none.

Supporters of the resolution would be unable to argue that it had any near-term positive effect, while critics could point to its rejection by both sides, the solidification of a one-state reality in defiant response, and the increasing irrelevance of both the two-state solution and its international proponents. Obama's successor, meanwhile, could subvert it through side letters and private commitments made to Israel, much as George W. Bush undermined a US-supported Security Council resolution on settlements in an April 2004 letter to Ariel Sharon.[19]

Above all, there was internal politics in the United States. This was the largest obstacle to a parameters resolution, which for the Obama administration had always been a question as much of domestic politics as of foreign policy. In July 2016, the Republican Party amended its platform to remove support for a two-state solution, to oppose "any measures intended to impose an agreement or to dictate borders or other terms," and to call "for the immediate termination of all US funding of any entity that attempts to do so." Following Netanyahu's speech to AIPAC, 388 Democratic and Republican members of Congress sent a letter to Obama warning that support for a Security Council resolution on parameters would "dangerously hinder" the prospect of renewed negotiations. In September 2016, a bipartisan group of 88 senators urged Obama "to continue longstanding U.S. policy and make it clear that you will veto any one-sided UNSC resolution that may be offered in the coming months."[20] The Obama administration could justify challenging AIPAC and large numbers of Democrats in Congress for a goal as important to the United States as the agreement to limit Iran's nuclear program. But to confront widespread domestic opposition for something as marginal to US national security interests as the Israeli-Palestinian conflict was another matter.

* * *

Where US officials came down on a parameters resolution depended to a significant degree on whether they believed the two-state solution was dying or already dead. Those who thought it was merely dying—most in the Obama administration—saw a parameters resolution as having many beneficial effects. It could, they thought, give new hope to hopeless Palestinians; inject a dose of realism into both societies about the compromises that will be required; ratchet up pressure on Israel to reverse steps undermining a two-state solution; and provide grounds for the Palestinian leadership to claim that its hand was forced by international law.

Those who thought the two-state solution was already dead, however, worried that a parameters resolution would simply give new life to the lie of a "temporary occupation" that will end in the next round of talks, meanwhile wasting the time of the United States and the international community with plans, pleas, and bribes to gain the parties' acceptance as Israel expropriated more of Jerusalem and the West Bank.

In fact, the debate in Western capitals about whether to put forward a parameters resolution was a distraction from the more substantive question of what the resolution should say. Among the parties themselves, opposition was not really about the wisdom of such an intervention in the abstract but about what each side feared it would lose. Both sides were certain to be disappointed with the final text, and the same could be said of the various US officials who sought a resolution more favorable to one party or the other. The debate between those officials was, in their own minds, one between relatively pro-Israeli and pro-Palestinian positions. But it was closer to one between the stances of Republican and Democratic groups, all of them pro-Israel and Zionist.

On one side of the debate was AIPAC, an organization that distances itself from the Israeli government only when it is not led by Likud; on the other side were organizations like J Street, which had aligned itself with an Israeli center whose positions on borders and Jerusalem did not differ from Netanyahu's. J Street had sought to overcome a boycott by the past several Israeli governments by trying to build ties to Likud ministers and offering to help Netanyahu's government combat BDS.[21]

The inevitable outcome of this process was either no resolution (some officials called instead for a nonbinding and easily dismissed speech, endorsed, perhaps in a formal paper, by a number of allies) or one that was of far greater benefit to Israel than to the Palestinians. This was a particular irony, since AIPAC and Israel were strongly opposed to a parameters resolution in principle, while the Palestinians had been asking for US guidelines or internationally imposed terms of reference for well over a decade.[22]

* * *

Any resolution the United States could support would contain clauses that are difficult for each side to accept. The hardest issues for Israel are that the borders would be based on the pre-1967 lines and that the Palestinian capital would be in Jerusalem. The most onerous clauses for the Palestinians relate to recognition of Israel as a Jewish state, the absence of a timeline for Israel's withdrawal from the West Bank, and a resolution of the refugee problem that would rule out any more than a symbolic return to Israel.

When we examine these painful concessions for each side, a striking disparity emerges: the two compromises for Israel are battles that the country already lost long ago, in numerous UN resolutions, presidential statements, official declarations of EU policy, and the Arab Peace Initiative, which has been welcomed by the Quartet and the Security Council.[23] A Security Council call for a Palestinian state on the pre-1967 boundaries with East Jerusalem as its capital is consistent with the views of virtually all UN member states and is neither a significant gain for the PLO nor a substantial loss for Israel.

This is not true of the bitter pills for the Palestinians. A US-supported resolution would represent entirely new concessions to Israel. Settlements that the Security Council has determined must be dismantled would gain legitimacy as parts of a potential land swap. European and UN Security Council calls for a just and agreed solution to the refugee problem would be transformed into a strongly implied denial of a Palestinian right of return. And, for the first time in a Security Council resolution, the international community would offer some sort of recognition of Israel as a Jewish state, which the Quartet had previously refused to do.[24]

Palestinians and Israelis would be trading fundamentally unlike assets, one tangible, the other intangible. Palestinians would give up moral claims, acquiescing in the denial of their right to return and bestowing legitimacy on their dispossessors by recognizing the vast majority of their homeland as a Jewish state. Israelis, by contrast, would be committing to a physical withdrawal from land under their full control. The crucial difference between these two types of assets is that, once the parties had accepted the parameters, only the intangible ones would disappear. The land, by contrast, would remain in Israel's possession until the parties reached a comprehensive settlement, an outcome that an agreed framework by no means guarantees.

For the United States, the purpose of any parameters would be to make negotiations more likely to succeed by securing the largest concessions from each side in advance. But even with agreed guidelines, the power disparity in the negotiating room would remain, which means that the worst possible interpretation of the parameters, the full exploitation of every loophole, is what would be presented to the weaker party as the alternative to continued occupation. The onus, then, was on the drafters to include as much detail as possible, immunizing the terms against the legal and semantic circumventions for which Netanyahu and his longtime envoy, Yitzhak Molho, are well known.

Yet the United States never considered drafting detailed Security Council parameters of this sort. Instead, the guidelines considered by the United States consisted of just a few short paragraphs, which sought to arrive at compromise positions:

- Between those who call for land swaps to be equal not just in size but quality, and those who call merely for "mutually agreed" swaps, thereby enabling Israel to annex valuable territory, including in Jerusalem, while offering smaller, inferior patches of desert land in return;
- Between those who put an upper limit on Israel's West Bank annexation of no more than 3 percent, and those who do not, allowing Israel to annex settlements like Ariel that lie halfway across the West Bank;
- Between those who stress that the settlements remain illegal violations of the Fourth Geneva Convention until a peace agreement is reached, and those who describe the possibility of land swaps in a manner that permits Israel to claim that construction in settlement blocs has been sanctioned by the Security Council;
- Between those who call for two capitals in Jerusalem, and those

who call merely for a shared capital, wording that empowers Israel to insist on a unified city with limited or no Palestinian sovereignty;

- Between those who specify that a Palestinian capital will be in East Jerusalem within its pre-1967 municipal borders, and those who more vaguely propose that there be two capitals in Jerusalem—that is, in the expanded, Israeli-defined boundaries of the city, which extend to the edges of Ramallah and Bethlehem. That allows Israel to demand that the Palestinian capital be located in a place like Kafr Aqab, which is the northern-most neighborhood of the present-day municipality, but was never considered part of Jerusalem before June 1967; it lies on the West Bank side of the separation wall, and is closer to Ramallah than to the city center;

- Between those who state that some limited land swaps may be negotiated in Jerusalem, and those who call for all "Jewish neighborhoods" (that is, settlements) in East Jerusalem to be annexed by Israel, thereby legalizing all Jerusalem settlements, depriving Palestinians of the right to negotiate the status of some of their most valued land, and giving Israel license—and incentive—to increase construction of Jerusalem settlements in advance of a peace agreement;

- Between those who call for Palestinian sovereignty over the Noble Sanctuary/Temple Mount and Israeli sovereignty over the Wailing Wall/Buraq Wall, and those who call for a "special regime" in the Old City or say nothing about it, allowing Israel to insist on control or sovereignty over the al-Aqsa Mosque;[25]

- Between those who set a deadline for Israeli withdrawal from the West Bank once an agreement has been reached, as the Clinton Parameters did, and those who reject a timeline or state merely that Palestinians and Israelis should agree on one, enabling Israel to demand that its withdrawal be contingent on its own determination of satisfactory Palestinian performance;[26]

- Between those who propose resolving the Palestinian refugee issue through both symbolic and practical concessions by Israel (for example, permitting return to all living refugee survivors of the 1948 war, of whom there are estimated to be as few as 30,000 today), and those who explicitly deny that any refugees will return or insist that they do so only on a "humanitarian" basis, at Israel's sole discretion, indicating a rejection of any meaningful return;

- And, finally, between those who say that any "narrative" concessions—concerning the history of the conflict—should include Israeli acknowledgment of partial responsibility for the expulsion and flight of Palestinian refugees and full responsibility for denying them the ability to return, and those who say that the Palestinians must recognize Israel as a Jewish state without any reciprocal concession.

It was clear that on many of these issues, any US-supported resolution would favor Israeli positions over Palestinian ones. There were some Palestinians who were nevertheless prepared to take US-endorsed, legally binding parameters, with all their flaws and detrimental effects, as an improvement on existing international law that the US mediator has ignored. The choice for the PLO has never been between inadequate US parameters and existing UN resolutions. It has been, rather, between refusing to negotiate while Israel's occupation grows more deeply entrenched, and negotiating with no parameters at all. The latter meant talks being held on Israel's terms. That was why some Palestinians saw a parameters resolution as a risky but perhaps worthwhile gamble, weakening their position on paper in the hope of strengthening it in practice. And it was why the prospect of US guidelines seemed to them very much like the Obama administration itself: disappointing, unjust, and ineffectual, and yet perhaps still the best they were going to get.

—September 2016

CODA

In the end, the Palestinians didn't get even that. Obama finished his presidency much as he had started it: bold in words, timid in deeds. In the intensive debate about how to secure an Israel-Palestine legacy, he chose the most cautious path: abstaining from a UN Security Council resolution on settlements that, by the administration's own admission, contained nothing new. It was, in fact, not even a reiteration but rather a watered-down version of a far stronger Security Council resolution that had been supported by the Carter administration.

Several days later, during his final month in office, Obama allowed his secretary of state to put forward parameters in a lengthy speech. Israel rejected both the speech and the UN resolution, with no apparent consequences. In his final remarks, Kerry once again warned Israel that if it did not separate from the Occupied Territories it would have to choose between being Jewish or democratic. But Kerry seemed unable or unwilling to appreciate that his threats carried no weight: he had been making the same admonition for several years, without forcing any such choice on Israel.

Until its final day in power, the Obama administration continued to believe that Israel would move toward a two-state solution if only the United States explained that the alternative was apartheid. The logic was irrefutable, they believed, so it was inevitable that Israel would eventually grasp its truth. Eight years of failed policy were founded on the stubborn delusion that with sufficiently impassioned rhetoric Israel could be persuaded to make concessions that it did not consider to be in its interest. Obama achieved less than any of his recent predecessors because, when it came to Israel, force was a language he could not—or would not—understand.

—January 2017

Notes

The notes below have been consolidated, in most cases, to one per paragraph. English sources have been cited where possible; Arabic and Hebrew sources appear in English translation and are marked Hebrew or Arabic. Transliterations provided by publishers have been retained.

PART I. FORCING COMPROMISE

Laura M. James, "Military/Political Means/Ends: Egyptian Decision-Making in the War of Attrition," *The Cold War in the Middle East: Regional Conflict and the Superpowers 1967–73*, Nigel J. Ashton, ed. (New York: Routledge, 2007), p. 93.

1. THE ONLY LANGUAGE THEY UNDERSTAND

1. For the first Carter quote ("be harder on the Israelis"), see Zbigniew Brzezinski, *Power and Principle: Memoirs of the National Security Adviser, 1977–1981* (New York: Farrar, Straus and Giroux, 1985), pp. 277–78. For the second ("no strong feelings"), see Jimmy Carter, *Keeping Faith: Memoirs of a President* (New York: Bantam Books, 1982), p. 282. For details of Carter's trip to Israel and the West Bank, see Carter, *Keeping Faith*, p. 281; Jimmy Carter, *The Blood of Abraham: Insights into the Middle East* (New York: Houghton Mifflin, 1985), p. 25. For the final Carter quote ("profound impact"), see E. Stanly Godbold, Jr., *Jimmy and Rosalynn Carter: The Georgia Years, 1924–1974* (New York: Oxford University Press, 2010), pp. 250–51.

2. Throughout the book I have used the phrase pre-1967 lines to refer to the 1949 armistice lines, which are also commonly called the "1967 borders" or the "pre-1967 borders." On Carter as the first American president to call publicly for almost total Israeli withdrawal, see Avi Shlaim, *The Iron Wall: Israel and the Arab World* (New York: W. W. Norton & Company, 2014), p. 356. For more on Carter's approach to the pre-1967 lines, see William B. Quandt, *Peace Process: American Diplomacy and the Arab-Israeli Conflict Since 1967* (Washington, DC, and Berkeley: Brookings Institution Press and University of California Press, 1993), pp. 260–61;

Dennis Ross, *Doomed to Succeed: The U.S.-Israel Relationship from Truman to Obama* (New York: Farrar, Straus and Giroux, 2015), p. 151. For Carter's declaration ("has to be a homeland"), stated at a March 16, 1977, town hall meeting in Clinton, Massachusetts, see "Editorial Note," in Adam M. Howard, ed., *Foreign Relations of the United States, 1977–80,* volume VIII: *Arab-Israeli Dispute, January 1977–August 1978* (Washington, DC: United States Government Printing Office, 2013), p. 164. Henceforth this volume will be cited as *FRUS,* VIII. For Carter's use of Palestinian and PLO interchangeably, see Quandt, *Peace Process,* p. 259. For the Brookings paper, see "Toward Peace in the Middle East," Brookings Institution Middle East Study Group, December 1975.

3.   For Ford's written assurance, see Quandt, *Peace Process,* pp. 169–70. For Carter's PLO outreach, see William B. Quandt, *Camp David: Peacemaking and Politics* (Washington, DC: Brookings Institution Press, 2016), p. 104; *FRUS,* VIII, pp. 498–517; Jimmy Carter, *White House Diary* (New York: Farrar, Straus and Giroux, 2010), p. 44. On the handshake, see *FRUS,* VIII, p. 189. For Ford's September 1975 letter, see "Letter from President Ford to Israeli Prime Minister Rabin," Document 234, *Foreign Relations of the United States, 1969–1976,* volume XXVI, *Arab-Israeli Dispute, 1974–1976,* 1976, pp. 838–40. For the Carter quote ("put as much pressure as we can"), see his diary entry on April 25, 1977: Carter, *White House Diary,* p. 44. On "showdown," see Carter, *Keeping Faith,* p. 313; Carter, *White House Diary,* p. 168. Aides also described Carter as favoring a showdown. See Quandt, *Camp David,* p. 108; Brzezinski, *Power and Principle* (1983 hardcover edition), pp. 105–6.

4.   Carter, *Keeping Faith,* p. 284.

5.   On Carter spending more time on the Arab-Israeli conflict than any other, see Ross, *Doomed to Succeed,* p. 145. On the Carter-Rabin meeting and "fresh perspective," see *FRUS,* VIII, pp. 618–40. On Israeli disappointment in the meeting, see Quandt, *Camp David,* p. 48; Shlaim, *The Iron Wall,* pp. 356–57. For Carter's warning ("a blow to U.S. support for Israel"), see *FRUS,* VIII, p. 622.

6.   For Carter quotes on Rabin, King Hussein, Hafez al-Assad, and Sadat, see Carter, *Keeping Faith,* pp. 287, 292, 286, 291. Carter's account appeared in his memoirs, published in 1983, two years after Sadat's assassination. Yet the reverential tone can be found in Carter's diary as well. For the quotes from the diary, see Carter, *White House Diary,* pp. 38–39. For Carter's quote to his wife, see Carter, *Keeping Faith,* p. 291. For the final quote ("Arab leaders want to settle it"), see Carter, *White House Diary,* p. 44.

7.   For the death of Begin's parents and brother, see Daniel Gordis, *Menachem Begin: The Battle for Israel's Soul* (New York: Schocken Books, 2014), pp. 35–36. For the execution of nearly all of the Jews in Brest, see Christopher R. Browning, *Nazi Policy, Jewish Workers, German Killers* (Cambridge, UK: Cambridge University Press, 2000), pp. 118–42. On Begin's opposition to the 1952 reparations agreement, see Anita Shapira, *Israel: A History* (Waltham, MA: Brandeis University Press, 2012), p. 264. For Begin on Jabotinsky, whom he called his "master," see Shlaim, *The Iron Wall,* p. 360. On Begin's pioneering use of simultaneous bombings and improvised explosive devices, see Lawrence Wright, *Thirteen Days in September: The Dramatic Story of the Struggle for Peace* (New York: Vintage, 2015), p. 106. On IRA use of *The Revolt,* see J. Bowyer Bell, *The Secret Army: The IRA* (London: Transaction Publishers, 1997), p. 164; Wright, *Thirteen Days,* p. 106. On admiration for *The Revolt*

by Nelson Mandela and the ANC, see Nelson Mandela, *Conversations with Myself* (New York: Farrar, Straus and Giroux, 2010), pp. 106–7. On the al-Qaeda training camp and Osama bin Laden, see Wright, *Thirteen Days*, pp. 82, 303. On the King David Hotel bombing, in which ninety-one people were killed, as well as one of the Irgun attackers, see Bruce Hoffman, *Anonymous Soldiers: The Struggle for Israel, 1917–1947* (New York: Vintage, 2016), p. 300. Of the ninety-one victims, there were thirteen soldiers, three policemen, and twenty-one first-rank government officials. See Thurston Clarke, *By Blood & Fire: July 22, 1946: The Attack on the King David Hotel* (New York: G. P. Putnam's Sons, 1981); Benny Morris, *1948: The First Arab-Israeli War* (New Haven: Yale University Press, 2008), p. 35. On Haganah involvement in and Irgun blame for the Deir Yassin killings and the King David Hotel bombing, see Gordis, *Menachem Begin*, pp. 70–75.

8. On Begin's opposition to partition in 1937 and 1947, see Shlaim, *The Iron Wall*, p. 360. For the Irgun emblem, see Bernard Reich and David H. Goldberg, *Historical Dictionary of Israel* (Lanham, MD: Rowman & Littlefield, 2016), p. 261. For the Herut platform, see Ehud Sprinzak, *The Ascendance of Israel's Radical Right* (New York: Oxford University Press, 1991), p. 33. For the Likud platform, see Shlaim, *The Iron Wall*, p. 360.

9. For the American plan, known as the Second Rogers Plan, which was initiated on June 19, 1970, and agreed to by the Israeli government on July 31, 1970, see State of Israel, Knesset, "Rogers Plan," accessed August 2, 2016; Richard Nixon, "Second Annual Report to the Congress on United States Foreign Policy," Feburary 25, 1971, http://www.presidency.ucsb.edu/ws/index.php?pid=3324&st=policy&st1=. For Begin's remarks on "Judea and Samaria" and annexation, see Gordis, *Menachem Begin*, p. 164. For Begin's quote ("excuse my emotions"), see *FRUS*, VIII, p. 343. On Begin's view that if Jews had no right to the West Bank they had no right to Tel Aviv, see Quandt, *Camp David*, pp. 272, 67. For the Begin quote ("the Eastern part is the real Jerusalem"), see *Foreign Relations of the United States, 1977–80*, volume IX: *Arab-Israeli Dispute, August 1978–December 1980* (Washington: United States Government Printing Office, 2014), p. 1186. The two figures—55 percent in the 1947 partition plan and conquest of an additional 23 percent—come from two of Israel's leading mapping experts, Dan Rothem and Shaul Arieli. Some texts use slightly different numbers, putting the allotment to the Jewish state in the 1947 partition plan at 56 percent, with a conquest of an additional 22 percent during the war. Part of the discrepancy stems from the existence in the partition plan of a separate UN-controlled regime for Jerusalem and Bethlehem, taking up less than 1 percent of Mandatory Palestine and under the sovereignty of neither the Jewish nor the Arab state. Personal correspondence, Dan Rothem, March 28, 2016.

10. For background on Ezer Weizman, see Wright, *Thirteen Days*, pp. 54–55; Gordis, *Menachem Begin*, p. 168. For Sharon's role in the Qibya massacre, see Benny Morris, *Israel's Border Wars, 1949–1956: Arab Infiltration, Israeli Retaliation, and the Countdown to the Suez War* (New York: Oxford University Press, 1994), pp. 258–59. On Dayan's goal to prevent the West Bank from continuing to have an Arab majority, see Wright, *Thirteen Days*, p. 181. On Dayan's preference for Sharm el-Sheikh without peace, see Ezer Weizman, *The Battle for Peace* (New York: Bantam Books, 1981), p. 130. For Begin's quote ("The Arabs would not dare go to war"), see Shlaim, *The Iron Wall*, p. 361.

11. On the similarities and differences between Labor and Likud positions on the

Palestinian issue in the late 1970s, see Shlaim, *The Iron Wall*, pp. 330–40, 354–62; Quandt, *Camp David*, pp. 2, 46–51. On Labor's positions in August 1977, see *FRUS*, VIII, pp. 454–58. Labor too was opposed to Palestinian self-determination, relinquishment of East Jerusalem, acceptance of the pre-1967 lines with only minor modifications, an end to Jewish settlement in the West Bank, and recognition of the PLO.

12. Quandt, *Camp David*, p. 69.

13. All of the above quotes from Goldmann appear in *FRUS*, VIII, pp. 732, 731.

14. For Walter Mondale's speech, see Quandt, *Camp David*, p. 73. For the public campaign by US diplomats against Begin's interpretation of UN Resolution 242, see Quandt, *Camp David*, p. 75. For the drafting of principles that were taken to Arab leaders, see Quandt, *Camp David*, pp. 76–89; *FRUS*, VIII, pp. 369–472.

15. For Arafat's message, see "Memorandum from the President's Assistant for National Security Affairs (Brzezinski) to President Carter," in *FRUS*, VIII, p. 335. For Carter's message to Vance, see Quandt, *Camp David*, p. 89. For Begin's pleas and Carter's refusal, see Quandt, *Camp David*, p. 87.

16. For the Vance telegram, see *FRUS*, VIII, pp. 412–14. For Carter's statement on US-PLO dialogue, see Quandt, *Camp David*, p. 93. For Vance dropping US insistence on the PLO changing its charter and Begin's comparison of US actions to appeasement of Hitler, see Quandt, *Camp David*, p. 94. For Begin's quote ("excluded forever") and his reading aloud from the PLO charter (in particular "those articles which negated Israel's right to exist and which called for the expulsion of Israelis who arrived after 1917"), see *FRUS*, VIII, p. 432.

17. For Vance's request for draft peace treaties, see *FRUS*, VIII, pp. 382–84, 423–24. For Vance's more detailed ideas on Palestinian self-determination, including a transitional period of self-rule, see Quandt, *Camp David*, p. 109; *FRUS*, VIII, pp. 380, 384–88, 477–78. For State Department announcements in September, see Quandt, *Camp David*, p. 105; *FRUS*, VIII, p. 512. For US backchannel outreach to the PLO through Bolling, see *FRUS*, VIII, pp. 498–520. Bolling was president of Earlham College, in Indiana, from 1958 to 1973.

18. For Dayan's quote ("most unpleasant"), see Moshe Dayan, *Breakthrough: A Personal Account of the Egypt-Israel Peace Negotiations* (New York: Knopf, 1981), p. 59. For Qaddumi's quote as well as Arafat's welcome of the US statement and acceptance of 242 with modifications, see Yezid Sayigh, *Armed Struggle and the Search for State: The Palestinian National Movement, 1949–1993* (New York: Oxford University Press, 1999), pp. 421–22. In September 1977, Arafat conveyed to Carter through Landrum Bolling that he was willing to accept Security Council Resolution 242 if the United States would declare its support for a Palestinian state, which Carter was not prepared to do. *FRUS*, VIII, pp. 506, 503; Quandt, *Camp David*, p. 101. Later that month, Arafat was asked by Barbara Walters of ABC Television whether he would accept Resolution 242 if it were supplemented by a new UN Security Council resolution declaring that Palestinians were entitled to a national homeland or entity. *The New York Times* reported: "Yasir Arafat, chairman of the Palestine Liberation Organization, says he would accept a United Nations Security Council Resolution acknowledging the right of Israel to exist if it were supplemented by a resolution specifying recognition of the right of the Palestinians to an independent homeland." David Binder, "Arafat Hints Easing of P.L.O. Stand," *The New York Times*, September 25, 1977; Quandt, *Camp David* p. 106.

19. On settlement building, steps toward annexation, and the stern warning to Begin, see "Telegram from the Department of State to the Embassy in Israel": "The Israeli Government announced on August 15 [1977] that it would extend services to the West Bank and the Gaza Strip, raising fears that it was planning to annex the area, and on August 17 announced the construction of three new settlements on the West Bank." *FRUS*, VIII, p. 480. On "showdown," see Quandt, *Camp David*, p. 108; Brzezinski, *Power and Principle*, pp. 105–6. On US drafting of model peace treaties, including one involving a transitional regime in the West Bank, see Quandt, *Camp David*, pp. 101–102.

20. On Moshe Dayan's August 22, 1977, meeting in London with Jordan's King Hussein, see Shlaim, *The Iron Wall*, pp. 364–65; Quandt, *Camp David*, p. 112.

21. On Dayan's meeting with Anwar Sadat's envoy, see Dayan, *Breakthrough*, pp. 38–54; Shlaim, *The Iron Wall*, pp. 365–66; Sidney Zion and Uri Dan, "Untold Story of the Mideast Talks," *The New York Times Magazine*, January 21, 1979; Quandt, *Camp David*, pp. 112–14. For Dayan's quote ("one overriding principle"), see Dayan, *Breakthrough*, p. 45. For Tuhami and Sadat's rejection of an Egyptian-Israeli peace that excluded the Palestinian issue, see Dayan, *Breakthrough*, p. 47.

22. For Dayan's "wipe out" comment and quotes from Lewis, see *FRUS*, VIII, p. 418. For Israel's arming of Lebanese Christians, see comments by Ezer Weizman: *FRUS*, VIII p. 436. For Lewis's telegram, see *FRUS*, VIII, pp. 415–16. Lewis's warning was then echoed by an Egyptian official, who told the United States: "Israel might be planning to strike at the PLO in Lebanon to ensure that the moderate tendency in the PLO would be put on the defensive." Quandt, *Camp David*, p. 95.

23. For Carter warning Begin of "gravest consequences," see Quandt, *Camp David*, p. 103. For Begin's violation of the 1976 Arms Export Control Act and US-Israeli defense assistance agreements, see *FRUS*, VIII, p. 565. For US intelligence confirmation that Israeli statements were untrue, see Quandt, *Camp David*, p. 106.

24. For Carter's letter of warning, see *FRUS*, VIII, p. 566. For Carter's threat that US military assistance "will have to be terminated," see "Telegram from the Department of State to the Embassy in Israel," *FRUS*, VIII, pp. 564–66. For Begin's promise to withdraw and his raised glass of whiskey, see *FRUS*, VIII, pp. 566–70; Quandt, *Camp David*, p. 107.

25. For the US-Soviet joint statement, see Quandt, *Camp David*, p. 122. For the Sadat quote ("brilliant maneuver"), see Quandt, *Peace Process*, p. 268. For Israel's announcement ("harden Arab demands"), see Bernard Gwertzman, "U.S. and Soviet Set Mutual Guidelines for Mideast Peace," *The New York Times*, October 2, 1977. For *The New York Times* on "growing strain," see "Israel Reacts to Statement," *The New York Times*, October 2, 1977, p. 16.

26. For the administration's failure to cover its flanks, see Quandt, *Camp David*, p. 126. See also comments by Carter's press secretary: Jody Powell, *The Other Side of the Story* (New York: William Morrow, 1984), p. 57, cited in Daniel Patrick Strieff, "The President and the Peacemaker: Jimmy Carter and the Domestic Politics of Arab-Israeli Diplomacy, 1977–1980," Doctoral Thesis Submitted to the Department of International History of the London School of Economics, October 2013, p. 111. For Quandt's quotes ("time to put their friends on notice" and "otherwise peaceful Saturday"), see Quandt, *Camp David*, p. 126. For Jody Powell quote, see "Interview with Jody Powell, December 17–18, 1981," Carter Presidency Project, The Miller Center, 2003, p. 57, accessed September 28, 2016, http://web1

.millercenter.org/poh/transcripts/ohp_1981_1217_powell.pdf. For condemnations from American Jewish groups and many more details on the opposition to the communiqué, see Daniel Strieff, *Jimmy Carter and the Middle East: The Politics of Presidential Diplomacy* (New York: Palgrave Macmillan, 2014), chapter 3; Daniel Patrick Strieff, "The President and the Peacemaker."

27. For Carter's UN address (in which he added, to great Israeli satisfaction, "We do not intend to impose a settlement on the nations of the Middle East"), see Jimmy Carter, "United Nations Address Before the General Assembly," The American Presidency Project (online), October 4, 1977, accessed September 28, 2016, http://www.presidency.ucsb.edu/ws/?pid=6744. For Carter's quote ("rather commit political suicide"), see Martin Tolchin, "Carter Assures Representatives on Israel," *The New York Times*, October 7, 1977. Carter had been "increasingly concerned about criticisms of our peace initiatives from within the American Jewish community." Carter, *Keeping Faith*, p. 296.

28. For quotes from Dayan and Carter, see "Memorandum of Conversation," *FRUS*, VIII, pp. 658–59. In his diary, Carter wrote of the meeting: "I told the group that there was no doubt that, of all the nations with whom we had negotiated on the Middle East, Israel was by far the most obstinate and difficult. This seemed to cause them [the Israelis] genuine concern and they kept coming back to the point, but of course Cy and Zbig and all of us know that it's absolutely a fact." Carter, *White House Diary*, pp. 112–13.

29. For Carter defending himself against the charge of selling out Israel, see Quandt, *Camp David*, pp. 134–36. For Brzezinski on "blackmail," see Quandt, *Camp David*, p. 144, n. 41, citing Brzezinski, *Power and Principle*, p. 108. For Dayan and Carter quotes, see "Memorandum of Conversation," *FRUS*, VIII, pp. 673–74.

30. For Carter's quote ("would be a blow to your position"), see *FRUS*, VIII, p. 674. For the US official's assessment ("exploited the opportunity brilliantly"), see Quandt, *Camp David*, p. 138. For Dayan's quote ("it would be bad"), see *FRUS*, VIII, p. 676. For Quandt's quote ("clear priority to domestic political concerns"), see Quandt, *Camp David*, p. 135.

31. On Sadat's statement that Carter's note convinced him of the need to take a bold step, see *FRUS*, VIII, pp. 741–42. On Sadat having been motivated by despair over Carter's capitulation, see Quandt, who writes, "It was not the U.S.-Soviet communiqué that disillusioned him; it was Carter's apparent inability to stand up to Israeli pressure . . . that seems to have convinced Sadat to strike out on his own." Quandt, *Peace Process*, 1993, pp. 267–68. In another book, Quandt writes, "It has often been said that Sadat's decision to go to Jerusalem was a direct response to the U.S.-Soviet communiqué. Such comments usually come from Israeli sources. But he makes no such statement in his autobiography, and other Egyptians who were involved in the talks at the time have denied it." Quandt, *Camp David*, p. 127.

32. For quotes on the "Zionist lobby" from Sadat (who also said: "The inspiration for my initiative itself came from President Carter"), see *FRUS*, VIII, p. 992. Egypt's foreign minister later implied that Carter's confession of impotence, including private admissions to Egypt that further pressuring Israel would be "political suicide," had been decisive in Sadat's decision-making. Quandt, *Camp David*, p. 118. For Sadat's November 9 announcement ("ends of the earth for peace"), see Shlaim, *The Iron Wall*, p. 367.

33. On Mordechai Gur's fear of a ruse, see Shapira, *Israel*, p. 366; Shlaim, *The Iron Wall*,

p. 367. On Yigael Yadin's call for a mobilization of reserves, see Shlaim, *The Iron Wall*, p. 367. On Israeli sharpshooters in case Sadat's plane was a Trojan horse, see Quandt, *Camp David*, p. 151. For Golda Meir quote, see Shapira, *Israel*, p. 367.

34. For quotes from Sadat's speech, see Israel Ministry of Foreign Affairs, "Statement to the Knesset by President Sadat—20 November 1977," accessed September 29, 2016, http://www.mfa.gov.il/mfa/foreignpolicy/mfadocuments/yearbook3/pages/73 Statement to the Knesset by President Sadat-20.aspx. For Weizman's note to Begin (who accepted the note and nodded), see Wright, *Thirteen Days*, pp. 28–29. For Sadat sweating profusely, see Quandt, *Camp David*, p. 151.

35. For the Arab reaction to Sadat's trip to Jerusalem—including flag burning, a diplomatic and economic boycott by the PLO and four Arab states, a day of national mourning declared by Syria, and Iraq's cancelation of celebrations of the Islamic holiday of Eid al-Adha—see Sabri Jiryis, "The Arab World at the Crossroads: An Analysis of the Arab Opposition to the Sadat Initiative," *Journal of Palestine Studies* 7 (1977–1978): 26–61; Shlaim, *The Iron Wall*, p. 371.

36. On US expectations of Begin (Carter insisted that during an upcoming regional tour he would not stop in Israel unless Begin made a proposal that went beyond a mere Egyptian-Israeli bilateral agreement), see the following endnote, as well as Quandt, *Camp David*, p. 155. On the public opinion poll of Americans, see *FRUS*, VIII, p. 845. On Vance's delivery of a personal, written appeal from Carter, see *FRUS*, VIII, p. 813.

37. For quotes from the meeting at which Begin informed Vance of a plan for Palestinian "home rule," see *FRUS*, VIII, pp. 814–15. During a discussion six days later, Carter opened by telling Begin that the ball was now in his court: "President Sadat's action was dramatic and far-reaching. It was almost the ultimate concession that he could make, a guarantee of real peace. He will even agree to withdraw most of his troops from Sinai. The world is now awaiting your response." *FRUS*, VIII, p. 862.

38. On prior approval for Begin's plan by the security cabinet, see Shlaim, *The Iron Wall*, p. 372. *FRUS*, VIII, p. 870. For Begin's quotes ("including perhaps sovereignty" and "He can take credit"), see *FRUS*, VIII, p. 881.

39. For the text of Begin's plan for "Home Rule for Palestinian Arabs, Residents of Judea, Samaria and the Gaza District," see *FRUS*, VIII, pp. 871–72. Points 14, 15, and 16 state: "14. Residents of Judea, Samaria and the Gaza district, without distinction of citizenship, or if stateless, will be granted free choice (option) of either Israeli or Jordanian citizenship. 15. A resident of the areas of Judea, Samaria and the Gaza district who requests Israeli citizenship will be granted such citizenship in accordance with the citizenship law of the State. 16. Residents of Judea, Samaria and the Gaza district who, in accordance with the right of free option, choose Israeli citizenship, will be entitled to vote for, and be elected to, the Knesset in accordance with the election law." Point 19 states: "Residents of Israel will be entitled to acquire land and settle in the areas of Judea, Samaria and the Gaza district. Arabs, residents of Judea, Samaria and the Gaza district will be entitled to acquire land and settle in Israel." The plan approved by the Knesset later that month was modified to remove the provision for unrestricted land purchase for all Arabs, making land purchase in Israel available only to those Arabs who had chosen Israeli citizenship. Compare Point 19 of the original plan to Point 20 of the plan approved by the Knesset. For the Knesset-approved plan and Begin's quotes ("fairness," "Rhodesia," and "anti-racialism"), see Israel Ministry of Foreign Affairs, "Statement to the Knesset by Prime Minister Begin

Presenting Israel's Peace Plan—28 December 1977," accessed September 29, 2016, http://mfa.gov.il/MFA/ForeignPolicy/MFADocuments/Yearbook3/Pages/103 Statement to the Knesset by Prime Minister Beg.aspx.

40. *FRUS*, VIII, p. 671.

41. For text of the Framework for Peace, see "The Camp David Accords: The Framework for Peace in the Middle East," Jimmy Carter Presidential Library (online), accessed September 29, 2016, http://www.jimmycarterlibrary.gov/documents/campdavid /accords.phtm/. For the Framework serving as the basis of Oslo, see Dennis Ross, who writes: "Yitzhak Rabin would insist in the secret Oslo talks that the essential elements from the CDA [Camp David Agreement] framework provide the basis for the Declaration of Principles that would be signed at the Clinton White House in September 1993." Ross, *Doomed to Succeed*, p. 168. For the invitation letter to the 1991 Madrid Peace Conference, which reproduced the main points of the 1978 Camp David Framework, see Israel Ministry of Foreign Affairs, "Letter of Invitation to Madrid Peace Conference, October 30, 1991," accessed October 7, 2016, http://www.mfa.gov.il/mfa/foreignpolicy/peace/guide/pages/madridletterofinvita tion.aspx; see also Yossi Beilin, *The Path to Geneva: The Quest for a Permanent Solution, 1996–2003*, (New York: RDV Books/Akashic Books, 2004), pp. 47–48.

42. For the texts of the two agreements, see "The Camp David Accords," cited above, and Israel Ministry of Foreign Affairs, "Declaration of Principles on Interim Self-Government Arrangements September 13, 1993," accessed September 29, 2016, http://www.mfa.gov.il/mfa/foreignpolicy/peace/guide/pages/declarationofprinci ples.aspx. For Security Council Resolution 242, see "S/RES/242 (1967)," United Nations, November 22, 1967.

43. On Sadat and Carter colluding on a plan to force an agreement on Begin, see *FRUS*, VIII, pp. 984–87. Quandt writes that "the idea arose of trying to work out with Sadat a means for resuming the negotiating process that would put pressure on Begin. . . . Sadat should put forward an Egyptian plan for the West Bank and Gaza. . . . Carter would have an understanding in advance with Sadat that at a mutually agreed moment an American compromise proposal would be put forward—and Sadat would accept it. Then the full burden of American influence could be turned on Begin, without Carter being vulnerable to the charge of applying one-sided pressure on Israel." Quandt, *Camp David*, pp. 173, 175–77. For Carter's statement to Begin on Israel as "the main obstacle to peace," see *FRUS*, VIII, p. 1079. For Dayan's quote ("fury in his cold blue eyes") and Begin's admission that the meeting was one of the most difficult moments of his life, see Shlaim, *The Iron Wall*, p. 378. For Carter's quote to a group of Senate leaders, see Ross, *Doomed to Succeed*, pp. 385–86. For Israel's failed effort to block arms sales to the Saudis, see Quandt, *Camp David*, pp. 195–96, 200, 210. For Sharon's quote ("sowing the seeds for war"), see Quandt, *Camp David*, p. 202.

44. For the texts of the two agreements, see "The Camp David Accords," cited above, and Israel Ministry of Foreign Affairs, "Declaration of Principles on Interim Self-Government Arrangements September 13, 1993," accessed September 29, 2016. For Security Council Resolution 242, see "S/RES/242 (1967)," United Nations, November 22, 1967. On Carter's threat to Begin of American censure and warning to Sadat of the end of US-Egyptian relations, see Quandt, *Camp David*, pp. 246–47. On the eleventh day of the summit, Carter asked his aides to draft a "failure speech" blaming Begin for the collapse of the negotiations. On the same day, Car-

ter warned Sadat against leaving the talks: "'It will mean first of all an end to the relationship between the United States and Egypt. There is no way we can ever explain this to our people. It would mean an end to this peacekeeping effort, in which I have put so much investment. It would probably mean the end of my Presidency because this whole effort will be discredited. And last but not least, it will mean the end of something that is very precious to me: my friendship with you.' . . . Sadat appeared to be shaken by the force of Carter's argument." At the time Carter made this threat, Egypt was receiving over $900 million per year in US assistance, a figure that would rise considerably after the peace agreement. According to the Congressional Research Service, "In the late 1970s, U.S. aid to Egypt was substantial when compared to both the size of the Egyptian economy and the government's budget." Jeremy M. Sharp, "Egypt: Background and U.S. Relations," Congressional Research Service, February 25, 2016, pp. 18–19, 24.

45. Charles D. Freilich, *Zion's Dilemmas: How Israel Makes National Security Policy* (Ithaca, NY: Cornell University Press, 2012), pp. 82–83. Although Carter threatened Begin with the end of US aid, his threats against Sadat—the end of US-Egyptian relations—were more severe, and the final framework agreements reflect the greater pressure placed on Sadat: they took Begin's earlier concessions from his December 1977 autonomy plan and coupled them with an Egyptian-Israeli agreement on Sinai. Quandt writes of Sadat: "Instead of cornering Begin with his strategy of brinkmanship, in which Carter was to be assigned the crucial role as co-conspirator, Sadat found himself the target of relentless pressures for concessions." And of Carter, Quandt writes: "once again, faced with the choice of pressuring Begin or Sadat for concessions, he turned to Sadat." Quandt, *Camp David*, pp. 226, 266, 174.

46. On Begin's December 1977 autonomy plan as the basis of the Camp David agreement, see Quandt, *Camp David*, p. 218. Quandt describes an American strategy paper prepared in advance of the Camp David summit: "The key idea was to refashion Begin's autonomy plan into a proposal for an interim regime for the West Bank and Gaza that would offer the Palestinians a serious measure of self government." He writes that the Americans entered Camp David thinking that Israel's withdrawal from Sinai would be easy to resolve and that the greatest difficulty, toward which "almost all the American effort was aimed," was the Palestinian issue. Quandt, *Camp David*, p. 223.

47. Sayigh, *Armed Struggle and the Search for State*, p. 337.

48. For the Ben Gurion quote, the Soviet letter, and Eisenhower's ultimatum, see Shlaim, *Iron Wall*, pp. 191–92.

49. Abraham Rabinovich, *The Yom Kippur War: The Epic Encounter That Transformed the Middle East* (New York: Schocken, 2007), p. 209.

50. On Israel's two withdrawals in 1974, see Avi Kober, *Israel's Wars of Attrition: Attrition Challenges to Democratic States* (New York: Routledge, 2009), p. 81: "In order to pressure Israel to withdraw its forces from the heart of their country, the Egyptians adopted coercive diplomacy, accompanying negotiations with Israel on a disengagement agreement with continuous barrages on Israeli troops on the west bank of the Suez Canal. Violence ended only after the signing of the disengagement agreement on 18 January 1974. In the Golan Heights, an eighty-day war of attrition accompanied the U.S.-mediated talks between Syria and Israel. The war peaked between 12 March 1974 and the signing of the disengagement agreement

in May 1974." Shlaim writes of the first Sinai agreement: "Israel made greater concessions in return for a military disengagement with Egypt in 1974 than those it
had refused to make in return for an interim agreement in the first half of 1971."
Still heavier US pressure forced Israel's reluctant acceptance of a second Sinai
withdrawal, in September 1975, during one of the most difficult periods in US-
Israel relations. The crisis began when President Gerald Ford blamed Israeli
intransigence for the collapse of talks over a second Sinai withdrawal in
March 1975. Ford sent a harsh letter to Prime Minister Yitzhak Rabin concerning
his "deep disappointment over the position taken by Israel." It stated that "vital
interests of the United States" had been at stake, that Israel's rejection of a "reasonable" proposal would "have far-reaching effects in the area and on our relations,"
and that the United States would now begin a period of "reassessment" of its
regional policies, "including our relations with Israel." In the middle of the reassessment, during which the United States refused to sign any new arms deals with
Israel, Ford offered Rabin two ways out: an Arab-Israeli conference for a comprehensive peace agreement based on Israeli withdrawal to the pre-1967 lines, which
Rabin wanted to avoid; or a second withdrawal from Sinai. Rabin agreed to
another Sinai withdrawal, and the reassessment came to an end. For more on the
first and second Sinai withdrawal agreements, see Shlaim, *The Iron Wall*, pp. 327,
340–46. For the quote from Israel's prime minister ("worst periods"), see Yitzhak
Rabin, *The Rabin Memoirs* (Berkeley: University of California Press, 1979), p. 261.
For the United States suspending consideration of economic assistance, see Nadav
Safran, *Israel: The Embattled Ally* (Cambridge, MA: Belknap Press, 1981), p. 548.

51. For the number killed during the Coastal Road massacre, see Israel Ministry of
Foreign Affairs, "32nd Anniversary of the Coastal Massacre," March 11, 2010,
accessed September 29, 2016, http://mfa.gov.il/MFA/ForeignPolicy/Terrorism
/Palestinian/Pages/32nd_anniversary_coastal_massacre_11-Mar-2010.aspx.
Other sources state that thirty-five or thirty-seven Israelis were killed. For the latter, see Ian Black and Benny Morris, *Israel's Secret Wars: A History of Israel's Intelligence Services* (New York: Grove Press, 1991), pp. 361–62. They write that, in
addition, nine of the eleven perpetrators were killed. Other sources state that the
number of perpetrators was twelve. For the Carter quotes, see Carter, *White House
Diary*, p. 179.

52. For the 1982 invasion and sense of quagmire, see Shlaim, *The Iron Wall*, pp. 430,
433, 437–40. For the recommendation of unilateral withdrawal, see Shlaim, *The
Iron Wall*, pp. 430, 433; Shapira, *Israel*, p. 383. For Begin's torment and the Begin
quotes ("war of choice" and "I cannot go on"), see Shlaim, *The Iron Wall*, pp. 431–
32; Shapira, *Israel*, p. 380. For the commission of inquiry, see Israel Ministry of
Foreign Affairs, "Report of the Commission of Inquiry into the Events at the Refugee Camps in Beirut—8 February 1983," accessed September 29, 2016, http://www
.mfa.gov.il/mfa/foreignpolicy/mfadocuments/yearbook6/pages/104 report of the
commission of inquiry into the e.aspx. For estimates of the number killed at Sabra
and Shatila, see Ze'ev Schiff and Ehud Ya'ari, *Israel's Lebanon War* (New York:
Simon & Schuster, 1984), p. 282. For the stages of Israel's pullout from Lebanon,
see Shlaim, *The Iron Wall*, pp. 430, 433–36, 437–42.

53. For Operation Grapes of Wrath and civilian deaths in Qana, see Shlaim, *The Iron
Wall*, pp. 580–84. (Sources vary on how many civilians were killed, with most citing
one of two numbers: 102 or 106. The figure of 102 comes from Amnesty Interna-

tional, "Unlawful Killings During Operation 'Grapes of Wrath,'" July 23, 1996.) For Netanyahu's departure from the previous Israeli insistence on a peace treaty for any withdrawal from Lebanon, see Shlaim, *The Iron Wall*, pp. 616–17, 619. (When Netanyahu's "Lebanon first" proposal—for withdrawal in return for the dismantlement of Hezbollah—was not accepted, he made several others: a multinational force to replace Israeli troops after they withdrew or a guarantee by the Lebanese government that it would take over the evacuated buffer zone and prevent attacks against Israel.) For the Israeli names for Lebanon (which also included "that cursed place," "the Valley of Death," and that "Moloch"), see Shlaim, *The Iron Wall*, p. 617. For the group of bereaved mothers, see "Israeli Mothers Who Called for Lebanon Pullout Say Work Is Done," Associated Press, June 6, 2000; Shlaim, *The Iron Wall*, p. 617. For Hezbollah's growing strength, the weakening of the South Lebanon Army, and the greater burden placed on Israel, see Shlaim, *The Iron Wall*, pp. 616–19, 670–73. For Barak's campaign promise, see Shlaim, *The Iron Wall*, p. 643. For the objections of the IDF chief of staff, see Shlaim, *The Iron Wall*, pp. 670–73.

54. For the doubling and tripling of IDF deployments in the West Bank and Gaza, see remarks by IDF Chief of Staff Dan Shomron in "Israel Prepares for Violence on Anniversary of Al Fatah," Associated Press, December 29, 1987; see also Hillel Frisch, "The West Bank and the Gaza Strip: The Intifada," in *Middle East Contemporary Survey*, vol. 12: 1988, Ami Ayalon and Haim Shaked, eds. (Boulder, CO: Westview Press, 1990), p. 292; Sayigh, *Armed Struggle and the Search for State*, p. 619. For King Hussein's quotes, see Shlaim, *The Iron Wall*, p. 473. Members of the Israeli right and a few Jordanian figures have continued to discuss the possibility of Jordanian rule in the West Bank, but Jordan and the PLO are both opposed to the idea. See Hassan A. Barari, "Four Decades After Black September: A Jordanian Perspective," *Civil Wars* 10, no. 3 (2008): 231–43.

55. On the same day, in another UN resolution, 138 member states welcomed the PLO's declaration, called for its participation at an international peace conference, and affirmed that among the principles necessary for peace were "the withdrawal of Israel from the Palestinian territory occupied since 1967, including Jerusalem, and from the other occupied Arab territories"; "dismantling the Israeli settlements"; and "resolving the problem of the Palestine refugees in conformity with General Assembly Resolution 194 (III) of 11 December 1948, and subsequent relevant resolutions." Israel and the United States were the only countries to vote against the two resolutions (43/176 and 43/177).

56. For the understanding of Israeli leaders that military means were insufficient, see comments by IDF Chief of Staff Dan Shomron ("there is no such thing as eradicating the intifada because in its essence it expresses the struggle of nationalism") in Glenn Frankel, *Beyond the Promised Land: Jews and Arabs on the Hard Road to a New Israel* (New York: Simon & Schuster, 1994), p. 88. For comments by the IDF chief of staff, the head of central command, and the head of the analysis branch of military intelligence, all of whom said that military measures were insufficient to stop the violence, see Beilin, *The Path to Geneva*, p. 290; Aluf Benn, "The Army Is Dictating Policy," *Haaretz*, August 8, 2002; Tamir Libel and Shlomo Shpiro, "Israeli Intelligence Threat Perceptions of Palestinian Terrorist Organizations, 1948–2008," in *The Image of the Enemy: Intelligence Analysis of Adversaries Since 1945*, Paul Maddrell, ed. (Washington, DC: Georgetown University Press, 2015),

p. 201. For the US push for Israel to accept or produce a new peace plan, see Dan Fisher, "Shamir Shuns U.S. Deadline on Peace Plan: Won't Bring Initiative to Cabinet Vote Before His Washington Visit," *The Los Angeles Times*, March 7, 1988; Shlaim, *The Iron Wall* pp. 470–72, 483. For Rabin's 1989 proposal, see Shlaim, *The Iron Wall*, p. 483. For Shamir's plan, see Shlaim, *The Iron Wall*, pp. 483–86.

57. For Rabin's election and the increasing strength of Hamas and Islamic Jihad, see Shlaim, *The Iron Wall*, p. 533. For the growing violence of the intifada (Hamas and Islamic Jihad killed six IDF soldiers in seven days, resulting in the deportation of 415 of their members to Lebanon), see Graham Usher, *Dispatches from Palestine: The Rise and Fall of the Oslo Peace Process* (London: Pluto Press, 1999), p. 18; Shlaim, *The Iron Wall*, p. 527; Michael Parks, "Palestinians Return from Lebanon Exile," *The Los Angeles Times*, December 16, 1993. For the violence in March, the sealing of the Occupied Territories "until further notice," and the near hysteria of the Israeli press at this time, see Usher, *Dispatches from Palestine*, pp. 12–13, 15. For Israelis stressing the urgency of a political solution and asking Palestinians in Oslo to stop the intifada, see Shlaim, *The Iron Wall*, p. 533; Mahmoud Abbas, *Through Secret Channels: The Road to Oslo, Senior PLO Leader Abu Mazen's Revealing Story of the Negotiations with Israel* (London: Garnet Publishing, 1995), pp. 179–80. For the debate over withdrawal from Gaza and the summer 1993 poll, see Shlaim, *The Iron Wall*, pp. 531–32; Abbas, *Through Secret Channels*, p. 199. For Rabin's quotes ("take Gaza out of Tel Aviv" and "swarming around here"), see Usher, *Dispatches from Palestine*, p. 13. For reports to Rabin on Oslo, see Shlaim, *The Iron Wall*, pp. 530–41; Hilde Henriksen Waage, "Norway's Role in the Middle East Peace Talks: Between a Strong State and a Weak Belligerent," *Journal of Palestine Studies* 34, no. 4 (2004–2005): 6–24.

58. For the text of Oslo, see Israel Ministry of Foreign Affairs, "Declaration of Principles on Interim Self-Government Arrangements September 13, 1993," accessed September 29, 2016. For attacks on Oslo by the Israeli right (Likud leader Benjamin Netanyahu promised to cancel Oslo, called the agreement appeasement, and said to Peres, "You are even worse than Chamberlain. He imperiled the safety of another people, but you are doing it to your own people"), see Shlaim, *The Iron Wall*, p. 539. On Rabin's insistence that the Camp David framework agreement serve as the basis of the Oslo negotiations, see Ross, *Doomed to Succeed*, p. 168; see also Beilin, *The Path to Geneva*, pp. 47–48. For Rabin's quote ("less than a state"), see Israel Ministry of Foreign Affairs, "Address to the Knesset by Prime Minister Rabin on the Israel-Palestinian Interim Agreement," October 5, 1995, accessed October 1, 2016, http://www.mfa.gov.il/mfa/foreignpolicy/mfadocuments/yearbook10/pages /address to the knesset by prime minister rabin on.aspx. A Palestinian negotiator during the early Oslo period told me that he and others hoped Rabin's statement to the Knesset represented a harder line than his private views and that, whatever Rabin's true beliefs regarding Palestinian statehood, it seemed to the Palestinian team that several of the Israeli negotiators had come around to the idea. Phone interview by the author with Palestinian negotiator, August 18, 2016. In his memoir, former Israeli foreign minister Shlomo Ben-Ami wrote that Rabin—his colleague in the Labor Party—did not support Palestinian statehood: "As a matter of fact, neither Rabin nor, especially, Peres wanted autonomy to usher in a Palestinian state. As late as 1997—that is, four years into the Oslo process when, as the chairman of the Labour Party's Foreign Affairs Committee I proposed for the first

time that the party endorse the idea of a Palestinian state—it was Shimon Peres who most vehemently opposed the idea." Shlomo Ben-Ami, *Scars of War, Wounds of Peace: The Israeli-Arab Tragedy* (New York: Oxford University Press, 2007), p. 220.

59. For the sharp rise in violence after the Oslo signing, see Israel Ministry of Foreign Affairs, "Terrorism Deaths in Israel-1920–1999," January 1, 2000, accessed October 1, 2016, http://mfa.gov.il/MFA/MFA-Archive/2000/Pages/Terrorism deaths in Israel-1920–1999.aspx; Israel Ministry of Foreign Affairs, "Fatal Terrorist Attacks in Israel (Sept 1993–1999)," September 24, 2000, accessed October 1, 2016, http://www.mfa.gov.il/MFA/ForeignPolicy/Terrorism/Palestinian/Pages/Fatal Terrorist Attacks in Israel Since the DOP -S.aspx. For the "first—and last" quip, for which Shlaim gives original credit to Mahmoud Darwish and for which others have credited Shafiq al-Hout, see Shlaim, *The Iron Wall*, p. 540; Barry M. Rubin, *Revolution Until Victory?: The Politics and History of the PLO* (Cambridge, MA: Harvard University Press, 1994), p. 203.

60. On Oslo allowing Israel to repackage rather than end its control and making resistance easier to contain, see Shlaim, *The Iron Wall*, p. 542. For the Rabin quote ("do what they will do"), see Usher, *Dispatches from Palestine*, p. 74. Rabin's mention of the Association for Civil Rights in Israel was not accidental. During the First Intifada, when he was defense minister, the organization had brought a case to the Supreme Court that had cast Rabin in a terrible light. In the village of Hawara, south of Nablus, IDF soldiers took twelve young men, handcuffed them, shackled their legs, placed them facedown on the ground, and beat them with clubs, breaking their arms and legs. Court testimony from the local officers later revealed that before the incident Rabin had traveled to Nablus and given the following orders: 'You must catch them and break their arms and legs. . . . Go in and break their bones.'" Frankel, *Beyond the Promised Land*, pp. 75–82.

61. Counting each calendar year from the beginning of 1975 to the end of 1993. According to the Israeli government, the last year prior to 1994 in which as many died from Palestinian attacks was 1974, when 67 were killed. Of the 64 killed by suicide bombing from July 1994 to September 1995, 61 were Israeli, two were American, and one was Dutch; the number does not include perpetrators killed in the attacks. Israel Ministry of Foreign Affairs, "Terrorism Deaths in Israel-1920–1999," January 1, 2000, accessed October 1, 2016; Israel Ministry of Foreign Affairs, "Fatal Terrorist Attacks in Israel (Sept 1993–1999)," September 24, 2000, accessed October 1, 2016; "Yasser Arafat Ends 27-Year Exile," BBC, July 1, 1994.

62. The Temple Mount is considered by many Jews to be the holiest site of their faith, although a majority of Israelis (69 percent) say they believe the holiest site in Judaism is the Western Wall. See Kobi Nachshoni, "Poll: Israel's Jews Abandoning Temple," *Ynet*, July 16, 2013. The Noble Sanctuary refers to an elevated plaza housing two main structures, the al-Aqsa Mosque and the Dome of the Rock. In Islam, the entire Noble Sanctuary, not just its two main structures, has the sanctity of a mosque, and it is common for Muslims to refer to the Noble Sanctuary as al-Aqsa Mosque. See International Crisis Group, "The Status of the Status Quo at Jerusalem's Holy Esplanade," *Middle East Report*, no. 159, June 30 2015, p. 1. For the Netanyahu quote ("expresses our sovereignty"), see Anthony Lewis, "Which Israel?," *The New York Times*, September 30, 1996. For two common

estimates of the number of Palestinians killed in the tunnel riots (Shlaim: 80 Palestinians; Herzog: 84 Palestinians), see Shlaim, *The Iron Wall*, p. 598; Chaim Herzog (updated by Shlomo Gazit), *The Arab-Israeli Wars: War and Peace in the Middle East* (New York: Vintage, 2005), p. 422. For the worst violence since the height of the intifada, see Shlaim, *The Iron Wall*, pp. 598–99; Usher, *Dispatches from Palestine*, p. 117. Names used by Palestinians for the tunnel riots include "the tunnel upheaval" (*habba al-nafaq*) and, more commonly, "the tunnel uprising" (*intifada al-nafaq*).

63. For the Security Council resolution, see "S/RES/1073 (1996)," United Nations Security Council, September 28, 1996. For the summit and Netanyahu's promise, see Ross, *The Missing Peace: The Inside Story of the Fight for Middle East Peace* (New York: Farrar, Straus and Giroux, 2004), pp. 266–68. For details of the Hebron Protocol and the attached "Note for the Record" (the latter called on Israel to release prisoners and set a March 1997 deadline for Israel's redeployment), see "Note for the Record, January 15, 1997," United States Institute of Peace, Peace Agreements Digital Collection, accessed October 1, 2016, http://www.usip.org /sites/default/files/file/resources/collections/peace_agreements/note_for_record .pdf; Israel Ministry of Foreign Affairs, "Protocol Concerning the Redeployment in Hebron, 17 January 1997," accessed October 1, 2016, http://www.mfa.gov.il/mfa /foreignpolicy/peace/guide/pages/protocol concerning the redeployment in hebron .aspx; Shlaim, *The Iron Wall*, pp. 601–603; Ross, *The Missing Peace*, pp. 302–24. For the release of 31 prisoners (Ross writes that he was negotiating the release of 29 female prisoners), see "Question of the Violation of Human Rights in the Occupied Arab Territories, Including Palestine," United Nations, Commission on Human Rights, 53rd Session, February 19, 1997, https://unispal.un.org/DPA/DPR/unispal .nsf/0/B4BF26CDEC8333A8802564530035E48D. For the Wye Memorandum and the failure to implement much of it, see Israel Ministry of Foreign Affairs, "The Wye River Memorandum, 23 October 1998," accessed October 1, 2016, http://www .mfa.gov.il/mfa/foreignpolicy/peace/guide/pages/the wye river memorandum.aspx; Shlaim, *The Iron Wall*, pp. 633–39.

64. For Sharon as "the bulldozer," see Shlaim, *The Iron Wall*, p. 712. For Sharon's demand that an IDF general be fired, see Kobi Finkler, "Friends Tell of Dan Shomron," *Arutz Sheva* [Hebrew], November 16, 2014; Mazal Mualem, "Right Wing Declares Open Season on IDF Chief of Staff," *Al-Monitor*, February 22, 2015. For the quote ("Sharon offered a freeze") by Indyk, who accompanied Sharon on his first visit to President George W. Bush in March 2001, see Martin Indyk, *Innocent Abroad: An Intimate Account of American Peace Diplomacy in the Middle East* (New York: Simon & Schuster, 2009), pp. 377, 380.

65. For the refusal to visit by the Saudi Crown Prince (who also canceled a high-level defense meeting with the United States), as well as the quotes ("how can you possibly tolerate," "put U.S.-Saudi relations in the balance," and "responding to Saudi pressure"), see Elliott Abrams, *Tested by Zion: The Bush Administration and the Israeli-Palestinian Conflict* (Cambridge, UK: Cambridge University Press, 2013), pp. 14–15. For more details on the Saudi threats and the US endorsement of Palestinian statehood that resulted, see Robert G. Kaiser and David B. Ottaway, "Saudi Leader's Anger Revealed Shaky Ties," *The Washington Post*, February 10, 2002. According to a senior Saudi official quoted in the above article, in late August 2001 Crown Prince Abdullah instructed his ambassador to the United States, Prince

Bandar bin Sultan, to deliver the following message to national security adviser Condoleezza Rice and secretary of state Colin Powell: "'Starting from today, you're from Uruguay, as they say. You [Americans] go your way, I [Saudi Arabia] go my way. From now on, we will protect our national interests, regardless of where America's interests lie in the region.'" Bandar, the article states, "was instructed to cut off further discussion between the two countries. . . . over the next two days, the United States went to extraordinary lengths to try to repair the relationship, its closest with any Arab country, finally satisfying the Saudis with a personal letter to Abdullah from the president himself. . . . Bush's letter, according to Saudi officials, endorsed the idea of a viable Palestinian state on the West Bank and Gaza Strip." Abrams writes (pp. 36–37) that Crown Prince Abdullah made a similar threat to relations with the United States several months later, in April 2002, demanding that the United States end Israel's siege of Arafat at his headquarters in Ramallah. Bush wrote of that moment in his memoir: "America's pivotal relationship with Saudi Arabia was about to be seriously ruptured." For the change in policy reflected in the US endorsement of Palestinian statehood (which was first made privately, in the August 2001 letter to Crown Prince Abdullah, then publicly in an October 2001 statement to the press and a November 2001 speech to the UN), see Ross, *The Missing Peace*, p. 786, p. 848; Abrams, pp. 15, 22. Ross writes that it was Bush who had "establish[ed] for the first time that U.S. policy henceforth would be to support a two-state solution. . . . While the Clinton parameters presented to the two sides in December 2000 would have provided for an independent Palestinian state, the parameters represented ideas to resolve the differences between the two sides, were never stated as formal policy, and were withdrawn at the end of the administration." For Bush's first public support of Palestinian statehood and the administration's leaked plans for creating a Palestinian state in fall 2001, see James Bennet, "Sharon Apologizes over Dispute With U.S.," *The New York Times*, October 7, 2001; Abrams, pp. 21–24; "Bush 'Endorses' Palestinian State," BBC, October 2, 2001, http://news.bbc.co.uk/2/hi/middle_east/1575090.stm.

66. For the Security Council resolution on Palestinian statehood, see "S/RES/1397 (2002)," United Nations Security Council, March 12, 2002. The formal endorsement by Sharon's government was made in 2003, but Sharon himself had stated that he accepted a demilitarized Palestinian state in October 2001. See "World-Wide," *The Wall Street Journal*, October 17, 2001, p. A1; Jonathan Karp, "Radical Palestinian Group Assassinates Israeli Minister, Hurting Peace Process," *The Wall Street Journal*, October 18, 2001. Sharon's fall 2001 statement, the first of its kind that he had made as prime minister, did not put an unrealistic limit on the size of the Palestinian state, unlike his claim during his 2001 election campaign that he would offer the PLO something it would never accept: a demilitarized state in no more than 42 percent of the West Bank. See Anthony H. Cordesman (with the assistance of Jennifer Moravitz), *The Israeli-Palestinian War: Escalating to Nowhere* (Westport, CT: Praeger, 2005), p. 52. In November 2001, Sharon's chief foreign policy adviser, Zalman Shoval, described a new Israeli peace plan that included Palestinian statehood. See Sam Kiley, "Sharon Backs a Palestinian State," *Evening Standard*, November 8, 2001; Simon Jeffrey, "Sharon Endorses Palestinian State," *The Guardian*, June 4, 2003. (Sharon issued another statement of support for Palestinian statehood in 2002. "Sharon Tentatively Backs Plan for Palestinian State," *The New York Times*, December 5, 2002.) For Sharon leading the first Israeli government

to endorse Palestinian statehood, see James Bennet, "The Mideast Turmoil: Jerusalem; Israel Approves Bush's Road Map to New Palestine," *The New York Times*, May 26, 2003.

67. For Clinton's proposal, see Ross, *The Missing Peace*, pp. 809–13. Clinton's plan also called for a Palestinian state in Gaza and 95 to 99 percent of the West Bank; withdrawal of nearly all Israeli forces within three years (and the remainder—in the Jordan Valley—within another three); recognition of the right of Palestinian refugees to return to their homeland or to historic Palestine, subject to Israel's sovereign discretion; and the release of Palestinian prisoners. For details of the 2002 polls, see Ben-Dror Yemini, "Palestinians Are Not Exempt from Blame over Failure of Peace Talks," *Yediot Aharonot*, July 26, 2015; Raviv Drucker, "History Will Fault Netanyahu, but Not for Iran Deal," *Haaretz*, July 20, 2015. Similarly, in annual polls from 1987 to 2005, support for the establishment of a Palestinian state reached an all-time high (59 percent) in 2003. Yehuda Ben Meir and Olena Bagno-Moldavsky, "The Voice of the People: Israeli Public Opinion on National Security 2012," The Institute for National Security Studies, April 2013, p. 78. For the Abrams quote ("the bloodshed was so great"), see Abrams, *Tested by Zion*, pp. 27–28. For the open letters to Sharon, see David Landau, *Arik: The Life of Ariel Sharon* (New York: Knopf, 2014), pp. 456–57; Amos Harel, "13 Elite Reservists Refuse to Serve in Territories," *Haaretz*, December 22, 2003. For the interview with four former chiefs of the Shin Bet, see Landau, *Arik*, pp. 457–58.

68. For the April 2001 report, see "Sharm el-Sheikh Fact-Finding Committee—The Mitchell Plan, April 30, 2001," The Avalon Project, Yale Law School, accessed October 3, 2016, http://avalon.law.yale.edu/21st_century/mitchell_plan.asp. For Sharon's Czechoslovakia speech—which, according to Sharon's foreign minister, Shimon Peres, as well as a Sharon adviser who spoke to Abrams, was impelled by the news of an imminent US peace plan that would establish a Palestinian state—see Israel Ministry of Foreign Affairs, "Statement by Israeli PM Ariel Sharon–4 Oct 2001," accessed October 2, 2016, http://mfa.gov.il/MFA/PressRoom/2001/Pages/Statement by Israeli PM Ariel Sharon - 4-Oct-2001.aspx; James Bennet, "Sharon Apologizes over Dispute with U.S.," *The New York Times*, October 7, 2001. The United States postponed the plan and then took up a different one, the Roadmap, instead. For the Arab Peace Initiative, which was welcomed by the Security Council and included in the Quartet's 2003 Roadmap (see below) as one of the foundations of a settlement, see Israel Ministry of Foreign Affairs, "A Performance-Based Roadmap to a Permanent Two-State Solution to the Israeli-Palestinian Conflict," April 30, 2003, accessed October 2, 2016, http://www.mfa.gov.il/mfa/foreignpolicy/peace/guide/pages/a performance-based roadmap to a permanent two-sta.aspx; "S/RES/1397 (2002)," United Nations Security Council, March 12, 2002. For the People's Voice Initiative and its endorsement, see Abrams, *Tested by Zion*, pp. 84–85; Landau, *Arik*, pp. 457–58. For the Geneva Initiative and the official responses to it, see Abrams, pp. 85–86.

69. For text of the Roadmap, see above. For Israel's reservations, see "Israel's Road Map Reservations," *Haaretz*, May 27, 2003. For Sharon's statement to the Likud conference ("yes, it is occupation"), see Gideon Alon, "Irate Likud MKs Put PM on the Defensive," *Haaretz*, May 27, 2003. For the Security Council's endorsement of the Roadmap, see "Security Council Adopts Resolution Endorsing Road Map

Leading Towards Two-State Resolution of Israeli-Palestinian Conflict," United Nations, November 19, 2013, http://www.un.org/press/en/2003/sc7924.doc.htm; "S/RES/1515 (2003)," United Nations Security Council, November 19, 2003. For Sharon's statement to Bush ("better to take steps ourselves"), see Abrams, *Tested by Zion*, p. 131. In a 2004 interview with *Haaretz*, Sharon's close adviser and chief of staff, Dov ("Dubi") Weissglas, gave a similar explanation for the withdrawal: "In the fall of 2003 . . . Arik grasped that this state of affairs would not last. That they [the Americans] wouldn't leave us alone, wouldn't get off our case. Time was not on our side." Ari Shavit, "The Big Freeze," *Haaretz*, October 7, 2004.

70. On the origins of the security barrier, see Lev Luis Grinberg, *Politics and Violence in Israel/Palestine: Democracy Versus Military Rule* (New York: Routledge, 2009), pp. 78–81; David Makovsky, "How to Build a Fence," *Foreign Affairs*, March/April 2004; Robert B. Lloyd, "On the Fence: Negotiating Israel's Security Barrier," *The Journal of the Middle East and Africa* 3 (2012); Shlaim, *The Iron Wall*, pp. 751–56. Israel began constructing a fence around Gaza shortly after the establishment of the Palestinian Authority in 1994. In early 1995, Rabin established a committee to consider building a security barrier in the West Bank as well. A precursor of the West Bank separation barrier was erected between the Jewish community of Bat Hefer and the Palestinian city of Tulkarm in the mid-1990s. Tracy Wilkinson, "Some Israelis Hoping for a Concrete Line in the Sand," *Los Angeles Times*, September 10, 2001. On the share of the West Bank separated by the barrier (the original route took up a higher percentage), see B'Tselem, "The Separation Barrier—Statistics," July 16, 2012, accessed October 3, 2016, http://www.btselem .org/separation_barrier/statistics. On the opposition from settlers (one settler leader said that "a separation fence within Judea and Samaria and little [pre-1967] Israel would in effect establish that to the east of the fence the Palestinian state would arise, and to the west, the state of Israel would remain in what Abba Eban called 'Auschwitz borders' "), see Grinberg, *Politics and Violence in Israel Palestine*, p. 221. For Sharon's December 2003 speech, see Israel Ministry of Foreign Affairs, "Address by PM Ariel Sharon at the Fourth Herzliya Conference—Dec 18, 2003," accessed October 3, 2016, http://mfa.gov.il/MFA/PressRoom/2003/Pages/Address by PM Ariel Sharon at the Fourth Herzliya.aspx.

71. For details on rocket attacks from Gaza (from 17 in 2002 to 123 in 2003 to more than double that number in 2004), see Israel Security Agency, "Analysis of Attacks in the Last Decade—Rocket Launching," accessed October 3, 2016, http://www .shabak.gov.il/English/EnTerrorData/decade/Rocket/Pages/default.aspx; Israel Security Agency, "Analysis of Attacks in the Last Decade—Mortar Shell Launching Attacks," accessed October 3, 2016, http://www.shabak.gov.il/English/EnTerrorData /decade/Mortar/Pages/default.aspx. For more on the first rocket and mortar attacks from Gaza (Hamas announced that it had fired a "Qassam 1" rocket at Israel in November 2001, and Palestinians began firing mortars at Israel and Gaza settlements earlier that year), see "Rocket Threat from the Gaza Strip, 2000–2007," Israel Intelligence Heritage and Commemoration Center, December 2007, pp. 4, 6, 32. For Sharon's first quote ("sorry, a relocation"), see James Bennet, "Angering Settlers, Sharon Says Most May Have to Leave Gaza," *The New York Times*, February 3, 2004. For Sharon's second quote ("friction between us and the Palestinians"), see Israel Ministry of Foreign Affairs, "Address by PM Ariel Sharon at the Fourth

Herzliya Conference—Dec 18, 2003," accessed October 3, 2016. For more on Sharon's reasoning at the time, see the comments by his adviser, Dov Weissglas: "Gaza cost us over 100 casualties that could not be explained, in the sense that [Sharon] knew that in the long term we will not stay in Gaza. However the final status negotiations start or end, there will be no Israelis in Gaza. So, what are the casualties for? And as to the internal situation, public support and public opinion regarding the government, we were in the very worst shape we had ever been." Abrams, *Tested by Zion*, p. 90.

72. For Sharon's stroke, see Conal Urquhart, "Israel Plunged into Crisis as Sharon Suffers Massive Stroke," *The Guardian*, October 5, 2006; Harriet Sherwood, "Former Israeli PM Ariel Sharon Dies After Eight-Year Coma," *The Guardian*, January 11, 2014. For Hamas's victory, see Scott Wilson, "Hamas Sweeps Palestinian Elections, Complicating Peace Efforts in Mideast," *The Washington Post*, January 27, 2006. For Olmert's promise to withdraw from the West Bank east of the barrier, see Jim Rutenberg and Steven Erlanger, "West Bank Pullout Gets a Nod from Bush," *The New York Times*, May 24, 2006; David Makovsky, "Olmert's Unilateral Option: An Early Assessment," The Washington Institute for Near East Policy, May 2006. For Olmert's cancelation of the withdrawal plan after the 2006 Lebanon war, see Doug Struck, "Israel Shelves Plan to Pull Out of Settlements in West Bank," *The Washington Post*, August 23, 2006.

73. For more on the fall 2015 violence, as well as the shorter-lived precursor that came one year earlier, see chapter 8. For the numbers killed during the first six months of the unrest, see Peter Beaumont, "Israel-Palestine: Outlook Bleak as Wave of Violence Passes Six-Month Mark," *The Guardian*, March 31, 2016; "U.N. Expert Decries Israeli Soldier's Killing of Palestinian Attacker," Reuters, March 30, 2016; B'Tselem, "Five Palestinians Killed When Israeli Military Fired at Protesters Near Gaza Perimeter Fence, December 2015–January 2016, February 22, 2016. (Several of the Palestinians were Gazans killed by Israeli fire at protests along the border. Four foreign nationals were also killed. Other news sources stated that "at least 190"—rather than "over 200"—Palestinians had been killed during this period. Israel says that more than 130—roughly two-thirds—of the Palestinians killed were assailants.) For the third intifada statements, see, for example, comments by the Labor Party's Omar Bar-Lev and Isaac Herzog, in Tamar Pileggi, "Labor Approves Herzog's Unilateral Pullout Plan," *The Times of Israel*, February 7, 2016; Daniel K. Eisenbud, "Herzog: There Must Be Immediate Disengagement Between Jews, Palestinians," *The Jerusalem Post*, March 15, 2016; "More Israeli-Palestinian Violence Fuels Talk of a Third Intifada," Reuters, October 10, 2015. For comments from senior generals on the need for larger political concessions, see statements by such figures as the head of military intelligence and the deputy head of COGAT in "IDF's Plan to Beat Terror: Peace Talks with the PA," *Israel National News*, February 22, 2016; "Senior IDF Official: Diplomatic Steps Have 'Weight' in Restraining Palestinian Violence," *The Jerusalem Post*, October 28, 2015.

74. In late 2014, 38 percent of the Israeli public supported withdrawing from Palestinian neighborhoods of East Jerusalem as part of a peace agreement. By late 2015, 69 percent expressed support. Zipi Israeli, "Public Opinion and National Security, Strategic Survey for Israel 2015–2016," The Institute for National Security Studies, p. 119. Numerous polls over the preceding years had shown large Israeli majorities opposed to dividing Jerusalem as part of a peace agreement. Polls by Israel's Insti-

tute for National Security Studies from 1994 to 2012 found majority support for withdrawing from "Arab neighborhoods of Jerusalem," excluding the Old City, in only one year—2001, the first full year of the Second Intifada—when support was 51 percent. From 2004 to 2012, a separate question was asked about withdrawal from the Old City's Temple Mount/Noble Sanctuary, and support never exceeded the level of 2004: 30 percent. "The Peace Index: July 2008," The Israel Democracy Institute, accessed October 3, 2016; Yehuda Ben Meir and Olena Bagno-Moldavsky, "Vox Populi: Trends in Israeli Public Opinion on National Security 2004–2009," The Institute for National Security Studies, November 2010, p. 80; Yehuda Ben Meir and Dafna Shaked, "The People Speak: Israeli Public Opinion on National Security 2005–2007," The Institute for National Security Studies, May 2007, p. 56; Yehuda Ben Meir and Olena Bagno-Moldavsky, "The Voice of the People: Israeli Public Opinion on National Security 2012," The Institute for National Security Studies, April 2013, p. 78. For text of the Labor Party plan and analysis of it, see Ameinu, "Labor Party Security and Peace Plan," February 11, 2016; Ofer Zalzberg, "The Israeli Labor Party's Separation Plan," Friedrich Ebert Stiftung, April 2016.

75. The desire to deny the effectiveness of force can be found in groups and individuals who object to any pressure on Israel, such as AIPAC, as well as in groups that more narrowly object to violence or sanctions or boycotts. Individuals often claim that whatever methods of coercion they oppose on moral grounds also happen to be ineffective. This is an example of what Robert Jervis has described as "irrational consistency." Robert Jervis, *Perception and Misperception in International Politics* (Princeton, NJ: Princeton University Press), 1976, pp. 128–43. For George W. Bush on "no daylight," as well as the claim by the former Israeli ambassador to the United States, Michael Oren, that "no daylight" is a "time-honored principle in the U.S.-Israel alliance," see Abrams, *Tested by Zion*, pp. 169, 308; Michael B. Oren, *Ally: My Journey Across the American-Israeli Divide* (New York: Random House, 2015), p. 113. For more on AIPAC and its influence in Washington, see Connie Bruck, "Friends of Israel," *The New Yorker*, September 1, 2014. The quote from the national security official comes from an interview with the author, Washington, DC, December 8, 2015.

76. For more on AIPAC, where Indyk was a deputy director of research, and the Washington Institute for Near East Policy (WINEP), where Indyk was the founding executive director and for which Ross wrote the first research paper, see "Martin S. Indyk—Biography," Brookings Institution, accessed October 3, 2016, https://www.brookings.edu/experts/martin-s-indyk; "Dennis Ross' 'Doomed to Succeed' Wins Prestigious Jewish Book Council Award," Washington Institute for Near East Policy, January 13, 2016; Helena Cobban, "Confessions of an AIPAC Veteran," *The Nation*, October 14, 2009. According to former AIPAC staffer M. J. Rosenberg, the Washington Institute was "created by AIPAC. How do I know? As an AIPAC staffer, I was in the room when AIPAC decided to establish WINEP.... WINEP was to be AIPAC's cutout. It was funded by AIPAC donors, staffed by AIPAC employees, and located one door away, down the hall, from AIPAC headquarters." Rosenberg quotes another AIPAC staff member who was present at the same meeting: "It was suggested ... that we split the AIPAC research department into two parts, a minor part to service the legislative lobbying, and the major part to become a 501(C)3 that could raise big bucks tax-free, unlike AIPAC itself." M. J. Rosenberg, "The Think Tank AIPAC Built: The Washington Institute for Near East

Policy," Political Correction, Media Matters Action Network, April 13, 2010. For Indyk's quote, see Indyk, *Innocent Abroad*, p. 408.

77. For the quotes from Ross's book, see Ross, *Doomed to Succeed*, pp. 50, 349. In the first quoted passage ("we never benefited"), Ross is speaking specifically of benefits that the United States received from Arab states. But elsewhere, such as in the jacket copy, he makes the broader claim that "distancing the United States from Israel . . . never yielded any benefits." For an incisive review of Ross's book, see Ahmad Samih Khalidi, "Fantasies of a Middle East Envoy," *The Cairo Review of Global Affairs*, Spring 2016. For Ross's statement to a Jewish audience at a New York synagogue, where he appeared alongside former Israeli prime minister Ehud Barak and Rabbi Angela Buchdahl, see Philip Weiss, "Dennis Ross Tells American Jews, 'We Need to Be Advocates for Israel'—and Not for Palestinians," Mondoweiss.net, June 17, 2016. Weiss was the only journalist to report on the event. At the bottom of his article he noted: "The Central Synagogue has objected to us that the event was off the record. The invitation to the event did not say so, and when a synagogue brings in a foreign leader to attack the president's foreign policy in front of 500 cheering people—with no demurral from the rabbi sitting at his side, after everyone in the synagogue has stood to sing the national anthem of that foreign country (yes, along with the Star-Spangled Banner)—other Americans have a right to know about it."

78. Ross, *Doomed to Succeed*, p. 389.

79. Menachem Begin, *The Revolt* (New York: Nash Publishing, 1977), p. 36.

80. At several junctures, it seemed the PLO's path to statehood would be closed, either through Israeli annexation, establishing limited autonomy led by local leaders in the West Bank and Gaza at the expense of the PLO in exile, or Israel and Jordan reaching a separate agreement over the West Bank.

81. In 1947, just under 32 percent of the population of Palestine was Jewish (630,000 Jews out of a total population of 1,970,000). In 1946, the figure was just under 30 percent. See Sergio DellaPergola, "Demographic Trends in Israel and Palestine: Prospects and Policy Implications," *American Jewish Yearbook*, 2003, p. 11; *Israel in the Middle East: Documents and Readings on Society, Politics, and Foreign Relations, Pre-1948 to the Present*, Itamar Rabinovich and Jehuda Reinharz, eds. (Waltham, MA: Brandeis University Press, 2008), pp. 571–72. On the figure of less than 7 percent of the land, see Rashid Khalidi's response to Kenneth W. Stein, "Letters," *Journal of Palestine Studies* 17, no. 4 (Summer 1988): 254–56; Gershon Shafir, *Land, Labor and the Origins of the Israeli-Palestinian Conflict, 1882–1914* (Berkeley: University of California Press, 1996), p. 198; and for a similar figure—of exactly 7 percent—see *Encyclopedia of the Palestinians*, edited by Philip Mattar (New York: Facts on File, 2005), p. 125. On Israel outnumbering Arab forces at every stage of the 1948 war, see Avi Shlaim, "Israel and the Arab Coalition in 1948," in *The War for Palestine: Rewriting the History of 1948*, Eugene L. Rogan and Avi Shlaim, eds. (Cambridge, UK: Cambridge University Press, 2001), p. 81. See also Mattar, p. 44; Benny Morris, *The Birth of the Palestinian Refugee Problem Revisited* (Cambridge, UK: Cambridge University Press, 2004), pp. 16–17. Shlaim writes: "at each stage of the war, the IDF outnumbered all the Arab forces arrayed against it, and, after the first round of fighting, it outgunned them too. The final outcome of the war was therefore not a miracle but a faithful reflection of the underlying military balance in the Palestine theater. In this war, as in most wars, the stronger side prevailed."

82. On the US and UK peace plan, codenamed Alpha, see Shapira, *Israel*, pp. 278–79; Michael R. Fischbach, *Records of Dispossession: Palestinian Refugee Property and the Arab-Israeli Conflict* (New York: Columbia University Press, 2003), p. 226. The plan also called on Israel to allow an international regime in Jerusalem, repatriate 75,000 to 100,000 refugees, pay £100 million in compensation for refugee property, and give up large parts of the Negev desert to Jordan and Egypt, creating a land bridge between the two. For the Shapira quote, see Shapira, p. 283, who writes on the same page: "the Sinai Campaign was a turning point in Israel's standing in both the Middle East and the world. The IDF's power and military capability convinced the Great Powers that Israel was there to stay, and would not disappear from the map."

83. For the Khartoum summit and the statement from Aharon Yariv, see Shlaim, *The Iron Wall*, p. 277. For a more detailed account showing that Egypt and Jordan's acceptance of Security Council Resolution 242 later that year was the culmination of the Khartoum Conference, not a contradiction of it, see Yoram Meital, "The Khartoum Conference and Egyptian Policy After the 1967 War: A Reexamination," *Middle East Journal* 54, no. 1 (Winter 2000): 64–82.

84. For the number killed in Black September, see Sayigh, *Armed Struggle and the Search for State*, p. 267, who writes that the dead included over 600 Jordanian soldiers, 910–960 Palestinian fighters (of whom over 400 belonged to Fatah), and 1,500–3,500 civilians, mostly Palestinians in Amman. For the group that joined the pragmatic camp (the Democratic Front for the Liberation of Palestine), see Sayigh, p. 683. For the quote from a deputy chief of the PLO (Salah Khalaf), see Rubin, *Revolution Until Victory?*, p. 37.

85. For the loss of hope in a liberation strategy of people's war modeled on China and Vietnam, see Sayigh, *Armed Struggle and the Search for State*, p. 683. For the shift toward increasing terrorism, see Sayigh, pp. 280–81, 683–84; Rubin, *Revolution Until Victory?*, pp. 37–42. Sayigh writes that the final battle in Jordan "represented a defeat of the strategy of people's war championed by the various guerrilla groups since 1967, and posed a fundamental challenge to their professed aims, political programs, and organizational structure. . . . The phase of revolutionary *élan* and fervor was over."

86. Rubin, *Revolution Until Victory?*, p. 40.

87. For text of the quoted 1968 PLO charter and discussion of the revisions made from the 1964 version, see "The Palestinian National Charter: Resolutions of the Palestine National Council, July 1–17, 1968," The Avalon Project, Yale Law School, accessed October 4, 2016; Asher Susser, *Israel, Jordan, and Palestine: The Two-State Imperative* (Waltham, MA: Brandeis University Press, 2012), pp. 26–27; Hussam Mohamad, "PLO Strategy: From Total Liberation to Coexistence," *Palestine-Israel Journal* 4, no. 2 (1997). For the PNC quote ("including Muslims, Christians, and Jews") and Arafat quote ("allow Jews to live in dignity"), see Rubin, *Revolution Until Victory?*, p. 40. For more on the PLO's call for a secular democratic state, formally approved at the eighth PNC session, in Cairo, from February 28 to March 5, 1971, see "The PNC: Historical Background," *Journal of Palestine Studies* 16, no. 4 (Summer 1987): 151. For a skeptical view of this slogan, see Salim Tamari, "The Dubious Lure of Binationalism," *Journal of Palestine Studies* 30, no. 1 (Autumn 2000): 85.

88. This was the head of the PLO's second-largest faction, Sa'iqa, which was under strong Syrian influence. Shafiq al-Hout, *My Life in the PLO* (London: Pluto Press, 2011), p. 120.

89. For the PLO's struggle for influence in the West Bank in the 1970s, see Moshe Ma'oz, *Palestinian Leadership on the West Bank: The Changing Role of the Mayors Under Jordan and Israel* (New York: Routledge, 2015), pp. 110–19. For the Kissinger quote ("Arafat will be the spokesman"), see Henry Kissinger, *Years of Upheaval* (Boston: Little, Brown, 1982), p. 972. For the quotes from the PLO's weekly publication ("handover of our Palestinian land") and the head of a PLO faction ("relinquished the Bank and the Strip to the Jordanian regime"), see Sayigh, *Armed Struggle and the Search for State*, pp. 337–38.

90. The ten-point program also moderated the 1968 charter's insistence that "armed struggle is the only way to liberate Palestine," stating instead that the PLO would "employ all means," of which armed struggle was now "foremost." See *Middle East Contemporary Survey*, vol. I: 1976–77, Colin Legum, ed. (New York: Holmes and Meier, 1978), p. 187. For the Arab League endorsement, see Shlaim, *The Iron Wall*, pp. 337–39.

91. For text of the Tripartite Communiqué (signed by Arafat while Jordan and Israel were holding talks over dividing the West Bank), see "Arab Documents on Palestine and the Arab-Israeli Conflict," *Journal of Palestine Studies* 4, no. 2 (Winter 1975): 164–165. For the Jordan-Israel talks held when the PLO signed the communiqué, see Shlaim, *The Iron Wall*, p. 338. For Syria and Egypt's acceptance of Israel in Resolutions 242 and 338 and their use of Occupied Territories to refer to those conquered in 1967, see Sayigh, *Armed Struggle and the Search for State*, p. 149; *FRUS*, VIII, pp. 243–44. Syria stated its willingness to accept Resolution 242 (offering peace and recognition to Israel in exchange for withdrawal) in March 1972, and within a day of the adoption of Resolution 338 both countries had accepted it (Resolution 338 called for immediate implementation of Resolution 242). For Syria's acceptance of Resolution 338, see Israel Ministry of Foreign Affairs, "Syria Accepts the Cease-Fire—Letter from the Deputy Minister of Foreign Affairs of Syria—23 October 1973," accessed December 28, 2016, http://mfa.gov.il/MFA/Foreign Policy/MFADocuments/Yearbook1/Pages/11 Syria Accepts the Cease-Fire- Letter from the D.aspx. For the Popular Front quote ("drop by drop"), see Sayigh, *Armed Struggle and the Search for State*, p. 344.

92. For the PLO defeats in Lebanon and the intervention by Syria, which also feared that a Palestinian victory could have led to a partition of the country or invited an Israeli invasion, see Sayigh, *Armed Struggle and the Search for State*, pp. 376–91; Rubin, *Revolution Until Victory?*, p. 50; Benny Morris, *Righteous Victims: A History of the Zionist-Arab Conflict, 1881–2001* (New York: Vintage, 2001), p. 500. For more on Syria's calculations, see Henry Kissinger, *Years of Renewal* (New York: Simon & Schuster, 1999), p. 1040.

93. For Jordan's revival of the idea of confederation, see Sayigh, *Armed Struggle and the Search for State*, pp. 414–415; Ma'oz, *Palestinian Leadership on the West Bank*, p. 147. For the February 1977 meeting at which Egypt told the United States that it favored Jordanian-Palestinian confederation, see *FRUS*, VIII, p. 338. Arafat's close aide Hani al-Hasan attacked Sadat's endorsement of the idea three days later. See Sayigh, p. 415.

94. On PLO dialogue with Israeli doves, see Sayigh, *Armed Struggle and the Search for State*, p. 414. For more on Abbas, who was among the founders of Fatah and joined the PLO Executive Committee in November 1984, see "The PNC: Historical Background," *Journal of Palestine Studies* 16, no. 4 (Summer 1987): 152; Mattar, *Ency-*

clopedia of the Palestinians, p. 3. For the quote from the head of Sa'iqa ("we may accept a truce"), see Sayigh, p. 414. For more on Sa'iqa, which had been the second-largest PLO faction but suffered massive defections following Syria-PLO clashes in 1976, see Rubin, *Revolution Until Victory?*, p. 50; Helena Cobban, *The Palestinian Liberation Organisation: People, Power and Politics* (Cambridge, UK: Cambridge University Press, 1985), p. 79. For Arafat's message to Egypt's foreign minister, see *FRUS*, VIII, pp. 25, 57–66. For the PLO announcement of willingness to attend the new conference, see Sayigh, p. 415.

95. For Qaddumi's statement regarding a national authority in the West Bank and Gaza alone, see al-Hout, *My Life in the PLO*, p. 117; Sayigh, *Armed Struggle and the Search for State*, p. 417. For the PLO's message to the White House, see section i of this chapter; *FRUS*, VIII, pp. 335–36. For Qaddumi's statement on abandoning the armed struggle and accepting a modified version of Resolution 242, see Sayigh, p. 421.

96. For the number of Lebanese and Palestinian civilians killed during the invasion, see the Lebanese police report cited by Rashid Khalidi, *Under Siege: P.L.O. Decisionmaking During the 1982 War* (New York: Columbia University Press, 2014), p. 200. For Palestinian estimates of the number of PLO fighters killed (560 "fulltime" personnel and approximately an equal number of militiamen), see Sayigh, *Armed Struggle and the Search for State*, p. 540. For much higher numbers of dead PLO combatants claimed by Israel (IDF Chief of Staff Rafael Eitan: 2,000; Amir Drori, the commander of the Israeli invasion: 3,000), see Eric Pace, "Israeli General Says Mission Is to Smash P.L.O. in Beirut," *The New York Times*, June 15, 1982; "Casualties of Mideast Wars," *Los Angeles Times*, March 8, 1991. For the number of PLO personnel evacuated (8,500 by sea to Tunisia and another 2,500 by land to Syria, Iraq, and Yemen), see Shlaim, *The Iron Wall*, p. 425. In addition, several thousand Syrian soldiers were evacuated, making a total of 14,398 PLO personnel and PLA and Syrian soldiers who left by sea or land. Sayigh, p. 537. For US written assurances to the PLO, see Quandt, *Peace Process*, p. 344.

97. For estimates of the number killed, which range from 700 to 2,750, see Sayigh *Armed Struggle and the Search for State*, p. 539; Shlaim, *The Iron Wall*, p. 428. For Sharon's quote ("clean out"), see Schiff and Ya'ari, *Israel's Lebanon War*, p. 285. For details of the IDF role in the massacre, see Linda A. Malone, "The Kahan Report, Ariel Sharon and the Sabra-Shatilla Massacres in Lebanon: Responsibility Under International Law for Massacres of Civilian Populations," *Utah Law Review*, no. 2 (1985): 373–433; Seth Anziska, "A Preventable Massacre," *The New York Times*, September 16, 2012; and especially Sayigh, *Armed Struggle and the Search for State*, p. 539. Sayigh writes: "The IDF transported several hundred [Phalange] militiamen to Shatila . . . and provided wireless communications, ammunition, food rations, and night-time illumination for the next 48 hours while the Lebanese Forces conducted a systematic slaughter of every living thing, human or animal, they met. . . . hundreds of prisoners were herded into the nearby sports stadium, where, in the presence of Israeli officers, Maronite gunmen led young men away for execution. Sharon, Eitan, Drori, and military intelligence chief Yehoshua Saguy all knew what was happening by the evening of 17 September, according to their own subsequent testimony, but the massacre was allowed to continue for twelve more hours. . . . the IDF also provided bulldozers which the Lebanese Forces hurriedly used to dig mass graves."

98. For the PLO's sense that the Lebanon War had demonstrated the futility of seeking to liberate Palestine from neighboring bases, see al-Hout, *My Life in the PLO*, p. 229. For Abu Iyad's quip ("betray the PLO"), see Rubin, *Revolution Until Victory?*, p. 58. For the 70,000 Palestinians flying out of Beirut in 1983, see al-Hout, p. 219. For the drop in crude oil prices (from 1981 to 1986, the inflation-adjusted price of imported crude oil was reduced to less than one-third of its original value, from $98.12 to $30.55 per barrel), see "Short-Term Energy Outlook, Real Prices Viewer," US Energy Information Administration, accessed October 7, 2016, http://www.eia .gov/forecasts/steo/realprices/.

99. For Arafat's March 1983 agreement to negotiate on the basis of the Reagan Plan (as part of a joint Jordanian-Palestinian delegation) and the PLO's opposition to Arafat's concession, see Sayigh, *Armed Struggle and the Search for State*, pp. 557–58. In April 1983, Arafat gave his verbal support to the plan, though the PLO did not approve it. David B. Ottaway, *The King's Messenger: Prince Bandar bin Sultan and America's Tangled Relationship with Saudi Arabia* (New York: Walker & Company, 2008), p. 76. For the PLO statement on "some positive elements" to the Reagan Plan, see Sayigh, p. 538. For the secret PLO-US discussions in the months leading up to the Reagan Plan, see Bernard Gwertzman, "Reagan Administration Held 9-Month Talks with P.L.O.," *The New York Times*, February 19, 1984.

100. For the Fez plan, see "Text of Final Declaration at Arab League Meeting," Associated Press, September 10, 1982; Sayigh, *Armed Struggle and the Search for State*, pp. 551–53. For the PLO's conditional willingness to state that it would live in peace with Israel in 1977, see section i of this chapter and n. 95 of this section. For the Fahd Plan that Arafat had quietly helped formulate, see Sayigh, pp. 511–12. The Fahd plan was published two weeks after Israel and the PLO agreed to a cease-fire that ended what was known as the "artillery war." The PLO had fired rockets from south Lebanon and Israeli aircraft had destroyed the PLO headquarters, killing 150 civilians. Sayigh, p. 506. Arafat came under withering PLO criticism for the Saudi Plan that he had discreetly helped create, especially for article 7, which called for "all states in the region" to live in peace, implying recognition of Israel.

101. For the Geneva Declaration, made at the International Conference on the Question of Palestine that convened from August 29 to September 7, 1983, see United Nations, "Letter Dated 10 October 1983 from the Chairman of the Committee on the Exercise of the Inalienable Rights of the Palestinian People addressed to the Secretary-General," October 12, 1983.

102. For Arafat's engagement with Jordan, which again sought to subsume Palestinian national aspirations under the confines of confederation, see Sayigh, *Armed Struggle and the Search for State*, pp. 551–55; *The Middle East and North Africa 2004* (New York: Routledge, 2003), p. 66–67. For Arafat persuading Fatah to accept a plan for Jordanian-Palestinian union and the PLO breaking the Arab boycott of Egypt, see Sayigh, p. 553.

103. For the split in Fatah in 1983 and the decision by two leftist factions to suspend activity in the PLO, see Rubin, *Revolution Until Victory?*, p. 62. For the call for Arafat's overthrow, see Rubin, p. 64. For the paper on the PLO's dead-end, see Sayigh, *Armed Struggle and the Search for State*, p. 605. In 1985–1986, hundreds of PLO fighters died in what was known as "the war of the camps" in Lebanon. Joshua Teitelbaum, "The Palestine Liberation Organization" in *Middle East Contemporary*

Survey, vol. X: 1986, Itamar Rabinovich and Haim Shaked, eds. (Boulder, CO: Westview Press, 1986), pp. 194–96; Sayigh, p. 584. For the scene at Arafat's office in 1987, see Sayigh, p. 606. For the snub by King Hussein, who had recently expelled PLO officials from Jordan and didn't greet Arafat at the airport, see "Jordan Expels Arafat Again," *The New York Times,* July 13, 1986. For the concluding statement of the Arab Summit, see Sayigh, p. 606.

104. For the outbreak of the First Intifada, see Ann M. Lesch, "Prelude to the Uprising in the Gaza Strip," *Journal of Palestine Studies* 20, no. 1 (Autumn 1990): 1–23. For Arafat's interview, Abbas's announcement on an international peace conference, and statements by Abbas and the PLO weekly publication, see Sayigh, *Armed Struggle and the Search for State,* p. 616.

105. For Abu Jihad's worry that Arafat would seek diplomatic gains prematurely, see Sayigh, *Armed Struggle and the Search for State,* p. 618. For the quote by Abu Iyad (who added: "They faced us with a *fait accompli*"), see Rubin, *Revolution Until Victory?,* p. 92.

106. For PLO anxiety over the possibility that the United States and Israel could strike a separate deal with leaders in the Occupied Territories, see Sayigh, *Armed Struggle and the Search for State,* p. 635. See also Ghassan Khatib, *Palestinian Politics and the Middle East Peace Process: Consensus and Competition in the Palestinian Negotiating Team* (New York: Routledge, 2010), pp. 56–58. For Abu Iyad's statement that there would have been no intifada if the PLO had remained in Beirut, see Rubin, *Revolution Until Victory?,* p. 92. For the fourteen-point political program, see David K. Shipler, "Palestinian Turmoil Could Provide the Seeds of Peace," *The New York Times,* February 7, 1988; Sayigh, p. 635; Rubin, p. 96.

107. For Jordan's surrender of all claims on the West Bank, see al-Hout, *My Life in the PLO,* p. 231; "Hussein Surrenders Claims on West Bank to the PLO," *The New York Times,* August 1, 1988. For the quote from an Arafat adviser ("only the PLO"), see Rubin, *Revolution Until Victory?,* p. 97.

108. For the Soviet Union's pressure on the PLO to recognize Israel, see Rubin, *Revolution Until Victory?,* p. 96. For video of the Shultz speech, see "George Shultz, Address to the Washington Institute for Near East Policy, September 16, 1988," C-Span, September 16, 1988, accessed October 16, 2016.

109. For PLO fears of Israeli annexation, see Sayigh, *Armed Struggle and the Search for State,* p. 623. See also Rubin, *Revolution Until Victory?,* p. 97, who quotes one PLO official stating: "We felt we had to move fast in case the Israelis decided to step in and fill the vacuum."

110. For the declaration of independence and the PNC's approval, see "Palestinian Declaration of Independence, Palestine National Council, Algiers, 15 November 1988," *Journal of Palestine Studies* 18, no. 2 (Winter 1989): 214; "Political Communiqué, Palestine National Council, Algiers, 15 November 1988," *Journal of Palestine Studies* 18, no. 2 (Winter 1989): 220. The declaration was drafted in Arabic by Darwish and in English by Edward Said. Rashid Khalidi, *The Iron Cage: The Story of the Palestinian Struggle for Statehood* (Boston: Beacon Press, 2006), p. 194. Other Palestinians affiliated with the PLO and Fatah also contributed to the draft. Interview by the author with former Arafat adviser, August 2016. For the PLO's use of the term "historic compromise" to refer to the acceptance of a two-state solution, as embodied in the declaration of independence's acceptance of UN General Assembly Resolution 181—partitioning Palestine into two states, one Arab

and one Jewish—and the political communiqué's acceptance of UN Security Council Resolution 242 and its call for Israel to withdraw from territories occupied in 1967, see PLO Negotiations Affairs Department, "The Historic Compromise: The Palestinian Declaration of Independence and the Twenty-Year Struggle for a Two-State Solution," November 2008, accessed December 29, 2016, http://carim-south.eu/carim/public/polsoctexts/PS2PAL005_EN.pdf.

111. According to B'Tselem, 326 Palestinians were killed during the first year of the intifada; for a number closer to 400, see Zachary Lockman and Joel Beinin, eds., *Intifada: The Palestinian Uprising Against Israeli Occupation* (Cambridge, MA: South End Press, 1999), p. 317. For more details, see chapter 7.

112. Giving up claims to political sovereignty over any part of Israel within its pre-1967 boundaries was the clear meaning of the declaration to all PLO members. There was, and remains, considerable ambiguity about whether this also meant the abandonment of the right of all refugees to return to their homes. A number of PLO officials were explicit about it meaning just that, stating that while they wanted Israel to recognize the principle that refugees are entitled to return or compensation, in practice Israel's demographic balance could not be upset and a return of large numbers was not possible. In 1990, Abu Iyad wrote: "We accept that a total return is not possible. . . . We recognize that Israel would not want to accept large numbers of Palestinian returnees who would tip the demographic balance against the Jewish population. Nonetheless, we believe it is essential that Israel accept the principle of the right of return or compensation with the details of such a return to be left open for negotiation. . . . We shall for our part remain flexible regarding its implementation." And, in 2002, Arafat wrote: "We seek a fair and just solution to the plight of Palestinian refugees who for 54 years have not been permitted to return to their homes. We understand Israel's demographic concerns and understand that the right of return of Palestinian refugees, a right guaranteed under international law and United Nations Resolution 194, must be implemented in a way that takes into account such concerns. However, just as we Palestinians must be realistic with respect to Israel's demographic desires, Israelis too must be realistic in understanding that there can be no solution to the Israeli-Palestinian conflict if the legitimate rights of these innocent civilians continue to be ignored. Left unresolved, the refugee issue has the potential to undermine any permanent peace agreement between Palestinians and Israelis." Salah Khalaf, "Lowering the Sword," *Foreign Policy*, Spring 1990, pp. 92–112; Yasir Arafat, "The Palestinian Vision of Peace," *The New York Times*, February 3, 2002.

113. On PLO factions having been founded by Palestinians from cities and villages in pre-1967 Israel, see Sayigh, *Armed Struggle and the Search for State*, p. 677. For the quote from Fatah dissidents ("homeland for a state"), see Sayigh, p. 644. For the Shafiq al-Hout quote ("tears in my eyes"), see al-Hout, *My Life in the PLO*, pp. 231–32.

114. For al-Hout's words ("a just solution . . . a possible one"), see al-Hout, *My Life in the PLO*, p. 252.

115. An additional argument the PLO had to confront was that Israel could not withdraw from the West Bank because of its topography and proximity to Israeli urban centers. To nullify these rationales for continued occupation, the PLO eventually acquiesced to the demand that the entire Palestinian state be demilitarized. On Egypt as the strongest Arab army (since the 1950s it had more than twice as many army personnel and far more tanks and planes than the next largest Arab military,

Iraq), see Elie Podeh, *The Quest for Hegemony in the Arab World: The Struggle Over the Baghdad Pact* (Leiden: E. J. Brill, 1995), p. 21.

116. On the number of Palestinians in Kuwait at the time, see Mattar, *Encyclopedia of the Palestinians*, pp. 288–90. On PLO financial and military ties with Iraq, which had grown closer ever since Syria supported a Fatah rebellion in 1983, see Joshua Teitelbaum, "The Palestine Liberation Organization," in *Middle East Contemporary Survey*, vol. XIV: 1990, Ami Ayalon, ed. (Boulder, CO: Westview Press, 1992), pp. 221–27; Sayigh, *Armed Struggle and the Search for State*, p. 641. For Arafat's 1990 statement about the far greater aid given to the Afghan mujahiddin ($19 billion since 1981) than to the PLO ($2.6 billion since 1964), see Sayigh, p. 640.

117. For details of the PLO's initially ambiguous position on the Iraqi invasion, as well as its votes at the Arab summit (initially it voted against the Saudi position and the day after changed its vote to one of abstention), see Bruce Maddy-Weitzman, "The Inter-Arab System and the Gulf War: Continuity and Change," The Carter Center, November 1991; Sayigh, *Armed Struggle and the Search for State*, pp. 641–42. For the PLO's shift from ostensible neutrality to unmistakable support for Iraq, see Sayigh, pp. 641–43. An Arafat associate stressed to me that the PLO chairman genuinely wished to mediate the crisis between Iraq and the Gulf states. Arafat, he said, had sympathy for Kuwait, where he had worked as an engineer and where Fatah had been informally founded. His decision was driven not just by a calculation that Iraq was capable of confronting Israel and the coalition led by the United States, but also by his desire not to antagonize Saddam Hussein. Phone interview by the author with Arafat associate, August 18, 2016.

118. For the PLO flight from Kuwait (six months after the war, in August 1991, only 70,000 Palestinians were left in Kuwait; Jordan alone absorbed some 250,000), see Mattar, *Encyclopedia of the Palestinians*, p. 290. For the PLO's inability to pay the families of workers, see Rubin, *Revolution Until Victory?*, p. 96. For the PFLP leader's quote ("we burdened the uprising"), see Sayigh, *Armed Struggle and the Search for State*, p. 647. For the public exultation at the Soviet coup attempt, see Sayigh, p. 643.

119. For more on the period following the Soviet collapse, see Sayigh, *Armed Struggle and the Search for State*, pp. 643–50, 690–91; see also Khatib, *Palestinian Politics*, pp. 51–55. For figures on Soviet emigration to Israel (from several hundred per year during the mid-1980s to 185,227 in 1990), see "Total Immigration, from Former Soviet Union (1948–Present)," Jewish Virtual Library, accessed October 5, 2016, http://www.jewishvirtuallibrary.org/jsource/Immigration/FSU.html.

120. For details of the Madrid conference, see Menachem Klein, *Jerusalem: The Contested City* (London: C. Hurst & Co. Publishers, 2001), p. 131; Elie Rehkess, "The West Bank and the Gaza Strip," in *Middle East Contemporary Survey*, vol. XV: 1991, Ami Ayalon, ed. (Boulder, CO: Westview Press, 1993), pp. 260–62; Youssef M. Ibrahim, "The Middle East Talks: 2 Scholars Act as Palestinians' Data Base," *The New York Times*, October 30, 1991. The PLO sought to circumvent the ban on Jerusalem residents in two ways: first, the renowned Palestinian historian Walid Khalidi, a Jerusalemite who was a research fellow at Harvard and had not lived in the city in decades, was a member of the Jordanian delegation; second, the Jerusalem leader Faisal Husseini headed a PLO committee—which included other Jerusalemites—that was sent to the Madrid talks but not permitted in the negotiating room. For the Qaddumi statement ("join the peace process or exit history"), see Sayigh, *Armed Struggle and the Search for State*, p. 643.

121. For Shimon Peres's remark, see Shlaim, *The Iron Wall*, p. 530. For Arafat's quote ("a male bee that fertilizes"), see Sayigh, *Armed Struggle and the Search for State*, pp. 654–55. For the PLO Executive Committee member's quote ("paranoid enough already"), see al-Hout, *My Life in the PLO*, p. 267. For Sayigh's quote, see Sayigh, p. 655.

122. For Arafat's strategy of obstruction, see Sayigh, *Armed Struggle and the Search for State*, p. 655; Indyk, *Innocent Abroad*, p. 79. For Rabin's decision to leave the Washington talks when he discovered that the Palestinian negotiators were taking orders from the PLO leadership in Tunis, see Itamar Rabinovich, *The Lingering Conflict: Israel, the Arabs, and the Middle East, 1948–2012* (Washington, DC: Brookings Institution Press, 2012), p. 37. For more detail on Arafat's use of the Jerusalem issue to end the Washington talks and force Israel to deal directly with the PLO leadership in Tunis (which, as an enticement, took a softer line on Jerusalem), see Klein, *Jerusalem*, pp. 134–35. Klein writes: "Under pressure from the PLO leadership and from Arafat personally, the Palestinian delegation in Washington demanded that all Palestinian legislation apply to Jerusalem. Israel, of course, refused. . . . The Palestinians fiercely opposed the American proposal [to postpone discussion of Jerusalem until final status negotiations], both because of the instruction Arafat had given (intended to bring the talks to a dead end) and because of the fact that several members of the delegation lived in East Jerusalem. . . . While the Palestinians in Washington were raining down fire and brimstone on the U.S., the PLO had already agreed in its secret contacts with Israel in Oslo to put off discussion of Jerusalem to the talks on the permanent settlement." See also chapter 8.

123. For the Rabin quote ("on the ropes") and the statement to Rabin from the head of Israeli military intelligence, see Shlaim, *The Iron Wall*, p. 533. For the PLO cutting payments to up to one-third of personnel, the severe drop in assistance to the West Bank and Gaza, the PLO budget being halved, and the thousands of Fatah layoffs, see Sayigh, *Armed Struggle and the Search for State*, pp. 656–57. For the protests in front of the home of the PLO representative in Lebanon and the deaths from conditons that went untreated due to lack of funds, see al-Hout, *My Life in the PLO*, p. 271.

124. For the concessions contained in the Camp David framework, see section i of this chapter; for the pressures that pushed Israel toward Oslo, see section ii of this chapter. For the Brzezinski "Basutoland" analogy, which he mentioned twice to Begin, see *FRUS*, VIII, pp. 870, 1077. For the Amos Oz quote, see Edward Said, *Peace and Its Discontents: Essays on Palestine in the Middle East Peace Process* (New York: Vintage, 1996), p. 8.

125. For Abbas as "holy spirit" of Oslo and his quotes ("achievement" that "ended a twentieth-century conflict"), see Abbas, *Through Secret Channels*, pp. 38, 175. For Nabil Sha'ath quote ("full peace with Israel"), see Usher, *Dispatches from Palestine*, p. 43. For Arafat's quote ("it is a bad agreement"), see Graham Usher, *Palestine in Crisis: The Struggle for Peace and Political Independence After Oslo* (London: Pluto Press, 1995), p. 1.

126. Before 1993, the year of the first Oslo agreement, unemployment in the West Bank and Gaza hovered at 5 percent. By May 1996, despite the fact that the PA had created new jobs, unemployment had reached 28.4 percent, and then lowered to 18 percent in September 1997. See Leila Farsakh, "Under Siege Closure, Separation and the Palestinian Economy," *Middle East Report*, no. 217, Winter 2000; Leila Farsakh, "Palestinian Employment in Israel: 1996–1997," MAS—Palestine Economic Policy Research Institute, August 1998, p. 36; see also chapter 7.

127. For the first Said quote ("before that occupation had ended"), see Said, *Peace and Its Discontents*, p. xxix. For Said on the African National Congress and the second quote ("rid of an unwanted insurrectionary problem"), see Said, *The Politics of Dispossession*, p. xxxviii; Said, *Peace and Its Discontents*, pp. 6, 8. For Said's growing skepticism that a Palestinian state would arise and his later support of a single binational state, see "The One-State Solution," *The New York Times Magazine*, January 10, 1999. For the resignations of Darwish and al-Hout, see Sayigh, *Armed Struggle and the Search for State*, p. 658. Whereas the vote in the PLO Executive Committee barely approved the agreement, thanks only to these resignations and the absence of several other opponents, there were just two abstentions in the Israeli cabinet, which approved Oslo unanimously. See Shlaim, *The Iron Wall*, p. 534.

128. For an example of an Israeli leader admitting that negotiations were used cynically to continue settlement construction and unilaterally shape the contours of a final settlement, see comments by Prime Minister Yitzhak Shamir shortly after he lost power in June 1992, following more than half a year of Israeli-Palestinian talks in Madrid and then Washington: "What is this talk about 'political settlements'? I would have carried on autonomy talks for ten years, and meanwhile we would have reached half a million people in Judea and Samaria." Shlaim, *The Iron Wall*, p. 517. This was why the Palestinian intellectual and future Knesset member Azmi Bishara said Oslo was Israel's "brilliant chess move." Under the agreement, he asked, "Where is the incentive for Israeli withdrawal? The aim of autonomy is separation without withdrawal, and it's realizable. Why would the Israelis throw it away?" See Usher, *Dispatches from Palestine*, pp. 60, 63. When Israel first conquered the West Bank and Gaza in 1967, Golda Meir asked Prime Minister Levi Eshkol what he planned to do with a million Arabs. Eshkol jokingly replied, "The dowry pleases you but the bride does not." Oslo provided a perfect solution to Meir's dilemma: Israel could keep all the dowry while rejecting the bride, so long as it called the arrangement temporary. For the Eshkol quote, see Shlaim, *The Iron Wall*, p. 273.

129. For the number of settlers (out of 547,000 settlers, 350,010 lived in the West Bank outside Jerusalem at the end of 2013, and 196,890 lived in the area of East Jerusalem at the end of 2012), see B'Tselem, "Statistics on Settlements and Settler Population," May 11, 2015. For the Netanyahu-led boom in settlement construction during the 2013–2014 talks, see Peace Now, "9 Months of Talks, 9 Months of Settlement Development," April 29, 2014.

130. For the Israel-Jordan Peace Treaty, which delimited the international border "with reference to the boundary definition under the Mandate," returned 147 square miles of Israeli-occupied land to Jordan, provided for equal swaps of territory (11.5 square miles) in Wadi Araba, and outlined leasing arrangements in two small boundary areas (totaling 700 acres), see Avi Shlaim, *Lion of Jordan: The Life of King Hussein in War and Peace* (New York: Knopf, 2008), pp. 547–48; Clyde Haberman, "Israel and Jordan Sign a Peace Accord," *The New York Times*, October 26, 1994; Israel Ministry of Foreign Affairs, "Israel-Jordan Peace Treaty," October 26, 1994, accessed December 30, 2016, http://www.mfa.gov.il/MFA/ForeignPolicy/Peace/Guide/Pages/Israel-Jordan Peace Treaty.aspx. For Israel's full withdrawal in Lebanon to the UN-mandated "Blue Line," which is so close to the 1923 international boundary and 1949 armistice line that, according to the Congressional Research Service, the difference cannot be detected except on very large maps, see Alfred B. Prados, "The Shib'a Farms Dispute and Its Implications," Congressional Research

Service, August 7, 2001. (According to UN maps, the Shib'a Farms are in the Israeli-occupied Golan territory of Syria.) See also David Eshel, "The Israel-Lebanon Border Enigma," IBRU Boundary and Security Bulletin, Winter 2000–2001, pp. 72–83. For Israel's 1998 proposal—in a ten-point document, Netanyahu offered Hafez al-Assad full Israeli withdrawal from Syrian lands occupied in 1967—see Shlaim, *The Iron Wall*, pp. 622–23.

131. For Peres's quotes (as well as the "greatest achievement" quote in the following paragraph), see Amira Lam, "Peres: I Will Get to See Peace," *Yediot Aharonot*, August 2, 2010. In this interview, Peres seems to confuse the Palestinian concessions made in the 1980s and those made in Oslo, referring incorrectly to Oslo as the point at which Palestinians accepted a state on the pre-1967 lines.

132. Shlaim, *The Iron Wall*, pp. 646–47.

133. For the 1980 UN Security Council Resolution (465), see "S/RES/465 (1980)," United Nations, March 1, 1980. The resolution demands that Israel dismantle all settlements, including in Jerusalem, and calls on all states not to provide Israel with any assistance to be used in connection with settlements.

134. For the Abba Eban quote ("History teaches us"), see Robert Andrews, *Famous Lines: A Columbia Dictionary of Familiar Quotations* (New York: Columbia University Press, 1997), p. 330.

135. For an example of the "absence of personal chemistry" argument, see Alon Ben-Meir, "Why Have Past Israeli-Palestinian Negotiations Failed?," *The Huffington Post*, November 18, 2015. For a prominent example of the "lack of trust" argument, see the December 28, 2016, speech by Secretary of State John Kerry: "In the end, I believe the negotiations did not fail because the gaps were too wide, but because the level of trust was too low." US Department of State, "Secretary of State John Kerry—Remarks on Middle East Peace," December 28, 2016. For more on mistaken assumptions of would-be peace brokers, see International Crisis Group, "The Emperor Has No Clothes: Palestinians and the End of the Peace Process," *Middle East Report*, no. 122, May 7, 2012; Tal Becker, "The End of the 'Peace Process'?," The Washington Institute for Near East Policy, March 2012.

136. For more on the direct talks between Abbas and Netanyahu, see Hillary Rodham Clinton, *Hard Choices* (New York: Simon & Schuster, 2014), pp. 323–28, as well as chapter 12. The negotiations began on September 2, 2010, in Washington and ended in a final bilateral meeting on September 15, 2010, in Jerusalem, though the formal date the talks concluded is often recorded as September 26, when a ten-month partial halt on some types of settlement construction expired. For the backchannel negotiations, see Nahum Barnea, "Netanyahu's Secret Peace Offer Concessions to Palestinians Revealed," *Yediot Aharonot*, March 6, 2015; Ross, *Doomed to Succeed*, pp. 385–86.

137. For the growing share of religious infantry officers (from 2.5 percent in 1990 to 31.4 percent in 2007), see "Sharp Rise in Number of Religious IDF Officers," *Haaretz*, September 15, 2010. For Israeli profits from occupation, including extraction of Palestinian natural resources, see Human Rights Watch, "Occupation, Inc.: How Settlement Businesses Contribute to Israel's Violations of Palestinian Rights," January 19, 2016. For Israeli profits from collecting customs for the PA (according to the World Bank, the fee charged "significantly outstrips costs incurred by [Israel] to handle Palestinian imports"), see The World Bank, "Economic Monitoring Report to the Ad Hoc Liaison Committee," April 19, 2016. For an estimate of the

amount of aid to the Palestinians that ends up in the Israeli economy (72 percent), see Shir Hever, Aid Watch, "How Much International Aid to Palestinians Ends Up in the Israeli Economy?," September 2015.

138. See Alan M. Milner, Robert Fink, and Rabbi Ephraim Rubinger, reply by Arthur Herzberg, "Begin and the Jews: An Exchange," *The New York Review of Books*, April 29, 1982. For the quote from Benvenisti, see Meron Benvenisti, *Conflicts and Contradictions* (New York: Villard Books, 1986), pp. 11–12.

139. For figures on US military aid to Israel, see chapter 12; Jeremy M. Sharp, "U.S. Foreign Aid to Israel," Congressional Research Service, June 10, 2015. For a survey of subjective well-being in which Israel ranked fifth among members of the Organization for Economic Cooperation and Development, see "How's Life? 2015: Measuring Well-Being," Organization for Economic Cooperation and Development, 2015, accessed October 5, 2016.

140. The number of settlers to be evacuated in a final status agreement depends primarily on two questions: whether Israelis and Palestinians decide that some settlers will remain in their homes and live under Palestinian sovereignty, and what adjustments to the pre-1967 lines are specified in the peace treaty. The 2003 draft permanent status agreement known as the Geneva Accord called for Israel to annex 2.2 percent of the Occupied Territories and provide the Palestinians an equivalent amount of Israeli land. In 2008, Prime Minister Olmert proposed to President Abbas that Israel annex approximately 6 percent of the Occupied Territories and provide slightly less to the Palestinians in exchange. During those same discussions, Abbas proposed that Israel annex 1.9 percent and provide an equal amount in return. Using figures from Israel's Central Bureau of Statistics, Israeli policy analyst and territorial expert Dan Rothem calculated the number of settlers that would have to be removed in 2015 (the number of settlers increases every year) under several potential territorial agreements: if Israel annexed the roughly 6 percent that Olmert had proposed, 102,220 settlers (18 percent of all Israelis living in the Occupied Territories). If Israel annexed the 1.9 percent Abbas suggested, 239,591 settlers (41 percent of the settler population). If Israel annexed the 2.2 percent outlined in the Israeli-Palestinian Geneva Accord, 182,970 settlers (31 percent). And if Israel annexed 3 percent, 156,100 settlers (27 percent). Dan Rothem, "Border Scenarios Data," unpublished paper, December 2016.

141. Jews have been a minority in Israel-Palestine since 2012. At the end of April 2012, the Israeli government announced that there were a total of 5,931,000 Jews in Israel and the Occupied Territories. The total number of non-Jews at this time was 5,948,313, including 1,623,000 Palestinian citizens of Israel or residents of East Jerusalem; 2,354,020 Palestinian residents of the West Bank (excluding 295,000 Christian and Muslim residents of Jerusalem counted above); 1,644,293 Palestinian residents of Gaza; and 327,000 immigrants to Israel and their offspring not registered as Jews. (These figures do not include the 217,000 foreign residents of Israel.) Note that the Israeli figures for Christian and Muslim residents of Jerusalem have been subtracted from the total number of West Bank Palestinians counted by the Palestinian Central Bureau of Statistics (PCBS). Prior to this deduction, the West Bank total was 2,649,020, which included residents of the Jerusalem governorate (an area that includes all of municipal East Jerusalem and territory beyond it). By mid-2016 there were 6,377,000 Jews in Israel-Palestine compared to 6,645,503 non-Jews (of whom 6,271,503 were Arab). Of the non-Jews, there were 1,771,000 Palestinian citizens of

Israel and residents of East Jerusalem; 374,000 others ("non-Arab Christians, members of other religions, and persons not classified by religion in the Ministry of Interior"); 2,619,368 Palestinians in the West Bank, excluding 316,000 Arabs in Jerusalem (at the end of 2014); and 1,881,135 Palestinians in Gaza. The 2016 figures do not include 192,000 foreign residents of Israel. For Jewish, Palestinian, and non-Jewish citizens of Israel, see "On the Eve of Israel's 64th Independence Day," Israel Central Bureau of Statistics, April 25, 2012; "Selected Data on the Occasion of Jerusalem Day (2014–2015)," Israel Central Bureau of Statistics, May 31, 2016, both accessed October 14, 2016. For non-Jewish (Muslim, Christian, and other) population of Jerusalem, see "Selected Data on the Occasion of Jerusalem Day," Israel Central Bureau of Statistics, May 16, 2012; "68th Independence Day—8.5 Million Residents in the State of Israel," Israel Central Bureau of Statistics, May 9, 2016, both accessed October 14, 2016. For the Palestinian population of the West Bank and Gaza, see "Estimated Population in the Palestinian Territory Mid-Year by Governorate, 1997–2016," Palestinian Central Bureau of Statistics, accessed October 14, 2016.

142. For the Eisenhower and Ford examples, see section ii of this chapter. For the Carter examples, see section i. Freilich, *Zion's Dilemmas*, pp. 82–83; Quandt, *Camp David*, pp. 246–47. For the James Baker example, see Shlaim, *The Iron Wall*, p. 503.

143. For some advocates of a boycott of settlements, the not so hidden purpose of the ban is to shield Israel from the Boycott, Divestment, and Sanctions (BDS) movement, as the first sentence of a 2016 open letter signed by numerous liberal Zionists makes clear: "We, the undersigned, oppose an economic, political, or cultural boycott of Israel itself as defined by its June 4, 1967, borders." See Todd Gitlin, Peter Beinart, Peter Brooks, Michael Walzer, and Edward Witten, et al., "For an Economic Boycott and Political Nonrecognition of the Israeli Settlements in the Occupied Territories," *The New York Review of Books,* October 13, 2016. For a rebuttal by advocates of BDS, see Angela Y. Davis, Chandler Davis, Richard A. Falk, Rashid Khalidi, and Alice Rothchild, et al., "On the Boycott of Israeli Settlements," *The New York Review of Books*, November 10, 2016.

144. US interests in an Israeli-Palestinian peace agreement declined substantially when the Soviet Union collapsed, after which there was no longer the same risk that an Arab-Israeli war could lead to some degree of great power confrontation, as occurred in 1956, 1967, 1973, and 1982. Quandt, *Camp David*, p. 334.

145. Shlaim, *The Iron Wall*, p. 320.

PART II. DOMINATION

Joshua 24:13, in *The New American Bible, Revised Edition* (New York: HarperCollins, 2012), p. 255.

2. FEELING GOOD ABOUT FEELING BAD

This chapter was updated in September 2016.

1. For Bentwich's trip to Jaffa, his acquaintance with Herzl, and the report for the First Zionist Congress, see Ari Shavit, *My Promised Land: The Triumph and Tragedy of Israel* (New York: Spiegel & Grau, 2013), pp. 3–4, 10.

2. For background on Bentwich, see Shavit, *Promised Land*, p. 3. For the motives of Herzl and most early Zionists, see Shapira, *Israel*, pp. 16–23; see also Laurel Plapp, *Zionism and Revolution in European-Jewish Literature* (New York: Routledge, 2007), pp. 28–29. For Bentwich's worries, see Shavit, pp. 5–10.

3.   For the 6,500 Jews in Palestine at the end of the eighteenth century, see Shapira, *Israel*, p. 27. Others have written that the number was approximately two thousand lower or higher. For an estimate of the Jewish population that "did not exceed 5,000–6,000 in 1800" and "consisted of mainly Sephardi Jews," see Ruth Kark and Joseph B. Glass, "The Jews in Eretz-Israel/Palestine: From Traditional Peripherality to Modern Centrality," *Israel Affairs* 5, no. 4 (June 1999): 73–107. For a historical table on the proportion of "Orientals and Sephardim" in the world and Palestine, which states that the number of Jews in 1800 was 8,000, of whom 60 percent were "Orientals and Sephardim," see Sammy Smooha, *Israel: Pluralism and Conflict* (Berkeley, CA: University of California Press, 1978), p. 281. For the Jewish share of Palestine's population at the time of Bentwich's visit, see Justin McCarthy, *The Population of Palestine: Population History and Statistics of the Late Ottoman Period and the Mandate* (New York: Columbia University Press, 1990), pp. 10, 20, 24; Sergio DellaPergola, "Demographic Trends in Israel and Palestine: Prospects and Policy Implications," p. 11; Smooha, p. 281; *In Vigilant Brotherhood: The American Jewish Committee's Relationship to Palestine and Israel* (New York: American Jewish Committee, 1964), p. 6. In 1882, according to numerous Zionist sources, the Jewish population of Palestine was 24,000 (of whom 15,300 were Ottoman citizens) out of a total of 468,089 Ottoman citizens (not including foreigners), making up 5 percent of the total; in 1890, according to Zionist sources, it was 43,000 (of whom 17,991 were Ottoman citizens) out of a total of 532,000, making up 8 percent; in 1895, according to Zionist sources, it was 47,000 out of a total of 569,000, making up 8 percent. These figures are almost certainly inflated: they assume a number of noncitizen Jews in Palestine that is greater than the total number of foreigners (of any religion) registered by the Ottomans. The demographer and historian Justin McCarthy writes, "In 1893, the only year for which such data are available, the Ottomans registered 5,457 resident foreign nationals in the Jerusalem Sanjak and 2,742 in the entire Beirut Vilayet [that is, all of Palestine, plus three territorial units outside it—the sanjaks of Latakia, Tripoli, and Beirut]. Obviously all the enumerated foreigners were not Jews in Palestine, but even if they had been it would have added only 8,199 Jews to the 1893 figure [of 19,257 Jewish Ottoman citizens in Palestine], bringing the total number of Jews (Ottoman subjects plus foreigners) in Palestine to 28,000." If one assumes a Jewish population of 27,456 in 1893 (19,257 citizens and 8,199 noncitizens, including those outside Palestine, in the Beirut Vilayet), Jews made up 5 percent of the 543,477 total population that year (535,278 Ottoman citizens and 8,199 noncitizens). If one assumes arbitrarily that half of the 2,742 foreigners in the Beirut Vilayet lived in the north (outside Palestine) and half in the south (inside it), then there were 6,828 foreigners in Palestine (1,371 in the Beirut Vilayet and 5,457 in the Jerusalem Sanjak). Assuming all of them were Jews, the Jewish share of the population would have been under 5 percent: 26,085 Jews (19,257 citizens and 6,828 noncitizens) out of a total population of 542,106 (535,278 Ottoman citizens and 6,828 noncitizens). McCarthy estimates that by 1914 the total number of Jews in Palestine was 56,754 (of whom 38,754 were Ottoman citizens) out of a total of 722,143 Ottoman citizens, making up just under 8 percent (and even lower if one were to include noncitizens who were not Jews). Both McCarthy and Zionist sources put the number of Jews in Palestine in 1918 at approximately 60,000, though they differ on the size of the total population, creating estimates of the share of Jews ranging from 8 percent

(McCarthy) to 9 percent (Rabinovich and Reinharz). McCarthy, p. 37; Rabinovich and Reinharz, eds., *Israel in the Middle East*, pp. 571–72. According to Smooha (p. 281), by 1895, the majority of Jews in Palestine were Ashkenazi.

4. For Bentwich's alleged failure to see the Arabs surrounding him, see Shavit, *Promised Land*, pp. 10–13.

5. For Shavit's argument on the necessity of Zionism for Jewish survival, see Shavit, *Promised Land*, pp. 5–6. For the Kishinev pogrom, see Edward H. Judge, *Easter in Kishinev: Anatomy of a Pogrom* (New York: New York University Press, 1995), p. 72. On the 35,000–40,000 Jews who immigrated to Palestine during the Second Aliya (1904–1914) and the far greater number (1.2 million) who went to the United States at this time, see Shapira, *Israel*, pp. 12, 42; Shafir, *Land, Labor, and the Origins of the Israeli-Palestinian Conflict*, pp. 74–75. On the secularism and idealism of those who went to Palestine then, see Shapira, *Israel*, pp. 42–62.

6. For the share of Jews in Palestine (27 percent) at the end of 1935, a year in which nearly 62,000 Jews emigrated there, see Roger Owen and Şevket Pamuk, *A History of Middle East Economies in the Twentieth Century* (Cambridge, MA: Harvard University Press, 1999), p. 249; McCarthy, *The Population of Palestine*, p. 35. For the quoted article by the leader of Rehovot's orange growers, see Shavit, *Promised Land*, p. 62.

7. For the number killed during the Arab Revolt, see Abdel Monem Said Aly, Shai Feldman, and Khalil Shikaki, *Arabs and Israelis: Conflict and Peacemaking in the Middle East* (New York: Palgrave Macmillan, 2013), p. 21. For other estimates of the number of Arab deaths, ranging from 3,000 to 6,000, see Matthew Hughes, "The Banality of Brutality: British Armed Forces and the Repression of the Arab Revolt in Palestine, 1936–39," *English Historical Review* 124, no. 507 (2009): pp. 314–54; Morris, *Righteous Victims*, p. 157. For Shavit on the end of Zionism's utopian phase and the realization that conflict was unavoidable, see Shavit, *Promised Land*, pp. 52–53, 73–76.

8. For the Jewish share of the population in 1947 (just under 32 percent), see Sergio DellaPergola, "Demographic Trends in Israel and Palestine: Prospects and Policy Implications," p. 11. The previous year, in 1946, the figure was just under 30 percent. Rabinovich and Reinharz, eds., *Israel in the Middle East*, pp. 571–72. For the amount of land owned by Jews, see chapter 1, section iii, n. 81. On the number of casualties on each side, those for early April 1948—875 Jews and 967 Arabs—are known from official British figures, while the numbers by mid-May 1948 are not as clear. For an estimate of 2,000 Jewish deaths by mid-May 1948 (out of a total of 6,000 killed during the war), see Morris, *The Birth of the Palestinian Refugee Problem Revisited*, p. 35. For an estimate of 4,000 Palestinian deaths by mid-May 1948, see figures by the Palestinian historian 'Arif al-'Arif cited in Efraim Karsh, *Fabricating Israeli History: The "New Historians"* (New York: Routledge, 2000), p. 23. For the British figures, see David Tal, *War in Palestine, 1948: Israeli and Arab Strategy and Diplomacy* (New York: Routledge, 2004), p. 100. For estimates of the number of Palestinian refugees at this time, which vary from 250,000 to 350,000, see the following: for "over a quarter of a million," see United Nations, "Cablegram from the Secretary-General of the League of Arab States to the Secretary-General of the United Nations," May 15, 1948, http://www.un.org/Docs/journal/asp/ws.asp?m=S /745; for 300,000, see Shapira, *Israel*, p. 162; for 350,000, see Rashid Khalidi, *The Iron Cage: The Story of the Palestinian Struggle for Statehood* (Boston: Beacon

Press, 2006), p. 131. Benny Morris estimates there were 250,000–300,000 Palestinians who fled or were expelled in what he calls the "second wave" of the Palestinian exodus, from April to June 1948, and states that some 200 Palestinian villages and towns had been conquered by the time of the Arab invasion in mid-May 1948. Morris, *The Birth of the Palestinian Refugee Problem Revisited*, pp. 262, 34.

9. For details of the attack on Lydda, see Shavit, *Promised Land*, pp. 107–8, 113–14, 125; for the number killed and Rabin's order ("must be expelled quickly"), see Shavit, p. 108. For a rebuttal to Shavit's account of the murders and expulsions at Lydda, disputing that a massacre had taken place, see Martin Kramer, "What Happened at Lydda," *Mosaic Magazine*, July 1, 2014. For a response to Kramer—"Lydda was simultaneously the biggest massacre and biggest expulsion of the 1948 war. . . . [the] disproportion speaks massacre, not 'battle'"—see Benny Morris, "Zionism's 'Black Boxes,'" *Mosaic Magazine*, July 13, 2014.

10. For Shavit on "cleansing," see Shavit, *Promised Land*, p. 110. For the Shavit quotes ("Lydda could not be" and "I'll stand by the damned"), see Shavit, pp. 108, 131.

11. For the Holocaust going unmentioned, the marginalization of Middle-Eastern Jewish culture, the forgetting of Palestinian refugees, the erasure of history, the replacement of Arab town names with Hebrew ones, and the demolition of Palestinian villages and building of Israeli ones, see Shavit, *Promised Land*, pp. 150–51, 160–62.

12. For the doubling of the Jewish population, see Shapira, *Israel*, p. 208; Shavit, *Promised Land*, p. 148. For Shavit on Israel as an egalitarian and democratic state in these years, see Shavit, pp. 151, 355. For the flourishing of science and agriculture and the building of the nuclear reactor, see Shavit, pp. 149–51, 188–93.

13. For Shavit's realization that "the promise of peace was unfounded," see Shavit, *Promised Land*, pp. 253–54. For Shavit on the narrow base and dilettantish, "adolescent" leadership of the Israeli left, see Shavit, p. 244. For Shavit on peace as a "plaint against the Right and the settlers," see Shavit, p. 253. For Shavit on the peace camp's misleading focus on 1967 as a way of distracting from and denying 1948, its ignoring "Arab political culture," its delusions about the nature of the conflict, see Shavit, pp. 245, 254, 265–66. For Shavit on Palestinian citizens of Israel wanting to change the Jewish character of the state, see Shavit, pp. 313–24. For Shavit on the 1948 problem having no solution (in his shorthand, all of the Palestinian population centers that were taken over by Israel in 1948 are invoked when he mentions the name of one of two towns, Lydda and Hulda, which are used interchangeably), see Shavit, pp. 265, 267.

14. Ibid., p. 205.

15. Ibid., p. 253. On camps surrounded by barbed wire and guarded by police, see Shapira, *Israel*, p. 225. On DDT, see Shavit, *Promised Land*, pp. 157, 280, 286. For Shavit's quote ("had no Arabs"), see Shavit, p. 252.

16. For Shavit congratulating himself for having "dared touch the fire," see his December 2, 2013, talk at the Jewish Community Center of San Francisco. Video is available at www.youtube.com/watch?v=UnA-kDX9BY8, accessed August 23, 2016. A similar quote can be found in video of his November 19, 2013, speaking event at the 92nd Street Y in New York: www.youtube.com/watch?v=aeDxRFeNs_o, accessed August 23, 2016.

17. For Shavit's use of the Holocaust (he describes the concentration camps of the Holocaust as "Zionism's ultimate arguments," implying that the movement's

justification before the Second World War is primarily retroactive), see Shavit, *Promised Land*, p. 394.

18. Likewise, Shavit assumes but does not attempt to defend the notion of Jewish proprietary rights to Palestine by virtue of hereditary links to ancient residents. The historian Anita Shapira could as well have been referring to Shavit when she wrote of early Zionists that "the continuity of rights in the past and the future was not subject to questioning." (When Chaim Weizmann, Israel's first president, was asked by a British commission by what right the Jews claimed ownership of Palestine, he is said to have replied, "Memory is right.") Shapira, *Land and Power: The Zionist Resort to Force, 1881–1948* (Stanford, CA: Stanford University Press, 1999), p. 41; for the Weizmann quote, see Amos Elon, *The Israelis: Founders and Sons* (New York: Holt, Rinehart and Winston, 1971), p. 37. Highly influential Zionist figures, such as the journalist Micha Josef Berdyczewski, did, however, question the historical right: "The country is not ours," Berdyczewski wrote, "inasmuch as for a thousand years it was forsaken by us, and other peoples conquered it in blood, saturating its soil. Thus, doubt speaks in our hearts, on occasion, adding another burden for us to carry." Shapira, *Land and Power*, pp. 45–46.

19. On the centrality of religious ideas, traditions, and texts in early Zionism, see Shapira, *Israel*, p. 15; Shapira, *Land and Power*, p. 41. The idea of the Jews returning to their ancient homeland in order to hasten the arrival of the Messiah and redeem the world, Shapira writes, coincided with a rise in Christian missionary activity in Palestine and seems to have originated among a group of evangelical English Protestants in the 1840s. The Jewish left bitterly opposed the idea because it was based on religion, while Jewish conservatives, like much of the anti-Zionist ultra-Orthodox community today, considered it sacrilegious interference with God's plan. For the Shapira quote ("seminal text"), see Shapira, *Israel*, p. 58. In *Land and Power* (p. 28), Shapira writes that "the Bible was the battlefield on which the struggle over the nature of the new national ethos was waged." For the piety of Eastern European Jews as the reason the Zionist movement chose Palestine over other territories, see Shapira, *Israel*, pp. 22–23; Shapira, *Land and Power*, p. 9.

20. Estimates of the number of Jews who entered Palestine during the First Aliya vary widely, but most sources share in common the assertion that the majority of immigrants did not stay. For an estimate of 60,000, of whom between half and 70 percent left the country, see Shapira, *Israel*, p. 33. For an estimate of 30,000 immigrants, of whom only half remained in Palestine, see Aviva Zeltzer-Zubida and Hani Zubida, "Patterns of Immigration and Absorption," *Israel Studies: An Anthology*, 2012, p. 5, available at: http://www.israel-studies.com/anth_pdf/Zubida .pdf. For an estimate of 20,000–30,000 immigrants who entered Palestine, see Robert Bachi, *The Population of Israel* (Jerusalem: Scientific Translations International), p. 79, available at: http://www.cicred.org/Eng/Publications/pdf/c-c26.pdf.

For an argument that even Bachi's lower estimate of 20,000 is too high and doesn't account for the large number of immigrants who left Palestine, see McCarthy, *The Population of Palestine*, pp. 20, 23. In the Second Aliya (1904–1914), according to Shapira (p. 33), "some 40,000 immigrants came to Palestine, and more than 60 percent of them eventually left, with some estimates putting that figure even higher." See also Shafir, *Land, Labor, and the Origins of the Israeli-Palestinian Conflict*, pp. 74–75. For Shavit's quote ("the national moral leader"), see Shavit, *Promised Land*, p. 43. For Ahad Ha'am's views, see Shapira, *Israel*, pp. 21–22.

21. For Shavit on Palestine's emptiness (echoing the old Zionist slogan "a land without a people for a people without a land"), see Shavit, *Promised Land*, p. 12. For the Zionist slogan, which was common at the end of the nineteenth and beginning of the twentieth centuries, see Shapira, *Land and Power*, p. 42. For the Ahad Ha'am quote, see Ahad Ha'am, "A Truth from Eretz Yisrael," translated by Hilla Dayan, in *Wrestling with Zion: Progressive Jewish-American Responses to the Israeli-Palestinian Conflict*, Tony Kushner and Alisa Solomon, eds. (New York: Grove Press, 2003), pp. 15–16.

22. For text of Epstein's lecture, see Yitzhak Epstein, "The Hidden Question," Qumsiyeh.org, accessed August 21, 2016, http://qumsiyeh.org/yitzhakepstein/. In *Land and Power*, Anita Shapira quotes Hillel Zeitlin, a member of the territorialist camp: "What all the Palestinians [he means the Zionists of Zion] forget, mistakenly or maliciously, is that Palestine belongs to others, and it is totally settled. . . . For what reason and why would they give you Palestine . . . at the same time that they themselves want to be the lords of the land, who are the ones who are settled there and till the land and who wish to rule over it?" The Zionists of Zion, Shapira writes, "answered these pointed questions by the reply that if Palestine were not given to them, they would take it by force." Shapira, *Land and Power*, pp. 46–47.

23. For Shavit's quote ("absolute, universal justice that cannot be refuted"), see Shavit, *Promised Land*, p. 52. For Sharett's quote ("not a single Arab"), see Shapira, *Land and Power*, p. 227. For the Ben Gurion quote ("we are the aggressors"), see Morris, *Righteous Victims*, p. 676.

24. For Shavit's quote ("unjust colonial movement"), see Shavit, *Promised Land*, p. 31. For the promotion of Jewish labor, the efforts to close the economy to Arab workers, the Arab petitions against Jewish immigration, and the urban lifestyle chosen by most immigrants, see Shapira, *Land and Power*, p. 220; Shapira, *Israel*, pp. 96, 106–7, 145, 147. For Shapira's quote ("Despite all the preaching"), see Shapira, *Israel*, p. 112.

25. For Shavit's quote ("from a state of utopian bliss"), see Shavit, *Promised Land*, p. 73. For the 1886 riots and subsequent ones, see Shapira, *Land and Power*, pp. 57–58, 110–11, 129; Shapira, *Israel*, p. 81.

26. For Shavit's quote ("inevitable phase of the Zionist revolution"), see Shavit, *Promised Land*, p. 131. For a map of the discontinuous thirds of the 1947 partition plan, see Shapira, *Israel*, Plate 3, located between pages 242 and 243. For the Shapira quote ("ill-equipped, partially trained"), see Shapira, *Israel*, p. 148. On the relative size of Israeli and Arab forces during the war, see chapter 1, section iii, n. 81; Avi Shlaim, "Israel and the Arab Coalition in 1948," in *The War for Palestine*, Eugene L. Rogan and Avi Shlaim, eds., p. 81. For Shapira's quote ("did his utmost to avoid that snare"), see Shapira, *Israel*, p. 280.

27. For Shavit's quote ("at the core of the Zionist enterprise"), see Shavit, *Promised Land*, p. 245. For the argument made by a group of Palestinian leaders ("What confusion would ensue"), see the Palestine Arab Delegation's "Observations on the High Commissioner's Interim Report on the Civil Administration of Palestine During the Period 1st July 1920–30th June 1921," as cited in Natasha Gill's valuable essay, "The Original 'No': Why the Arabs Rejected Zionism, and Why It Matters," Middle East Policy Council, June 19, 2013. I am grateful to Natasha Gill for generously providing me with the original documents and numerous related ones.

28. For Shavit's quote ("an aberration, a grotesque reincarnation"), see Shavit, *Promised Land*, p. 221.

29. For the several thousand Palestinians killed while trying to sneak back to their homes, see Shapira, *Israel*, pp. 274–75; Morris, *Israel's Border Wars*; Morris, *Righteous Victims*, pp. 272–78. For the tens of thousands of Palestinians encouraged to leave or forcibly displaced, see the estimate by Morris of 30,000–40,000 in 1948–1950 alone: Morris, *The Birth of the Palestinian Refugee Problem Revisited*, p. 536.

30. For the restrictions on Palestinians in Israel until 1966, see Shapira, *Israel*, pp. 196–98. For the plans to transfer tens of thousands of Christian Arabs to Argentina and Brazil, see Arik Ariel, "Revealed from Archive: Israel's Secret Plan to Resettle Arab Refugees," *Haaretz*, December 19, 2013. For Shavit's quote ("a just social democracy"), Shavit, *Promised Land*, p. 151.

31. For restrictions on the growth of Arab villages and efforts to "Judaize" the Arab-inhabited areas, see Shapira, *Israel*, pp. 350–51. For the push by the Labor Party and leading intellectuals for settlement growth and territorial expansion, see Gorenberg, *The Unmaking of Israel* (New York: Harper, 2011), p. 68; Shapira, *Israel*, p. 345.

32. For restrictions on the sale and lease of land to Arabs, punishment of commemoration of the Nakba, and the plans to "Judaize Galilee," see Zafrir Rinat, "WZO Pushing New Jewish Towns to 'Balance' Arab Population in Israel's North," *Haaretz*, December 1, 2013; "'Judaization' of the Galilee Means Racism," *Haaretz*, December 2, 2013; The Association for Civil Rights in Israel, "'The Nakba Law' and Its Implications," May 15, 2011; Human Rights Watch, "Off the Map: Land and Housing Rights Violations in Israel's Unrecognized Bedouin Villages," 2008; Adalah–The Legal Center for Arab Minority Rights in Israel, "New Data on 39th Land Day: Gross Housing Discrimination Continues Against Palestinian Citizens of Israel," March 30, 2015; Adalah, "Challenging ILA Policy of Tenders Open Only to Jews for Jewish National Fund Lands"; Adalah, "Land Rights and the Indigenous Palestinian Arab Citizens of Israel: Recent Cases in Law, Land and Planning," submitted to the Secretariat, UN Working Group on Indigenous Populations, April 26, 2004. For the *Haaretz* headline, see "'Judaization' Is Racism," *Haaretz*, January 20, 2013.

33. For the blurbs for Shavit's book and the Natan Book Award, see the following page at the Random House website: www.randomhouseacademic.com/book?isbn =9780385521703, accessed August 23, 2016. For AIPAC's distribution of the book to the Saban Leadership Seminar in 2014 and its sponsorship of several events for the book, see, for example, Jewish Federation of Cincinnati, "AIPAC Presents: An Evening with Ari Shavit," October 28, 2014; Jewish Boston, "AIPAC PRESENTS: My Promised Land with Ari Shavit," April 2, 2014. For the laudatory columns by Thomas Friedman and David Brooks, see Thomas L. Friedman, "Something for Barack and Bibi to Talk About," *The New York Times*, November 17, 2013; David Brooks, "The Tragic Situation," *The New York Times*, December 20, 2013. For David Remnick's first quote, see the November 18, 2013, episode of the television program *Charlie Rose*. For Remnick's second quote ("an argument for liberal Zionism"), see "A Conversation About Israel," Council on Foreign Relations, December 4, 2013. For the Leon Wieseltier quote ("unblinkered by Zionism"), see Leon Wieseltier, "The State of Israel," *The New York Times*, November 24, 2013.

34. This desire to have it both ways is not foreign to Shavit's American Jewish fans, nor to the major leaders of their communities: when Spain decided to grant citizenship to descendants of Jews who were expelled during the Inquisition,

Malcolm Hoenlein, executive vice chairman of the Conference of Presidents of Major American Jewish Organizations, the central representative body of the American Jewish establishment, said: "We saw a country confronting history, although 500 years late. [The] fact is that the Spanish government, in this action, is saying they recognize what happened. While they can't undo it, they can at least acknowledge to those of Spanish descent that they are welcome in Spain." Despite all of Shavit's emphasis on 1948, he, like Hoenlein, does not call for Israel to offer its own recognition and to welcome the descendants of those who were expelled. For Hoenlein's quote, see Judy Maltz, "U.S. Jewish Leader: BDS is '21st Century Form of 20th Century Anti-Semitism,'" *Haaretz*, February 17, 2014. For a public opinion poll showing that most American Jews identify as liberals and Democrats and feel affection for Israel, see "A Portrait of Jewish Americans," Pew Research Center, October 1, 2013. For Shavit's quotes ("have to leave that behind" and "we are the ultimate victims"), see "'Promised Land' Wrestles with Israel's Brutal Contradictions," *NPR*, November 18, 2013, http://www.npr.org/2013/11/18 /245952983/promised-land-wrestles-with-israels-brutal-contradictions.

35. The Shavit and Remnick quotes appear between minutes 34 and 36 of the following recording of a November 19, 2013, event at the 92nd Street Y in New York: www .youtube.com/watch?v=aeDxRFeNs_o, accessed August 23, 2016.

36. Shavit's quote ("moral and reasonable obligation") appears between minutes 6 and 7 of the November 18, 2013, episode of the television program *Charlie Rose*.

37. For Shavit's quotes ("a collective act of messianic drunkenness"; "military campaign patiently, wisely, and calmly"; "We're a tiny minority nation under attack"; "no partner"; and "liable to foment tidal waves of violence"), see Ari Shavit, "Why We Hate Him: The Real Reason," *Haaretz*, December 26, 1997; "The Israelis' Victory," *Haaretz*, April 22, 2004; "The Challenge of Anti-Semitism," *Haaretz*, August 21, 2014; "Thinking Outside Two Boxes," *Haaretz*, March 19, 2009; "So Mature, This New Israeli Majority," *Haaretz*, August 16, 2005. For the 71 Israelis and more than 2,250 Palestinians killed in the Gaza war, as well as one foreign worker in Israel, see chapter 9, nn. 16 and 18. For Shavit's quotes on the Olmert plan ("unconditional surrender of Zionism"), his statement that withdrawal from even part of the West Bank would be a mistake, and his advocacy of cautious and gradual change while Israeli soldiers remain in place, see Ari Shavit, "Olmert's Arrogance," *Haaretz*, March 14, 2006; "The State of Israel: Past, Present, and Future," Council on Foreign Relations, November 20, 2013. For a catalogue of Shavit's many false and hysterical predictions, see "Ari Shavit: Apocalypse Now, Apocalypse Forever," *+972*, November 21, 2013.

38. For Wieseltier's quote ("least tendentious"), see Leon Wieseltier, "The State of Israel," *The New York Times*, November 24, 2013. For Shavit's quote ("prophet"), see Shavit, *Promised Land*, p. 397. For a citation of the Jabotinsky passage, from his essay, "The Iron Wall," see chapter 3, n. 6.

3. GOING NATIVE

This chapter was updated in September 2016.

1. For the numbers killed and injured during the first weeks of October 2015, see Israel Ministry of Foreign Affairs, "Wave of Terror 2015/16," July 11, 2016; "Palestinians Killed in the OPT and Israel Since 1 October 2015," *Al-Haq*, October 19, 2015.

2. For the T-shirt, see Ian Black, "Wave of Violence Fuels Arab-Jewish Suspicions in Israel's Heartland," *The Guardian*, November 6, 2015. For the attack on the Eritrean asylum seeker, see Raoul Wootliff, "New Video Exposes Severity of Eritrean Man's 'Lynching,'" *The Times of Israel*, October 23, 2015.

3. On the government taking harsher measures than recommended by the security establishment, see Barak Ravid, "Police Chief Rebuffs Ministers' Calls to 'Enforce Israeli Sovereignty in East Jerusalem,'" *Haaretz*, October 14, 2015; "Police Given Authority to Impose East Jerusalem Closures," *The Times of Israel*, October 14, 2015. On the proposal to destroy illegally built homes in Jerusalem, see Barak Ravid, "Police Chief Rebuffs Ministers' Calls to 'Enforce Israeli Sovereignty in East Jerusalem,'" *Haaretz*, October 14, 2015. For estimates on the share of Palestinian homes in East Jerusalem that lack Israeli-issued building permits, ranging from 33 to 39 percent, see "EU HoMs Report on Jerusalem," European Union Heads of Mission in Jerusalem and Ramallah, March 18, 2014, accessed June 4, 2016; Association for Civil Rights in Israel, "East Jerusalem 2015: Facts and Figures," May 12, 2015.

4. For the interior minister's call to deport Palestinian attackers from East Jerusalem and revoke some of the rights of their relatives, see Judah Ari Gross, Raoul Wootliff, and *Times of Israel* staff, "Minister Says Residency of 19 East Jerusalem Terrorists to Be Revoked," *The Times of Israel,* October 14, 2015. For the government's refusal to return some Palestinian bodies, see "Israel Won't Return Bodies of Dead Palestinian Assailants," *The Jerusalem Post*, October 14, 2015.

5. On the criminalization of Palestinian political activity, see International Crisis Group, "Extreme Makeover? (II): The Withering of Arab Jerusalem," *Middle East Report*, no. 135, December 20, 2012, p. 1.

6. For the article by Jabotinsky, first published in Russian on November 4, 1923, in *Rassvyet*, with the title *O Zheleznoi Stene*, see Lenni Brenner, *The Iron Wall: Zionist Revisionism from Jabotinsky to Shamir* (London: Zed Books, 1984), pp. 146–49. Jabotinsky published it under his birth name, Vladimir.

7. For more on these exceptions, see Avi Shlaim, *The Iron Wall: Israel and the Arab World* (New York: W. W. Norton & Company, 2014), pp. 40, 48, 64–71, 76–80, 318–19, 337. Subsequent to them were the Fahd Plan of 1981 and the Fez Initiative of 1982; a January 1982 Syrian offer of peace in return for full Israeli withdrawal from the territories occupied in 1967 and the establishment of a Palestinian state under the PLO; Jordanian-Israeli negotiations over the West Bank in the 1980s; the Arab Peace Initiative of 2002; and Syrian-Israeli talks over the Golan in the 1990s, 2000, 2007–2008, and 2010. In February 1971, Egypt also proposed an interim deal, short of a full peace agreement, in which Egypt would open the Suez Canal to Israeli shipping and Israel would withdraw its forces from part of Sinai, including the eastern bank of the canal. See Shlaim, pp. 305–12. For the January 1982 offer from Syria, see Yezid Sayigh, *Armed Struggle and the Search for State: The Palestinian National Movement, 1949–1993* (New York: Oxford University Press, 1999), p. 513. For the Jordanian-Israeli talks, see Shlaim, pp. 457–63. For the talks with Syria in the 1990s and 2000, see Shlaim, pp. 549–56, 573–74, 619–25, 656–68, 660–65. For the 2007–2008 Syria-Israel talks, see Peter Walker, "Syria and Israel Officially Confirm Peace Talks," *The Guardian*, May 21, 2008. For the 2010 Syria-Israel talks, see Isabel Kershner, "Secret Israel-Syria Peace Talks Involved Golan Heights Exit," *The New York Times*, October 12, 2012.

8. For the role of Ben Gurion and the first heads of the Mossad, see Yossi Alpher,

Periphery: Israel's Search for Middle East Allies (London: Rowman & Littlefield, 2015), p. xvii.

9. Despite appearances to the contrary, Alpher insists that some of the alliances were driven by more than just realpolitik. Arguing that ethics and morality were important drivers of aid to the Iraqi Kurdish struggle for independence, Alpher tells of the answer that Prime Minister Yitzhak Rabin gave to a parliamentary question about the motive for Israel's support: "Because we're Jews." Alpher fails to note that a sense of Jewish morality did not cause Israel to support the quest for independence of the far larger Kurdish populations in Turkey and Iran. For the Rabin quote, see Alpher, *Periphery*, p. 51.

10. For some of the achievements of the periphery doctrine that were not directed primarily at Israel's adversaries, including economic benefits such as Israeli imports of Omani and Iranian oil for export to Europe, as well as the receipt of Iranian funds for the development of Israeli weapons programs, see Alpher, *Periphery*, pp. 7, 73. For Israel's marketing of the periphery alliances to the United States, see Alpher, pp. 5, 19. For Egypt's fears concerning Israel's periphery alliances and the northward flow of Nile River water, see Alpher, p. 113. For the share of Egyptian troops tied down in Yemen, see Alpher, p. 37, who provides a number of one-third, a figure also cited by Eugene Rogan and Tewfik Aclimandos, "The Yemen War and Egypt's War Preparedness," in *The 1967 Arab-Israeli War: Origins and Consequences*, Wm. Roger Louis and Avi Shlaim, eds. (Cambridge, UK: Cambridge University Press, 2012), p. 155. For an argument that these figures are inflated, see Kenneth M. Pollack, *Arabs at War: Military Effectiveness, 1948–1991* (Lincoln, NE: University of Nebraska Press, 2002), pp. 593–94. For Alpher's quote on Uganda ("all fruits of"), see Alpher, p. 39.

11. For the allure of using Israeli influence in Washington, see Alpher, *Periphery*, pp. 63–73, 136. For the Alpher quote ("could manipulate U.S. policy in their favor"), see Ronen Bergman, "The Officer Who Saw Behind the Top-Secret Curtain," *Yediot Aharonot*, June 21, 2015. Alpher also writes of the issue at several points in his book (pp. 63, 379, 73), including an anecdote involving a Turkish official who told the CIA that Israel was an essential component of efforts to combat recognition of the Armenian genocide: "The reason we are so friendly to Israel," said the Turkish official, "is that . . . AIPAC . . . is the solution to the Armenian problem." Alpher, p. 17.

12. For the lack of help from periphery allies in 1967 and the antagonistic behavior of Morocco and Iran in 1973, see Alpher, *Periphery*, pp. 139, 71. For the Kurdish failure to open a front against Iraq, and pressure on the Kurds by Iran and the United States, see Alpher, pp. 55, 66, 71, 88, 139. For Iran's support of the Arab oil embargo, see Alpher, p. 15. For the United States' lack of enthusiasm for Israel's periphery alliances and the failure of the periphery doctrine to "aggrandize [Israel's] political stock in Washington," see Alpher, pp. 139–40.

13. For the Algiers Agreement between Iran and Iraq, Israel's hope of bringing to power a friendly Lebanese regime that would expel the Palestinians to Jordan, and the lesson of the Lebanese failure for Israel, see Alpher, *Periphery*, pp. 58–59, 47, 96, xxi, 73.

14. For the Arafat quote ("handful of Sinai sand"), see Lawrence Wright, *Thirteen Days in September: Carter, Begin, and Sadat at Camp David* (New York: Knopf, 2014), p. 287.

15. For the quotes from Kamel ("a separate peace") and Sadat ("bluster and empty slogans"), see Wright, *Thirteen Days*, p. 243.

16. For more on the 1982 Arab plan, which was a slightly modified version of Saudi Arabia's "Fahd Plan" of 1981, see chapter 1. For Shamir's quote ("declaration of war") and the Foreign Ministry statement ("danger to Israel's existence"), see "Israel Rejects Arab Summit Plan as 'Declaration of War on Israel' and Terms It Worse Than Fahd Plan," Jewish Telegraphic Agency, September 13, 1982.

17. For the Arabic-speaking countries with diplomatic representation in Israel, see Alpher, *Periphery*, p. 95; Israel Ministry of Foreign Affairs, "Israel Among the Nations: Middle East & North Africa," accessed August 21, 2016, http://mfa.gov.il /MFA/AboutIsrael/Nations/Pages/Israel Among The Nations- Middle East - North Afri.aspx. For Peres's quote, see Alpher, *Periphery*, p. 98.

18. For more on the suppression and defeat of the Muslim Brotherhood, see chapter 9; Carlotta Gall, "Islamist Party in Tunisia Concedes to Secularists," *The New York Times*, October 27, 2014. For the Yadlin quote ("third-order threats"), see Amos Yadlin, "Undermining Assad," in "Israel's Northern Border and the Chaos in Syria: A Symposium," *Jewish Review of Books*, Summer 2015. On Hamas seeking a long-term cease-fire, see "Abu Marzouk: No Truce Before Israel Lifts Siege on Gaza," The Palestinian Information Center, September 6, 2015.

19. For the steps taken by Saudi Arabia and other Gulf states toward increasingly public cooperation with Israel, see Herb Keinon, "Top Diplomat: Israel Has Contacts with Almost Every Arab State," *The Jerusalem Post*, January 19, 2016; "Netanyahu: Some Arab Countries See Israel as an Ally," *Israel National News*, February 15, 2016; Barak Ravid, "Ya'alon: Israelis Secret Meeting with Officials from Gulf States," *Haaretz*, February 14, 2016; Barak Ravid, "Former Saudi General Visits Israel, Meets with Foreign Ministry Director-General," *Haaretz*, July 22, 2016; Chemi Shalev, "Saudi Prince al-Faisal Tells *Haaretz*: Desire for Peace Exists Both in Gaza and Ramallah," *Haaretz*, November 12, 2015; J. J. Goldberg, "Top Israeli, Saudi Ex-Spy Chiefs in Rare Dialogue," *The Forward*, May 26, 2014; Eric Cortellessa, "In Rare Joint Appearance, Saudi Prince, Ex-Netanyahu Adviser Spar over Peace," *The Times of Israel*, May 6, 2016; Elliott Abrams, "Reading *The Jerusalem Post* in Riyadh," Council on Foreign Relations, October 8, 2016. For the Israeli diplomatic office in Abu Dhabi and the joint aerial combat exercise with the UAE and Pakistan, see "Israel to Open Representative Office in Abu Dhabi, First in UAE," Reuters, November 27, 2015; Judah Ari Gross, "Israeli Pilots Return Home After Flying Alongside Pakistan, UAE in U.S. Drill," *The Times of Israel*, September 1, 2016. For Sudan's announcement of possible normalization with Israel, as well as Israel's lobbying of the United States and EU member states to improve ties with Sudan, see Sue Surkes, "Sudan Said Willing to Consider Normalizing Ties with Israel," *The Times of Israel*, January 21, 2016; Barak Ravid, "Israel Urges U.S., Europe to Bolster Ties with Sudan," *Haaretz*, September 7, 2016. For Peres's address to Arab and Muslim foreign ministers, see Spencer Ho, "Peres Addressed 29 Arab and Muslim Foreign Ministers," *The Times of Israel*, December 2, 2013. For the softening of the Arab League's peace offer, see "In Sea Change, Arab League Backs Land Swaps in Peace Talks," *The Times of Israel*, April 30, 2013; "Arab States 'Willing to Change Peace Initiative, Waiting to Hear from PM,'" *The Times of Israel,* May 20, 2016. For attempts to help Israel and its Arab allies work together toward Israeli-Palestinian peace, see William Booth and Ruth Eglash, "What Is Egypt's Sissi up to? Maybe an Israel-Palestinian Peace Deal," *The Washington Post*, July 11, 2016; "Arab States 'Willing to Change Peace

Initiative, Waiting to Hear from PM,'" *The Times of Israel*, May 20, 2016. For more on Israeli exports to Arab states such as Tunisia, Morocco, the UAE, and Qatar, see Tani Goldstein, "'Arabs Dying to Do Business With Israel,'" *Ynet*, April 3, 2011.

20. For the Menachem Begin quip, see "Menachem Begin," New World Encyclopedia, accessed August 20, 2016, http://www.newworldencyclopedia.org/entry/Menachem _Begin; Eran Etzion, "Israel on the Outer in Syria's Civil War," Middle East Institute, July 19, 2016. For the old idea of a Druze buffer state in southern Syria, see Alpher, *Periphery*, pp. 43–44. On the hope of Israel's right wing that the international community will reverse its opposition to Israeli annexation of the Golan, see Isabel Kershner, "Israel Will Never Give Golan Heights to Syria, Netanyahu Vows," *The New York Times*, April 17, 2016.

21. For the 2016 Turkish-Israeli reconciliation, see Cengiz Çandar, "Erdogan Displays Survival Instinct in Israel Reconciliation," *Al-Monitor*, June 27, 2016. For Turkey-Israel trade during the period of downgraded ties, see Ora Coren, "Israeli Trade with Turkey on Track to Reach Record," *Haaretz*, July 4, 2014. For EU trade with Israel, see "European Union, Trade in Goods with Israel," European Commission, June 21, 2016, accessed August 21, 2016, http://trade.ec.europa.eu/doclib/docs/2006 /september/tradoc_113402.pdf. For Israel as one of the world's top arms exporters (ranked ten in the world from 2010 to 2015), see "SIPRI Arms Transfers Database," Stockholm International Peace Research Institute, accessed October 18, 2016, http://armstrade.sipri.org/armstrade/page/toplist.php. For Israel's approval of contracts to sell natural gas to Egypt and Jordan, see "Government Approves First Gas Export Contract from Israel to Egypt," *Natural Gas World*, December 24, 2015; Sharon Udasin, "Israel to Supply Gas to Jordan in $10 Billion Deal," *The Jerusalem Post*, September 26, 2016. For Israel's energy exports prior to the natural gas deals (e.g., crude oil, electricity, and refined petroleum products), see "Israel," CIA World Factbook, accessed August 20, 2016, http://www.cia.gov/library/publications/the -world-factbook/geos/is.html. For Israel's strengthening ties with India and China, see Dan Blumenthal, "Is China a Friend of Israel?," *Mosaic Magazine*, November 16, 2015; Tanvi Madan, "Why India and Israel Are Bringing Their Relationship out from 'Under the Carpet,'" Brookings Institution, February 11, 2016; "India Successfully Testfires Indo-Israeli Barak-8 Missile," Xinhua, December 30, 2015. For Israel's efforts to join the African Union as an observer and growing ties with African states, see Ken Karuri, "Guinea, Israel Restore Diplomatic Ties after 49 Years of Severed Relations," *Africa News*, July 20, 2016; "Kenya Set to Help Restore Israeli Ties with Africa," Jewish News Service, July 5, 2016; "Ethiopia Backs Israeli Bid for AU Observer Status," *Al Jazeera*, July 7, 2016. For Israel's permanent office at NATO headquarters and its election as chair of a UN permanent committee, see Julian E. Barnes and Emre Parker, "Israel to Open Office at NATO Headquarters," *The Wall Street Journal*, May 4, 2016; "Israel Elected to Head Permanent U.N. Committee for First Time," Reuters, June 13, 2016.

22. Barak Ravid, "Mossad Chief: Palestinian Conflict Top Threat to Israel's Security, Not Iran," *Haaretz*, July 5, 2014; Barak Ravid, "Mossad Chief: Nuclear Iran Not Necessarily Existential Threat to Israel," *Haaretz*, December 29, 2011.

23. For more details, see chapter 12; "Fact Sheet: Memorandum of Understanding Reached with Israel," White House, Office of the Press Secretary, September 14, 2016.

PART III. COLLABORATION

"Abbas Vows to Uphold 'Sacred' Security Coordination with Israel," *The Times of Israel*, May 28, 2014.

4. OUR MAN IN PALESTINE

This chapter was updated in September 2016.

1. For the August 31, 2010, attack and the statement from Hamas, see "4 Israelis Killed in Shooting Attack Shattering Years of Relative West Bank Calm," *Haaretz*, September 1, 2010. For a report on Palestinian security reform, see International Crisis Group, "Squaring the Circle: Palestinian Security Reform Under Occupation," *Middle East Report*, no. 98, September 7, 2010.

2. For use of the phrase "Dayton forces," which Hamas sometimes applied only to the subset of PA security forces trained by the United States (primarily the National Security Forces) but most often applied collectively to all PA security agencies in the West Bank, see "Hamas Prisoners: The PA Security Became More Dangerous than the Occupation," The Palestinian Information Center, June 11, 2009; "Squaring the Circle." On Fayyad's day-to-day control of the security forces (despite the fact that the president is the commander-in-chief), the above cited report by the International Crisis Group states: "today each branch [of PA security] has three masters: the interior minister, prime minister and president. Of the three, the ministry is the weakest; the president is the commander-in-chief and theoretically the strongest, but since Abbas often is abroad and rarely involves himself in daily affairs, much of the authority in practice falls to Fayyad. A ministry official commented: 'This means that any chief worth his salt cultivates his relations with both the prime minister and the president. Fayyad has the money and some operational control, but being on good terms with Abbas give[s] you leverage with Fayyad.' . . . According to a PA security official, 'although the security campaigns were condoned by the president, Fayyad was the main driving force.'"

3. "Salam Fayyad—Full Bio," Atlantic Council, accessed August 27, 2016, http://www.atlanticcouncil.org/about/experts/list/salam-fayyad#fullbio; "Profile: Salam Fayyad," BBC, June 17, 2007, http://news.bbc.co.uk/2/hi/middle_east/6757273.stm.

4. For Fayyad's suggestion that Palestine would offer citizenship to Jews, see "Fayyad: Jews Can Be Equal Citizens in a Palestinian State," *Haaretz*, July 5, 2009. For an example of the sort of approbation Fayyad received, see several columns by Roger Cohen, who called Fayyad "the most important phenomenon in the Middle East"; and Thomas Friedman, who coined a term for the prime minister's brand of "transparent, accountable administration and services"—"Fayyadism"—which Friedman called "the most exciting new idea in Arab governance ever." Roger Cohen, "Beating the Mideast's Black Hole," *The International Herald Tribune*, April 27, 2010; Thomas Friedman, "Green Shoots in Palestine," *The New York Times*, August 4, 2009. For Bush greeting Fayyad with the "Hook 'em Horns" sign, see Steven Erlanger, "An Economist's Task: Building a Model for His People," *The New York Times*, August 25, 2007. On Fayyad and Sharon at the wedding, see an article by Sharon's adviser, Dov Weisglass: "The Visionary of the Palestinian State," *Yediot Aharonot*, February 7, 2010.

5. For Peres comparing Fayyad to Ben Gurion, see Akiva Eldar, "A Day in the Life of the Palestinian Ben Gurion," *Haaretz*, February 11, 2010. For Fayyad's quote ("the

reality of the state will impose itself'"), see Fadi Elsalameen, "Fayyad: 'Build, Build Despite the Occupation,'" *The Palestine Note*, July 30, 2010. For support for Fayyad's plan, see "Middle East Quartet Communiqué," Office of the United Nations Special Coordinator for the Middle East Peace Process, September 24, 2009; "Joint Statement by the Quartet," US State Department Office of Press Relations, March 19, 2010. For a lengthy interview with Fayyad about the plan, see Khalid Farraj, Camille Mansour, and Salim Tamari, "A Palestinian State in Two Years: Interview with Salam Fayyad, Palestinian Prime Minister," *Journal of Palestine Studies* 39, no. 1 (2009–2010).

6. For Lieberman's warning, see Merav Michaeli, "Lieberman: Israel's Gestures to Palestinians Met with 'Slaps in the Face,'" *Haaretz*, May 13, 2010.

7. For Fayyad's quote ("intended to generate pressure"), see Elsalameen, "Fayyad-Build, Build." The Israeli-Palestinian talks that started in September 2010 and were quickly aborted had a late summer 2011 deadline that coincided with Fayyad's. Herzog's quotes are taken from an interview with the author, Tel Aviv, April 2010.

8. Much was made of a report by the International Monetary Fund stating that real GDP in the West Bank grew by 8.5 percent in 2009. For a source arguing that the IMF's report of West Bank economic growth was greatly exaggerated, see Bassim S. Khoury, "Putting the Palestinian 'Carriage Behind the Horse,'" ForeignPolicy.com, July 1, 2010, http://foreignpolicy.com/2010/07/02/putting-the-palestinian-carriage-behind-the-horse/. Ghassan Khatib's quote comes from an interview with the author, Ramallah, April 2010.

9. For data on joint Israeli-Palestinian security operations, see "Measures Taken by Israel in Support of Developing the Palestinian Economy, the Socio-Economic Structure, and the Security Reforms," Report of the Government of Israel to the Ad Hoc Liaison Committee, April 13, 2010.

10. For the quotes and figures from the Shin Bet, see Israeli Security Agency. "2010 Annual Summary—Data and Trends in Palestinian Terrorism"; "2009 Annual Summary—Data and Trends in Palestinian Terrorism." See also previous Israeli Security Agency reports and Israel Ministry of Foreign Affairs, "Four Years of Conflict: Israel's War Against Terrorism," October 3, 2004. The 2010 Shin Bet report states that the number of attacks from Jerusalem and the West Bank was 1,309 in 2006, 946 in 2007, 893 in 2008, and 636 in 2009. Of these, West Bank and Jerusalem shooting and explosive attacks had gone from 744 in 2006 to 464 in 2007, 137 in 2008, and 33 in 2009.

11. Herzog's quote is taken from an interview with the author. Mona Mansour's quote comes from an interview with the author, Nablus, April 2010.

12. For figures on the Palestinian security forces, see Jim Zanotti, "U.S. Foreign Aid to the Palestinians," Congressional Research Service, March 18, 2016, p. 15. Four of these battalions had been trained by January 2010 and nine by the end of 2012. In addition, the United States trained two battalions of the Presidential Guard. According to the Congressional Research Service, between 2007 and 2012, there were 6,000 personnel (nine special battalions of the National Security Forces and two battalions of the Presidential Guard) trained under the auspices of the United States. By 2016, the PA security forces in the West Bank had grown to 31,913 personnel, of whom 8,000 were NSF. See "Securing Gaza: Challenges to Reunifying the Palestinian Security and Justice Sectors," Geneva Centre for the

Democratic Control of Armed Forces (DCAF), 2016. On the size of the NSF in 2010, see the estimates made in "Palestinian Authority: U.S. Assistance Is Training and Equipping Security Forces, but the Program Needs to Measure Progress and Faces Logistical Constraints," US Government Accountability Office (Washington, DC, May 2010); and "Squaring the Circle." The number used in this chapter falls between the figures provided in those two reports and represents a slight adjustment, presented to me by a spokesman for the European Union Police Mission for the Palestinian Territories (EUPOL COPPS) in April 2010, of a previous estimate made by US officials. See "West Bank: Palestinian Security Forces," US Security Coordination Road Warrior Team, June 2008.

13. For more on the leadership courses (open to members of each of the seven security services: the National Security Forces, Presidential Guard, Civil Police, Civil Defense, and three intelligence services—Military Intelligence, General Intelligence, and Preventive Security), see GAO report, p. 17. (Military Police is usually counted as part of Military Intelligence, and the very small Military Justice service is counted as part of the National Security Forces.) For the figures on State Department allocations, see Zanotti, "U.S. Foreign Aid," p. 3; GAO report, May 2010, pp. 3, 14.

14. For the number of USSC personnel and private contractors, see GAO report, May 2010, p. 12. For the training of nine battalions, one for every governorate except Jerusalem (the PA security sector treats Jenin and Tubas as a single governorate), as well as Dayton's plan to train a tenth battalion to be held in reserve, see "US Security Assistance to the Palestinian Authority," Congressional Research Service, January 8, 2010, pp. 13, 16; "Squaring the Circle," p. 11.

15. On Israel granting greater responsibility to Palestinian forces, see "Squaring the Circle," pp. 18–21. For Israel's removal of some restrictions in the West Bank, see UN Office for the Coordination of Humanitarian Affairs (UN OCHA), "West Bank Movement and Access Update," June 2010, pp. 2–13.

16. For Dermer's report, see Colonel Philip J. Dermer, "Trip Notes on a Return to Israel and the West Bank: Reflections on US Peacemaking, the Security Mission, and What Should Be Done," *Journal of Palestine Studies* 39, no. 3 (Spring 2010): 66–81. For Oren's quote ("the only viable model"), see James Kitfield, "United They Fall; Divided They Stand," *National Journal*, March 28, 2009.

17. The statement by Abrams comes from an interview with the author, Washington, DC, June 2010.

18. For the burning of synagogues and looting of greenhouses, see Said Ghazali, "Synagogues Burn as Palestinians Retake Gaza," *The Telegraph*, September 13, 2005; "Looters Strip Gaza Greenhouses," Associated Press, September 13, 2005. For the fighting in Gaza that followed Israel's withdrawal, see "Top Gaza Figure Assassinated," *The Scotsman*, September 8, 3005; "Inside Gaza: The Challenge of Clans and Families," International Crisis Group, *Middle East Report*, no. 71, December 20, 2007.

19. On Dayton's task shifting toward helping prevent Hamas from controlling the security forces, see Adam Entous, "Abbas Builds Up Forces Amid Palestinian Crisis," Reuters, October 5, 2006; David Rose, "The Proof Is in the Paper Trail," *Vanity Fair*, March 5, 2008. David Welch, a former assistant secretary of state for Near Eastern affairs who helped oversee the Dayton mission until December 2008, told me, "We were essentially trying to carve an uneasy middle ground between

cleaning the security forces up and defeating the enemy." Phone interview with the author, July 2010. By the fall of 2006, the Israeli daily *Haaretz* had reported that Dayton planned to push Abbas to confront Hamas in Gaza: Welch and Abrams, on a visit to Israel in early November, had "arrived with an ambitious plan that was formulated by Lieutenant General Keith Dayton. . . . The United States wants to push Abu Mazen into a military confrontation in Gaza, which will topple the Hamas government." Aluf Benn, "Words, Words, Words," *Haaretz*, November 2, 2006. For Abbas's decrees to limit the new government's powers, see International Crisis Group, "Palestinians, Israel, and the Quartet: Pulling Back from the Brink," *Middle East Report*, no. 54, June 13, 2006, p. 7. On US advice, Abrams told me that US officials had said to Abbas, "Could you issue a presidential decree that says, 'I hereby say that this force—Force 17—is no longer under the minister of interior'? But the question was always more legal and formal. In the real world, we—Abbas, Fatah, the PA, the PLO—were in control the whole time." Abrams interview with the author. On the violent clashes in Gaza, see Adam Entous and Haitham Tamimi, "Hamas, Abbas Rivalry Spurs Palestinian Arms Race," Reuters, June 8, 2006; "'This Must End Before It's Like Iraq," *The Jerusalem Post*, December 20, 2006.

20. For Mish'al's speech, see "Political Office Leader Khalid Mashal Speech: No Way We Will Bend to U.S., Israeli & Fateh Pressure to Be Subservient to the Zionists—Fateh Leaders in an Uproar," *Palestine News Network*, April 22, 2006. For Fayyad's statement on American pressure, see Fayyad interview in *Journal of Palestine Studies* 39, no. 1 (Autumn 2009): 58–74. For de Soto's report, see Alvaro de Soto, "End of Mission Report," May 2007. A week before Mecca, de Soto wrote, "the U.S. envoy declared twice in an envoys' meeting in Washington how much 'I like this violence.'" In my July 2010 interview with Welch, he told me: "I did say that. But what I also said was, 'Were there no violence, the good guys would already have capitulated.'" At the end of April 2007, a Jordanian newspaper published leaked US documents outlining a strategy to collapse the national unity government, bolster Fatah, and eliminate Hamas's new security force. Hamas officials would later say that these plans, together with the arrival from Egypt of troops trained under Dayton, prompted them to go on the offensive in Gaza in late spring. See Rose, "The Proof Is in the Paper Trail"; International Crisis Group, "After Gaza," *Middle East Report*, no. 68, August 2, 2007, p. 11; and comments by Mahmoud Zahar and Fawzi Barhoum in David Rose, "The Gaza Bombshell," *Vanity Fair*, April 2008.

21. For the Hamas attack on USSC-trained troops, see Ibrahim Barzak, "Hamas Kills 7 in Gaza Border Clash," Associated Press, May 15, 2007. For Dayton's testimony, see "U.S. Assistance to the Palestinians," Hearing before the Subcommittee on the Middle East and South Asia of the Committee on Foreign Affairs, House of Representatives, 110th Congress, May 23, 2007. For Sourani's quote ("just a few days"), see Paul McGeough, *Kill Khalid: The Failed Mossad Assassination of Khalid Mishal and the Rise of Hamas* (New York: The New Press, 2009), p. 381.

22. The Abrams quote ("the project was needed") comes from an interview with the author, June 2010. For dissenting views about the Dayton mission within the Bush administration, albeit from officials who did not have much influence over the policy they criticized, see quotes in Rose, "The Gaza Bombshell." This article also quotes UN ambassador John Bolton ("Having failed to heed the warning not to hold the elections, they tried to avoid the result through Dayton") and the Middle

East adviser to Vice President Cheney, David Wurmser: "What happened wasn't so much a coup by Hamas but an attempted coup by Fatah that was pre-empted before it could happen."

23. Welch's quotes ("the best Palestinian Authority government in history" and "a lot cleaner to do in the West Bank") are taken from an interview with the author, June 2010. For details of the PA's campaign in the West Bank, see International Crisis Group, "Ruling Palestine II: The West Bank Model?" *Middle East Report*, no. 79, July 17, 2008, p. 4.

24. Mohammed Najib, "Palestinian Officers Graduate from Jordanian Special Ops Training Course," *Jane's Defence Weekly*, May 2, 2008.

25. Ghaith al-Omari's quote ("nationalist, respectable endeavor") comes from an interview with the author, June 2010. For the poll on the attack in Dimona, which was supported by 77 percent of Palestinians surveyed, and the attack in Jerusalem, which was supported by 84 percent, see "Palestinian Public Opinion Poll, no. 27," Palestinian Center for Policy and Survey Research, March 24, 2008.

26. For the report in *Yediot Aharonot*, see Nahum Barnea, "Last Chance," *Yediot Aharonot*, September 19, 2008. See also "Shocking Details of PA-Israeli Security Meetings," *Palestine Times*, September 29, 2008; Jon Elmer, "A Prescription for Civil War," *Al-Jazeera*, February 8, 2010, http://english.aljazeera.net/focus/2009/12/2009121311331278355.html.

27. For the events in Hebron, see B'Tselem, "Hebron: Willful Abandonment by Security Forces," December 10, 2008; Ethan Bronner, "Israeli Troops Evict Settlers in the West Bank," *The New York Times*, December 4, 2008. For Olmert's quote ("pogrom"), see "Olmert Condemns Settler 'Pogrom,'" BBC, December 7, 2008. For the disappearance of the Palestinian security forces, see Jared Malsin, "Witnesses: Israeli Police, Soldiers 'Deeply Involved' in Settler Attacks," Ma'an News Agency, December 7, 2008; Tony Karon and Aaron J. Klein, "Israeli Settler Youth on the Rampage in Hebron," *Time*, December 5, 2008. The statements from the former governor of Hebron and the NSF commander of Hebron are taken from interviews with the author, Hebron, April 2010.

28. For actions by the West Bank security forces during the Gaza war, see Robert Blecher, "Operation Cast Lead in the West Bank," *Journal of Palestine Studies* 38, no. 3 (Spring 2009): 64–71; "Squaring the Circle," p. 10. For Dayton's quote ("a good portion of the Israeli army"), see Keith Dayton, "Peace Through Security: America's Role in the Development of the Palestinian Authority Security Services," Washington Institute for Near East Policy, Program of the Soref Symposium, Michael Stein Address on U.S. Middle East Policy, May 7, 2009. The quote from Ben-Zur ("in Israeli Arab cities") comes from an interview with the author, Tel Aviv, April 2010. For Lieberman's quote ("Abbas himself called and asked us"), see Merav Michaeli, "Lieberman: Israel's Gestures to Palestinians Met with 'Slaps in the Face,'" *Haaretz*, May 13, 2010.

29. For Dayton's quote ("new men"), see "Peace Through Security." For the PA's formal complaint, the refusal of senior PA officials to meet Dayton, and the quote ("owing to tensions"), see Mohammed Najib, "Palestinian Authority Seeks Changes in Security Training," *Jane's Defence Weekly*, August 5, 2009; and "Palestinian Authority to Opt Out of U.S. Training Programme," *Jane's Defence Weekly*, March 17, 2010.

30. For the poll on the PA's legitimacy and the large demonstrations against the PA,

see "Palestinian Public Opinion Poll, no. 31," Palestinian Center for Policy and Survey Research, December 22, 2008; "Massive Hamas Demonstrations Denounce Beitawi Shooting as 'Assassination Attempt,'" Ma'an News Agency, April 19, 2009. For the strafing of Beitawi's car, see Palestinian Centre for Human Rights, "Car of PLC Member Fired Upon by Unknown Persons in Nablus," September 4, 2008. For Beitawi's chairmanship of the Palestinian Islamic Scholars Association, see Matthew Levitt, *Hamas: Politics, Charity, and Terrorism in the Service of Jihad* (New Haven: Yale University Press, 2006), p. 102. For the PA's ban of Beitawi's sermons and the arrest of Beitawi's sons, see "Hamas Sheikh Banned from Delivering Sermons," Ma'an News Agency, August 16, 2010; "PA Night Raids Target 2 Leaders," Ma'an News Agency, September 12, 2010; "Source: 20 Hamas Leaders Detained, Funds Seized," Ma'an News Agency, July 31, 2010. The Beitawi quote ("corruption and coordination with the Israelis") comes from an interview with the author, Nablus, April 2010. Beitawi died in 2012.

31. For the funeral and protest, see "20,000 Attend Funeral for Slain Nablus Fatah Men," Ma'an News Agency, December 26, 2009; "Squaring the Circle." For video of the cartoon, which depicts a Palestinian officer offering a white dove to an Orthodox Jewish settler who has murdered Palestinian children and drunk their blood, see "New Anti-Semitic Animated Film Vilifies the Palestinian Authority—PA Security Forces Help Stereotypical Blood-Drinking Jews," Middle East Media Research Institute, January 1, 2010.

32. For Abbas's statement, see "U.S. Security Assistance to the Palestinian Authority," Congressional Research Service, January 8, 2010, p. 30. For Qaradawi's quote ("stoned to death"), see "Qaradawi Slams Abbas," *Al-Ahram*, January 21–27, 2010; "Sheik Al-Qaradhawi Suggests that Mahmoud Abbas Should Be Stoned to Death and Is Rebuked by PA Minister of Religious Endowments," Middle East Media Research Institute, January 7, 2010.

33. For the quote by the critic of the PA, Bassem Eid (a former senior researcher for the Israeli human rights organization B'Tselem who then founded the Palestinian Human Rights Monitoring Group—which focused on violations of human rights by the PA until it was shut down in 2011—and later became a prominent opponent of the Boycott, Divestment, and Sanctions movement), see Bassem Eid, "Jericho's Stasi," *The Jerusalem Post*, June 24, 2009. For the assertion by Mamdouh al-Aker ("a police state"), see "Palestinian Group Accuses Hamas, Fatah of Abusing Human Rights," Reuters, May 27, 2008. For the accusations of torture, see Human Rights Watch, "Internal Fight," July 29, 2008. "Hamas and Fatah Split Their Differences," *Jane's Foreign Report*, March 12, 2009. The NSF shared responsibility for malpractices of other security forces: one of its officers was always the "local area commander" in each governorate, with overall security responsibility. Regarding NSF authorities for arrests, Jari Kinnunen, the lead police adviser of EUPOL COPPS, the European Union Police Mission for the Palestinian Territories, told me, "All of the Palestinian security services are making arrests. But not all have the authority to do so." Interview with the author, Ramallah, April 2010.

34. On the relative legitimacy of the two governments, see, "Palestinian Public Opinion Poll, no. 27," Palestinian Center for Policy and Survey Research, March 24, 2008; and "Palestinian Public Opinion Poll, no. 31," Palestinian Center for Policy and Survey Research, March 5–7, 2009. For corruption rankings, see "Global Integrity Report 2008, West Bank," Global Integrity, 2008.

35. Civilians were regularly tried in military courts, and the PA dissolved elected municipal councils controlled by Hamas. See "Palestinian Authority, Amnesty International Report 2010"; and "The Detention of Civilians by Palestinian Security Agencies with a Stamp of Approval by the Military Judicial Commission," Palestinian Independent Commission for Human Rights, December 2008.

36. Shawan Jabarin's statement on routine torture comes from a phone interview with the author, July 2010. On feelings of security in Gaza and the West Bank, see "Palestinian Public Opinion Poll, no. 31" and other polls by the Palestinian Center for Policy and Survey Research. On the Ministry of Religious Affairs dictating sermons, see, for example, "PA Dictates Content of Friday Sermons," *The Arab American News*, February 1, 2010. On press freedom, see Reporters Without Borders, "Press Freedom Index 2007," https://rsf.org/en/worldwide-press-freedom-index-2007; and "Press Freedom Index 2008," https://rsf.org/en/world-press-freedom-index-2008. On Freedom House's rating, see "Palestinian Authority-Administered Territories, Freedom in the World 2010," https://freedomhouse.org/report/freedom-world/2010/palestinian-authority-administered-territories?page=22&year=2010&country=7964.

37. Sam Bahour's quote ("window dressing") comes from an interview with the author, Ramallah, April 2010. For the violent breakup of a protest by PA security forces, see "PA Forces Assault Press and Rights Workers at Anti-talks Protest," Ma'an News Agency, August 28, 2010.

38. For Hamas's boycott of municipal elections, see "Hamas to Boycott W. Bank Elections," *The Jerusalem Post*, May 24, 2010. Shikaki's quote ("further weaken Hamas") comes from an interview with the author, Ramallah, April 2010. For the PA's cancelation and denial, see "Controversy over Elections Decision Continues," Ma'an News Agency, June 11, 2010. At Fatah headquarters in Ramallah in April 2010, Muhammad Madani, a member of Fatah's Central Committee, told me the elections were not meant to help Fatah, all of whose troubles, he stressed, were over. Interview with the author, April 2010. The Jabarin quote ("Hamas followers were questioned") comes from an interview with the author, July 2010. Shikaki's quote ("more accurate reporting") comes from an interview with the author.

39. For Dermer's report, see "Trip Notes on a Return to Israel and the West Bank." Ghandi Amin's quote ("no hope for the Fayyad plan") comes from an interview with the author, Ramallah, April 2010.

40. For the State Department's 2011 request that the USSC receive its largest ever appropriation—$150 million—as well as a comparison to USSC budgets in previous years, see "Palestinian Authority: U.S. Assistance Is Training and Equipping Security Forces." For the statement by Mustafa Barghouti ("It's shameful. The people cannot live with two occupations at once"), see Andrew Lee Butters, "Casualties of War: Palestinian Moderates," *Time*, January 10, 2009.

5. PALESTINIAN PARALYSIS

This chapter was updated in September 2016.

1. See, for example, Barak Ravid, "Fayyad's Resignation: The Beginning of the End of the PA?," *Haaretz*, April 14, 2013.

2. For Fayyad's 2.4 percent of the vote in 2006, see "The Final Results for the Electoral Lists," Palestinian Central Election Commission, accessed June 7, 2016, http://web.archive.org/web/20081029054121/http://www.elections.ps/pdf/Final

_Results_PLC_Summary_Lists_Seats_2_En.pdf. For more on Fayyad, see chapter 4. For Fayyad's quotes ("open-ended commitment" and "our problem much more" and "better relationship with the Central Bank of Israel"), see "PM Fayyad and PMA Governor al-Wazir Discuss Proposed Designations and Palestinian Banking Sector with Treasury DAS Glaser," US Department of State cable, published by Wikileaks.org, August 7, 2008, https://wikileaks.org/plusd/cables /08JERUSALEM1450_a.html; "Fayyad Asks U/S Levey for Help with Qatar and Trade-based Money Laundering," US Department of State cable, published by Wikileaks.org, August 17, 2007, https://wikileaks.org/plusd/cables/07JERUSALEM1719_a.html.

3.   For Israeli sanctions and Fatah-fueled demonstrations against Fayyad, see Jim Zanotti, "U.S. Foreign Aid to the Palestinians," Congressional Research Service, March 18, 2016, p. 2; International Crisis Group, "Buying Time? Money, Guns and Politics in the West Bank," *Middle East Report*, no. 142, May 29, 2013, p. 13. On the Bush administration's efforts to create the new position of prime minister in order to weaken Arafat and empower Abbas, see Elliott Abrams, *Tested By Zion* (Cambridge, UK: Cambridge University Press, 2013).

4.   As discussed later in this chapter, the reference to "sustained public talks" is as opposed to the abortive "exploratory" talks held in Jordan for several weeks in early 2012 and the back-channel talks that envoys of Abbas and Netanyahu pursued for several years until December 2013.

5.   On the exploratory talks, see "PLO Cabinet to Meet Monday over Failed Talks," Ma'an News Agency, January 28, 2012.

6.   For Israel's threat to annul Oslo, see Barak Ravid, "Israel: We Will Annul Oslo Accords if Palestinians Seek Upgraded UN Status," *Haaretz*, November 14, 2012. For Palestine's upgrade at the UN, see Ethan Bronner and Christine Hauser, "U.N. Assembly, in Blow to U.S., Elevates Status of Palestine," *The New York Times*, November 29, 2012. For use of the phrase "doomsday weapon" by Netanyahu's advisers and "nuclear option" by Israeli journalists, see Ariel Kahana, "The Application to the Hague Will Become the Chairman's Job Accident," *Makor Rishon* [Hebrew], January 10, 2015; Barak Ravid, "Israel's Troubles Are Just Beginning: Enter the Palestinian 'Nuclear Option,'" *Haaretz*, January 1, 2015. For Palestinians joining the International Criminal Court, see Diaa Hadid and Marlise Simons, "Palestinians Join International Criminal Court, but Tread Cautiously at First," *The New York Times*, April 1, 2015.

6. THE END OF THE ABBAS ERA

This chapter was updated in September 2016.

1.   Peter Beaumont, "Israel-Palestine: Outlook Bleak as Wave of Violence Passes Six-Month Mark," *The Guardian*, March 31, 2016.

2.   For Abbas's secret contacts with the Israelis, see Abbas, *Through Secret Channels*. For Barghouti's withdrawal, see "Barghouti Out of Race for Palestinian Presidency," *The Globe and Mail*, December 13, 2004. On the Bush administration's support for Abbas, which began before Arafat had died, see Abrams, *Tested by Zion*.

3.   For more on the efforts to undermine Hamas, see chapter 4; International Crisis Group, "Palestinians, Israel and the Quartet: Pulling Back from the Brink," *Middle East Report*, no. 54, June 13, 2006. For polls that showed Palestinians wanted Abbas to resign, see "Palestinian Public Opinion Poll, no. 60," Palestinian Center for Policy and Survey Research, June 21, 2016; "Palestinian Public Opinion Poll,

no. 59," Palestinian Center for Policy and Survey Research, March 17–19, 2016; "Palestinian Public Opinion Poll, no. 58," Palestinian Center for Policy and Survey Research, December 10–12, 2015; "Palestinian Public Opinion Poll, no. 57," Palestinian Center for Policy and Survey Research, September 17–19, 2015.

PART IV. CONFRONTATION

Rubin, *Revolution Until Victory?*, p. 21.

7. NOT POPULAR ENOUGH

1. For the nonviolence that predominated during the first several decades of Zionist immigration, see Wendy Pearlman, *Violence, Nonviolence, and the Palestinian National Movement* (Cambridge, UK: Cambridge University Press, 2011), pp. 27–39. See also Ben Ehrenreich, *The Way to the Spring: Life and Death in Palestine* (New York: Penguin Press, 2016), p. 193, who writes: "In his official report to the British Parliament on the 1929 'disturbances,' Sir Walter Shaw acknowledged that 'there had been no recorded attacks of Jews by Arabs' in the previous eight decades and 'representatives of all parties' had concurred 'that before the [First World] War the Jews and Arabs lived side by side if not in amity, at least with tolerance.' The aggravating factor, Shaw was forced to admit, was the 1917 Balfour Declaration, which promised British support for the creation of a Jewish homeland in Palestine, such that 'the Arabs have come to see in the Jewish immigrant not only a menace to their livelihood but a possible overlord of the future.'"

2. For the 93 percent of Palestine's land outside Jewish hands, see chapter 1, section iii, n. 81. For the land owned by Jews having been sold mostly by absentee landlords, many of them non-Palestinian, see Hillel Cohen, *Army of Shadows: Palestinian Collaboration with Zionism, 1917–1948* (Berkeley, CA: University of California Press, 2008), p. 4; see also Rashid Khalidi's response to Kenneth W. Stein, "Letters," *Journal of Palestine Studies* 17, no. 4 (Summer 1988): 254–56.

3. For the number of Palestinian combatants in 1948 (including local militias, the Army of the Holy War, and the Arab Salvation Army), see Cohen, *Army of Shadows*, p. 3. On Palestinian combatants in 1956, see Sayigh, *Armed Struggle and the Search for State*, pp. 60–65; and Martin Van Creveld, *Sword and the Olive: A Critical History of the Israeli Defense Force* (New York: Public Affairs, 2008), p. 146, who writes that the Palestinian units under Egyptian command in Gaza "had not been issued with heavy weapons by their Egyptian masters and had never been intended for anything more than purely holding operations." See also Yagil Henkin, *The 1956 Suez War and the New World Order in the Middle East: Exodus in Reverse* (London: Rowman & Littlefield, 2015), p. 170, who writes: "In a war, the [Palestinian] 8th Division would be not much more than cannon fodder. . . . the Egyptian defense plan for Sinai, dated August 1956, made no mention whatsoever of the Gaza strip." On Palestinian fighting in 1967 and 1973, see Hillel Frisch, *The Palestinian Military: Between Militias and Armies* (New York: Routledge, 2008), pp. 54–58, 63–64; Sayigh, *Armed Struggle and the Search for State*, pp. 169–73, 329–33.

4. For the number of Jews killed per year by Palestinian violence, according to Israeli government statistics, see Israel Ministry of Foreign Affairs, "Terrorism Deaths in Israel—1920–1999," January 1, 2000, accessed October 20, 2016. Israel Ministry of Foreign Affairs, "Victims of Palestinian Violence and Terrorism Since September 2000," accessed June 16, 2016. According to the above, Palestinian violence and

terrorism killed 2,500 Jews from 1920 to 2000 and 1,364 Israelis from 2000 to the end of June 2016, for a total of 3,863 in a period of 96.5 years (40 per year). (The figures above contain the following adjustments to the Israel Foreign Ministry totals: included are 66 soldiers declared dead or missing in the 2014 Gaza war and 8 Jewish soldiers killed [4 from friendly fire] in the 2008–2009 Gaza war, both of which had been excluded from the Israeli Foreign Ministry total; excluded are at least 9 Arabs and 18 foreign nationals killed by Palestinian violence between 2000 and June 2016. Note that both the Foreign Ministry total and the adjusted figures above include some Israelis killed by non-Palestinian militants, such as the July 2012 Hezbollah attack in Bulgaria that killed 5 Israelis and a local bus driver; the July 2002 attack at the Los Angeles airport by an Egyptian national; and attacks from Sinai that Israel claims were orchestrated in Gaza.) The fewer than 4,000 Jews killed by Palestinian violence between 1920 and the end of June 2016 is some thirteen times fewer than the number of French combatants, settlers, and allies killed by Algerian nationalists in less than eight years of fighting, and it is nineteen times less than the number of French forces killed by Vietnamese nationalists in an equally short period. For the approximately 75,000 French soldiers killed in the First Indochina War, see Edward Berenson, Vincent Duclert, Christophe Prochasson, eds., *The French Republic: History, Values, Debates* (Ithaca: Cornell University Press, 2011), p. 259; Alistair Horne, *A Savage War of Peace: Algeria 1954–1962* (New York: New York Review Books Classics, 2006), p. 538. For the more than 50,000 French forces, settlers, and allies killed in the Algerian War, see Horne, p. 67.

5.   For British repression of the Arab Revolt, see Gudrun Krämer, *A History of Palestine: From the Ottoman Conquest to the Founding of the State of Israel*, trans. Graham Harman (Princeton, NJ: Princeton University Press, 2011), p. 274. For the number killed during the Arab Revolt, see chapter 2, n. 7.

6.   For the estimate of 326 Palestinians killed during the first year of the intifada, see B'Tselem, "Fatalities in the First Intifada," accessed June 18, 2016, http://www.btselem.org/statistics/first_intifada_tables. For an estimate of 390 Palestinians killed (including a list of names), see Zachary Lockman and Joel Beinin eds., *Intifada: The Palestinian Uprising Against Israeli Occupation*, p. 317. For the IDF statement that "we have no record that soldiers have been killed as a result of rock-throwing," see Ehrenreich, *The Way to the Spring*, pp. 44–45, who adds: "In the many demonstrations I went to in Nabi Saleh—I lost count, but it was probably around twenty—I only once saw a soldier hit with a stone." For stone throwing by undercover Israeli security forces, see Chaim Levinson, "'Undercover Israeli Combatants Threw Stones at IDF Soldiers in West Bank,'" *Haaretz*, May 7, 2012; Ishaan Tharoor, "Watch: Israeli Undercover Cops Brutally Beat Palestinian Protesters," *The Washington Post*, October 8, 2015. Video of the undercover agents throwing stones prior to the arrests can be found in Sheren Khalel, "Video: Israeli Undercover Police Help Palestinians Throw Stones Before Drawing Guns on Them," *Middle East Eye*, October 7, 2015.

7.   For figures on Palestinians killed in the first days of the intifada, see Menachem Klein, *The Jerusalem Problem: The Struggle for Permanent Status*, trans. Haim Watzman (Gainesville, FL: University Press of Florida, 2003), pp. 97–99. For the killing of 12 Palestinian citizens of Israel (as well as a resident of Gaza who was present), see Adalah—The Legal Center for Arab Minority Rights in Israel, "The October 2000 Killings," September 17, 2015.

8. For Jayyous as the largest olive-producing region of Qalqilya and details on the wells, irrigated land, and olive trees closed off by the barrier, see UN OCHA, "The Humanitarian Impact of the West Bank Barrier on Palestinian Communities," March 2005; Sharif Omar, "Israel's Wall Hems in Livelihoods—and Dreams," *USA Today*, August 17, 2003.

9. For the ICJ advisory opinion, see "Legal Consequences of the Construction of a Wall in the Occupied Palestinian Territory," International Court of Justice, July 9, 2004. For changes in the barrier from 2003 to 2009, including its rerouting around Budrus in 2005, see UN OCHA, "Five Years After the International Court of Justice Advisory Opinion: A Summary of the Humanitarian Impact of the Barrier," July 2009; Ray Dolphin, *The West Bank Wall: Unmaking Palestine* (London: Pluto Press, 2006), pp. 190–91. For the previous route of the barrier, encircling Budrus and eight nearby villages, see Mark Sorkin, "Letter from Budrus: Palestinians Are Organizing a Grassroots, Nonviolent Resistance to Israel's Separation Barrier," *The Nation*, June 14, 2004; "Budrus Discussion Guide," Just Vision, 2011. For more on Budrus, see the documentary directed by Julia Bacha, *Budrus*, Just Vision Films, 2010; and interviews with Ayed Morrar and Abd al-Nasser Morrar: Jody McIntyre, "Interview: Budrus 'Built a Model of Civil Resistance,' " *The Electronic Intifada*, November 4, 2010; Ida Audeh, "A Village Mobilized: Lessons from Budrus," *The Electronic Intifada*, June 13, 2007.

10. For the court decision on the single home near Jerusalem, see Ehrenreich, *The Way to the Spring*, pp. 86–87. For the quote from the president (often translated as chief justice) of the Supreme Court ("We were not convinced"), see Mohammed Daraghmeh, "Court: Israel Must Re-Route Barrier," Associated Press, September 4, 2007.

11. For the protests in Kafr Qaddum, see B'Tselem "Background on the Protests in Kafr Qadum," December 4, 2013. For more on restrictions in Area C, Israeli approval of only 5.6 percent of applications for building permits between 2000 and 2012, the inability of Palestinians to build in more than 99 percent of Area C, and Israel's demolition of nearly three thousand Palestinian structures, see B'Tselem, "Acting the Landlord: Israel's Policy in Area C," June 2013, pp. 15, 19–20. See also UN OCHA, "Humanitarian Factsheet on Area C of the West Bank," July 2011 (updated through December 2011).

12. For the more than 120 physical obstacles deployed by the Israeli military in Hebron, the shuttering of 512 businesses, the closure of 1,100 other businesses due to restricted access, and the abandonment of over 1,000 Palestinian homes in restricted areas, see UN OCHA, "The Humanitarian Impact of Israeli Settlements in Hebron City," November 2013. For the closure of Shuhada Street, see "Ghost Town: Israel's Separation Policy and Forced Eviction of Palestinians from the Center of Hebron," B'Tselem, 2007, pp. 22–36, https://www.btselem.org/download /200705_hebron_eng.pdf. For the Goldstein massacre, see Chris Hedges with Joel Greenberg, "West Bank Massacre; Before Killing, Final Prayer and Final Taunt," *The New York Times*, February 28, 1994.

13. For the Israeli government statistics obtained by Peace Now, see Peace Now, "GUILTY! Construction of Settlements upon Private Land—Official Data," March 2007, pp. 1, 6, 12, accessed June 19, 2016, http://peacenow.org.il/wp-content /uploads/2016/05/Breaking_The_Law_formal-data_March07Eng.pdf. For the history of Nabi Saleh and Halamish, the imposition of a closed military zone, the

marches toward the spring used by settlers, and the occasion on which villagers finally reached it, see Ehrenreich, *The Way to the Spring*, pp. 13–15, 27–30, 75–76.

14. For the marches on Nakba day, see Ethan Bronner, "Israeli Troops Fire as Marchers Breach Borders," *The New York Times*, May 15, 2011; Harriet Sherwood, "Thirteen Killed as Israeli Troops Open Fire on Nakba Day Border Protests," *The Guardian*, May 15, 2011; "Egyptians Rally at Rafah for Palestinian Rights," Ma'an News Agency, May 15, 2011. Several reports state that tens of thousands assembled in Lebanon at the border with Israel. See Nicholas Blanford, "A Third Intifadah? Deadly Nakba Protests Spark Fears of Israel-Lebanon Border Escalation," *Time*, May 15, 2011. For Israeli officials commenting on the growth of BDS at this time, see Ben Caspit, "Did Israel's Reaction to BDS Drive Movement's Growth?," *Al-Monitor*, April 27, 2016.

15. For the Palestinian Freedom Riders, see Joel Greenberg, "Palestinian 'Freedom Riders' Arrested on Bus to Jerusalem," *The Washington Post*, November 15, 2011; Hugh Naylor, "Police Arrest Palestinians on Bus to Jerusalem," *The National*, November 16, 2011. For the protesters blocking a road exclusively for Israeli cars and a related demonstration, see Elior Levy, "Palestinians Protest Against Settlement Goods," *Ynet*, October 24, 2012.

16. For the US veto, see "United States Vetoes Security Council Resolution on Israeli Settlements," UN News Centre, February 18, 2011. For Palestine joining UNESCO, see Steven Erlanger and Scott Sayare, "Unesco Accepts Palestinians as Full Members," *The New York Times*, October 31, 2011. For the PLO's unsuccessful application for Palestine to be admitted to the UN as a full member state, see "UN Security Council Panel Fails to Agree on Palestinian Statehood Bid," *Haaretz*, November 11, 2011. For Palestine's admission to the UN as a nonmember observer state, see "General Assembly Votes Overwhelmingly to Accord Palestine 'Non-Member Observer State' Status in United Nations," United Nations, November 29, 2012. For Abbas's signature of instruments of accession to treaty bodies in April 2014, see Human Rights Watch, "U.S.: Stop Blocking Palestinian Rights: Support Commitment to Abide by International Law," April 5, 2014. For Abbas's December 31, 2014, signature of the Rome Statute, Palestine's deposit of the instrument of accession on January 2, 2015, and the Rome Statute entering into force on April 1, 2015, see "Preliminary Examination—Palestine," International Criminal Court, accessed June 20, 2016.

17. For the Israeli army's support of settlements and restrictions that forbid soldiers from preventing settler attacks, see Ehrenreich, *The Way to the Spring*, pp. 201–2; Breaking the Silence, *Our Harsh Logic: Israeli Soldiers' Testimonies from the Occupied Territories, 2000–2010* (New York: Metropolitan Books, 2012). For the evacuation of Bab al-Shams, see Irene Nasser, "In Bab Al-Shams, Palestinians Create New Facts on the Ground," *+972*, January 25, 2013; "Security Forces Evacuate E1 Outpost," *Ynet*, January 13, 2013. For the four other protest villages—"Bab al-Karameh" in Beit Iksa, northwest of Jerusalem; "al-Asra," northwest of Jenin; "al-Manatir" in Burin, south of Nablus; and "Canaan," near al-Tuwani, south of Hebron—see "Activists Construct New Protest Village in South Hebron," Ma'an News Agency, February 9, 2013; Linah Alsaafin, "Israeli Military Cracks Down on Palestinian Tent Villages," *Al-Monitor*, February 14, 2013.

18. For labor statistics, see chapter 1, section iii, n. 126. See also Leila Farsakh, "Palestinian Employment in Israel: 1996–1997," MAS—Palestine Economic Policy Research Institute, August 1998.

19. For the 3 percent fee and Israel's profits from it, see chapter 1, section iv, n. 137.
20. For the 165 islands, see B'Tselem, "Acting the Landlord: Israel's Policy in Area C," June 2013, pp. 5, 12. For the control by Jewish settlements and local and regional councils of 42.8 percent of the West Bank in 2009, see B'Tselem, "By Hook and by Crook: Israeli Settlement Policy in the West Bank," July 2010, p. 11. For the 90 percent of the West Bank's Palestinian population that resides in Areas A and B, see B'Tselem, "Impact of Construction and Planning Policy on Communities in Areas A and B," October 23, 2013.
21. For Israel's Military Order 101 and other regulations, see Ehrenreich, *The Way to the Spring*, pp. 19, 160.
22. For the share of Palestinian men who have been imprisoned, see "Palestinian Political Prisoners in Israeli Prisons," Addameer Prisoner Support and Human Rights Association, January 2014. For Tamimi having spent three years in prison, see Ehrenreich, p. 12; "Military Court Rejects Motion to Release Bassem Tamimi," Popular Struggle Coordination Committee, October 12, 2011. For the charges against Tamimi and his conviction, see "Military Court Rejects Motion to Release Bassem Tamimi," Popular Struggle Coordination Committee, October 12, 2011; "Palestinian Activist, Bassem Tamimi, Convicted; Prosecution Criticized by Court," Popular Struggle Committee, May 20, 2012; Ehrenreich, pp. 19–20. For the 99.74 percent of tried Palestinians who were convicted (of 9,542 cases in 2010, 25 resulted in full acquittal, while 4 percent resulted in conviction with the acquittal of some charges), see Chaim Levinson, "Nearly 100% of All Military Court Cases in West Bank End in Conviction, *Haaretz* Learns," *Haaretz*, November 29, 2011.
23. For the 1.4 percent of complaints against soldiers resulting in indictment, see Yesh Din—Volunteers for Human Rights, "Israel's Compliance with the International Covenant for Civil and Political Rights," September 8, 2014. For the three hundred inquiries concerning Shin Bet torture (the Justice Ministry has not revealed how many complaints it received that did not result in inquiries in the first place), see Yotam Berger, "Department Fails to Investigate Complaints About Shin Bet Torture," *Haaretz*, December 7, 2016. According to the Israeli human rights lawyer Irit Ballas, of the hundreds of complaints of torture at the hands of the Shin Bet between mid-2002 and 2012, there was "not even one found worthy of a criminal investigation." See Irit Ballas "Regimes of Impunity," in "On Torture," Adalah—The Legal Center for Arab Minority Rights in Israel, June 2012, p. 42, cited in Ehrenreich, *The Way to the Spring*, p. 158.
24. For divisions in Nabi Saleh, see Ehrenreich, *The Way to the Spring*, pp. 66–67, 122–25. For the 155 injured, 70 arrested, and damage done to homes, see Ehrenreich, p. 15. For the two protesters killed—Mustafa Tamimi in 2011, and Rushdi Tamimi in 2012—see Phoebe Greenwood, "Israeli Soldiers Clash with Mourners at Funeral of Palestinian Protester," *The Guardian*, December 11, 2011; "Palestinian Dies of Wounds in Nabi Saleh Protest," Ma'an News Agency, November 19, 2012.
25. For the PLO Central Council's vote, see Peter Beaumont, "PLO Leadership Votes to Suspend Security Cooperation with Israel," *The Guardian*, March 5, 2016. For Abbas's threat, see Emily L. Hauser, "Abbas Threatens to Dismantle PA—Again," *The Daily Beast*, December 28, 2012. For Abbas's first two quotes ("sacred" and "we will not give it up"), see Elhanan Miller, "Abbas Vows to Uphold 'Sacred'

Security Coordination with Israel," *The Times of Israel*, May 28, 2014; Linah Alsaafin, "Abbas Vows No Collapse of Palestinian Authority," Middle East Eye, January 6, 2016. For Abbas's third quote ("Our people will continue"), see Stephen Foley, "Abbas Tells the World: It Is Time for Palestinian People to Gain Their Freedom," *The Independent*, September 24, 2011. For examples of suppression by PA security forces—stopping protests from marching on settlements and checkpoints, discouraging leaders of village protests from demonstrating in Area A, infiltrating protests to direct them away from Israelis, threatening a leader of demonstrations in Hebron, and breaking up numerous popular protests, including ones that called for unity (March 2011) or that opposed US-led negotiations (July 2013)—see Ehrenreich, *The Way to the Spring*, pp. 73, 128, 178, 220, 335–36.

26. Ehrenreich, *The Way to the Spring* pp. 335–36.

8. RAGE IN JERUSALEM

This chapter was updated in September 2016.

1. For the Palestinian share of Jerusalem's population, see "Selected Data on the Occasion of Jerusalem Day 2014–2015 [Hebrew]," Israel Central Bureau of Statistics, May 31, 2016, which reports that at the end of 2014 there were 850,000 residents of Jerusalem, of whom 316,000 were Palestinian, making up 37.18 percent of the population. (The population had grown to 870,000 by the end of 2015.) For beatings by Jewish nationalist youths, see, for example, Nir Hasson, "In Suspected Jerusalem Lynch, Dozens of Jewish Youths Attack 3 Palestinians," *Haaretz*, August 17, 2012; "Young Palestinian 'Beaten by Jewish Mob' in Jerusalem Hotel," Ma'an News Agency, October 18, 2014; "Palestinian Youth Beaten by Israelis Near Jerusalem Old City," Ma'an News Agency, November 22, 2014.

2. For the share of Palestinian Jerusalemites who have refused to apply for citizenship, see International Crisis Group, "Extreme Makeover? (II): The Withering of Arab Jerusalem," *Middle East Report*, no. 135, December 20, 2012, p. 22: "About 13,000 Palestinians in Jerusalem (roughly 5 percent of the Arab population) are reported to have citizenship, though it seems likely a significant proportion are members of Israel's Palestinian minority who have moved to Jerusalem for work or family reasons. . . . While no precise figure is available, a study estimates some 6,000 to 10,000 Israeli-Palestinians immigrated to Jerusalem from other localities in Israel." The source for the 13,000 Palestinians with citizenship is Laurent Zecchini, "Le passeport qui brule les doigts," *Le Monde*, January 12, 2012. The source for the 6,000–10,000 Israeli-Palestinians who immigrated to Jerusalem is Asmahan Masry-Herzalla et al., "Jerusalem as an Internal Migration Destination for Israeli-Palestinian Families," Jerusalem Institute for Israel Studies, July 2011. For the steadily dropping approval rates of Palestinian applications for citizenship (from 37 percent in 2013 to 2.8 percent in 2015), see "Sharp Drop in Granting of Citizenship to Jerusalem's Arabs," *The Jerusalem Post*, June 5, 2016. For the 14,416 revocations of residency between 1967 and 2014, see HaMoked—Center for the Defence of the Individual, "Israel Continues Its 'Quiet Deportation' Policy: in 2014, the Ministry of Interior Revoked the Residency Status of 107 Palestinians from East Jerusalem," March 23, 2015. For the boycott by over 99 percent of Palestinians in Jerusalem, see "Municipal Elections: Barkat Takes J'lem, Huldai

Carries TA," *Ynet*, October 23, 2013; Daoud Kuttab, "Palestinians Again Boycott East Jerusalem Elections," *Al-Monitor*, October 24, 2013. For the turnout among Palestinian residents of Jerusalem in 2008 (2 percent), see "Extreme Makeover? (II)," p. 23.

3. For the population and proportion of the municipal budget in 2014, see n. 1 of this chapter; European Union Heads of Mission in Jerusalem and Ramallah, "EU HoMs Report on Jerusalem," March 18, 2014, accessed June 4, 2016. For a slightly higher figure (10.1 percent) for 2013, see Ir Amim, "Jerusalem Municipality Budget Analysis for 2013: Share of Investment in East Jerusalem," December 2014. For the figures on unequal service provision and the share of Palestinians below the poverty line, see Association for Civil Rights in Israel, "East Jerusalem 2014–By the Numbers," May 24, 2014. For the number of playgrounds per capita, see Nir Hasson, "Jerusalem Must Plan Playgrounds for Palestinian Neighborhoods, Court Orders," *Haaretz*, January 10, 2016. For figures on classrooms, see Association for Civil Rights in Israel, "New Report—Failing East Jerusalem Education System," September 2, 2013.

4. For the absence of new Palestinian neighborhoods, see Middle East Task Force, "Occupation Realities," American Friends Service Committee, Winter 2004. For restrictive zoning and permit allocation (between 2010 and 2015, only 7.5 percent of building permits in Jerusalem were given to Palestinian neighborhoods, where nearly 40 percent of the population lives), see Nir Hasson, "Only 7% of Jerusalem Building Permits Go to Palestinian Neighborhoods," *Haaretz*, December 7, 2015. For land allocation in Jerusalem, see United Nations Conference on Trade and Development, "The Palestinian Economy in East Jerusalem: Enduring Annexation, Isolation and Disintegration," 2013. For the share of Palestinian homes in Jerusalem built without permits and at risk of demolition, see the estimate of 33 percent in European Union Heads of Mission in Jerusalem and Ramallah, "EU HoMs Report on Jerusalem," March 18, 2014, accessed June 4, 2016; and the estimate of 39 percent in Association for Civil Rights in Israel, "East Jerusalem 2015: Facts and Figures," May 12, 2015. See also chapter 3.

5. For the demolition of homes of Palestinian attackers but not Jewish ones, see Akiva Eldar, "Why Isn't IDF Razing Homes of Jewish Terrorists," *Al-Monitor*, January 7, 2016, http://www.al-monitor.com/pulse/originals/2016/01/demolition-palestinian-terrorists-jewish-undeground.html. For the eviction of Palestinians but not Jews from homes abandoned in 1948, see Association for Civil Rights in Israel, "East Jerusalem 2015: Facts and Figures," May 12, 2015, p. 9.

6. For the rationale for the route of the wall in Jerusalem, see Ir Amim, "The Separation Barrier," accessed June 4, 2016; "Extreme Makeover? (I): Israel's Policies of Land and Faith in East Jerusalem," pp. 11–12. For the 3 percent of the wall that follows the pre-1967 line, see "EU HoMs Report on Jerusalem," p. 6. For the one-quarter to one-third of Palestinian residents on the West Bank side of the barrier, see Association for Civil Rights in Israel, "East Jerusalem 2015—Facts and Figures," May 12, 2015, p. 1; in 2014, the same organization estimated that the number of Palestinians in Jerusalem neighborhoods on the West Bank side of the barrier was more than 120,000, which is more than one-third of the city's Palestinian population: "different surveys estimate that between 60,000 and 80,000 residents live in the Shuafat Refugee Camp, and [a] similar number in Kfar Akab. Both are located within Jerusalem's municipal boundaries, but on the east side of

the Separation Barrier." "East Jerusalem 2014—By the Numbers," n. 20, http://www.acri.org.il/en/2014/05/24/ej-numbers-14/. For the Palestinian communities entirely encircled by the wall, such as the 15,000 people in the Bir Nabala enclave, see UN OCHA, "The Humanitarian Impact of the West Bank Barrier on Palestinian Communities: East Jerusalem," June 2007, pp. 4, 14.

7. For Israel's neglect of the areas on the West Bank side of the barrier, where residents do not receive the most basic services yet still pay Jerusalem municipal taxes, see UN OCHA, "The Humanitarian Impact of the West Bank Barrier," June 2007, pp. 8–49; "East Jerusalem 2014—By the Numbers," http://www.acri.org.il/en/2014/05/24/ej-numbers-14/.

8. For the operation of the Israeli security forces in East Jerusalem and the behavior of paramilitary units—known in Hebrew by the acronym Magav (Mishmar HaGvul), the Israeli Border Police is a gendarmerie that operates primarily in Jerusalem, the West Bank, and on Israel's borders, and it is one of the forces in which Israelis may do their compulsory military service—see Ruth Eglash, "Heavy-handed or heroes? Israel border police are on the front line," The Washington Post, April 24, 2016.

9. For the slogans chanted by Jewish demonstrators—including "a Jew is a brother, an Arab is a bastard," "we want war," and "Kahane was right"—and the attacks on Palestinian workers and passersby, see Nir Hasson, "Extreme Rightists Attack Palestinians in Jerusalem as Teens Laid to Rest," Haaretz, July 1, 2014; Isabel Kershner, "Arab Boy's Death Escalates Clash over Abductions," The New York Times, July 2, 2014. For the murder of Abu Khdeir, see Peter Beaumont, "Palestinian Boy Mohammed Abu Khdeir Was Burned Alive, Says Official," The Guardian, July 5, 2014.

10. "Damage to Light Rail by Arab Rioters Could Take 'Months' to Fix," Israel National News, July 3, 2014.

11. For Israel's policy of "dilution" at the Temple Mount/Noble Sanctuary—imposing age and gender restrictions on Muslim access during visits by Jewish activists, including those calling for building a Third Temple in place of the Dome of the Rock—see International Crisis Group, "The Status of the Status Quo at Jerusalem's Holy Esplanade," Middle East Report, no. 159, June 30, 2015. For the growing number of Jewish visitors to the site (from 5,658 in 2009 to 10,906 in 2014), see "Jewish Visits to Temple Mount Increase by 92% Since 2009," The Jerusalem Post, January 27, 2015. For advocacy of prayer at the site or the construction of a Jewish temple, see statements by numerous Knesset members and by ministers of the Netanyahu governments formed in 2009, 2013, and 2015: by Minister of Housing and Construction Uri Ariel (2013–2015); by Deputy Religious Affairs Minister and Deputy Defense Minister Eli Ben-Dahan (2013–2015); by Deputy Defense Minister Danny Danon (2013–2014); and by Deputy Minister of Transport, National Infrastructure, and Road Safety Tzipi Hotovely (2013–2015), see International Crisis Group, "The Status of the Status Quo at Jerusalem's Holy Esplanade," Middle East Report, no. 159, June 30, 2015, p. 10; "Far-Right Israel Minister Makes Brief Visit to Al Aqsa," AFP, March 16, 2014; "Likud's Hotovely Gets Death Threats After Temple Mount Visit," The Times of Israel, November 26, 2014; "MK Ben Dahan Vows to Enable Temple Mount Prayer," Israel National News, July 16, 2013; "Minister Calls for Third Temple to Be Built," The Times of Israel, July 5, 2013; "'We're Not Embarrassed to Say It: We Want to Rebuild the Temple,'" Israel National

News, August 14, 2016. For the deputy defense minister's financial support of an institution that advocates building a Third Temple where the Dome of the Rock now stands, see "Israeli Deputy Minister, Netanyahu Donor Gave to Temple Mount Groups," JTA, December 9, 2015. For the newly established Knesset Temple Mount Lobby, whose launch event was attended by three cabinet ministers, the speaker of parliament, and three lawmakers, see Nir Hasson, "Israeli Ministers Join Call to Permit Jewish Prayer at Temple Mount," *Haaretz*, November 8, 2016.

12. For Barkat's statement, see "Mayor Reveals Jerusalem Went from 200 to 5,000 Monthly Attacks," *Israel National News*, October 27, 2014. For the more than 1,000 detained, see "2 Palestinians to Be Detained Without Trial for 6 Months," Ma'an News Agency, November 28, 2014; "PLO: Israel Has Detained 1266 Palestinian Children in 2014," *Al-Akhbar*, December 30, 2014. For the 240 arrests in Jerusalem for security-related offences in the 2000 to 2008 period, see Daniel Seidemann and Lara Friedman, "Jerusalem 2014: No New Stable Status Quo, No Return to Status Quo Ante," Terrestrial Jerusalem, August 22, 2014. In the period between October 2015 and October 2016, when violence in Jerusalem resurged, Israel detained nearly 1 percent of the city's Palestinian population—2,355 Palestinians, 866 of them children—according to the Committee of Prisoners' Families: "Israel Detained 2,355 Palestinians in Jerusalem in the Last Year," Middle East Monitor, October 3, 2016.

13. For the deployment of special forces officers and extra border police units, the large-scale raids, the new checkpoints and barricades, the call for Israelis with firearms to join a volunteer security force, the demolition of homes of Palestinian attackers and the arrest of their relatives, the use of "skunk" water, the threats to fine parents, the proposed twenty-year prison sentences for throwing stones, and the fines for spitting out shells of sunflower seeds, see "Mayor Barkat Releases New Jerusalem Security Plans," *The Times of Israel*, November 21, 2014; Peter Beaumont, "Jerusalem on the Edge as Tensions over Holy Site Threaten to Boil Over," *The Guardian*, November 11, 2014; "Netanyahu Promises to Crack Down on Jerusalem Riots," *The Times of Israel*, October 26, 2014; "Israel Eases Gun Control Rules After Jerusalem Terror Attack," *The Jerusalem Post*, November 20, 2014; "Israel Begins Demolishing Homes over Attacks," *Al Jazeera*, November 20, 2014; "IDF Arrests Family Members of Suspects Behind Monday's Terrorist Attacks," *The Jerusalem Post*, November 11, 2014; John Reed, "Israeli Use of Skunk Water Fuels Anger in East Jerusalem," *Financial Times*, November 21, 2014; "Children Throwing Stones? Parents to Pay the Price," *i24 News*, October 27, 2014; Kate Shuttleworth, "Palestinian Stone Throwers Could Face 20 Years in Jail," *The Guardian*, November 4, 2014; "East Jerusalem 2015: Facts and Figures," p. 16.

14. For the Palestinian teenager abducted, beaten, and left alive, as well as a similar incident several weeks earlier, see "Unidentified Assailants Kidnap Jerusalem Teen," Ma'an News Agency, November 5, 2014; "Witnesses: Settlers Try to Kidnap 11-Year-Old Jerusalem Boy," Ma'an News Agency, September 24, 2014. For Palestinians in the West Bank who were run over, see, for example, "Israeli Settler Runs Over Hebron Child with Car," International Middle East Media Center, September 11, 2014; "Ten-Year-Old Injured in Settler's Deliberate Hit and Run," Wafa—Palestinian News & Info Agency, September 25, 2014; "Palestinian Girl Dies in Hit-and-Run by Jewish Driver," *The Times of Israel*, October 19, 2014; "Jewish Settler Runs Over 7-Year-Old Palestinian Child Near Hebron," Ma'an News Agency,

December 28, 2014; "Jewish Settler Runs Over Palestinian Child Walking to School in Tuqu," Ma'an News Agency, December 31, 2014. For the shooting of the supporter of Jewish prayer in the Noble Sanctuary/Temple Mount, see "Temple Mount Activist Shot, Seriously Hurt Outside Jerusalem's Begin Center," *The Times of Israel*, October 29, 2014. For the attack at the West Jerusalem synagogue (the fourth rabbi, Haim Rothman, was critically injured and died of his wounds eleven months later, on October 24, 2015), see Jodi Rudoren and Isabel Kershner, "Israel Shaken by 5 Deaths in Synagogue Assault," *The New York Times*, November 18, 2014. For the 13 people killed by Palestinians in Israel and the West Bank between September 16, 2014, and November 18, 2014 (including those who were attacked during this period but died of their injuries later), compared to the 6 Israelis killed in 2013 and none in 2012 (excluding those killed by exchanges of hostilities with militants in Gaza), see Israel Ministry of Foreign Affairs, "Victims of Palestinian Violence and Terrorism Since September 2000," accessed June 4, 2016.

15. For Israeli claims that Abbas incited the violence, see "Netanyahu Blames Abbas Incitement for Jerusalem Attack," *The Times of Israel*, October 22, 2014; "Abbas Is Inciting Jihad, Has Joined Ranks with IS, Liberman says," *The Times of Israel*, October 18, 2014; "Netanyahu Lashes Abbas for Inciting Violence Among Arabs," *The Times of Israel*, November 9, 2014; "Palestinian Driver Rams Jerusalem Station Killing Baby," Reuters, October 22, 2014. For senior Israeli security officials contradicting the claim by politicians that Abbas was responsible, see, for example, the statement by Shin Bet chief Yoram Cohen in Attila Somfalvi, "Shin Bet Chief: Abbas Is Not Inciting to Terror," *Ynet*, November 18, 2014.

16. For Rabin's opposition to dividing Jerusalem ("If they told us that peace is the price of giving up on a united Jerusalem under Israeli sovereignty, my reply would be, 'Let's do without peace'"), see Dore Gold, *The Fight for Jerusalem: Radical Islam, the West, and the Future of the Holy City* (Washington, DC: Regnery Publishing, 2009), p. 177; and Rabin's October 5, 1995, Knesset speech ("First and foremost, united Jerusalem, which will include both Ma'ale Adumim and Givat Ze'ev—as the capital of Israel, under Israeli sovereignty"). Israel Ministry of Foreign Affairs, "PM Rabin in Knesset- Ratification of Interim Agreement," accessed June 4, 2016. For Rabin's decision to bypass the West Bank and Gaza Palestinians in the Madrid-Washington talks and negotiate directly with senior PLO leaders based in Tunis, see chapter 1, section iii, n. 122. The PLO had deliberately encouraged local leaders to take harder line positions in the Madrid-Washington talks to persuade Israel to negotiate directly with it in Oslo. Nevertheless, beneath the tactical ploy there appeared to be substantive differences between Husseini and Arafat on negotiating Jerusalem. For a discussion of these differences (albeit one that neglects the coordination between the PLO and the Palestinian representatives at the Madrid-Washington talks), see Gold, pp. 162–63.

17. For the deportation of Palestinian legislators from Jerusalem and Shin Bet monitoring of political subversion, see Daoud Kuttab, "Israeli Court to Rule on Minister's Deportation Case," *Al-Monitor*, May 11, 2015, http://www.al-monitor.com /pulse/originals/2015/05/Israel-interior-minister-jerusalem-palestinian-residents .html; "Extreme Makeover? (II)," p. 1.

18. For the assault on a former religious affairs minister and close associate of Abbas, see "Abbas Adviser Forced to Flee Temple Mount," *The Jerusalem Post*, June 29, 2014; chapter 9, n. 10. For the PA Minister of Jerusalem Affairs, Adnan

al-Husseini, who was expelled from the Abu Khdeir family home, see Asmaa al-Ghoul, "Palestinian Press Losing Media War in Current Crisis," *Al-Monitor*, July 8, 2014.

19. For details of the 2011 agreement and quotes from Hamas officials confirming that Mish'al agreed with Abbas to a strategy of popular resistance, see International Crisis Group, "Light at the End of Their Tunnels? Hamas & the Arab Uprisings," *Middle East Report*, no. 129, August 14, 2012, pp. 18–25, 33. For Mish'al's May 2011 speech in which he stated that Hamas was willing to suspend attacks on Israel ("We have given peace, from Madrid to now, twenty years. I say: We are ready to agree as Palestinians, in the arms of the Arabs and with their support, to give an additional chance for agreement on how to manage it"), see the following video, available at: www.youtube.com/watch?v=k6z FDivGgCs. For Hamas's previous agreement to a strategy of popular resistance in the so-called Prisoners' Document (Wathiqat al-Asra) of 2006, officially known as the National Conciliation Document of the Prisoners, see "Text of Agreement Reached by Palestinian Factions," *The New York Times*, June 28, 2006. For leaked minutes of an August 21, 2014, Doha meeting between Abbas and Mish'al in which both confirm that they had agreed to a program of nonviolence and in which Mish'al complains that Abbas had obstructed nonviolent protests, see "Palestinian Authority President Abbas to Qatari Emir Tamim: Meshaal Is Lying," *Al-Akhbar*, September 5, 2014. See also "Abbas and Mashaal Agree on Peaceful Intifada," *The Jerusalem Post*, February 23, 2013. For complaints of PA obstruction by leaders of nonviolent protests against Israel, see, for example, "Jamal Juma': PA 'Killing Popular Resistance,'" Stop the Wall, August 10, 2011. For more on PA efforts to quell Palestinian protests, see Ahmad Azem, "West Bank Uprisings Dampened by PA," *Al-Monitor*, August 7, 2014; "Abbas Tells PA Forces to Urgently Quell West Bank Protests," *The Times of Israel*, October 5, 2015; "PA at Odds with Palestinians as West Bank Protests Escalate," Ma'an News Agency, October 9, 2015; "Caught Between Protesters and Israel, Palestinian Security Forces Shift Tactics," *The New York Times*, October 25, 2015. For Abbas's refusal to endorse a nonviolent boycott of Israel, see "Abbas: Don't Boycott Israel," *The Times of Israel*, December 13, 2013.

20. For the Israeli-Jordanian understandings and Israel's breach of them, see International Crisis Group, "How to Preserve the Fragile Calm at Jerusalem's Holy Esplanade," Middle East Briefing, no. 48, April 7, 2016, pp. 1–3, 4–6.

21. For more on the uncoordinated attacks prior to the outbreak of the First Intifada, see Lisa Hajjar, Mouin Rabbani, and Joel Beinin, "Palestine and the Arab-Israeli Conflict for Beginners," and Salim Tamari, "What the Uprising Means," both in Zachary Lockman and Joel Beinin, eds., *Intifada*, pp. 110, 132; Pearlman, *Violence, Nonviolence, and the Palestinian National Movement*, p. 101. For the local elections in 1976—when legitimate Palestinian representatives were toppled and deported, and more compliant, unelected figures were put in their place—see Ma'oz, *Palestinian Leadership on the West Bank* (London: Frank Cass, 1984), pp. 133–161.

9. HAMAS'S CHANCES

This chapter was updated in September 2016.

1. For the 2012 cease-fire agreement, see "Text: Cease-fire Agreement Between Israel and Hamas," Reuters, November 21, 2012.

2. For the Shin Bet report that recorded only a single attack, see "Monthly Summary—December 2012," Israel Security Agency, accessed May 24, 2016, https://www.shabak.gov.il/SiteCollectionImages/english/TerrorInfo/reports/Dec12report-en.pdf. For the regular incursions into Gaza, the firing at farmers and boats, and the restrictions on fisherman, see International Crisis Group, "The Next Round in Gaza," *Middle East Report*, no. 149, March 25, 2014.

3. For more on crossings, buffer zones, imports, exports, and exit permits, see "The Next Round in Gaza."

4. For quotes from Israeli officials explaining the delays in holding substantive Hamas-Israel negotiations over implementing the cease-fire (as distinct from regular Israel-Egypt discussions about Gaza that took place before and after the war), see "The Next Round in Gaza," p. 5. A few press reports indicated that there may have been preliminary preparations for indirect Hamas-Israel talks; in February 2013, the Israeli media, without quoting any officials, stated that some indirect discussions had reportedly taken place in Cairo, and the Egyptian press reported that an Israeli defense delegation met with senior Egyptian intelligence officials to discuss regional issues, including Syria, Hezbollah, Sinai, Palestinian reconciliation, and regional peace talks, but there was no mention of Gaza. See "Israel and Hamas Said to Hold Indirect Talks in Cairo," *The Times of Israel*, February 15, 2013. This report was contradicted by Israeli officials who subsequently stated that indirect talks had been repeatedly delayed; see "The Next Round in Gaza."

5. For Egypt's blame of Hamas and the Muslim Brotherhood and its convictions against members of the latter, see Patrick Kingsley, "Muslim Brotherhood Banned by Egyptian Court," *The Guardian*, September 23, 2013; "Egypt Court Bans Palestinian Hamas Group," *Al-Jazeera*, March 5, 2014; Kashmira Gander, "Egypt Mass Deaths: Muslim Brotherhood Leader Badie Among Hundreds Sentenced to Death," *The Independent*, April 28, 2014. For the number of Gaza civil servants on the Hamas payroll (in 2014, there were about 40,000, not including 7,000 on short-term contracts), see International Crisis Group, "No Exit? Gaza & Israel Between Wars," *Middle East Report*, no. 162, August 26, 2015, p. 25; "The Next Round in Gaza."

6. For more details on electricity shortages, see UN OCHA, "The Humanitarian Impact of Gaza's Electricity and Fuel Crisis," July 2015; see also chapter 10. In the period preceding the 2014 war, electricity was typically on only half the time (eight hours on, followed by eight hours off). But in some parts of Gaza, particularly the eastern neighborhoods close to the Israeli border, electricity was off for as much as eighteen hours per day. And there were times, such as November–December 2013, when I experienced blackouts of fifteen to eighteen hours per day in Gaza City. For Gaza's contaminated aquifer, see B'Tselem, "Over 90% of Water in Gaza Strip Unfit for Drinking," February 9, 2014.

7. For the April 2014 agreement, available only in Arabic, see "Hamas and Fatah Are Putting an End to the Split," Ma'an News Agency, April 23, 2014; "Towards Palestinian National Reconciliation," Geneva Centre for the Democratic Control of Armed Forces, 2011, pp. 58–59. The agreement, signed at Gaza's Shati (Beach) refugee camp, is a short seven-point document that is in essence an accord to implement a previous, more detailed reconciliation pact, signed in Cairo in May 2011. The 2011 Cairo agreement states that the government's role would be largely

apolitical, limited to the following tasks: preparing for elections, unifying institutions, solving problems caused by the division, reconstructing Gaza property damaged during the 2008–2009 war, and reopening NGOs and charities.

8. For the statements from Israeli security officials, see Isabel Kershner, "New Light on Hamas Role in Killings of Teenagers That Fueled Gaza War," *The New York Times*, September 4, 2014.

9. For the commitments Israel made in the Shalit deal, see "Egyptian Official: Shalit Deal Includes Improvement of Prison Conditions," *Ynet*, October 17, 2011. For a detailed assessment of the Shalit deal, see Yoram Schweitzer, "A Mixed Blessing: Hamas, Israel, and the Recent Prisoner Exchange," *INSS Strategic Assessment* 14, no. 4 (January 2012): 23–40.

10. For the assault and censure of allies of Abbas, see "Video: Habbash Expelled from al-Aqsa," *As-Sabeel* [Arabic], June 28, 2014; Amira Hass, "Abbas' Cooperation with Israel Sinking Him at Home," *Haaretz*, July 8, 2014; Asmaa al-Ghoul, "Palestinian Press Losing Media War in Current Crisis," *Al-Monitor*, July 8, 2014; see also chapter 8, n. 18.

11. For Israel's killing of nine militants, seven of them from Hamas, see "Hamas Vows Revenge on Israel After Seven Members Die in Air Strike," Associated Press, July 7, 2014. Operation Protective Edge is the Israeli government's translation of the Hebrew "Tsuk Eitan" (literally "Operation Firm Cliff").

12. For the July 2014 US cease-fire proposal, which called for the "transfer [of] funds to Gaza for the payment of salaries of public employees," see Barak Ravid, "Kerry's Cease-Fire Draft Revealed: U.S. Plan Would Let Hamas Keep Its Rockets," *Haaretz*, July 28, 2014. For the July 21, 2014, statement by Defense Minister Moshe Ya'alon to the Knesset Foreign Affairs and Defense Committee that Israel wished to see PA forces take control of Gaza's border crossings, see "UN Chief Due in Israel to Press for Cease-fire," *Haaretz*, July 22, 2014. For the payment to employees in Gaza and an Israeli security official explaining the "miscalculation" that led to the war ("when you have somebody by the throat, you shouldn't be surprised when they knee you in the groin. We knew after closing the tunnels that the cage [around Gaza] had to have some more room, within limits of course. But we underestimated it"), see International Crisis Group, "Toward a Lasting Ceasefire in Gaza," Middle East Briefing, no. 42, October 23, 2014.

13. For the reclassification of the two soldiers, see Gili Cohen and Noa Shpigel, "Two Fallen IDF Soldiers Recognized as 'Missing in Action or Captive,'" *Haaretz*, June 10, 2016.

14. For the shift in rhetoric of Ramallah leaders, see Orouba Othman, "Fatah's Sudden Volte-Face," *al-Akhbar*, July 23, 2014. For the Qalandiya demonstration, see "2 Killed as Tens of Thousands Protest Israeli Assault Across West Bank," Ma'an News Agency, July 25, 2014; Noa Yachot, "The Largest West Bank Protest in Decades," +972 July 25, 2014; Adiv Sterman, "Six Palestinians Killed in Rising West Bank Violence," *The Times of Israel*, July 26, 2014.

15. For a Shin Bet list of "the main attacks executed via tunnels" prior to the IDF withdrawal from Gaza, see "Hamas Use of Gaza Strip-based Subterranean Route," Israel Security Agency, accessed September 14, 2016: "a. On September 26 2001, IED explosion under Termit post on the Israel-Egypt border resulted in the collapse of the northern part of the post. Three IDF soldiers were injured. b. On June 27 2004, Explosion of Orhan Post in central Gaza Strip resulted in the col-

lapse of the post. One Israeli soldier was killed and 7 were injured. c. On December 12 2004, an offensive tunnel exploded under the JVT post close to Rafah Border Crossing. As a result, 5 IDF soldiers were killed and 6 injured," https://www.shabak.gov.il/English/EnTerrorData/Reviews/Pages/hamas-tunnel.aspx. On the third of these attacks, see "Attack Kills 5 Israeli Soldiers at Gaza Checkpoint," *CNN*, December 13, 2014, http://edition.cnn.com/2004/WORLD/meast/12/12/gaza.explosion/.

16. For the 10 members of the Israeli security forces killed during the 2008–2009 Gaza war, 4 of whom died from friendly fire, see B'Tselem, "Investigation of Fatalities in Operation Cast Lead," accessed October 25, 2016, https://www.btselem.org/download/20090909_cast_lead_fatalities_eng.pdf. For the 66 soldiers, 2 of whom—Oron Shaul and Hadar Goldin—were initially declared dead by Israel and later reclassified as missing in action or captive, see UN OCHA, "Occupied Palestinian Territory: Gaza Emergency," September 2014; 6 civilians, 5 of them Israeli citizens, were also killed during the war.

17. Video footage of armed drones that Hamas operated during the war is available on the Hamas military wing's website [Arabic]: http://www.alqassam.ps/arabic/videos/index/648. Other footage can be found in news reports uploaded to YouTube [Arabic]: https://www.youtube.com/watch?v=b6_f_pfVMGU. For admissions by the IDF that it had not removed all the tunnels penetrating Israel, see Ari Yashar, "IDF Commander Says Hamas Terror Tunnels Still Remain," *Israel National News*, October 16, 2014. For an estimate by the Israeli defense minister that direct military expenditure on the war had totaled $2.5 billion, see "Gaza war cost $2.5 billion, Ya'alon says," *The Times of Israel*, September 3, 2014. For an estimate by the head of the Israel Tax Authority, made weeks before the fighting had ended, that the war had cost the economy an additional $2 billion, not including direct expenditures, see Zvi Zrahiya, "As Fighting Eases, Gaza Conflict Costs Seen Totaling $8 Billion," *Haaretz*, August 6, 2014.

18. For figures from a UN commission of inquiry into the Gaza war—which found that of the 2,251 Palestinians who died, 1,462 were civilians, of whom 299 were women and 551 were children—see "Report of the Detailed Findings of the Independent Commission of Inquiry Established Pursuant to Human Rights Council Resolution S-21/1," UN Office of the High Commissioner for Human Rights, June 24, 2015, p. 153.

10. TRAPPED IN GAZA

This chapter draws on the author's report for the International Crisis Group, "No Exit? Gaza and Israel Between Wars," *Middle East Report*, no. 162, August 26, 2015. The chapter was updated in September 2016.

1. For the Gaza crossings, see "Gaza Economy on the Verge of Collapse, Youth Unemployment Highest in the Region at 60 Percent," World Bank, May 21, 2015. After the closure of three Gaza crossings—Karni (2007), Sufa (2008), and Nahal Oz (2010)—Gaza had three functioning ones: Rafah, on the southern border with Egypt (primarily for people, used for goods only exceptionally); Erez, on the northern border with Israel (for people); and Kerem Shalom, on the eastern border with Israel (solely for goods). For per capita income in 2015, which was 31 percent lower than in 1994, see "Gaza Economy on the Verge of Collapse, Youth Unemployment Highest in the Region at 60 Percent."

2.   For the arrangements regulating the PA's economic relations with Israel, see Israel Ministry of Foreign Affairs, "Gaza-Jericho Agreement Annex IV: Protocol on Economic Relations Between the Government of the State of Israel and the P.L.O., Representing the Palestinian People," April 29, 1994. For details on increased PA tax revenues (no amount of which came from the materials brought in by the UN and other donors, which were tax-exempt), see International Crisis Group, "No Exit? Gaza & Israel Between Wars," *Middle East Report*, no. 162, August 26, 2015.

3.   For an insightful overview of the separation policy, see Gisha—Legal Center for Freedom of Movement, "Separating Land, Separating People: Legal Analysis of Access Restrictions between Gaza and the West Bank," June 2015.

4.   For the 100,000 people still homeless in August 2015, see "Shelter Cluster Fact-sheet," Shelter Cluster Palestine, August 2015. Details on the disputes over how much construction material was needed for each square meter are taken from email correspondence between the author and Gisha executive director (at the time deputy director) Tania Hary, August 13, 2015.

5.   For the number living in temporary shelters, see "Report to the Ad Hoc Liaison Committee," Office of the UN Special Coordinator for the Middle East Peace Process, May 27, 2015. For the less than 6 percent of needed construction materials that arrived, see "The Gaza Cheat Sheet"; see also Gaza Reconstruction Mechanism website: http://grm.report.

6.   For Gaza's 2015 unemployment rates (41.5 percent overall and over 58 percent for youths), see "Labor Force Survey, Q2—2015," Palestinian Central Bureau of Statistics, August 6, 2015. Previous figures were slightly higher: overall unemployment, 43 percent; youth unemployment, over 60 percent. "Economic Monitoring Report." For food insecurity (defined as lacking reliable access to a sufficient quantity of affordable, nutritious food, including the inability to access such food due to poverty, even when there are no food shortages), see "The Gaza Cheat Sheet"; see also UNRWA, "Food Insecurity in Palestine Remains High," June 3, 2014. For the shrunken manufacturing sector, see "Gaza Economy on the Verge of Collapse, Youth Unemployment Highest in the Region at 60 Percent." For the amount of agricultural land and livestock destroyed, see "The National Early Recovery and Reconstruction Plan for Gaza, Submitted to the International Conference in Support of the Reconstruction of Gaza," State of Palestine, October 2014, p. 38.

7.   For Gaza's exports (approximately 5 percent of GDP, consisting mainly of furniture, textiles, and agricultural products), see Gisha, "Economic Monitoring Report"; "A Costly Divide: Economic Repercussions of Separating Gaza and the West Bank," February 2015. For figures on truckloads, see UN OCHA, "Gaza Crossings Activities Database," 2015.

8.   For a summary of the deteriorating conditions and the humanitarian repercussions of electricity shortages, see Association of International Development Agencies, "Charting A New Course: Overcoming the Stalemate in Gaza," April 13, 2015; UN OCHA, "The Humanitarian Impact of Gaza's Electricity and Fuel Crisis," July 2015. From 2013 to 2015, electricity was typically on only half the time (eight hours on, eight hours off) and was occasionally on for only six hours per day in certain areas and periods. By 2016, it was common for electricity to be on for just eight hours per day (six hours on, twelve hours off) throughout Gaza. For injuries from use of

generators, see Dr. Mads Gilbert, "Brief Report to UNRWA: The Gaza Health Sector as of June 2014," UNRWA, July 3, 2014, p. 8.

9. For the effect of electricity shortages on water desalination, agriculture, and hospitals, see "The Humanitarian Impact." For access to water and the destruction of the aquifer, see "Economic Monitoring Report"; "Gaza 2020: A Liveable Place?," UN Country Team, occupied Palestinian territory, 2012. For polluted drinking water (related to almost 40 percent of disease in Gaza) and increased infant mortality (12 percent of infant and young child deaths were caused by diarrhea), see UNICEF, "Protecting Children from Unsafe Water in Gaza: Strategy, Action Plan, and Project Resources," March 2011; B'Tselem, "Water Supplied in Gaza Unfit for Drinking; Israel Prevents Entry of Materials Needed to Repair System," August 23, 2010; "Protecting Children"; UNRWA, "Infant Mortality Rate Rises in Gaza for First Time in Fifty Years," August 8, 2015.

10. For details on bombings and clashes, see "No Exit?"

11. Interviews by the author with Beit Hanoun, Shujaiya, and Rafah residents, Beit Hanoun, Shujaiya, Rafah, March 2015.

12. For a detailed report on Salafi-jihadi groups in Gaza, see International Crisis Group, "Radical Islam in Gaza," *Middle East Report*, no. 104, March 29, 2011. For the attack on Hamas military personnel, see "Hamas Security HQ in Gaza Bombed After Threat," AFP, May 4, 2015. The dozens of checkpoints and four in an area of several blocks are from personal observations, Gaza City, Beit Lahiya, Nusseirat, Deir el-Balah, Khan Younis, and Rafah, May 2015. For the July 2015 bombings, see "Car Bombs Target Hamas, Islamic Jihad Armed Wings in Gaza," Ma'an News Agency, July 19, 2015.

13. For more on Palestinian rocket fire, Israeli strikes, strafing at individuals approaching the land and sea buffer areas, and the 25 Palestinian deaths and 1,375 injuries caused by Israeli forces in 2015, see UN OCHA, "Protection of Civilians 15–21 March 2015," March 24, 2016; "Israel Strikes Gaza After Rocket Fire," Associated Press, July 16, 2015; "IDF Strikes Hamas Target in Gaza After Rocket Attack," *The Times of Israel*, August 7, 2015. For clashes between Hamas and Salafi-jihadi groups and rockets fired by the latter, see "Gunman Killed in Clashes with Hamas Security in Gaza City," Ma'an News Agency, June 2, 2014; "Israeli Jets Strike 4 Targets in the Gaza Strip," Ma'an News Agency, June 4, 2015.

14. The quote from a Hamas leader ("why they should hold their fire") comes from an interview with the author, Gaza City, July 2015.

15. For data on crossings through Rafah (including the total closure of the crossing in four months of 2015 and three of the first four months of 2016, see UN OCHA, "Rafah Crossing: Movement of People into and out of Gaza," accessed May 31, 2016. After two attacks on Egyptian security forces in Sinai on October 24, 2014, Rafah was open for only fifteen days in the next seven months, and on several of those only for entrance into Gaza, not exit. "Report to the Ad Hoc Liaison Committee." The statement from the Egyptian official comes from an interview with the author, Tel Aviv, August 3, 2015.

16. For Egypt's operations against the tunnels, which began before President Sisi but did not make most of the tunnels inoperative until Sisi came to power, see "The Next Round in Gaza"; "Toward a Lasting Ceasefire." For Hamas taxes and partial salary payments to government employees and members of the military wing, see "No Exit?"; "Hamas Imposes New Taxes to Meet Payroll Dues," *Al-Monitor*, April 29, 2015.

17. For Israel's partial relaxation of some aspects of the closure regime (more imports, exports, and exit permits, but still far less than permitted ten or fifteen years earlier), see Gisha, "Entrance of Goods to Gaza from Israel," accessed May 31, 2016, http://www.gisha.org/graph/2387?datares=monthly. In the first half of 2015, 13,826 Gazans, most of them merchants (58 percent) and medical patients (18 percent), exited to Israel each month; in 2000, when Israel was in full control of Gaza, the number exiting to Israel per month was 780,000, more than fifty-six times greater than 2015 levels. For statements from Israeli security officials on the need to improve economic conditions in order to avoid a new conflagration, see "Toward a Lasting Ceasefire"; "No Exit?" For the payment by Qatar of $1,200 to each of the roughly 23,000 employees in all ministries, except the Interior Ministry's non-administrative employees, see "Qatar Offers Cash to Pay Some Staff in Gaza Strip," *The New York Times*, October 28, 2014. In July 2016, Qatar pledged to make another payment covering salaries for one month. "Qatar Says Gives $30 Million to Pay Gaza Public Sector Workers," Reuters, July 22, 2016.

18. For figures on the number of deaths, see chapter 9, nn. 16, 18. The sixty-six soldiers include two initially declared dead and later reclassified as missing; after the war, three additional Israeli citizens (a Jew of Ethiopian origin and two Bedouin) entered Gaza and did not return. See "Arab Israeli Jumps Security Fence, Enters Gaza Strip," Jewish Telegraphic Agency, July 12, 2016.

19. For the statement from the head of the Shin Bet, see "Shin Bet Chief: Hamas Gearing Up for Next Round with Israel," *The Times of Israel*, July 1, 2015. The same day, Hamas leader Ismail Haniyeh said Hamas was stronger than in 2014. "Hamas Chief Says Armed Wing 'Stronger' Now than During Gaza War," *The Times of Israel*, July 1, 2015. For Hamas's rebuilding and test-fire of rockets, see "No Exit?"

20. For statements by Israeli officials on the country's goals in Gaza, the unlikelihood of reoccupation unless there were a mass casualty attack, and the inability of the PA, Fatah, or international forces to take over, see "No Exit?" For the quote from the head of IDF southern command ("no substitute for Hamas as sovereign"), see "Israeli General Sees Common Interests with Hamas," Reuters, May 12, 2015.

21. For the minority opinion in the government, the statement from the security official, and the calls to overthrow Hamas by Avigdor Lieberman, who was then foreign minister and became defense minister in May 2016, see "No Exit?"; interviews by the author with Israeli security officials, Tel Aviv, April–May 2015; "Liberman: Topple Hamas and Give UN Control over Gaza," *The Times of Israel*, August 4, 2014.

22. For Israel's plans to evacuate border communities within 7 kilometers (4.3 miles) of Gaza in a future war, see "How Israel Plans to Evacuate Gaza Border Towns During Next War with Hamas," *The Jerusalem Post*, May 23, 2015. For the public opinion poll conducted three weeks into the war, see Ephraim Yaar and Tamar Hermann, "85% of the Public Supports Continuing Limited Ground Operations," *Walla! News* [Hebrew], July 29, 2014, http://news.walla.co.il/item/2770297.

23. The statements by residents of Gaza are taken from interviews by the author with Gaza residents, workers, and merchants, Gaza City, Beit Hanoun, and Shujaiya, March–April 2015. For Hamas proposals for a cease-fire, see "Abu Marzouk: No Truce Before Israel Lifts Siege on Gaza," Palestinian Information Center, September 6, 2015; interviews by the author with Hamas senior officials, Beit Lahiya, Gaza City, December 2014–May 2015. For statements by the head of Israeli military intelligence to the Knesset, see Barak Ravid, "IDF Intelligence Chief: Despite Hamas'

Efforts to Ensure Calm, Suffering in Gaza May Lead to Violence Against Israel," *Haaretz*, February 23, 2016.

24. On Israel's sense of reduced pressure, a security official said: "that there is no smuggling now gives us freedom to do more for Gaza with relatively little risk. If Hamas were smuggling a great deal . . . we would have to go to war much sooner to raze their capabilities." Interview by the author with Israeli security official, Jerusalem, May 2015. For similar statements, see "No Exit?"

25. For assessments by Hamas and Israel that a new war would not have a different outcome, Egyptian statements on hostility to Hamas and willingness to have Israel topple it, PA opposition to Israeli moves that would bolster Hamas, and Israeli and international opposition to direct relations with Hamas, see "No Exit?"; interviews by the author with Egyptian, PA, Israeli, Hamas, and international officials, Cairo, Ramallah, Jerusalem, Tel Aviv, Gaza City, March 2015, May 2015, April 2016.

26. For the 2015 arrest campaign (in mid-July, Hamas published the names of 250 members who were arrested by the PA in the West Bank in one of the largest PA operations against Hamas in eight years), see "Hamas Takes Hit After Latest PA Crackdown," *Al-Monitor*, July 16, 2015. For Islamic Jihad's threats over two different Palestinian prisoners, see "Islamic Jihad Threatens to End Truce if Adnan Dies," *al-Araby al-Jadeed*, June 22, 2015. "Islamic Jihad: If Hunger-Striker Dies, the Cease-Fire with Israel Is Over," *The Jerusalem Post*, August 14, 2015. For the flare-up in May 2016, see William Booth, "Israel and Hamas Using 'Rocket Language' Again in New Escalation," *The Washington Post*, May 6, 2016. For the incident months after the 2014 cease-fire in which a Hamas commander was killed, see "Israeli Forces Shoot Dead Hamas Militant after Gaza Border Firelight," *The Guardian*, December 24, 2014. The quote from a Hamas political committee member ("could have found ourselves in a new war") comes from an interview with the author, Gaza City, December 2014.

27. See interviews cited above; "No Exit?" For the Halevy quote ("What incentive will we have"), see Dalia Karpel, "A Former Spy Chief Is Calling on Israelis to Revolt," *Haaretz*, October 1, 2016.

28. For the State Comptroller's Report, see Amos Harel, "Bleak Gaza War Report Shows How Next Conflict Will Begin," *Haaretz*, May 10, 2016. For a list of Israel's shifts in policy after the war, see "Toward a Lasting Ceasefire."

V. NEGOTIATION

Shlaim, *The Iron Wall*, p. 517.

11. MORE THAN ONE STATE, LESS THAN TWO

This chapter was updated in September 2016.

1. For details of Olmert's proposal, see Abrams, *Tested by Zion*, pp. 276–95; Susser, *Israel, Jordan, and Palestine*, pp. 64–68; Rabinovich, *The Lingering Conflict*, p. 178; Aluf Benn, "*Haaretz* Exclusive: Olmert's Plan for Peace with the Palestinians," *Haaretz*, December 17, 2009; Bernard Avishai, "A Plan for Peace That Still Could Be," *The New York Times Magazine*, February 7, 2011; Josef Federman, "Abbas Admits He Rejected 2008 Peace Offer from Olmert," Associated Press, November 19, 2008; "Factbox: Israeli, Palestinian Papers Reveal Peace Deal Moves," Reuters, January 28, 2011; and the more than one thousand leaked documents

archived in "The Palestine Papers," *Al Jazeera* Investigations, accessed October 25, 2016.

2. For Olmert's quote ("I've been waiting"), see Avi Issachoroff, "Olmert: 'I Am Still Waiting for Abbas to Call,'" The Tower (online), May 24, 2013.

3. For Palestinians stating that they never heard back regarding their questions to Israel, see Abrams, *Tested by Zion*, p. 292. For a summary of the large gaps remaining, see comments to Abrams by Olmert's foreign policy adviser, Shalom Tourgeman: "There was no agreement on the land swap and where it will be, no agreement of the worth of the Gaza-West Bank passage and in principle on the size of land Israel will keep. We said the major [settlement] blocks are at least 6.3 percent, if not more, and they said not more than 1.9 percent. On foreign forces [replacing Israeli ones in the West Bank] I don't recall that it was ever an option; in all our talks we said it cannot be an option, not NATO and not other forces." Abrams, p. 290.

4. For discrepancies on the amount of land to be included in a swap, see Abrams, *Tested by Zion*, pp. 288–90; "The Palestine Papers." Throughout the 2008 Annapolis talks, Palestinian negotiators recorded what Israel claimed was the percentage of land to be annexed and then wrote in parenthesis beside this number a higher percentage, which they believed the Israeli proposed annexation actually represented. In calculating the percentages there was confusion not just about what denominator was used (representing the total area of the pre-1967 territories) but also the numerator (representing the amount of territory Israel would annex). Palestinian negotiators weren't sure that in the area to be annexed Israel included, for example, the 49-square-kilometer no-man's-land or the 70 square kilometers of East Jerusalem. (Abrams and others write of percentages of the West Bank, but a territorial expert who worked with Olmert told me the percentages were of the entire Occupied Territories.) The figure of 6.8 percent (in exchange for 5.5 percent) was what Abbas wrote in the upper left corner of his hand-drawn rendition of Olmert's September 16, 2008, map. These are the same figures a leaked PLO document states Olmert offered weeks earlier, on August 31. Abrams describes a November 24, 2008, White House meeting in which Olmert said it was an annexation of 6.5 percent, not 6.3 percent, that he proposed to Abbas; this number was repeated by the PLO's chief negotiator, Saeb Erekat, who himself has given inconsistent descriptions of Olmert's proposal.

5. For Abrams's quote ("looked very much the same"), see Abrams, *Tested by Zion*, p. 291.

6. For discrepancies on refugees (Palestinian negotiators insisted that Israel acknowledge responsibility for the refugee problem and viewed as insufficient Olmert's offer to "acknowledge the suffering" of Palestinian refugees) and for Qurei's quote ("territory is the easiest issue"), see ibid., pp. 288, 271.

7. For Abrams thinking Abbas shouldn't take the deal, Abrams telling Palestinians not to take the deal, and Abrams's quote ("The weaker he became"), see ibid., pp. 286, 288, 233.

8. For Abrams's quote ("too many lacunae"), Abbas's statement ("many people in the Israeli government"), see ibid., pp. 291, 285. For Rice's confirmation of Abbas's assertion ("Livni urged me (and, I believe, Abbas) not to enshrine the Olmert proposal"), see Condoleezza Rice, *No Higher Honor: A Memoir of My Years in Washington* (New York: Crown, 2011), p. 723. For Bush's statement ("dead simply because he was its sponsor"), see Abrams, *Tested by Zion*, p. 285.

9. For Shavit's quotes ("Abbas has not responded") and ("the whole world to the Palestinians"), see Ari Shavit, "Hamas Still Wants to Liberate 'All of Palestine,'" *Haaretz*, December 17, 2009; Ari Shavit, "Thinking Outside Two Boxes," *Haaretz*, March 19, 2009.

10. For a summary of the gap in Israeli and Palestinian perceptions, see the article by the former Palestinian negotiator Ghassan Khatib, "A Fundamental Difference of Understanding," BitterLemons.org, accessed May 4, 2016, http://www .bitterlemons.org/previous/b1290609ed25.html: "Israelis should understand that Palestinians have a concept of compromise that is different from theirs. The Israelis are coming to the table with the idea that they are going to compromise on the Occupied Territories, i.e., the West Bank, including East Jerusalem, and the Gaza Strip. The Palestinians, on the other hand, come to negotiations with the understanding that the original dispute with Israel is over historic Palestine, and the 1967 borders are themselves a compromise that cannot be further compromised." For the PLO's formal, written recognition of "the right of the State of Israel to exist in peace and security," which came in a September 9, 1993, letter from Arafat to Yitzhak Rabin, see "Israel-PLO Recognition-Exchange of Letters Between PM Rabin and Chairman Arafat—Sept 9–1993," Israel Ministry of Foreign Affairs, accessed May 4, 2016, http://www.mfa.gov.il/mfa/foreignpolicy /peace/guide/pages/israel-plo recognition - exchange of letters betwe.aspx. For the PLO's first recognition of Israel's right to exist in peace and security, which came in a December 14, 1988, statement by Yasir Arafat that mentioned "the right of all parties concerned in the Middle East conflict to exist in peace and security and, as I have mentioned, including the state of Palestine and Israel and other neighbors according to the Resolutions 242 and 338," see "Arafat: 'We Are Committed to Peace. We Want to Live in Our Palestinian State and Let Live," *The Washington Post*, December 15, 1988. Several days prior to this, Arafat stated at a news conference in Stockholm, "We accept two states, the Palestine state and the Jewish state of Israel." Steve Lohr, "Arafat Says PLO Accepted Israel," *The New York Times*, December 7, 1988.

11. For Abbas's 2009 statement ("The gaps were wide"), which came under withering criticism in the United States and Israel and which, three years later, he denied having made, see Jackson Diehl, "Abbas's Waiting Game on Peace with Israel," *The Washington Post*, May 29, 2009. For Abbas's subsequent denial, see Raphael Ahren, "Rebutting Abbas, Condoleezza Rice Confirms Her Account of Their 2008 Refugee Conversation," *The Times of Israel*, July 11, 2012. For a useful history of the territorial dimension of Israeli-Palestinian negotiations, see Michael Herzog, "Minding the Gaps: Territorial Issues in Israeli-Palestinian Peacemaking," Washington Institute for Near East Policy, December 2011. Between May 2000 and September 2008, Israeli negotiators made the following proposals: May 2000 in Eilat (66 percent, no swaps); May 2000 in Stockholm (76.6 percent, no swaps); the beginning of Camp David, in July 2000 (88.5 percent, no swaps); the end of Camp David, in July 2000 (91 percent, with a swap of Israeli land equivalent to 1 percent of the West Bank); Taba, in January 2001 (92 percent, no swaps); Livni-Qurei negotiations during the Annapolis process, in 2008 (92.7 percent, no swaps). The two offers in May 2000 proposed that additional territory (17 percent in the first offer in Eilat, 10.1 percent in Stockholm) remain under Israeli control for security reasons but ultimately become Palestinian territory.

12. For Kerry's quote ("or it's over"), see Josh Gerstein, "Kerry: 1–2 Years for Mideast Peace 'or It's Over,'" Politico, April 17, 2013, http://www.politico.com/blogs/politico44/2013 /04/kerry-1-2-years-for-mideast-peace-or-its-over-161945.

13. For Netanyahu's declaration of support for two states, see Address by PM Netan-yahu at Bar-Ilan University, Israel Ministry of Foreign Affairs, June 14, 2009, http://mfa.gov.il/MFA/PressRoom/2009/Pages/Address_PM_Netanyahu_BarIlan _University_14-Jun-2009.aspx. For the quote from a founder of the settler move-ment ("a revolutionary ideological turn"), see Israel Harel, "Likud's Final Term," *Haaretz*, January 31, 2013. For skepticism that Netanyahu meant it, aggravated by his statement prior to the 2015 Israeli election that a Palestinian state would not be created on his watch, see Jodi Rudoren and Michael D. Shear, "Israel's Netanyahu Reopens Door to Palestinian State, but White House Is Unimpressed," *The New York Times*, March 19, 2015. Netanyahu's statement prior to the election was retracted just after it: "I want a sustainable, peaceful two-state solution, but for that, circumstances have to change. . . . I was talking about what is achievable and what is not achievable. To make it achievable, then you have to have real negotia-tions with people who are committed to peace." Though Netanyahu's expressions of skepticism about a two-state solution have received a great deal more attention, his avowals of support for it have been far more frequent. For Netanyahu's demo-graphic argument in favor of two states, see Isabel Kershher, "Israeli Premier Backs Referendum on Any Peace Deal," *The New York Times*, May 3, 2013.

14. For polls showing that a majority of Israelis (and a greater majority of Israeli Jews) oppose a peace agreement based on the pre-1967 lines, see, for example, "Poll: Most Israelis Oppose Withdrawing to 1967," Reuters, August 6, 2013. Some polls are able to find greater support among Jews for dividing Jerusalem and a peace agreement based on the pre-1967 lines, but do so by coupling these two with numerous concessions that Palestinians have given little indication they would make, for example, recognizing Israel as the state of the Jewish people, renouncing totally any right of refugee return, and accepting Israeli annexation of the large settlement blocs. For Bennett's quote ("where exactly"), see "Bennett: A Palestin-ian State Will Never Be Formed," *The Jerusalem Post*, May 8, 2013.

15. For Eizenstat's quote ("commonly understood"), see Stuart E. Eizenstat, *The Future of the Jews: How Global Forces Are Impacting the Jewish People, Israel, and Its Rela-tionship with the United States* (Lanham, MD: Rowman and Littlefield, 2013), p. 152. For fierce fights over so-called "consensus" settlements such as Ma'ale Adu-mim, see Gregg Carlstrom, "'The Biggest Yerushalayim,'" *Al Jazeera*, January 23, 2011; "Meeting Minutes: Trilateral–United States, Israel and Palestine," The Pales-tine Papers, Al Jazeera Investigations, June 15, 2008.

16. For increased Israeli trade with countries where BDS has made large gains, see David Rosenberg, "Three Cheers for Yair Lapid," *Haaretz*, April 3, 2013: "Israeli exports to South Africa climbed 35.6% in the last three years, to Britain by 148%, and to Turkey by 32.3%." For the steady increase in the EU's trade of goods with Israel from 2013 to 2015, see "Israel—Trade Statistics," Directorate-General for Trade, European Commission, accessed September 23, 2016, http://trade.ec .europa.eu/doclib/docs/2006/september/tradoc_111672.pdf. For the steps against settlements so far taken by the EU, most notably the July 2013 approval of guide-lines that restrict the awards given by the European Commission—but not those by European Union member states—to Israeli entities operating in territories

Israel conquered in 1967, see "Guidelines on the Eligibility of Israeli Entities and Their Activities in the Territories Occupied by Israel Since June 1967 for Grants, Prizes and Financial Instruments Funded by the EU from 2014 Onwards," *Official Journal of the European Union*, July 19, 2013, C 205/9-11. The guidelines received considerable attention in the Israeli press but substantively changed very little: they were not binding on EU member states; though they restricted European Commission support—e.g., grants, prizes, and financial instruments—to Israeli entities in the West Bank and Golan Heights, such support was minimal to begin with; they did not affect trade between Israel and Europe; and they did not apply to Israeli government offices, such as the Ministry of Justice, that are located beyond Israel's pre-1967 boundaries.

17. For figures showing that the majority of the settlement workforce is employed outside the settlements, see Human Rights Watch, "Occupation, Inc.: How Settlement Businesses Contribute to Israel's Violations of Palestinian Rights," January 19, 2016. Among the minority of jobs inside the settlements, many are in the public sector, not in factories whose products could be boycotted; settlements receive a disproportionate share of the state budget, allowing them to hire greater numbers of state employees in such fields as education. For studies showing that municipalities and settlements east of the separation barrier have received about twice as much per resident and per student as communities in Israel proper, see MACRO—The Center for Political Economics, "A Comprehensive Analysis of the Settlements' Economic Costs and Alternative Costs to the State of Israel," February 19, 2015; Roby Nathanson and Itamar Gazala, "Allocation of Government Resources to Education by National Priority Areas and the West Bank," MACRO—The Center for Political Economics, July 20, 2015, p. 3.

18. American support for Israel has been quite consistent in annual surveys over the past decade. If anything, it has slightly increased in Israel's favor. In 2006, the share of Americans who stated that their sympathies lie with Israel was 59 percent; sympathy with the Palestinians was 15 percent; and sympathy with neither was 26 percent, http://www.jewishdatabank.org/studies/downloadFile.cfm?FileID =2772. In 2016, the numbers were almost identical: support for the Palestinians remained the same, support for neither dropped to 23 percent, and support for Israel rose to 62 percent. See "Americans' Views Toward Israel Remain Firmly Positive," Gallup, February 29, 2016, http://www.gallup.com/poll/189626/americans -views-toward-israel-remain-firmly-positive.aspx. For a separate study showing similar consistency over time, see "Public Uncertain, Divided over America's Place in the World," Pew Research Center, May 5, 2016, p. 41, http://www.people-press .org/files/2016/05/05-05-2016-Foreign-policy-APW-release.pdf. The same poll found that, compared to older generations, those born after 1980 ("Millennials") supported Israel (43 percent) much more than the Palestinians (27 percent), but this gap was smaller than that found among the population at large (54 percent support for Israel and 19 percent for the Palestinians). Among Jews, there may also be a generational gap, though both the findings and the possible causes of it have been disputed. For a 2013 Pew poll finding that 18- to 29-year-old American Jews are more attached to Israel than 30- to 49-year-olds (both overall and among Conservative Jews, Reform Jews, and Jews of no denomination), see chapter 5, "Connection with and Attitudes Toward Israel," in *A Portrait of Jewish Americans: Findings from a Pew Research Center Survey of U.S. Jews*, Pew Research Center's Religion

and Public Life Project, October 1, 2013, p. 82. For a 2012 poll finding young Jews have *greater* attachment to Israel than their elders, see Chemi Shalev, "Poll: Young American Jews Are Growing More Attached to Israel," *Haaretz*, July 9, 2012. For a study that finds younger Jews more distant from Israel than older Jews, but that attributes this more to intermarriage and generational effects than to political disagreements, see Steven M. Cohen and Ari Y. Kelman (with the assistance of Lauren Blitzer), "Beyond Distancing: Young Adult American Jews and Their Alienation from Israel," Jewish Identity Project of Reboot, 2007; see also Theodore Sasson, Benjamin Phillips, Graham Wright, Charles Kadushin, and Leonard Saxe, "Understanding Young Adult Attachment to Israel: Period, Lifecycle, and Generational Dynamics," *Contemporary Jewry* 32, no.1 (April 2012): 67–84. If current trends continue, the distancing of young non-Orthodox American Jews from Israel may be temporary. The majority of American Jews in their twenties today have one non-Jewish parent, but leading sociologists such as Steven Cohen expect that many of their children will not identify as Jewish at all; the result is that these offspring, self-identified non-Jews, will have attitudes toward Israel that resemble those of the rest of the US population (if the current trajectory does not change), while the remaining population that identifies as Jewish will be more Orthodox, conservative, and pro-Israel than the current generation.

19. For Kerry's quote ("left to choose"), see Paul Richter, "Kerry Presses Peace Deal at American Jewish Committee Meeting," *The Los Angeles Times*, June 3, 2013.
20. For protests that erupted in Jewish neighborhoods in which Palestinian families bought homes, see Noa Shpigel, "Hundreds Rally in Northern Israel Against Housing for Arabs," *Haaretz*, December 27, 2015. For more on the sense of a fading Green Line, see the interview with former Jerusalem deputy mayor Meron Benvenisti in Ari Shavit, "Jerusalem-Born Thinker Meron Benvenisti Has a Message for Israelis: Stop Whining," *Haaretz*, October 11, 2012.
21. See Susser, *Israel, Jordan, and Palestine*, p. 220; Yehouda Shenhav, *Beyond the Two-State Solution: A Jewish Political Essay*, Dimi Reider and Efrat Weiss, trans. (Cambridge: Polity, 2012). For Susser's quote ("little if any real progress"), see Susser, p. 218.
22. For the inequality in collective rights, see Dr. Yousef T. Jabareen, "The Politics of Equality: The Limits of Collective Rights Litigation and the Case of the Palestinian-Arab Minority in Israel," *Columbia Journal of Race and Law* 4, no. 1 (2013): 23–54; Amal Jamal, "On the Morality of Arab Collective Rights in Israel," Adalah Newsletter, vol. 12, April 2005; International Crisis Group, "Back to Basics: Israel's Arab Minority and the Israeli-Palestinian Conflict," *Middle East Report* no. 119, March 14, 2012. For restrictions on marriage, see "660,000 Israelis Unable to Get Married Here," *The Times of Israel*, January 12, 2016. Because Israel does not offer civil marriage and the Chief Rabbinate of Israel will not perform interfaith marriages, Jews who wish to marry those the Rabbinate considers non-Jews (a category that includes hundreds of thousands of immigrants from the former Soviet Union, many of whom consider themselves Jewish) must either have their partners convert to Orthodox Judaism (non-Orthodox conversions are not recognized), marry within a church (an option that very few Jews choose), or travel abroad to conduct a civil marriage. Approximately one in five Israeli couples register their marriages abroad. For the inequality in reclaiming homes abandoned in the 1948 war, see Association for Civil Rights in Israel, "East Jerusalem 2015: Facts

and Figures," May 12, 2015, p. 9; for a recent example, see Nir Hasson, "Five Palestinian Families in East Jerusalem Evicted from Homes," *Haaretz*, October 19, 2015.

23. For more on Palestinian citizens and residents of Israel who lived under military rule from 1948 until the end of 1966 and were unable to obtain citizenship until 1952 (and in many cases not until long after that, if they were not counted in the population registry or had no proof of identity), see chapter 2. For Shenhav on the "emulation" by West Bank settlers of what Zionists did within Israel proper prior to 1967, the "false distinction" between pre-1967 and post-1967 Israel, the inequality of Palestinians in Israel living under military rule until 1966, and the fact that pre-1967 Israeli settlements more often sit atop ruined Palestinian villages than post-1967 ones, see Shenhav, *Beyond the Two-State Solution*, pp. 15, 20, 23, 99–102.

24. For the Susser quote ("never a fully sovereign"), see Susser, *Israel, Jordan, and Palestine*, p. 220.

25. For Rabin's quote, see Israel Ministry of Foreign Affairs, "Prime Minister Yitzhak Rabin: Ratification of the Israel-Palestinian Interim Agreement—The Knesset," October 5, 1995.

26. The war that followed the November 1947 UN Partition Resolution, commonly referred to as the 1948 war, is typically divided by historians into two phases: first, a civil war in Mandatory Palestine, beginning just after the UN General Assembly passed the November 29, 1947, resolution calling for partition; and second, an Arab-Israeli war, which commenced with attacks by Arab states on Israel following the latter's May 14, 1948, declaration of independence (the day the British Mandate expired) and ended with the armistice agreements Israel and its neighbors signed in 1949. Many of the war's deaths and displacements took place during its first phase. By the time the second phase began, in May 1948, hundreds of thousands of Palestinians (most estimates range from 250,000 to 350,000) had already been displaced, and more than 2,000 Jews had already been killed (of a total of roughly 6,000 Jewish deaths during the war). For sources and more detailed figures, see chapter 2, n. 8.

12. Faith-Based Diplomacy

This chapter was updated in September 2016.

1. For American military aid to Israel, see Jeremy M. Sharp, "U.S. Foreign Aid to Israel," Congressional Research Service, June 10, 2015, pp. 5, 13. In the 2016 fiscal year, funds for Israel made up 53 percent of US foreign military financing worldwide. This figure does not include additional US aid for Israeli missile defense, which has averaged approximately $500 million per year ($729 million in 2014, $620 million in 2015). In September 2016, the United States pledged to increase military assistance to Israel to $3.8 billion per year, beginning in 2019. "Fact Sheet: Memorandum of Understanding Reached with Israel," White House, Office of the Press Secretary, September 14, 2016. From 2013 to 2016, the Israeli defense budget averaged $16 billion (60 billion NIS) per year, while US military assistance and aid for missile defense was approximately $3.5 billion per year, making up 22 percent of the Israeli defense budget. Figures for 2013 and 2014 can be found in Shmuel Even, "The Debate over Israel's Defense Budget," Institute for National Security Studies, 2015, p. 176; for 2015 in Yuval Azulai and Amiram Barkat, "Israel's Defense Budget Won't Be Above NIS 60b," *Globes*, November 12, 2015; and for 2016 in

Amos Harel, "Defense Ministry, Treasury Agree on $15.6 Billion Defense Budget for 2016," *Haaretz*, November 15, 2015. For figures on US foreign assistance to the West Bank and Gaza (not including aid to UNRWA) compared to the rest of the world, see "Congressional Budget Justification—Foreign Assistance—Summary Tables—Fiscal Year 2015," United States Department of State, accessed October 26, 2016.

2. For Kerry's quotes ("either being an apartheid" and "the window"), see Josh Rogin, "Exclusive: Kerry Warns Israel Could Become 'An Apartheid State,'" *The Daily Beast*, April 28, 2014; Harriet Sherwood, "Kerry: Two Years Left to Reach Two-State Solution in Middle East Peace Process," *The Guardian*, April 18, 2013.

3. In 2011 and again in summer 2013, Netanyahu privately agreed to enter talks based on the pre-1967 lines if Palestinians would cancel plans to gain recognition of the state of Palestine at international institutions and offer recognition of Israel as the nation-state of the Jewish people. The Palestinians have consistently refused the latter, seeing it as a ploy to have them relinquish refugee claims, consent to discrimination against non-Jewish citizens of Israel, and concede the primacy of Jewish rights to the land from which they were displaced.

4. Interviews with the author, Ramallah, May–June 2014.

5. For the Israeli cabinet decision that release of the fourteen prisoners would require a separate vote, see Haviv Rettig Gur and Ron Friedman, "Cabinet Votes to Free Prisoners, Paving Way for Peace Talks," *The Times of Israel*, July 28, 2013. Kerry's promise regarding Pollard comes from the author's interview with a former member of Kerry's negotiating team, Washington, DC, October 2014. (Kerry's discussions with Israel about releasing Jonathan Pollard started at the outset of the negotiations, in summer 2013, long before they were reported in the press, which mischaracterized them as a last-minute attempt to salvage the negotiations as they were unraveling.) At one point there was a proposal to have the fourteen prisoners released but exiled from Israel, a condition to which Palestinians objected. Interview by the author with a US official, Washington, DC, June 2014.

6. For Clinton's announcement of the Camp David summit, ("if we work hard, we can get it done in several days"), see John Lancaster, "Mideast Summit Set Next Week at Camp David," *The Washington Post*, July 6, 2000. For Rice's announcement at the outset of Annapolis, see "Rice Seeks Mideast Peace Deal While Bush in Office," Reuters, November 5, 2007. For Bush's statement at the same time (vowing to "make every effort to conclude an agreement before the end of 2008"), see "President Bush's Speech at Annapolis—November 27, 2007," United States Institute of Peace, accessed May 20, 2016. For the one-year timeline for the Annapolis talks, see Steven Lee Myers and Helene Cooper, "Framework Set by Palestinians and Israelis for Peace Talks," *The New York Times*, November 27, 2007. For Clinton's August 2010 statement ("to resolve all final status issues, which we believe can be completed within one year"), see Chris McGreal and Rachel Shabi, "Israel and Palestinians to Resume Peace Talks in Washington," *The Guardian*, August 20, 2010. Several weeks later, at the UN General Assembly, President Obama said, "When we come back here next year, we can have an agreement that will lead to a new member of the United Nations—an independent, sovereign state of Palestine, living in peace with Israel." "Remarks by the President to the United Nations General Assembly," White House, Office of the Press Secretary, September 23, 2010.

7. For Lieberman's views on negotiations as conflict management, see Elad Benari, "Lieberman: The Conflict with the Arabs Has No Solution," *Israel National News*, July 21, 2013.

8. Indyk, *Innocent Abroad*, p. 7.

9. Proponents of binationalism or a one-state solution, from either the left or right, have had no voice in the US government.

10. For more on US support for Fayyad's state-building program, see chapter 4.

11. Reproachers tend to neglect that even if Palestinians were to one day demand enfranchisement in a single state, Israel could probably thwart the move, and the accompanying international pressure, by withdrawing unilaterally from most areas of the West Bank, including large Palestinian population centers, and disclaiming responsibility for them.

12. For the push for a settlement freeze by Rahm Emanuel and others, see Scott Wilson, "Obama Searches for Middle East Peace," *The Washington Post*, July 14, 2012. For the settlement moratorium and the exemptions, see Peace Now, "Eight Months into the Settlement Freeze," August 2, 2010. For the offer to pay to extend the moratorium and Hillary Clinton's account of it ("Some in the United States also raised fair questions about whether it was wise to buy a ninety-day freeze for negotiations that might well lead nowhere. I wasn't happy either—I confided to Tony Blair that I found it to be 'a nasty business'—but it felt like a sacrifice worth making"), see Hillary Clinton, *Hard Choices*, pp. 326–29; Ross, *Doomed to Succeed*, p. 377; "U.S. Offers Israel Warplanes in Return for New Settlement Freeze," *Haaretz*, November 13, 2010. For figures on settlement construction starts and tenders during the moratorium (a nearly fourfold increase in East Jerusalem—from 170 tenders in 2009 to 663 in 2010—and a 7 percent drop in building starts in the West Bank, from 1,660 in 2009 to 1,550 in 2010), see Peace Now, "Torpedoing the Two State Solution: Summary of 2011 in the Settlements," January 2012; Peace Now, "Settlements and the Netanyahu Government: A Deliberate Policy of Undermining the Two-State Solution," January 2013.

13. See chapter 1, section ii, n. 64.

14. For Obama's statement, see Scott Wilson, "Obama Searches for Middle East Peace," *The Washington Post*, July 14, 2012.

15. Robert Satloff, the executive director of the Washington Institute for Near East Policy, which was cofounded by Dennis Ross and Martin Indyk (a former Embracer who has moved somewhat toward the Reproacher camp), praised the Obama administration for having moved toward the Embracer school: "In contrast to Obama 2009, the initial Kerry 2014 strategy has been to 'hug' Israeli prime minister Binyamin Netanyahu, essentially asking him, 'What do you need?'" See Washington Institute for Near East Policy, "Assessing U.S. Strategy in the Israeli-Palestinian Talks: A Mideast Trip Report," February 5, 2014.

16. For the text of the May 2011 speech, see "Remarks by the President on the Middle East and North Africa," White House, Office of the Press Secretary, May 19, 2011. Dennis Ross describes the policy debate that preceded the speech: "Before Mitchell left his post in April 2011, he favored laying out our positions on all the issues. He and I were in agreement that we needed to lean toward the Palestinians on territory and toward the Israelis on security. We disagreed, however, about outlining positions on refugees and Jerusalem. He wanted to present our positions on all four of the core issues; I felt that would guarantee only that we would get two nos. . . . On

this issue, my arguments prevailed, and the president decided we would do parameters only on borders and security." Ross, *Doomed to Succeed*, p. 382.

17. For Kerry's quotes ("unhelpful" and "expected"), see Joshua Mitnick, "Kerry Tries to Rekindle Israel-Palestinian Talks," *The Wall Street Journal*, November 6, 2013; "Kerry: Israeli Settlements Move Was Expected," BBC, August 13, 2013, http://www.bbc.com/news/world-middle-east-23677488.

18. For text of the Roadmap, which calls for all settlement activity to be frozen, "including natural growth," and demands the dismantlement of all outposts established since Sharon became prime minister in 2001, see "A Performance-Based Roadmap to a Permanent Two-State Solution to the Israeli-Palestinian Conflict," Israel Ministry of Foreign Affairs, April 30, 2003. For text of the Arab Peace Initiative, see "Arab Peace Initiative: Full Text," *The Guardian*, March 28, 2002.

19. Even the Clinton Parameters of December 2000, about which the PLO expressed major reservations, offered Palestinian sovereignty over Jerusalem's Noble Sanctuary/Temple Mount, an Israeli withdrawal from the West Bank within thirty-six months (and from the Jordan Valley within another thirty-six months), and Israeli recognition in principle, though with implementation left to Israel's sovereign discretion, of "the right of Palestinian refugees to return to historic Palestine." Ross, *The Missing Peace*, p. 810.

20. Territory was one domain in which the position of the Obama administration was more favorable to Palestinians than the position of the Clinton administration. Interviews by the author with US officials, Washington, DC, April 2016.

21. For statements from the head of Israel's Labor Party, Yitzhak Herzog ("Jerusalem must remain united as Israel's capital. Period."), see "Herzog: Jerusalem Must Remain United," *Israel National News*, March 13, 2015.

22. The details in this paragraph are taken from interviews by the author with former US officials and Palestinian negotiators, Ramallah and Washington, DC, July 2015, December 2015, April–May 2016, September 2016.

23. For quotes from the Clinton Parameters, see Ross, *The Missing Peace*, p. 812. The other details in this paragraph are taken from interviews by the author cited above. US and Palestinian officials differed on how strong was the implication of a Palestinian capital in Jerusalem. Two US officials characterized it as definitive; whereas Palestinians and one US offical said it was vague, offering the "possibility" of a capital in East Jerusalem. One Palestinian with first-hand knowledge of the framework said: "Of course it was vague on Jerusalem: the U.S. wanted both sides to accept it as the basis of negotiations, and anything that clearly implied East Jerusalem as the Palestinian capital would have been unacceptable to Netanyahu." Interview by the author with Palestinian negotiator, Ramallah, September 2016. Both Palestinian and US officials agreed that the 2014 framework read to Abbas was far more ambiguous on Jerusalem than was Clinton's proposal.

24. For Obama's quote ("too weak"), see Thomas L. Friedman, "Obama on the World," *The New York Times*, August 8, 2014. For a discussion of US policy toward the reconciliation agreement between Hamas and the PLO, see chapter 10.

25. On US views regarding the refugee issue, there is no constituency of American policy makers that calls for the return to Israel of an upper limit of 120,000–125,000 Palestinian refugees, as Israeli and Palestinian negotiators discussed at the Taba talks in 2001. (The Israeli team proposed absorbing 25,000 refugees over three years or 40,000 over five years, with refugee return to be resolved over a fifteen-

year period. Narrowly interpreted, this meant Israel accepted the return of 25,000 to 40,000 refugees. A broader interpretation is that it accepted 120,000 to 125,000 over the entire fifteen-year period.) For the figures at Taba, see Rex Brynen, "The 'Geneva Accord' and the Palestinian Refugee Issue," Palestinian Refugee Research Net, February 29, 2004, p. 4, http://prrn.mcgill.ca/research/papers/geneva_refugees _2.pdf. For the 2003 survey, see Palestinian Center for Policy and Survey Research, "Result of Refugees' Polls in the West Bank/Gaza Strip, Jordan and Lebanon," January–June 2003. For the US estimates prior to Camp David, see Michael Dumper, *Palestinian Refugee Repatriation: Global Perspectives* (New York: Routledge, 2006), p. 77. For the share of Palestinians who are refugees, see UN Relief and Works Agency for Palestine Refugees in the Near East, "UNRWA in Figures," November 2014. In July 2013 the population of registered refugees in Gaza was 1,221,110 and in the West Bank it was 748,899 making a total of 1,970,009. This was out of a total Palestinian population in the West Bank and Gaza of 4,420,549 at that time, according to the Palestinian Central Bureau of Statistics.

13. Obama's Palestine Legacy

1. See Ali Abunimah, "How Barack Obama Learned to Love Israel," The Electronic Intifada, March 4, 2007, https://electronicintifada.net/content/how-barack-obama -learned-love-israel/6786.

2. For Obama's quote ("my own blind spots"), see Peter Wallsten, "Allies of Palestinians See a Friend in Obama," *The Los Angeles Times*, April 10, 2008. For Obama's words of encouragement, see Ali Abunimah, "How Barack Obama Learned to Love Israel."

3. For Rice's comparison of Israeli practices in the West Bank to segregated Alabama, see Abrams, *Tested by Zion*, pp. 244–45. For Obama's replacement of Churchill's bust with one of Martin Luther King, Jr., see Michael D. Shear, "No Need for Holmes. Obama Sheds Light on a Winston Churchill Mystery," *The New York Times*, April 24, 2016.

4. For one of the first phone calls to a foreign leader, see comments by Abbas's spokesperson, Nabil Abu Rudeina, who quoted Obama as having told Abbas, "This is my first phone call to a foreign leader and I'm making it only hours after I took office." The White House has confirmed that Obama made four calls to foreign leaders on his first morning in office, and one of these was to Abbas, but it has refused to say who was called first. Of the four, only Abbas claims to have been told that he was called first. For the quotes from the pleased Abbas adviser, see "Obama Plunges Straight into Middle East Conflict," *The Sydney Morning Herald*, January 22, 2009.

5. For Mitchell's appointment and background, see "George Mitchell Named Special Envoy for the Middle East," CNN, January 22, 2009. For the administration's call for a complete freeze in settlement building and the vow to use tougher language, see Mark Landler and Isabel Kershner, "Israeli Settlement Growth Must Stop, Clinton Says," *The New York Times*, May 27, 2009; Helene Cooper, "Obama Calls for Swift Move Toward Mideast Peace Talks," *The New York Times*, May 28, 2009; Scott Wilson, "Obama Searches for Middle East Peace," *The Washington Post*, July 14, 2012. (While the Obama administration began using the stronger word "illegitimate" when referring to Israeli settlements, it refrained from calling settlements "illegal," as the United States had done decades earlier.) For the quote from a senior official traveling with Clinton ("it was apartheid"), see Peter Beinart, "Obama Betrayed Ideals on Israel," *Newsweek*, March 12, 2012.

6. For the observations from visitors to the White House, see Beinart, "Obama Betrayed." For the quotes from Obama's speech ("intolerable"), see "Remarks by the President at Cairo University, 6-04-09," White House, Office of the Press Secretary, June 4, 2009.

7. For Obama's quote ("what did we get"), see Scott Wilson, "Obama Searches for Middle East Peace," *The Washington Post*, July 14, 2012.

8. For the framework peace agreement obtained by Carter, see chapter 1, section i; "The Camp David Accords: The Framework for Peace in the Middle East," Jimmy Carter Presidential Library, September 17, 1978. For Reagan's opening of a dialogue with the PLO, see "Text of Reagan Statement," *The New York Times*, December 15, 1988. For Bush's support of Palestinian statehood and Sharon's endorsement, see chapter 1, section ii; Abrams, *Tested by Zion*, pp. 16–17, 32.

9. For the US view that Palestinians would be acting in "bad faith," see statement by George Mitchell in "The Palestine Papers: Meeting Minutes: Saeb Erekat and George Mitchell," *Al Jazeera*, October 21, 2009.

10. For the 2013 boom in settlement construction starts, greater than at any time since 2000, see Jodi Rudoren and Jeremy Ashkenas, "Netanyahu and the Settlements," *The New York Times*, March 12, 2015. For US complicity and Kerry's acceptance of settlement expansion as a necessary payoff to secure the right-wing government's acquiescence in the talks, see chapter 12; "Kerry: Israeli Settlements Move Was Expected," BBC, August 13, 2013. For Obama's sole veto of a UN Security Council resolution, see "Security Council Fails to Adopt Text Demanding That Israel Halt Settlement Activity as Permanent Member Casts Negative Vote," United Nations, February 18, 2011; "Security Council—Veto List," Dag Hammarskjöld Library, United Nations, accessed August 16, 2016. For figures on US military assistance and the United States having given more to Israel under Obama than under any other president, see chapter 12; Eli Lake, "Obama Wants to Stop Subsidizing Israel's Defense Industry," *Bloomberg View*, June 22, 2016. See also Colin H. Kahl, "Obama Has Been Great for Israel," *Foreign Policy*, August 16, 2012; Mitch Ginsburg, "Obama Is Best-ever U.S. President for Israel, Says Former Intel Chief," *The Times of Israel*, March 6, 2012. For the new aid package, see "Fact Sheet: Memorandum of Understanding Reached with Israel," the White House, Office of the Press Secretary, September 14, 2016.

11. For the more lenient terms that Israel sought (in particular on retaining its unique ability to spend a large share of US aid on non-US weapons), see Julie Hirschfeld Davis, "U.S. Offers to Increase Military Aid to Israel," *The New York Times*, July 1, 2016; Barak Ravid, "U.S. Seeks to Increase Aid to Israel—With More of It to Be Spent on American Equipment," *Haaretz*, July 3, 2016. For the trap Israel sensed, see comments by Michael Oren, Israel's former ambassador to the United States (and later a deputy minister in the Israeli government), who urged Netanyahu not to accept the package because, among other reasons, the deal could decrease Israeli leverage to oppose any peace initiatives that Obama might put forward in his final months. Gil Hoffman, "Michael Oren Advises Netanyahu Not to Sign U.S. Aid Deal," *The Jerusalem Post*, June 21, 2016. See also comments by Elliott Abrams: "If you do it this year, you will give Obama a talking point for why he is the best person for Israeli security, ever," he told *Bloomberg View*. "And Obama will misuse that in his last months in office to produce his parameters for the peace talks." Eli Lake, "Obama Wants to Stop Subsidizing Israel's Defense Industry," *Bloomberg View*, June 22, 2016.

12. See "Consulate General Staff," Government of Sweden, accessed July 15, 2016. Parliaments of the United Kingdom, France, and Spain also voted in favor of recognizing Palestine.

13. A "parameters resolution" had become the common shorthand for this option, even though the word "parameters" connotes something longer and more detailed than the short list of "principles"—similar in level of detail to Resolution 242—that the United States had in mind.

14. For the text of Netanyahu's speech, see "Prime Minister Benjamin Netanyahu's Speech at the AIPAC Policy Conference 2016," Israel Government Press Office, March 22, 2016. For similar statements by Netanyahu when Palestinians circulated draft resolutions in fall 2014 ("We will never agree to unilateral diktats. . . . He does not understand that they will result in a Hamas takeover in Judea and Samaria"), see "PM Netanyahu: 'Abu Mazen Thinks He Can Threaten Us with Unilateral Steps,'" press release, Israel Prime Minister's Office, December 18, 2014. In May 2016, Netanyahu tried to start a new, Egyptian-led peace process, an effort that, according to several Israeli cabinet ministers, was aimed at blocking the United States from introducing parameters, since Israel could have portrayed such a step as an attempt to interfere with the talks and quash a historical chance at peace. Shlomo Cesana, Daniel Siryoti, and *Israel Hayom* staff, "Report: Netanyahu Willing to Meet Abbas at Cairo Summit," *Israel Hayom*, July 12, 2016.

15. For quotes from George Ball's article, see George W. Ball, "How to Save Israel in Spite of Herself," *Foreign Affairs* 55, no. 3 (April 1977): 453–71.

16. Following the collapse of the Camp David summit, President Clinton presented both sides with the nonnegotiable "Clinton Parameters," but said the offer would disappear as soon as he left office less than one month later. At the end of the 2007–2008 Annapolis negotiations, Condoleezza Rice recalled in her memoir, the White House attempted to invite both sides to "accept the parameters" of an agreement, but, as with Clinton, it was during a US president's final months in office, and again based on the proposal of an outgoing Israeli prime minister, Ehud Olmert. And following Kerry's failure in 2014, Obama administration officials deliberated over whether to present an American framework for resolving the conflict, this time perhaps in a binding resolution at the UN Security Council. Rice, *No Higher Honor*, p. 723–24; Helene Cooper and Michael D. Shear, "Obama May Find It Impossible to Mend Frayed Ties to Netanyahu," *The New York Times*, March 18, 2015.

17. On the potential difficulty of obtaining a consensus in the Security Council, one senior US official said that the United States had received assurances from other members of the Security Council and Arab states that on the specific language of a resolution they would be flexible. Whether the United States could trust those assurances, particularly from the Arab states, who typically defer to the Palestinians, was another question. Phone interview by the author with a senior US official, September 2016.

18. There are precedents for backlashes against peace proposals: the discussion of sovereignty over the Noble Sanctuary/Temple Mount at the Camp David summit led directly to Ariel Sharon's controversial demonstration of Israeli control over the site, solidifying his support on the right and paving the path to the prime minister's office. Similarly, the Right of Return movement and the Palestinian Campaign for the Academic and Cultural Boycott of Israel, both precursors of the BDS movement, grew in reaction to the unofficial 2003 Geneva Accord. And the Camp

David proposal of land swaps in the Halutza sands near Gaza led Sharon as prime minister to attempt to foreclose the possibility by building new towns in those areas. Clyde Haberman, "Israeli Cabinet Rules Out Idea of Exchange of Territory," *The New York Times*, July 16, 2001. For the possibility of formal Israeli annexations, see "Knesset Speaker Calls for Annexation of Ma'ale Adumim," *The Times of Israel*, July 19, 2016. In 2016, the Land of Israel lobby in the Knesset proposed a draft law that would formally annex the settlement of Ma'ale Adumim and commissioned a poll that found that 78 percent of Israeli Jews favor it. For the proposal to require a supermajority to authorize negotiations over Jerusalem, see Aeyal Gross, "Should We Worry About Bill Requiring Knesset Supermajority to Negotiate on Jerusalem?" *Haaretz*, October 21, 2013. In March 2014, Israel passed a basic law requiring a two-thirds supermajority (and a national referendum if the share of votes were to fall between one-half and two-thirds) to approve any cession of land in which Israeli law applies; this includes East Jerusalem and the Golan Heights, but not Gaza or the West Bank. Unlike a separate draft law that failed to pass in 2013, the 2014 Basic Law requires a supermajority to approve a completed peace treaty, rather than to approve the mere holding of negotiations over a possible cession. Lahav Harkov, "Knesset Passes First Basic Law in 22 Years: Referendum on Land Concessions," *The Jerusalem Post*, March 12, 2014.

19. For Bush's April 2004 letter, see "Exchange of Letters Between PM Sharon and President Bush," Israel Ministry of Foreign Affairs, April 14, 2004.

20. For the quoted portion of the Republican Party platform, see "Republican Platform 2016," Republican National Committee, 2016, p. 46; Tal Kopan, "GOP Moves to the Right on Israel," CNN, July 11, 2016, http://edition.cnn.com/2016/07/11/politics/gop-platform-republican-convention-israel. For the letter from Republican and Democratic members of Congress to Obama, see Carol E. Lee, "Don't Back U.N. Council on Israeli-Palestinian Conflict, Lawmakers Urge Obama," *The Wall Street Journal* (online), April 14, 2016. For the letter from a bipartisan group of 88 senators (which also stated: "Any such resolution . . . will ultimately make it more difficult for Israelis and Palestinians to resolve the conflict. . . . Even well-intentioned initiatives at the United Nations (UN) risk locking the parties into positions that will make it more difficult to return to the negotiating table and make the compromises necessary for peace"), see "88 Senators Urge Obama to Veto 'One-Sided' Security Council Resolutions on Israel," Jewish Telegraphic Agency, September 20, 2016.

21. For J Street's attempts to build ties to Likud ministers and help Netanyahu's government combat BDS, see Barak Ravid, "Israel Engaging with J Street in Bid to Counter BDS on U.S. Campuses," *Haaretz*, June 20, 2016. A regional cochair of J Street's student wing, which is reputed to be more critical of Israel than the parent organization, issued a plea for Ron Dermer, a close Netanyahu adviser who became ambassador to the United States in 2013, to engage with the group. Sonia Brinn, "Ron Dermer, Meet with America's Pro-Israel Progressives, Not Only Its Hawks," *Haaretz*, June 22, 2016.

22. For Palestinian requests for the United States to present parameters after the collapse of the Camp David talks in 2000 and on other occasions in subsequent years, see Dennis Ross, *The Missing Peace*, p. 724; "Meeting Minutes: Saeb Erekat and George Mitchell, The Palestine Papers," *Al Jazeera*, October 21, 2009.

23. For EU declarations, see, for example, "Council Conclusions on the Middle

East Peace Process," Council of the European Union, December 13, 2010. For the Arab Peace Initiative being welcomed by the Quartet and the Security Council, see "A Performance-Based Roadmap to a Permanent Two-State Solution to the Israeli-Palestinian Conflict," Israel Ministry of Foreign Affairs, April 30, 2003; S/RES/1397 (2002), United Nations, March 12, 2002; S/RES/1515 (2003), United Nations, November 19, 2003.

24. The UN Partition Plan of 1947, adopted in UN General Assembly Resolution 181, described the partition of Palestine into a Jewish and an Arab state, but it did so as a matter of describing the demographic majority in each state, not in an effort to recognize the character of either state, both of which were to provide full and equal rights to all citizens. "General Assembly Resolution 181," United Nations, November 29, 1947.

25. During past negotiations, a distinction has been made between the Western Wall—the entire western retaining wall of the Noble Sanctuary/Temple Mount—the majority of which is located underground in the Muslim Quarter of the Old City, and the Wailing Wall, which is the section of the Western Wall that is exposed and faces the plaza in which Jews pray.

26. One of the points of dispute in discussions of security during the Kerry talks was if the determination of whether Palestinians had satisfied the security performance criteria stipulated in the agreement would be subject to Israeli veto. Interviews by the author with a Palestinian negotiator, an Israeli negotiator, US officials, Ramallah, Jerusalem, Washington, DC, September 2014, March 2015. For discussion of this issue, see "Advancing the Dialogue: A Security System for the Two-State Solution," Center for a New American Security, May 2016.

ACKNOWLEDGMENTS

If this book has added something of value to the extensive literature on Israel and Palestine, it is thanks to the many previous authors on whom I have relied. For the title chapter, I owe a particular debt to three: William B. Quandt, Yezid Sayigh, and Avi Shlaim, who have written the definitive accounts of American peacemaking in the Middle East, the Palestinian national movement, and Israeli diplomatic history, respectively.

This book began with an assignment in April 2010 from the editor of *The New York Review of Books*, Robert B. Silvers. He is in many ways responsible for launching my career. So, too, is Robert Malley, who, on the basis of the resulting piece, sent me to Gaza to write my first report for the International Crisis Group.

At Crisis Group I've been fortunate to work under three accomplished scholars, each of them experienced in Israel and Palestine: Robert Blecher, Rob Malley, and Joost Hiltermann. Few have influenced my thinking on this conflict more than my three local colleagues: in the West Bank, Suheir Freitekh, whose caustic wit sustained me through the dreariest of meetings; in Israel, Ofer Zalzberg, who commands a deep understanding of his society; and in Gaza, Azmi Keshawi, a veteran journalist, dogged researcher, fearless investigator, and cherished comrade.

A number of this book's chapters are based on pieces published in different form elsewhere, primarily in *The New York Review of Books* and the *London Review of Books*, but also in *Foreign Affairs* online and in a report for the International Crisis Group. At *The New York Review*, I am grateful to its polymath editor, Bob Silvers, as well as the editor of *NYR Daily*, Hugh Eakin, and Christopher Carroll. At the *London Review of Books*, Adam Shatz has been my champion and counselor, and I have been the recipient of the skillful editing of numerous others, including Christian Lorentzen and Daniel Soar. I owe thanks, too, to Gideon Rose at *Foreign Affairs*; Kate Lee at *Medium*; Mark Lotto at *Matter*; and, at *The New York Times*, Matt Seaton, Nick Fox, Sewell Chan, and, especially, Sasha Polakow-Suransky. During the past seven years, I have been a contributing editor at *Tablet*, whose editor-in-chief, Alana Newhouse, and literary editor, David Samuels, have generously offered me institutional backing and use of their beautiful home. David gave me one of my first breaks as a journalist many years ago. Another came from André Aciman.

In working on this book I have relied on the writings, research, and general assistance of numerous colleagues, officials, editors, language teachers, scholars, and interviewees, a number of whom will disagree with the conclusions they helped me reach. There are too many who should be named, and quite a few who do not wish to be. In the former category, several answered specific queries in their areas of expertise: Elliott Abrams, Tal Becker, Steven M. Cohen, Boaz Karni, Karim Nashashibi, William Quandt, Mouin Rabbani, Dan Rothem, Yezid Sayigh, Matti Steinberg, and Azzam Tamimi.

Two individuals deserve special acknowledgment. Hussein Agha worked behind the scenes to promote my career from an early stage, and he has enlightened, encouraged, and jovially taunted me in the years since. Ahmad Khalidi gave graciously of his time and vast erudition to provide detailed and astute feedback on the title chapter.

Five devoted friends have bolstered me over the course of this project. In July 2010, Joshua Yaffa and I took a writing retreat at a cabin in the Hudson Valley, and it was there that the earliest chapter was conceived. I'm beholden to Josh for his years of editorial assistance, but it is for his friendship that I am truly grateful. My closest companion from graduate school, Jesse James Wilkins III, has my copious appreciation for reading and editing nearly all my initial pieces, as well as several of the book's chapters. Rob Blecher has gone over every word herein. His dispassionate and exacting eye have improved my writing, and, on several occasions, saved me from myself. Finally, my confidants, guides, neighbors, and drinking partners, Adina Hoffman and Peter Cole, for whom no question—not even the choice of hues for the cover—was too slight. They have done more to support me as I wrote this book than I had any right to ask. The better part of it was completed in their marvelous, book-lined Musrara apartment, a writer's dream. I can never repay them.

When not in the field, at home, or at Adina and Peter's, I wrote at the Weizmann Institute of Science, the Abramov Library of Hebrew Union College, and the Musrara School of Art. In Gaza, I was privileged to do my earliest writing in the apartment of Amr Hamad.

No editor could have been more perfectly suited to working with me on this book than its tremendously talented, dedicated, and discerning steward, Riva Hocherman. Time and again, I was taken aback by her detailed knowledge of Israel and Palestine, which, though perhaps the least valuable of her many gifts, rescued me from missteps that only she could apprehend. I am profoundly indebted, too, to my publisher, Sara Bershtel. In Metropolitan she and Riva have created something truly uncommon: an imprint with a coherent worldview. I am honored to be published by them. I am thankful to the rest of the wonderful team at Metropolitan/Henry Holt, including Grigory Tovbis, Molly Bloom, Jolanta Benal, and Carolyn O'Keefe. For his innovative design, geniality, and patience with my meddling, I am obliged to Rick Pracher. Long before the first words of this book were written, I was lucky to find in Flip Brophy not only an agent but a nurturer, who welcomed me into her home and onto her list when I was just getting started.

My grandmother, Yulia, died seven years before I began this project, but I am sure that I would never have embarked on it without her. Nor could I have done it without the aid of the rest of my family, in particular my grandfather, Syoma, and my brother and parents. Sana'a Allan, who has come to be a beloved part of our family, made the work possible.

My wife, Judy, is a professional editor, and among the best I know.

Her parents like to joke that I wouldn't send a text message without first running it by her. Everything good in my life I owe to her: this book; her parents, who have become my parents; and, most of all, our girls, Zoe and Tessa. I would not trade the past six years we've had together for eternal life without them.

INDEX

About the Author

NATHAN THRALL is a leading analyst of the Arab-Israeli conflict. He is a regular contributor to *The New York Review of Books* and the *London Review of Books* and is a senior analyst with the International Crisis Group, for which he has covered Israel, the West Bank, and Gaza since 2010. His writing and analysis are often featured in print and broadcast media, including *The New York Times*, *The Washington Post*, *The Wall Street Journal*, Bloomberg News, the *Financial Times*, *The Guardian*, *The Economist*, *Time*, CNN, *Democracy Now!*, PRI, and the BBC. He lives in Jerusalem with his wife and daughters.